PATRICK HENRY ADDRESSING THE VIRGINIA ASSEMBLY

GREAT DEBATES IN AMERICAN HISTORY

From the Debates in the British Parliament on the
Colonial Stamp Act (1764–1765) to the Debates
in Congress at the Close of the Taft
Administration (1912–1913)

EDITED BY

MARION MILLS MILLER, Litt.D. (Princeton)

Editor of "The Life and Works of Abraham Lincoln," etc.

IN FOURTEEN VOLUMES

EACH DEALING WITH A SPECIFIC SUBJECT, AND CONTAINING A SPECIAL INTRODUC-
TION BY A DISTINGUISHED AMERICAN STATESMAN OR PUBLICIST

VOLUME ONE

Colonial Rights—The Revolution—The Constitution

With an Introduction by Henry Cabot Lodge, LL.D.
Senator from Massachusetts

CURRENT LITERATURE PUBLISHING COMPANY
NEW YORK

Copyright, 1913, by
CURRENT LITERATURE PUBLISHING COMPANY

49511

CONTENTS OF THE SERIES

VOL. XI. ECONOMIC AND SOCIAL QUESTIONS, PART 2.

Introduction by CHARLES R. VAN HISE, President of the University of Wisconsin.

VOL. XII. REVENUE: TARIFF AND TAXATION.

Introduction by IDA M. TARBELL, L. H. D., Associate Editor of the *American Magazine*.

VOL. XIII. FINANCE, PART 1.

Introduction by THEODORE E. BURTON, LL.D., Senator from Ohio.

VOL. XIV. FINANCE, PART 2.

Introduction by IRVING FISHER, Ph.D., Professor of Political Economy in Yale University.

CONTENTS OF VOLUME ONE

v

IV. FORCE OR CONCILIATION? (*Debates in the British Parlia-
    ment*)   99

    Debate in the Lords on the Removal of Troops from Boston:
    in favor, Lord CHATHAM (formerly WILLIAM PITT, Sr.),
    Lord CAMDEN, Lord SHELBURNE, and the MARQUIS of ROCK-
    INGHAM.
    Tilt in the Lords between Lord CHATHAM and Lord SAND-
    WICH over the character of BENJAMIN FRANKLIN.
    Plans of Conciliation by Lord CHATHAM, Dr. FRANKLIN,
    Lord NORTH, and EDMUND BURKE.
    BURKE'S great speech on "Conciliation with America."
    BURKE'S peroration on "The Right to Tax America."

V. COLONIES VS. PARLIAMENT (*American Debates and
   Speeches*)   150

    Speech of JAMES WILSON in the Pennsylvania Assembly: "In
    Vindication of the Colonies."
    Debate in the Virginia Convention on PATRICK HENRY'S reso-
    lutions to adopt Defensive Measures: in favor, Mr. HENRY
    (his "Liberty or Death" speech); opposed, RICHARD
    BLAND, ROBERT CARTER NICHOLAS, and EDMUND PENDLETON.
    Address of the Second Continental Congress to the British
    people, drafted by RICHARD HENRY LEE (Va.). Declaration
    of Congress to the World, drafted by JOHN DICKINSON (Pa.).

VI. COLONIES VS. THE CROWN (*Speeches and Debates on the
    Declaration of Independence*)   173

    The Mecklenburgh (N. C.) Declaration of Independence.
    Proposition of American Independence by THOMAS PAINE
    (Pa.) in his "Common Sense."
    Address of Judge WILLIAM HENRY DRAYTON (S. C.) on
    "America Created to Be Free."
    Declaration of Rights by Virginia, drafted by GEORGE MASON.
    Debate in Congress on the resolution of RICHARD HENRY LEE
    (Va.), declaring American Independence: in favor, Mr. LEE,
    JOHN ADAMS (Mass.), GEORGE WHYTE (Va.); opposed, JOHN
    HANCOCK (Mass.), JAMES WILSON (Pa.), ROBERT R. LIV-
    INGSTON (N. Y.), EDWARD RUTLEDGE (S. C.), JOHN DICKIN-
    SON (Pa.).

VII. THE DECLARATION OF INDEPENDENCE   .   .   .   200

    Original and Final Drafts of the Declaration.
    Speech of SAMUEL ADAMS (Mass.) on "American Independ-
    ence."

VIII. REVOLUTION OR REBELLION?   209

    Speeches in Parliament by Lord CHATHAM, CHARLES JAMES
    FOX, and JOHN WILKES against the American War.
    Address by Congress (drafted by SAMUEL CHASE) against
    British proposals of peace: "Be Not Deceived."
    Controversy between the EARL of SHELBURNE and THOMAS
    PAINE (Pa.) on Great Britain's Refusal to Grant Inde-
    pendence to America.

ILLUSTRATIONS IN VOLUME ONE

GREAT AMERICAN DEBATES

PREFACE OF THE SERIES

[INCLUDING BIBLIOGRAPHY]

ONE of the most notable scenes in ancient history
was the joint debate between Demosthenes and
Æschines, "On the Crown." The point at issue
was whether a civic crown should be granted to Demosthenes, the Athenian premier, for his policy toward
Philip of Macedon, who was attempting to subvert the
liberties of the peninsular Greeks. Æschines, the leader
of the anti-administration party, opposed the grant,
having deposited a large sum that he would prove his
charge of corruption against Demosthenes. The result
of the debate would be either that the whole national
policy would be reversed, and the man responsible for
it be deposed and disgraced, or that it would be vindicated and its impugner driven from the city a penniless
exile. It was the latter event which occurred.

So great and so widespread was the interest in the
debate that the open-air theater in which it was held
was packed with thousands of people, including visitors
from the farthest borders of the Greek world who had
been drawn to the capital by the importance of the issue
and the fame of the debaters. Under all these circumstances the two great statesmen, each a finished rhetori-
cian and a master of all the arts of public controversy,
as well as profoundly versed in constitutional law, made
the supreme efforts of their long and brilliant careers.
Each point in the speeches was thoroughly comprehended by the audience, and every oratorical period appreciated at its true æsthetic value, for the ancient
Greeks had developed to the highest two kindred passions, that for controversy and that for rhetoric, both
particularly in the domain of politics. Every man being

an intense partisan, stormy gusts of cheers and derisive shouts swept again and again in conflicting waves over the vast assembly, while the unperturbed speakers paused for their subsidence. In its physical aspect this was the greatest debate in all history.

But only in this aspect, for, despite a prevalent impression (based on the impossibility of paralleling such a spectacle in the modern world) that debate is in decay, never was forensic contest more keen than now, and never did it have more interested or appreciative auditors, nor—and this is the point of superiority over the ancients—has it ever had by millions so many.

When a statesman rises to-day in the American Congress, or the British Parliament, or any national assembly in the world, to speak upon a great issue, if this is vital to his country the mind of every patriot within the land attends, and if the question is one of world politics the furthest corner of the earth is agog to catch his utterance.

The telegraph, and its record, the newspaper, are the instruments which give such a speaker an audience larger and more representative of every shade of belief and form of interest than all the hearers combined who hung on the words of the entire roll of ancient orators.

Occasionally outside of the national capital there will be a debate between statesmen on a vital question, and, for the time, the place where it occurs, however insignificant otherwise, will be the Mecca of the nation, toward which the eyes of the faithful are turned. Such a place was Freeport, Illinois, where Abraham Lincoln by clever finesse forced from Stephen A. Douglas the proposal of "unfriendly legislation" toward slavery in the Territories, and thereby caused the ultimate schism in the Democratic party, and the triumph of the Republican party under his own leadership. The "Freeport doctrine" this proposal was called, and the name will be forever recorded in American political history.

However, it is Washington at which, with few exceptions, the great debates in American history have occurred. To our mind the academic discussion of some general principle which may take place in any non-legislative forum, including that of the magazine and newspaper, is not properly a political debate. No debate is complete unless it is followed by some concrete political action, preferably a vote upon a measure embodying the principle discussed. With such decision in prospect the controversy acquires the aspect of a real bout, a duel if there are two contestants, a field contest if there are many, and if these are, as is usually the case, divided into two parties, with the individual members of each so united in principle and program as to supplement the efforts of one another.

The duel, however, is the typical form of debate. Indeed, a field contest, in its general aspect of "team play," is a duel of one group against another, and in detail is a number of duels between coupled antagonists.

Each contestant maneuvers to gain the superior position over his adversary, and, when this is attained, to drive home his advantage. Direction is given his efforts by the fixed end in view, which, in both parliamentary law and finesse, is the question to be voted upon. Therefore, debate is law in the making, and legislation is the essence of political history.

All great historians recognize this, and so from Thucydides down have studied legislative debates. To what degree they have done so is probably the most accurate test of the value of their work. Certainly it is so in the case of American historians, for the United States is in all political aspects a constitutional democracy, and every important political event must be related to some legislative act, passed almost invariably after discussion, or to some constitutional function, which was originally a legislative act passed after extended debate.

Debate is thus the crucible of law, which is the metal of history. This symbol of the fusing pot is particularly apt in the case of American debate, for almost all the results of Congressional discussion have been of the nature of compromises. Even when a minority has been overborne, its protest has, if not at once some time thereafter, become effective in toning down the original purpose of the majority. Thus the overwhelming and imperious Radical majority in Congress after the Civil War failed to impeach President Johnson, and could not fasten permanently upon the South the Federal control of elections.

If, then, the historian profits by the study of debate, why should not everyone interested in politics follow his example? Why should he, too, not enjoy the enthusiasm of discovering the original materials of history and forming his own conclusions thereon?

Heretofore there has been a conclusive reason why this pleasure and profit, this high culture of intellectual insight and judgment, have been denied him. It has been impossible, without devoting, like the historian, many years to research work, and an equal period to comparison and selection, to acquire a discriminating knowledge of the debates in Congress and of their relation to each other. The records of our national assembly are presented in about five hundred large tomes, each averaging a thousand pages of two thousand words, making an approximate total of one billion words. Beginning with the *Annals of Congress,* and continuing with the *Congressional Globe* and the *Congressional Record,* this record is in strict chronological order, routine business being mingled with debates in a fashion most provoking to the investigator. Furthermore, it takes an expert to follow a subject through its widely separated installments by means of the index. Even when he has acquired this facility, the reader must dig his way through a mass of worthless material to find the vein of golden thought for which he is seeking.

Undoubtedly the superior grounding of our early statesmen in their subjects of discussion was due simply to the fact that the literature of debate was still of moderate extent, so that they could compass all that had been said before them on any given question. "Elliott's Debates," especially after their inclusion of the Madison Papers, rounded up the debates of the Confederation and the Constitutional Convention, although in undigested form. The *Annals of Congress* contained digests rather than verbatim reports of the debates in Congress for the first quarter of a century, and Senator

Thomas H. Benton's abridgment of Congressional debates down to the close of the first half of the nineteenth
century saved recourse to the official reports. Benton's
book can hardly be called a compilation, since it follows
the chronological order of the *Annals of Congress* and
the *Congressional Globe,* from which its material was
taken, and merely reduces these official records by ex-
cision and condensation. It is a digest rather than a
selection.

Although the need of a new selection and abridgment of American debates grew cumulatively greater
with every year that followed Benton's work, the labor
of preparing one increased apace, deterring editors
from the task, and none appeared before the present
year (1913).

It is true that the list of books relating to American
eloquence forms one of the largest bibliographies of
works published in the United States; and in this list
collections of political orations are notable for their
number and extent. But these are *disjecta membra* of
debates, and, while inciting the reader with desire to
possess the complete body, do not in any degree satisfy
the desire. Even when a debate is ostensibly presented
in one of these compilations, it is invariably the rhetorical, rather than argumentative, passages which are ex-
tracted and set over against each other. This is notably
the case with the "classic" debate between Senators
Webster and Hayne.

Believing that the practical American mind prefers
argument, the clash of mind against mind, to mere
rhetoric, which in its most interesting phase, the revelation of personality, is as far below debate as contrast
is below contest, and realizing the entire absence of any
work to satisfy this desire, Dr. Edward J. Wheeler, the
editor of *Current Opinion,* several years ago planned
a compilation of the great debates in our country's history from colonial times to the present, which should
contain in logical arrangement selected public discussions of the most important national events, and forensic controversies over leading political issues, as conducted by our ablest and most brilliant statesmen.

Dr. Wheeler honored me by asking that I compile this important work. Accepting the pleasing but onerous task, I set to work quarrying material in the rough out of the rich and well-nigh inexhaustible mines of colonial historical records and the official proceedings of Congress. Going over hundreds of volumes each of about a thousand pages, almost literally leaf by leaf, in order that no debate of prime importance should slip by, I unearthed at least a thousand debates all of interest to-day to the student of politics and economics. From these, with Dr. Wheeler's assistance, and that of Albert Ellery Bergh, the editor of "The World's Great Classics" and other important compilations, whom Dr. Wheeler called into consultation, I selected the two hundred or more which appear in the present work. While a very profound delver into American political history may regret to find that some debate which he considers of importance has been omitted, nevertheless the editor insists that, taking every element of selection into consideration, the inclusion of any such debate would have forced a better one out of a work which is necessarily limited in its extent.

These are the standards by which the selection has been made. They are arranged in the order of precedence:

1. Importance of the historical event, the legislative act, or the political or economic issue which forms the subject of the debate.

2. Argumentative force of the speeches.

3. Rhetorical brilliance of the speeches.

4. Distinguished rank of the speakers among American statesmen, with a minor preference for men of original views and interesting personality.

In preparing these debates the editor has faithfully tried to follow Herbert Spencer's great principle of literary composition: "economy of the reader's attention," and to this end has endeavored to give only that information which is essential to a proper understanding of each issue, and to present this in the place most available to the reader, whether it be preceding, during the debate, or following it. The work is not intended as a political history (although it is calculated to form a valuable supplement to such a history) and therefore only that information is presented which will connect the debate in hand with others related to it, and which will save the reader recourse to other works in order to understand the political situation at the time of the debate, and the unexplained allusions of the debaters. In this way it is believed that the ends of readability and reference are both attained.

In further obedience to this law, he has abandoned the rule, common among editors of speeches, of indicating omissions by asterisks. Had he continued this practise, so numerous were the omissions, owing to the great exigency of condensation, that the reader might at times think he was contemplating an astronomical chart rather than surveying the galaxy of American forensic eloquence.

In similar consideration, no less for the author quoted than for the reader, the editor has interpolated as an intrinsic part of the speeches certain phrases bridging over the omitted portions. Then, too, except where a grammatical solecism was plainly intended by a speaker, or is indicative of his personality, such a slip has been corrected. In so doing the editor has followed the example of the best Congressional reporters, certainly a sufficient, if not imperative, precedent in the case of editing Congressional speeches. Sticklers for exact phraseology may readily find this in the Congressional records themselves, by using the dates of the present work as indicators. In this connection it may be claimed that, on the important questions for which these vast and voluminous records are consulted in nine cases out of ten, the present work forms a very simple and practical guide book.

Where the substance of a speech, in whole or in part, is given by the editor, this is distinguished typographically from speeches or parts of speeches reported as delivered. However, condensations of speeches, changed from direct to indirect discourse, which was the rule in early reporting before the days of verbatim presentation, are represented in the same type as speeches printed as delivered.

Owing to this form of indirect discourse, the early speeches are not as lively as the later, but the reader should remember that what is lost in brilliance is more than compensated for by concentration of thought. In this work, as in any selection of American forensic oratory, there is fine rhetoric in overflowing measure for those who desire it, but, as has already been stated, "Great Debates" is intended for readers who primarily want clear and forcible argument.

Sources of Material

In gathering material resource was had to the many collected works of great American statesmen, such as John Adams, Daniel Webster, John C. Calhoun, Thomas Corwin, Joshua R. Giddings, William H. Seward, Abraham Lincoln, Charles Sumner, *et al.*, all of which will be found in the public libraries by the student who desires to read in full the speeches represented in this work.

Many collections of speeches were resorted to, of which it will be well to mention a few of the early ones which have been drawn upon by all the editors of the later collections. The chief early compilations are: "Eloquence of the United States," edited by E. B. Williston: Middletown, Ct., 1827, and "American Eloquence," edited by Frank Moore, and published by D. Appleton & Company, New York, 1857.

One of the modern compilations deserves special mention for the admirable taste shown in its selection of representative speeches, its illuminating notes, and its well-written biographies of the orators. This is "American Orations," edited by Professors Alexander Johnston of Princeton and James Albert Woodburn of Indiana University, and published by G. P. Putnam's Sons, New York. The first copyright was in 1896.

Professor Charles Kendall Adams, then of the University of Michigan, had compiled in similar manner "British Orations," published by the Putnams in 1884.

This has been largely drawn upon by the present editor in preparing the debates in Parliament on Colonial Rights.

The chief source of material for the debates in America during the Colonial and Revolutionary periods, the régime of the Confederation, and the administration of Washington, is "A Political and Civil History of the United States . . . to the close of the administration of President Washington," written by Timothy Pitkin, and published at New Haven, Ct., in 1828.

Mr. Pitkin was a representative in Congress, and took a leading part in its discussions. His biography will be found in the Index of Proper Names in Volume XIV. He shines as an editor no less than as an historian, since his work contains not only copious extracts from speeches, but also judicious selections of all the important protests and petitions of the Colonial legislatures, and the state papers of the Continental Congress, of the Congress under the Confederation, and those of the Washington Administration. The papers of the colonial legislatures and of the Continental Congress, being both argumentative in character and rhetorical in style, have been largely drawn upon in the present work, owing to the lack of preservation of the debates of this period.

For the period of the Revolution and the Confederation the "Journals of the Continental Congress 1774-1789," published by the Government Printing Office, 1906, have furnished considerable material.

Coming to the formation of the Constitution we find that "Debates on the Federal Constitution," by Jonathan Elliott (copyright 1836, and enlarged thereafter; now published by J. B. Lippincott Co., Philadelphia), is the standard work on its subject, being referred to constantly by both Northern and Southern statesmen from the time of its publication until the Civil War, upon the great questions of State Rights and Slavery. Abraham Lincoln made an exhaustive study of this work in preparing his great speech at Cooper Union in February, 1861, on "Slavery as the Fathers Viewed It."

Elliott (born in England 1784; died in Washington, D. C., 1846) emigrated to America about 1802, became a printer, and then a soldier, fighting for South American liberty, 1810-1813, and serving in the American army in the War of 1812. In 1814 he settled in Washington, editing for thirteen years the "Washington Gazette." He published a number of statistical and documentary works relating to American politics, chief of which is his famous "Debates." He also edited the "Madison Papers" (1845), published by the Government. Of the five volumes of the Debates the first contains Ante-Revolutionary history, the documents relating to American independence, and the documents and speeches relating to the Confederation and the Constitution, including Judge Yates's Minutes of the Convention of 1787; the second, third, and beginning of the fourth, the debates in the State legislatures and conventions in the ratification of the Constitution; the rest of the fourth, the documents, speeches, and judicial decisions relating to Constitutional questions debated in Congress 1789-1836; and the fifth, Madison's report of debates in the Congress of the Confederation and in the Constitutional Convention of 1787.

Recently the gaps in "Elliott's Debates" have been filled by "The Records of the Federal Convention of 1787," edited by Max Farrand, Professor of History in Yale University, and published by the Yale University Press, New Haven, Ct., in 1911. It is an exhaustive monograph on the subject, including most interesting notes on the speakers in the Convention made by agents of the French government in America and preserved in that government's archives. These vivacious pen-sketches appear in Volume XIV of "Great Debates" in connection with the biographies of the statesmen referred to. They were translated for us by Mrs. Helen E. Meyer, who has admirably preserved the sparkling spirit of the original French.

The official and semi-official records of Congress from the adoption of the Constitution to the present time (1912) have furnished, with a few exceptions such as the Lincoln-Douglas joint debates, the material for all the volumes after the first. The Lincoln-Douglas debates have been abridged from the complete report in

"The Life and Works of Abraham Lincoln" (1907), produced by the editor and publishers of the present work. This collection has also been used to supply introductory matter for various other speeches of Lincoln, and the debates in his administration.

The first records of Congress were "The Debates and Proceedings in the Congress of the United States, Compiled from Authentic Materials," edited and published in Washington by two Congressional reporters, Gales and Seaton. The first two volumes appeared in 1834, and the five remaining volumes in 1849-51. These records, known by the briefer title of *Annals of Congress,* have supplied the materials in the present work of all the Congressional debates down to 1824, with the exception of certain speeches, such as Daniel Webster's, where recourse has been had to fuller reports in published works.

Most of the speeches were reported in the *Annals* in condensed form, where indirect discourse was generally adopted, though the speeches of the more distinguished and rhetorical statesmen were presented as delivered, if not in full, at least by extracts of the important passages. The selection of these passages and the abstracting of the other speeches are remarkably well done, Joseph Gales, Sr., in particular having a keen eye for salient points of argument.

The *Annals* is thoroughly indexed by subjects, and has an appendix containing the important state papers and public documents and all laws of a public nature. Gales and Seaton were aided in their work by the suggestion and advice of a number of statesmen, notably Madison, whose experience covered the history of Congress from the beginning.

Francis Blair, Sr. (see biography in Volume XIV), and John Cook Rives, a departmental clerk at Washington, founded the *Congressional Globe* in the early part of Jackson's administration. Rives soon became sole proprietor, and continued so until 1864, when he retired with a fortune, of which he gave liberally to the wives of enlisted soldiers, and for the equipment of regiments. There was less editing done by Blair and Rives than by Gales and Seaton, the reports becoming more and more verbatim, until finally they were wholly so. The *Globe* continued until late in its life the practice of the *Annals* in recording the important public laws of Congress.

In 1857 Ex-Senator Thomas H. Benton, of Missouri, published an "Abridgment of the Debates of Congress from 1789 to 1856": D. Appleton and Company, New York.

Senator Benton derived the material for the first part of his work from the *Annals of Congress,* and for the latter part from the *Congressional Globe.*

These "Abridgments" are notable specimens of editing, as might be expected of a statesman of such profound ability and long service, as well as of the experienced author of "The Thirty Years' View." Nevertheless he slighted certain discussions which, owing to circumstances, have become of greater interest to readers of the present day than they were to those of his own era, and for these the present editor has reverted to the original sources. It should be remarked in this connection that many American historians have evidently been misled by following Benton. Thus Alexander Johnston, in his "American Political History," gives James Madison and Thomas Jefferson the credit for first presenting, in the Kentucky and Virginia Resolutions and the controversy concerning them, leading constitutional arguments against the Alien and Sedition Laws, which arguments, says Johnston, had been overlooked by the Anti-Federalist statesmen in Congress. Now the *Annals of Congress* show that Albert Gallatin and Edward Livingston had presented these very arguments most ably and completely. Benton, however, did not preserve them in his "Abridgement."

The *Congressional Record* succeeded the *Globe* on March 4th, 1873. As in the later issues of the *Globe,* the laws of Congress were omitted from its appendixes, since these now appeared by themselves in another form of public documents. Nevertheless the appendixes in time became larger than before, owing to the increasing practice of speakers, especially in the House, asking "leave to print" their speeches, in order that they might "frank" these to their constituents. Another practice which arose at this period was that of speakers "incorporating" in their remarks speeches of persons, chiefly candidates for office, who were not members of Congress, articles from magazines, and even entire books. One notable instance of the latter was the division of "Protection and Free Trade," written by Henry George, into six parts, and the incorporation of each by a Representative in his remarks on the McKinley Bill, the whole book thus becoming a public document, more than a million copies of which were franked by the so-called Free Trade Democrats all over the country, with the intention, and it is claimed, with the effect, of promoting the election of an anti-protection Congress.

The *Record* has thus become a great storehouse of valuable material of every sort of subject: political, social and economic. The present work makes available a select portion of its mass of heterogeneous information and argument, but this is necessarily in slight ratio to the whole. It would be a laudable act if Congress ordered a digest of the whole work arranged according to subjects. Failing this, the Government should certainly publish a logical index of all its published proceedings, with indications of what phase of each subject is treated on each page, that such an issue as the Tariff, for instance, could be intelligently followed by the student, with a great saving of his time and his temper.

WORKS OF REFERENCE

In view of the vast number of admirable treatises on American politics it seems invidious to single out any as specially helpful to readers of the present work who desire to pursue their researches beyond its pages. But the fact that a few works have been of special assistance to the editor should justify their mention.

The book which chiefly guided the author in the selection of debates before the Civil War is the "Constitutional and Political History of the United States" by Dr. Hermann von Holst, published by Callaghan and Company, Chicago, in 1889.

This is a work typical of German scholarship, containing views whose prevailing soundness is the almost mechanical result of a vast reading of original documents. Unfortunately the learned author's mind works along a line of thought the methodical principle of which it is difficult for the average American reader to perceive. Conclusions are often stated in advance of the information upon which they are based, so that the reader does not fully understand one point until he is in the throes of puzzlement over a new one. But, although the work is thus rendered difficult to read, it will repay study, so just are the author's judgments on both the political issues and the character of statesmen.

As has been mentioned, Senator Benton published a work entitled "Thirty Years' View": D. Appleton and Company, New York, 1854. This is a history of Congress from 1820 to 1850, during which period the author was a Senator from Missouri. He thus speaks of his qualifications:

I was in the Senate the whole time of which I write—an active business member, attending and attentive—in the confidence of half the administrations, and a close observer of the others—had an inside view of transactions of which the public only saw the outside, and of many of which the two sides were very different—saw the secret springs and hidden machinery by which men and parties were to be moved, and measures promoted or thwarted—saw patriotism and ambition at their respective labors, and was generally able to discriminate between them. So far, I have one qualification; but Mr. Macaulay says that Lord Lyttleton had the same, and made but a poor history, because unable to use his material. So it may be with me; but, in addition to my senatorial means of knowledge, I have access to the unpublished papers of General Jackson, and find among them some that he intended for publication, and which will be used according to his intention.

This work has been used by the present editor not only for historical reference, but also as a source of material, since it contains copious extracts from important

debates, chiefly on Slavery and Finance. He has, however, reduced somewhat the part which Senator Benton represented himself as performing in these controversies—the story is characteristic, if not well authen-
ticated, that the Senator once condescendingly remarked
of President Jackson that "Old Hickory" had been of
"considerable assistance" to him ("Old Bullion") in
the war against the United States Bank.

For the political history of the Civil War and the
causes leading up to it, "The American Conflict," by
Horace Greeley (published by O. D. Case and Company, Hartford, Ct., in 1865) is, though biased in favor
of the North, a work which cannot be overlooked by
any author, editor, or student dealing with the subject.
It has furnished the present editor not only with information for use in introductions, but also with the text
of several controversial speeches delivered outside of
Congress.

Of the many books containing digests of the speeches
at the outbreak of the Civil War, the "History, Civil,
Political, and Military, of the Southern Rebellion," by
Orville J. Victor (published by J. D. Torrey, New York,
in 1861) should be here mentioned, as it was largely
used by the present editor in preparing the debates on
the proposals of Conciliation made in Congress in
1860-61.

In similar fashion the "History of the Thirty-ninth
Congress," by William H. Barnes (Harper and
Brothers, New York, 1868) was of great assistance in
the preparation of the debates on Reconstruction, etc.,
in the period immediately following the Civil War.

The chief guide to the debates of the entire Reconstruction period was "Twenty Years of Congress," by
James G. Blaine (Henry Bell Publishing Company, Nor-
wich, Ct., 1884). On the issues subsequent to Reconstruction the book was unfortunately of little assistance,
for the last twelve years of the period discussed were
summarily disposed of in less than one-fourth of the
work, the author having apparently constructed the beginning on the basis of at least a four-volume book, only
to decide later to close it in two volumes. Thus the

great question of the Free Coinage of Silver, which arose in the closing part of the author's Congressional career, is hardly touched upon. Up to the close of Johnson's Administration, however, the work forms one of the best examples of American political history, so clear is the exposition of situations, so judicious the selection of argumentative points, so admirable the digest of speeches, and so sound are the author's own comments thereon.

A very valuable general guide to the editor was "American Political History, 1763-1876," by the editors of "American Orations," Professors Johnston and Woodburn [G. P. Putnam's Sons, 1905]. This work is logically arranged, covering the subject of the Revolution, the Constitution, the Growth of Nationality, Slavery, Civil War, and Reconstruction. The information is compact and well selected, and presented in clear and orderly fashion. The editorial conclusions, which are founded upon the historical statements, are convincing in tone, and can be overthrown or modified only by a more complete presentation of the basic facts.

As accompanying and supplementing this work almost down to date, the reader will find a little primer entitled "American Politics," by Professor Johnston and Professor Winthrop M. Daniels, also of Princeton, to be of great value for ready reference, the subject being treated by Presidential Administrations. Useful lists, such as of Cabinet officers, are included in the Appendix. The work is published by Henry Holt and Company, New York.

The larger work of Professor Johnston, "American Political History," contains extensive bibliographies upon each of its subjects, including almost every important book on American politics and economics which was published before 1905.

With this reference the reader will excuse us for not enlarging the present bibliography, beyond noting one important work recently published. This is "The Origin and Growth of the American Constitution," by Hannis Taylor, LL.D., ex-Minister to Spain: Houghton, Mifflin Company, Boston, 1911.

This historical treatise sets forth the documentary evidence as to Pelatiah Webster's "invention" of the plan of Federal Government, afterwards adopted in the main in the Constitution, and also discusses the adoption of the Constitution, and the constitutional issues in subsequent American political history. The documents appear in the appendix, and are very thoroughly annotated, the Constitution of the United States and its Amendments having citations appended of legal decisions concerning the same.

SCHEME OF THE SERIES

A logical order has been adopted for the presentation of the debates, which adheres so far as possible to the chronological order. Fortunately in presenting the early debates the logical and chronological orders exactly coincide, the subjects of Colonial Rights, Independence and Formation of the Constitution coming in causative succession, uninterrupted by any other issues. Volume I thus forms, as it were, an introduction to all the rest of the work. Having this character, those great documents of American constitutional history, the Declaration of Independence, the Articles of Confederation, and the Constitution, which are constantly referred to in the debates in the later volumes, are here inserted, as also are minor related state papers, such as the addresses of colonial assemblies, of the Continental Congresses, and of State Legislatures, an example of the last being the Virginia Bill of Rights. The "Federalist Papers" are also presented in the form of a digest, with a two-fold justification for their insertion: they are referred to constantly by the later debaters as the earliest and most authoritative commentaries on the Constitution, and have themselves the character of debates, since they quote and answer prevalent objections to the Constitution.

Formal debates were infrequent in colonial America, and only the substance of the few that occurred has been preserved. Accordingly it is to the recorded debates on colonial affairs, which took place in the British

Parliament, that we must chiefly turn, presenting the single speeches of American orators and the even more argumentative protests of the colonial assemblies as a supplement to the arguments of the British contenders for American rights. Volume I is therefore a record of public controversies, as well as of debates proper, and as such is more historical in character than the remaining volumes.

Since the most vital questions, when our new Government was struggling to establish its place among the nations of the earth, were those dealing with Foreign Relations, Volumes II and III contain the great debates upon this subject from Washington's Administration to the war with Spain and the diplomatic questions connected with the Panama Canal. Various debates on Foreign Affairs are inserted in other volumes because of their intimate connection with the subjects of these. Thus the Koszta affair appears in the first volume on Civil Rights.

Because our domestic history for the first three-quarters of our Constitutional history largely centered around slavery, this subject is taken up in Volume IV. The volume closes with the debate on the Dred Scott decision, and Volume V, reverting to the early debates on State's Rights Not Connected with Slavery (such as the Webster-Hayne debate), comes quickly down to the Lincoln-Douglas debates, the result of which precipitated upon the country the question of secession, in connection with slavery. The volume continues the debates on Secession and Slavery down to, and including, the debate on the Conciliation bill in the closing months of Buchanan's Administration.

Volume VI contains the debates of Lincoln's Administration, or the Civil War period, with the exceptions of debates on Reconstruction, which will be found in the succeeding volume on Civil Rights, and of debates on Revenue and Finance, which will be found in Volumes XII and XIII, bearing these titles.

Volumes VII and VIII are on Civil Rights. The first reverts to the early discussions on Naturalization, continues with the famous debates on the Alien and

Sedition Laws, and the related question of State Rights, and, touching upon the question of Nativism (the "Know-Nothing" movement), comes down to the Reconstruction period, and, taking up the question of Negro Rights where Volume VI left it, presents the debates on the Fourteenth Amendment. Volume VIII contains the debates on Negro Suffrage, ending with the Fifteenth Amendment, and then, the discussion of the negro being closed, takes up the debates on Indian Rights. The question of Woman's Rights is then presented, and the volume closes with debates on Polygamy, which, in its constitutional aspect, is a question of Civil Rights.

Volume IX contains debates on the powers and functions of the Departments of Government, Executive (President, Army, Navy), Legislative (Senate, House) and Judicial (Supreme Court), as well as debates on the related question of Civil Service Reform, and on the governmental powers and functions of the sovereign behind all the Departments—the People. Subjects treated in the last connection are Popular Election of President and Senators, Direct Legislation, and Recall of Judges and Judicial Decisions.

Volumes X and XI are on Economic and Social problems. In the first are debates on the Land Question (including the Homestead and Conservation laws and the Single Tax theory), and on the Railroad Question (centering around the power of the Federal Government over Interstate Commerce). The second volume contains debates on the Federal control of Trusts, on Labor legislation, on Socialism, Prohibition of the Liquor Traffic, National Regulation of Foods, etc.

Volume XII contains debates on Revenue, the chief subject being the Tariff, all the tariff acts from the revenue measures of the First Congress to the Payne-Aldrich Act being presented in chronological order, each clearly delimited from the rest by its specific issue. In close connection with the particular tariff or revenue bills which presented them, the subjects of Internal Revenue, Income, Inheritance and Corporation Taxes, and of Reciprocity with Canada are treated.

Volumes XIII and XIV contain debates on Finance. The main subjects of the first volume are Public Credit [questions of Repudiation, etc.], National Banks, "Greenback" or Specie Currency. The last volume deals exclusively with the Silver Question.

Volume XIV also contains the General Index of the Series. This is divided into two parts: an Index of Proper Names (persons and places), and an Index of Subjects.

These indexes are synoptical in character, enabling the reader to prepare from them his own debates, biographical sketches of debaters, etc.

INTRODUCTIONS

Never before, it is believed, has a work of this nature possessed as its editorial contributors persons of the eminence and authority which distinguish the authors of the introductions of the volumes of the present series. Here they are: the President of the United States; the two living ex-Presidents; the Secretary of State; two Senators, one a noted historian, and the other an eminent financial expert; three university presidents and one professor of economics, each an authority in the subject which he discusses; the dean of American journalists, and a woman whose rank both as a journalist and economic historian is exceeded by no other writer in America; and two representative men of letters, the one the chief living member of the most distinguished family of New England, the other the scion of an old Virginia house noted for service to nation and State— he himself being the American Ambassador to the Court of St. James.

Some of the introductions were written after the author had carefully read the proof sheets of the volume in which the introduction was to appear; others were composed upon a general knowledge of the contents of the volume, and the rest were adapted by the authors from former addresses or articles on subjects appropriate to the volume. Thanks for permission to use the adapted articles are herewith extended to the publishers as well as to the authors.

ILLUSTRATIONS

The volumes are illustrated with scenes of great debates and portraits of leading debaters, and with contemporary political cartoons relating to the subjects of the debate and the personality of the debaters. Indeed, the term "illustrated" is too weak a term to state the connection of the pictures with the text, for an apt cartoon is in itself the most effective of arguments, often exceeding in results the longest and most learned demonstration of an orator. Thomas Nast's cartoons of the Reconstruction period appealed on behalf of the Negro more movingly even than the pathetic periods of Charles Sumner, and Homer Davenport's symbolization of the Trust as a brutal giant was more convincing than the diatribes of any of the Populist orators against the "soulless corporations."

In this connection acknowledgment is made of the courtesy extended by the New York Public Library and the New York Historical Society in permitting the reproductions of many of the cartoons in their collections. To W. F. Brainard, of New York City, well known as an expert in "book-building," I would also extend thanks, for sifting the large number of editorially appropriate cartoons through the meshes of artistic and mechanical availability.

In conclusion I would express my appreciation of the services of my editorial assistant, Wilbert W. Blakeman. In such portions of the work as the early debates on the Tariff he has shown ability unusual in a young editor by selecting those points of the subject which are vital to-day, and reducing to the essential minimum those points which tempt the editor by their historical significance to expatiate upon them. By such procedure he has saved much needed space for the more important tariff debates of recent times.

M. M. Miller

VOLUME ONE

Colonial Rights—The Revolution
The Constitution

INTRODUCTION

The Constitution and Its Makers[1]

BESIDE the question of the maintenance or destruction of the Constitution of the United States all other questions of law and policy sink into utter insignificance. In its presence party lines should disappear and all sectional differences melt away like the early mists of dawn before the rising sun. The Constitution is our fundamental law. Upon its provisions rests the entire fabric of our institutions. It is the oldest of written constitutions. It has served as a model for many nations, both in the Old World and in the New. It has disappointed the expectations of those who opposed it, convinced those who doubted, and won a success beyond the most glowing hopes of those who put faith in it. Such a work is not to be lightly cast down or set aside, or, which would be still worse, remade by crude thinkers and by men who live only to serve and flatter in their own interest the emotion of the moment. We should approach the great subject as our ancestors approached it—simply as Americans with a deep sense of its seriousness and with a clear determination to deal with it only upon full knowledge and after the most mature and calm reflection. The time has come to do this, not only here and now, but everywhere throughout the country.

Let us first consider who the men were who made the Constitution and under what conditions they worked. Then let us determine exactly what they meant to do— a most vital point, for much of the discussion to which

[1] Adapted from an address delivered before the Literary and Historical Association of North Carolina, at Raleigh, on November 28, 1911.

1

we have been treated thus far has proceeded upon a complete misapprehension of the purpose and intent of the framers of the Constitution. Finally, let us bring their work and their purposes to the bar of judgment, so that we may decide whether they have failed, whether in their theory of government they were right or wrong then and now, or whether their work has stood the test of time, is broad based on eternal principles of justice, and, if rent or mangled or destroyed, would not in its ruin bring disaster and woes inestimable upon the people who shall wreck their great inheritance and, like

> The base Indian, throw a pearl away,
> Richer than all his tribe.

First, then, of the men who met in Philadelphia in May, 1787, with doubts and fears oppressing them, but with calm, high courage and with a noble aspiration to save their country from the miseries which threatened it, to lead it out from the wilderness of distractions in which it was wandering blind and helpless, into the light, so that the chaos, hateful alike to God and men, might be ended and order put in its place. It is the fashion just now to speak of the framers of the Constitution as worthy, able, and patriotic persons whom we are proud to have embalmed in our history, but toward whom no enlightened man would now think of turning seriously for either guidance or instruction, so thoroughly has everything been altered and so much has intelligence advanced. It is commonly said that they dealt wisely and well with the problems of their day, but that of course they knew nothing of those which confront us, and that it would be worse than folly to be in any degree governed by the opinions of men who lived under such wholly different conditions. It seems to me that this view leaves something to be desired and is not wholly correct or complete. I certainly do not think that all wisdom died with our fathers, but I am quite sure that it was not born yesterday. I fully realize that in saying even this I show myself to be what is called old fashioned, and I know that a study of history, which has been one of the pursuits of my life, tends to make a man give more weight to the teachings of the past than it is now thought they deserve. Yet, after all allowance is made, I can not but feel that there is something to be learned from the men who established the Government of the United States, and that their opinions, the result of much and deep reflection, are not without value, even to the wisest among us.

On questions of this character, I think, their ideas and conclusions are not lightly to be put aside; for, after all, however much we may now gently patronize them as good old patriots long since laid in their honored graves, they were none the less very remarkable men, who would have been eminent in any period of history and might even, if alive now, attain to distinction. Let us glance over the list of delegates to the Constitutional Convention in Philadelphia in 1787. I find, to begin with, that their average age was 43, which is not an extreme senectitude, and the ages range from Franklin, who was 81, to John Francis Mercer, of Virginia, who was 28. Among the older men who were conspicuous in the convention were Franklin, with his more than 80 years; Washington, who was 55; Roger Sherman, who was 66; and Mason and Wythe, of Virginia, who were both 61. But when I looked to see who were the most active forces in that convention, I found that the New Jersey plan was brought forward by William Paterson, who was 42; that the Virginia plan was proposed by Edmund Randolph, who was 34; while Charles Pinckney, of South Carolina, whose plan played a large part in the making of the Constitution, was only 29. The greatest single argument, perhaps, which was made in the convention was that of Hamilton, who was 30. The man who contributed more, possibly, than any other to the daily labors of the convention and who followed every detail was Madison, who was 36. The Connecticut compromise was very largely the work of Ellsworth, who was 42; and the committee on style, which made the final draft, was headed by Gouverneur Morris, who was 35. Let us note, then, at the outset that youth and energy, abounding hope, and the sympathy for the new times stretching forward into the great and unchartered future, as well as high ability, were conspicuous among the men who framed the Constitution of the United States.

Their presiding officer was Washington, one of the great men of all time, who had led the country through seven years of war, and of whom it has been said by an English historian that "no nobler figure ever stood in the forefront of a nation's life." Next comes Franklin, the great man of science, the great diplomatist, the great statesman and politician, the great writer; one of the most brilliant intellects of the eighteenth century, who in his long life had known cities and men as few others have ever known them. There was Hamilton, one of the greatest constructive minds that modern statesmanship has to show, to whose writings German statesmen turned when they were forming their empire forty years ago, and about whom in these later days books are written in England, because Englishmen find in the principal author of "The Federalist" the great exponent of the doctrines of successful federation. There, too, was Madison, statesman and lawmaker, wise, astute, careful, destined to be, under the Government which he was helping to make, Secretary of State and President. Roger Sherman was there, sagacious, able, experienced; one of the leaders of the Revolution and a signer of the Declaration of Independence, as he was of the Constitution. Great lawyers were present in Philadelphia in that memorable summer of 1787, such men as Ellsworth and Wilson and Mason and Wythe. It was, in a word, a very remarkable body which assembled to frame a constitution for the United States. Its members were men of the world, men of affairs, soldiers, lawyers, statesmen, diplomatists, versed in history, widely accomplished, deeply familiar with human nature. I think that, without an undue or slavish reverence for the past or for the men of a former generation, we may fairly say that in patriotism and in intellect, in knowledge, experience, and calmness of judgment, these framers of the Constitution compare not unfavorably with those prophets and thinkers of to-day who decry the work of

1787, would seek to make it over with all modern improvements, and who with unconscious humor declare that they are engaged in the restoration of popular government.

That phrase is in itself suggestive. That which has never existed cannot be restored. If popular government is to be restored in the United States it must have prevailed under the Constitution as it is, and yet those who just now are so devoured by anxiety for the rights of the people propose to effect the restoration they demand by changing the very Constitution under which popular government is admitted by their own words to have existed. I will point out presently the origin of this confusion of thought. It is enough to say now that for more than a century no one questioned that the government of the Constitution was in the fullest sense a popular government. In 1863 Lincoln, in one of the greatest speeches ever uttered by man, declared that he was engaged in trying to save government by the people. Nearly thirty years later, when we celebrated the one hundredth anniversary of the Constitution, the universal opinion was still the same. All men then agreed that the Government which had passed through the fires of civil war was a popular government. Indeed, this novel idea of the loss of popular government which it is proposed to restore by mangling the Constitution under which it has existed for more than a century is very new; in fact, hardly ten years old.

This first conception of our Constitution as an instrument of popular government, so long held unquestioned, was derived from the framers of the Constitution themselves. They knew perfectly well that they were founding a government which was to be popular in the broadest sense. The theory now sedulously propagated, that these great men did not know what they were about, or were pretending to do one thing while they really did another, is one of the most fantastic delusions with which agitators have ever attempted to mislead or perplex the public mind. The makers of the Constitution may have been right or they may have been wrong in the principles upon which they acted or in the work they accomplished, but they knew precisely what they meant to do and why they did it. No man in history ever faced facts with a clearer gaze than George Washington, and when, after the adjournment of the convention, he said, ''We have raised a standard to which the good and wise can repair; the event is in the hands of God,'' he labored under no misapprehension as to the character of the great instrument where his name led all the rest.

It is the fashion to say that since then great changes have occurred and wholly new conditions have arisen of which the men of 1787 could by no possibility have had any knowledge or anticipation. This is quite true. They could not have foreseen the application of steam to transportation, or of electricity to communication, which have wrought greater changes in human environment than anything which has happened to man since those dim, prehistoric, unrecorded days when some one discovered the control of fire, invented the wheel, and devised the signs for language, masterpieces of intelligence with which even the marvels of the last century cannot stand comparison. The men of the Constitution could as little have foreseen what the effects of steam and electricity would be as they could have anticipated the social and economic effects of these great inventions or the rapid seizure of the resources of nature through the advances of science and the vast fortunes and combinations of capital which have thus been engendered. Could they, however, with prophetic gaze have beheld in a mirror of the future all these new forces at work, so powerful as to affect the very environment of human life, even then they would not, I think, have altered materially the Constitution which they were slowly and painfully perfecting. They would have kept on their way, because they would have seen plainly what is now too often overlooked and misunderstood, that all the perplexing and difficult problems born of these inventions and of the changes, both social and economic, which have followed were subjects to be dealt with by laws as the questions arose, and laws and policies were not their business. They were not making laws to regulate or to affect either social or economic conditions. Their work was not only higher but far different. They were laying down certain great principles upon which a government was to be built and by which laws and policies were to be tested as gold is tested by a touchstone.

There is no greater fallacy than to suppose that new and fundamental principles of government are constantly to be invented and wrought out. Laws change and must change with the march of humanity across the centuries as it alteration finds in the conditions about it, but fundamental principles and theories of government are all extremely old.

If you will read "The Republic" and "The Laws" of Plato and supplement that study by an equally careful examination of what Aristotle has to say on government you will find that those great minds have not only influenced human thought from that time to this, but that there is little which they left unsaid. It is the fashion, for example, to speak of socialism as if it were something new, a radiant discovery of our own time which is to wipe away all tears. The truth is that it is very old, as old in essence as human nature, for it appeals to the strong desire in every man to get something for nothing and to have someone else bear his burdens and do his work for him. As a system it is amply discussed by Plato, who, in "The Republic," urges measures which go to great extremes in this direction. In the fourth century of our era a faction called the Circumcellions were active as socialists and caused great trouble within the weakening Empire of Rome. The real difficulty historically with the theories of socialism is not that they are new, but that they are very, very old, and wherever they have been put in practical operation on a large scale they have resulted in disorder, retrogression, and in the arrest of civilization and progress.

In order to reach the essence of what the makers of the Constitution tried and meant to do, which it is most important to know and reflect upon deeply before we seek to undo their work, let us begin by dismissing from our consideration all that is unessential or misleading.

Let us lay aside first the word republic, for a republic de-
notes a form and not a principle. A republic may be
democratic like ours, or an autocracy like that of Augustus Cæsar, or an oligarchy like Venice, or a changing
tyranny like some of those visible in South America.
The word has become as inaccurate, scientifically speaking, as the word monarchy, which may be in reality a
democracy as in England or Norway, constitutional as
in Italy, or a pure despotism as in Russia. Let us adhere in this discussion to the scientifically exact word
"democracy." Next let us dismiss all that concerns
the relations of the States of the National Government.
Federation was the great contribution of the Philadelphia convention to the science of government. The
framers of the Constitution, if they did not invent the
principle, applied it on such a scale and in such a way
that it was practically a discovery, a venture both bold
and new, as masterly as it was profoundly planned.
With the love of precedents characteristic of their race
they labored to find authority and example in such remote and alien arrangements as the Achaian League and
the Amphictyonic Council, but the failure of these precedents as such was the best evidence of the novelty and
magnitude of their own design. Their work in this respect has passed through the ordeal of a great war; it
has been and is to-day the subject of admiration and
study on the part of foreign nations, and not even the
most ardent reformer of this year of grace would think,
in his efforts to restore popular government, of assail-
ing the Union of Sovereign States. Therefore we may
pass by this great theme which was the heaviest part of
the task of our ancestors.

In the same way we may dismiss, much as it troubled
the men of 1787, all that relates to the machinery of
government, such as the electoral college, the tenure of
office, the methods of electing Senators and Representatives, and the like. These matters are important; many
active thinkers in public life seek to change them, not
for the better, as I believe, but none the less these provisions concern only the mechanism of government;
they do not go to the root of the matter, they do not

affect the fundamental principles on which the Government rests.

By making these omissions we come now to the vital point, which is, What kind of a government did the makers of the Constitution intend to establish and how did they mean to have it work? They were, it must be remembered, preparing a scheme of government for a people peculiarly fitted to make any system of free institutions work well. The people of the United Colonies were homogeneous. They came in the main from Great Britain and Ireland, with the addition of the Dutch in New York, of some Germans from the Palatinate, and of a few French Huguenots, whose ability and character were as high as their numbers were relatively small. But an overwhelming majority of the American people in 1787 were of English and Scotch descent, and they, as well as the others from other lands, were deeply imbued with all those principles of law which were the bulwarks of English liberty. In this new land men had governed themselves and there was at that moment no people on earth so fit or so experienced in self-government as the people of the thirteen colonies. Their colonial governments were representative and in essence democratic. They became entirely so when the Revolution ended and the last English governor was withdrawn. In the four New England colonies local government was in the hands of the town meetings, the purest democracies then or now extant, but it is best to remember, what the men of 1787 well knew, that these little democracies moved within fixed bounds determined by the laws of the States under which they had their being.

For such a people, of such a character, with such a past and such habits and traditions, only one kind of government was possible, and that was a democracy. The makers of the Constitution called their new Government a republic, and they were quite correct in doing so, for it was of necessity republican in form. But they knew that what they were establishing was a democracy. One has but to read the debates to see how constantly present that fact was to their minds. Democracy was then a very new thing in the modern world. As a system it had not been heard of, except in the fevered struggles of the Italian city republics, since the days of Rome and Greece, and although the convention knew perfectly well that they were establishing a democracy and that it was inevitable that they should do so, some of them regarded it with fear and all with a deep sense of responsibility and caution. The logical sequence as exhibited in history and as accepted by the best minds of the eighteenth century, struggling to give men a larger freedom, was democracy—anarchy—despotism. The makers of the Constitution were determined that so far as in them lay the American Republic should never take the second step, never revolve through the vicious circles which had culminated in empire in Rome, in the tyrants of the Grecian and the despots of the Italian cities, which is their turn had succumbed to the absolutism of foreign rulers.

The vital question was how should this be done; how should they establish a democracy with a strong government—for after their experience of the Confederation they regarded a weak government with horror—and at the same time so arranged the Government that it should be safe as well as strong and free from the peril of lapsing into an autocracy on the one hand, or into disorder and anarchy on the other? They did not try to set any barrier in the way of the popular will, but they sought to put effective obstacles in the path to sudden action which was impelled by popular passion, or popular whim, or by the excitement of the moment. They were the children of the "Great Rebellion" and the "Blessed Revolution" in the England of the seventeenth century, and they were steeped in the doctrine of limiting the power of the King. But here they were dealing with a sovereign who could not be limited, for, while a king can be limited by transferring his power to the people, when the people are sovereign their powers cannot be transferred to anybody. There is no one to transfer them to, and if they are taken away the democracy ceases to exist and another government, fundamentally different, takes its place.

The makers of the Constitution not only knew that the will of the people must be supreme, but they meant to make it so. That which they also aimed to do was to make sure that it was the real will of the people which ruled and not their momentary impulse, their well-considered desire and determination and not the passion of the hour, the child, perhaps, of excitement and mistake inflamed by selfish appeals and terrorized by false alarms. The main object, therefore, was to make it certain that there should be abundant time for discussion and consideration, that the public mind should be thoroughly and well informed, and that the movements of the machinery of government should not be so rapid as to cut off due deliberation. With this end in view they established with the utmost care a representative system with two chambers and an executive of large powers, including the right to veto bills. They also made the amendment of the Constitution a process at once slow and difficult, for they intended that it should be both, and indeed that it should be impracticable without a strong, determined, and lasting public sentiment in favor of change.

Finally they established the Federal judiciary, and in the Supreme Court of the United States they made an addition to the science of government second only in importance to their unequaled work in the development of the principle of federation. That great tribunal has become in the eyes of the world the most remarkable among the many remarkable solutions devised by the convention of 1787 for the settlement of the gravest governmental problems. John Marshall, with the intellect of the jurist and the genius of the statesman, saw the possibilities contained in the words which called the court into being. By his interpretation and that of his associates and their successors the Constitution attained to flexibility and escaped the rigidity which then and now is held up as the danger and the defect of a written instrument. In their hands the Constitution has been expanded to meet new conditions and new problems as they have arisen. In their hands also the Constitution has been the protection of the rights of States and the rights of men, and laws which violated its principles and its provisions have been set aside.

By making the three branches of the Government, the executive, the legislative, and the judicial, entirely separate and yet coördinate, and by establishing a representative system and creating a Supreme Court of extraordinary powers, the framers of the Constitution believed that they had made democracy not only all powerful but at the same time safe and that they had secured it from gradual conversion into autocracy on the one hand and from destruction by too rapid motion and too quick response to the passions of the moment on the other. If ever men were justified by results they have been. The Constitution in its development and throughout our history has surpassed the hopes of its friends and utterly disappointed the predictions and the criticisms of its foes. Under it the United States has grown into the mighty republic we see to-day. New States have come into the Union, vast territories have been acquired, population and wealth have increased to a degree which has amazed the world, and life, liberty, and property have been guarded beneath the flag which is at once the symbol of the country and of the Constitution under which the nation has risen to its high success.

CHAPTER I

THE STAMP ACT

Proposal in the British Parliament of a Colonial Stamp Act—Colonial Opposition—Passage of the Act: in favor, Sir George Grenville and Sir Charles Townshend; opposed, Gen. Henry Seymour Conway, Alderman Beckford, Mr. Jackson, Sir William Meredith, and Col. Isaac Barré—Tilt between Townshend and Barré—Debate on the Resolutions of Patrick Henry against the Act in the Virginia Assembly: in favor, Mr. Henry, George Johnson and Richard Henry Lee; opposed, Peyton Randolph—Stamp Act Congress—Boycott of Stamps—Sons of Liberty—Speech of John Adams [Mass.]: "Our Blood-bought Liberty"—Daniel Dulany [Md.] on the Stamp Act Riots.

THE acts of Parliament restraining the trade and manufacture of the colonies were deemed by the colonists, in some instances, a violation of their rights, and in others an unnecessary and improper sacrifice of their interest to the supposed interest of the parent country, or some other more favored part of the British empire; and they had, accordingly, been very little regarded.

A distinction had been made by the colonists between what were called external and internal taxes, the former being considered as imposed for the regulation of the trade of the empire, and not for the purpose of revenue. Plans of laying internal taxes and of drawing a revenue from the colonies had been at times suggested to the ministry, and particularly to Sir Robert Walpole and Mr. William Pitt during their respective administrations, but these statesmen were too wise and sagacious to adopt them.

The first attempt to draw a revenue directly from the colonies was made after the power of the French in America had been reduced. This was deemed a favorable moment to call upon the Americans for taxes to

13

assist in the payment of a debt which had been incurred, as was alleged, in a great measure for their protection against a powerful enemy, who was now no longer an object of their dread.

Soon after George Grenville became Prime Minister, the project of imposing internal taxes in America was carried into effect. In the winter of 1764 that minister called together the agents of the colonies, and gave them notice of his intention of drawing a revenue from the colonies, saying that for this purpose he should in the ensuing session of Parliament propose a duty on stamps.

Soon after this, resolutions were passed in the House of Commons continuing and making perpetual the duties on sugar, molasses, and some other articles imported into the colonies, with additions and amendments.

Memorials of the Colonies

These ministerial and parliamentary proceedings were soon communicated to the colonies by their agents. The colonists at once took the alarm, particularly at the contemplated stamp duty; and, instead of yielding to it, or providing an equivalent according to the suggestion of the minister, they reiterated, though in a more full and ample manner, the declarations so often made by their ancestors, that they could be taxed only in their colonial legislatures, where, and where alone, they were represented. The people of Boston, at their meeting in May, 1764, instructed their representatives to the general court on this important subject. In these instructions (which were drawn by Samuel Adams, one of the committee appointed for that purpose), after commenting on the sugar and molasses act, they proceed to observe:

But our greatest apprehension is that these proceedings may be preparatory to new taxes; for, if our trade may *be taxed*, why not our *lands*? Why not the products of our lands and every thing we possess or use? This, we conceive, annihilates our charter rights to govern and tax ourselves. It strikes at our British privileges, which, as we have never forfeited, we hold in common with our fellow subjects who are natives of Britain. If taxes are laid upon us, in any shape, without our having a legal representation where they are laid, we are reduced from the character of free subjects to the state of tributary slaves.

We, therefore, earnestly recommend it to you to use your utmost endeavors to obtain from the general court all necessary advice and instruction to our agent at this most critical juncture. We also desire you to use your endeavors that the other colonies, having the same interests and rights with us, may add their weight to that of this province; that by united application of all who are aggrieved all may obtain redress.

This was the first public act in the colonies in opposition to the ministerial plans of drawing a revenue directly from America; and it contained the first suggestion of the propriety of that mutual understanding and correspondence among the colonies which laid the foundation of their future confederacy.

The House of Representatives of Massachusetts, in June following, declared:

That the sole right of giving and granting the money of the people of that province was vested in them, or their representatives; and that the imposition of duties and taxes by the Parliament of Great Britain upon a people not represented in the House of Commons is absolutely irreconcilable with their rights. That no man can justly take the property of another without his consent; upon which original principles the power of making laws for levying taxes, one of the main pillars of the British constitution, is evidently founded.

The same sentiments are expressed, though in stronger language, in their letter of instructions to their agent:

If the colonists are to be taxed at pleasure without any representatives in Parliament, what will there be to distinguish them, in point of liberty, from the subjects of the most absolute prince? If we are to be taxed, at pleasure, without our consent, will it be any consolation to us that we are to be assessed by an hundred instead of one? If we are not represented we are slaves.

The House at the same time appointed a committee to sit in the recess of the court, to write to the other colonies requesting them to join in applying for a repeal of the sugar act, and in preventing the passage of the act laying stamp duties, or any other taxes, on the American provinces.

In the course of the year 1764 petitions to the King and both houses of Parliament were prepared in many of the colonies, and sent to their agents.

The petitions of the Assembly of New York were drawn with great ability, and breathed a spirit more bold and decided than those from any other colony.

An exemption from the burden of ungranted and involuntary taxes must be the grand principle of every free state. Without such a right vested in themselves, *exclusive of all others,* there can be no liberty, no happiness, no security; it is inseparable from the very idea of property; for who can call that his own which may be taken away at the pleasure of another? and so evidently does this appear to be the *natural right* of mankind, that even conquered tributary states, though subject to the payment of a fixed periodical tribute, never were reduced to so absolute and forlorn a condition as to yield to all the burdens which their conquerors might, at any future time, think fit to impose. The tribute paid, the debt was discharged; and the remainder they would call their own.

And if conquered vassals, upon the principle of mutual justice, may claim a freedom from assessments, unbounded and unassented to, without which they would suffer the loss of everything, and life itself become intolerable, with how much propriety and boldness may we proceed to inform the Commons of Great Britain, who to their distinguished honor in all ages asserted the liberties of mankind, that the people of this colony nobly *disdain* the thought of claiming that exemption as a *privilege.* They found it on a basis more honorable, solid, and stable; they *challenge it* and glory in it, as *their right.* That *right* their ancestors enjoyed in Great Britain and Ireland, their descendants returning to these kingdoms enjoy it again, and that it may be exercised by his Majesty's subjects *at home,* and justly denied to those who submitted to poverty, barbarian wars, loss of blood, loss of money, personal fatigues and ten thousand unutterable hardships, to enlarge the trade, wealth and dominion of the nation; or, to speak with the most incontestable modesty, that when, as subjects, all have equal merits, a fatal, nay the most odious, discrimination should nevertheless be made between them, no sophistry can recommend to the sober impartial decision of common sense.

While the Assembly of New York acknowledged that Parliament had a right to regulate the trade of the colonies, they declared that, in doing this, they had not the right of imposing duties for the purpose of *revenue*.

On this subject, they say to the House of Commons with equal boldness:

But a *freedom* to drive all kinds of traffic, in subordination to, and not inconsistent with, the British trade, and an *exemption from all duties in such a course of commerce,* is humbly claimed by the colonies as the most essential of all the *rights* to which they are entitled as colonists and connected in the common bond of liberty with the free sons of Great Britain. For, with submission, since all *impositions,* whether they be *internal taxes,* or *duties* paid for *what we consume,* equally diminish the estates upon which they are charged, what avails it to any people by which of them they are impoverished?

Everything will be given to preserve life; and, though there is a diversity in the means, yet the whole wealth of a country may be as effectually drawn off by the exaction of *duties* as by any other *tax* upon their estates.

In conclusion the Assembly declare:

They have no desire to derogate from the power of the Parliament of Great Britain; but they cannot avoid deprecating the loss of such rights as they have hitherto enjoyed, rights established in the first dawn of our constitution, founded upon the most substantial reasons, confirmed by invariable usage, conducive to the best ends; never abused to bad purposes, and with the loss of which, liberty, property, and all the benefits of life tumble into insecurity and ruin; rights, the deprivation of which will dispirit the people, abate their industry, discourage trade, introduce discord, poverty and slavery; or, by depopulating the colonies, turn a vast, fertile, prosperous region into a dreary wilderness, impoverish Great Britain, and shake the power and independence of the most opulent and flourishing empire in the world.

While the colonists in their various petitions denied the right of Parliament to tax them without their consent, they expressed their willingness to grant aids to the Crown according to their abilities through their own legislatures, whenever such aids should be required in the usual constitutional mode. As all aids granted to the Crown, agreeably to the British constitution, were the free gifts of the people, the colonists claimed the right of judging as to the amount and manner of these gifts; and were, therefore, unwilling indirectly to acknowledge or countenance the right of Parliament to tax them, by proposing any substitute for the stamp duty, which substitute Parliament might accept or reject at pleasure.

In the winter of 1764-1765 Dr. Benjamin Franklin and other agents of the colonies had a conference with Mr. Grenville on the subject of the stamp duty. They informed the minister of the great opposition to the proposed tax in America, and most earnestly entreated him that, if money must be drawn from the colonies by taxes, to leave it with the colonists to raise it among themselves in such manner as they should think proper and best adapted to their circumstances and abilities.

Debate Between Townshend and Barré

When the bill for laying the contemplated duties was brought before the House of Commons, it met with strong opposition. Though Mr. Pitt was absent on this occasion, confined to his bed by sickness, and General Conway and Alderman Beckford were the only persons in the House who opposed the bill on the ground that Parliament had no right to tax the colonies, Col. Isaac Barré, Mr. Jackson, Sir William Meredith, and others were against it on the ground of expediency, alleging generally that it was to the last degree impolitic, as well as unjust, for Great Britain to impose direct taxes upon the colonists while she retained the monopoly of their commerce. Sir George Grenville and Sir Charles Townshend were the principal supporters of the bill.

Mr. Townshend, in the conclusion of a speech in

favor of the measure delivered on February 7, 1765, exclaimed, "And now these Americans, *planted* by our care, *nourished* up by our indulgence, until they are grown to a degree of strength and importance, and *protected* by our arms—will they grudge to contribute their mite to relieve us from the heavy burden we lie under?" To this Col. Barré, in a style and manner peculiar to himself, instantly replied:

They *planted by your care!* No; your oppressions planted them in America! They fled from your tyranny to a then uncultivated and inhospitable country, where they exposed themselves to almost all the hardships to which human nature is liable; and, among others, to the cruelties of a savage foe, the most subtle, and I will take upon me to say the most formidable, of any people upon the face of the earth; and yet, actuated by principles of true English liberty, our American brethren met all the hardships with pleasure, compared with those they suffered in their own country from the hands of those that should have been their friends.

They *nourished by your indulgence!* They grew by your neglect of them. As soon as you began to take care about them; that care was exercised in sending persons to *rule* them in one department and another, who were deputies of deputies to some members of this house, sent to prey upon them; men whose behavior, on many occasions, has caused the blood of those *sons of liberty* to recoil within them; men promoted to the highest seats of justice, some [who], to my knowledge, were glad, by going to a foreign country, to escape being brought to a bar of justice in their own.

They *protected by your arms!* They have nobly taken up arms in your defence, have exerted their valor, amidst their constant and laborious industry, for the defence of a country whose frontier was drenched in blood, while its interior parts yielded all its little savings to your emolument.

And, believe me, that same spirit of freedom which actuated that people at first will accompany them still. But prudence forbids me to explain myself further.

God knows, I do not at this time speak from party heat. However superior to me in general knowledge and experience the respectable body of this house may be, yet I claim to know more of America than most of you, having seen and been conversant with that country. The people, I believe, are as truly loyal as any subjects the King has; but [they are] a people jealous of their liberties, and who will vindicate them if ever they should be violated—but the subject is too delicate, I will say no more.

REJECTION OF PETITIONS

The House was very forcibly struck with these sentiments, thrown out without premeditation, and for a while sat amazed and without answering a word. But when the petitions from Virginia, Connecticut, and South Carolina were offered in opposition to the bill, the House refused to receive them; in the first place because they questioned or denied the right of Parliament to pass the bill; and in the second place because it was contrary to an old standing rule of the House, *"that no petition should be received against a money bill."* The majority against receiving the petitions was very large, and those from the other colonies were not offered. The petition from New York was expressed in such strong language that no member of the House could be prevailed upon to present it. The bill passed the House 250 to 50; was adopted in the House of Lords with great unanimity, and on the 22d of March, 1765, received the royal sanction.

The act imposed duties on most of the instruments used in judicial and commercial proceedings, and, indeed, in almost all the ordinary transactions in the colonies; nor were pamphlets, newspapers and almanacs excepted. The literature of the colonists did not escape the notice of the ministers. A duty of two pounds sterling was required for every degree conferred by seminaries of learning. The ministry affected to believe, and indeed declared, that the act embraced so many objects that it would "execute itself." Apprehensive, however, of opposition, the government passed a bill during the same session authorizing the quartering of the troops in the colonies, and directing the assemblies to furnish them with certain articles of provisions not before usually required. During the pendency of this bill it was proposed that the troops might be quartered in private houses. This, however, was too palpable and flagrant a violation of the sacred rights of individuals to be

THE COUNCIL OF THE RULERS AND THE ELDERS AGAINST THE TRIBE
OF GREAT AMERICANITES

21

adopted, and the proposition was finally given up. No act of the parent country ever excited such universal alarm in the colonies as this. The colonists saw and felt that the act was not only a violation of their rights, but a fatal blow aimed at the future peace and prosperity of their country.

AMERICAN OPPOSITION TO THE ACT

The assembly of Virginia was the first public body that met after the news of the Stamp Act reached America. Those who had heretofore taken the lead in the popular branch of that body, the House of Burgesses, seemed unwilling to approach the subject. It was not until near the close of the session, about the first of May, that an action was taken regarding the act.

Then it was that a young lawyer from Hanover County, who had taken into his confidence only one or two of his colleagues, arose and introduced a set of resolutions, the boldness of which struck the timid assembly with consternation, although at the same time it excited their awe and admiration.

The speaker was Patrick Henry, who, though he was reputed the most eloquent speaker in the colony, had hitherto not distinguished himself in the assembly.

RESOLUTIONS OF PATRICK HENRY

The following are the resolutions which Mr. Henry introduced in the House of Burgesses on the Stamp Act:

Whereas the honorable House of Commons in England have of late drawn into question how far the General Assembly of this colony hath power to make laws for laying taxes and imposing duties, payable by the people of this His Majesty's most ancient colony; for settling and ascertaining the same to *all future times,* the House of Burgesses of the present General Assembly have come to the following resolutions.

Resolved, that the first adventurers and settlers of this, His Majesty's colony and dominion, brought with them, and transmitted to their posterity and all other His Majesty's subjects since inhabiting in this His Majesty's said colony, all the privileges, franchises, and immunities that have, at any time, been held, enjoyed, and possessed by the people of Great Britain.

Resolved, that by two royal charters granted by King James I, the colonists aforesaid are declared entitled to all the privileges, liberties, and immunities of denizens and natural born subjects, to all intents and purposes as if they had been abiding and born within the realm of England.

Resolved, that the taxation of the people by themselves, or by persons chosen by themselves to represent them, who can only know what taxes the people are able to bear, and the easiest mode of raising them, and are equally affected by such taxes themselves, is the distinguishing characteristic of British freedom, and without which the ancient constitution cannot subsist.

Resolved, that His Majesty's liege people of this most ancient colony have uninterruptedly enjoyed the right of being thus governed by their own Assembly, in the article of *their taxes and internal police;* and that the same hath never been forfeited, or any other way given up, but hath been recognized by the King and people of Great Britain.

Resolved, therefore, that the General Assembly of this colony have the *sole right and power to lay taxes and impositions* upon the inhabitants of this colony; and that every attempt to vest such power in any person or persons whatever, other than the General Assembly aforesaid, has a manifest tendency to destroy British as well as American freedom.

The above resolutions were found among the papers of Patrick Henry, after his death, sealed up, and with the following indorsement, "Inclosed are the resolutions of the Virginia assembly, concerning the Stamp Act. Let my executors open this paper." [1]

Chief Justice John Marshall, in his "Life of Washington," gives the resolutions which received the sanction of the Assembly with the third resolution omitted, and with slight differences in the phraseology of the others.

Judge Marshall adds, "Such were the resolutions as agreed to by that part of the Assembly which was most timid. The following resolutions were also introduced by Mr. Henry, and passed the committee, but were disagreed to in the House:

"Resolved, that His Majesty's liege people, the inhabitants

[1] Life of Patrick Henry, by William Wirt, p. 50.

of this colony, are not bound to yield obedience to any law or ordinance whatsoever, designed to impose any taxation whatsoever upon them, other than the laws and ordinances of the General Assembly aforesaid.

"Resolved, that any person who shall, by speaking or writing, maintain that any person or persons, other than the General Assembly of this colony, have any right or power to lay any taxation whatsoever on the people here, shall be deemed an enemy to this His Majesty's colony."

DEBATE ON THE RESOLUTIONS

Some of the resolutions offered by Mr. Henry occasioned a most violent and, as has been said by one who was present, a "most bloody" debate in that house. They were seconded by George Johnson, who was an able constitutional lawyer, and opposed by those who had before taken the lead, because not sufficiently conciliatory. The bold and powerful eloquence of the mover, however, prevailed over all opposition, though the most objectionable were carried by a single vote only. Mr. Henry did not hesitate to declare that the act imposing internal duties on the colonists was tyrannical, and that the king in assenting to it had acted the part of a tyrant; and when, in the heat of debate, alluding to the fate of other tyrants, he exclaimed, "Cæsar had his Brutus, Charles I his Cromwell, and George III"—he was interrupted by the speaker and others, with the cry of "Treason!" Mr. Henry, pausing for a moment, and fixing his eye on the speaker, deliberately concluded— "may profit by their example; if this be treason, make the most of it."

Henry was strongly supported in this debate by Richard Henry Lee. Says a historian of the time, "People knew not which most to admire: the overwhelming might of Henry, or the resistless persuasion of Lee." Mr. Lee also wrote many powerful articles upon the Stamp Act to the newspapers, as well as letters to patriots in the other colonies counseling a union of interests. In a letter to John Dickinson, dated July 25, 1768, on Parliament's declaration of its supremacy over the colonies, he wrote:

To prevent the success of this unjust system, an union of counsel and action among all the colonies is undoubtedly necessary. The politician of Italy delivered the result of reason and experience when he proposed the way to *conquest*, by *division*. How to effect this union, in the wisest and firmest manner, perhaps, time and much reflection only can show. But well to understand each other, and timely to be informed of what passes both here and in Great Britain, it would seem that not only select committees should be appointed by all the colonies, but that a private correspondence should be conducted between the lovers of liberty in every province.

Peyton Randolph was one of those who opposed Henry's resolutions as precipitate. Indeed, he was greatly alarmed at their probable effect in angering Parliament. As they were leaving the hall, Jefferson heard him say, referring to the closeness of the vote by which the resolutions were carried, "By God, I would have given five hundred guineas for a single vote!"

The proceedings of Virginia were immediately circulated through the colonies, and roused them to action. The various assemblies, at the suggestion of Massachusetts, determined upon a Stamp Act congress of the colonies, to be held at New York on the first Tuesday of October, 1765.

THE STAMP ACT CONGRESS

This was the first general meeting of the colonies for the purpose of considering their rights and privileges, and obtaining a redress for the violation of them on the part of the parent country.

The commissioners were generally instructed to prepare suitable petitions and representations to the King and Parliament on the subject of the late acts regarding the colonies, and to pray for relief.

After having duly organized, and resolved that the commissioners of each colony should have *"one voice"* only in determining questions that should arise, this congress, on the 8th of October, took into consideration "the rights and privileges of the colonists, with the several inconveniences and hardships to which they were

and must be subjected by the Stamp Act and other late
acts of Parliament.'' This important subject was under
consideration until the 19th of October, when a declaration of the *rights and grievances* of the colonists was
agreed to.

In this declaration, consisting of fourteen articles, after acknowledging their allegiance to the King, and *"all due subordination"* to Parliament, they, among other things, assert
and declare that the colonists are entitled to all the *inherent
rights and liberties* of His Majesty's natural born subjects in
the kingdom of Great Britain; and that it is inseparably essential to the freedom of a people, and the undoubted right of
Englishmen, that no taxes be imposed on them but with their
own consent, given personally or by their representatives—that
the colonists *are not* and, from their local circumstances, *cannot*
be represented in the House of Commons in Great Britain—
that the only representatives of the people of these colonies are
persons chosen *therein* by themselves, and that no taxes *ever*
have been or can be constitutionally imposed on them but by
their respective legislatures—that, all supplies to the Crown being the free gifts of the people, it is unreasonable and inconsistent with the principles and spirit of the British constitution
for the people of Great Britain to grant to His Majesty the
property of the colonists—that trial by jury is the inherent and
invaluable right of every British subject in the colonies, and that
the Stamp Act, and other acts extending the jurisdiction of the
Admiralty Court beyond its ancient limits, ''have a manifest
tendency to subvert the rights and liberties of the colonists.''
They also declared that the restrictions imposed by several
late acts of Parliament on the *trade* of the colonies were burdensome, and would render them unable to purchase the manufactures of Great Britain; and that it was the indispensable duty
of the colonies to the best of sovereigns, to the mother country,
and to themselves, to endeavor by a loyal and dutiful address
to the King and humble application to Parliament to procure a
repeal of the act imposing stamp duties, of all parts of such acts
as extend the admiralty jurisdiction, and of the other late acts
for the restriction of American commerce.

This declaration was drafted by John Cruger, Mayor
of New York, who was one of the delegates.

This congress then prepared an address to the King,
and a petition to each house of Parliament, drawn by

committees appointed for that purpose. The committee to draw an address to the King were Robert R. Livingston, William S. Johnson, and William Murdock; to draw the petition to the House of Lords were John Rutledge, Edward Tilghman, and Philip Livingston; and to draw the petition to the House of Commons were Thomas Lynch, James Otis, and Thomas McKean.

These state papers evince the talents as well as firmness, tempered with wisdom and moderation, of this first American congress; composed as it was of some of the most distinguished statesmen from the several colonies therein represented.

ADDRESS TO THE KING

In their address to the King, drawn up principally by Mr. Johnson from Connecticut, one of the ablest lawyers and most accomplished scholars in America, the congress remind him that:

Animated with the spirit of liberty, encouraged by his predecessors, and confiding in the public faith, their ancestors, for the enjoyment of all the rights essential to freedom, emigrated to the American continent; and in the midst of innumerable dangers and difficulties, and at a great expense of their blood and treasure, added "these vast and valuable dominions to the empire of Great Britain." That, for the enjoyment of their rights and privileges, governments were early formed in the colonies with full powers of legislation, agreeably to the principles of the English constitution; and that, under these governments, the liberties, thus vested in their ancestors, and transmitted to their posterity, have been exercised and enjoyed, and by the inestimable blessings thereof, under the favor of Almighty God, the inhospitable deserts of America have been converted into flourishing countries. Science, humanity, and the knowledge of divine truths have been diffused through remote regions of ignorance, infidelity, and barbarism; the number of British subjects wonderfully increased; and the wealth and power of Great Britain proportionally augmented. That, by means of these settlements, and the unparalleled success of His Majesty's arms, a foundation was now laid for rendering the British empire the most extensive and powerful of any recorded in history.

"Our connection," they add, "with this empire we esteem our greatest happiness and security, and humbly conceive it may now be so established by your royal wisdom as to endure to the latest period of time. This, with most humble submission to Your Majesty, we apprehend will be most effectually accomplished by fixing the pillars thereof on *liberty and justice,* and securing the inherent rights and liberties of your subjects *here,* upon the principles of the English constitution." To this constitution, they say, "these two principles are essential, the right of your faithful subjects freely to grant to Your Majesty such aids as are required for the support of your government over them and other public exigencies, and trial by their peers. By the one they are secured from unreasonable impositions, and by the other from arbitrary decisions of executive power. The continuance of these blessings to the inhabitants of America we ardently implore as absolutely necessary to unite the several parts of your widely extended dominions in that harmony so essential for the preservation of the whole."

PETITION TO PARLIAMENT

In their petition to the House of Commons they claim the same rights as in their address to the King; and they complain not only of the act imposing the stamp duties, but of several other acts imposing duties in the colonies, and laying their trade under burdensome restrictions.

They stated "that the remote situation and other circumstances of the colonies render it impracticable that they should be represented but in their respective subordinate legislatures"; and they "humbly conceived that the Parliament, adhering strictly to the principles of the constitution, have never hitherto taxed any but those who were actually therein represented; for this reason, we humbly apprehend they never have taxed Ireland, or any other of the subjects without the realm.

"But were it ever so clear," they add, "that the colonies might in law be represented in the honorable House of Commons, yet we conceive that very good reasons, from inconvenience, from the principles of true policy, and from the spirit of the British constitution, may be adduced to show that it would be for the real interest of Great Britain, as well as her colonies, that the late regulations should be rescinded, and the several acts of Parliament imposing duties and taxes on the colonies, and extending the jurisdiction of the courts of admiralty here beyond their ancient limits, should be repealed.

"We shall not attempt," they say, "a minute detail of all the reasons which the wisdom of the honorable house may suggest on this occasion, but would humbly submit the following particulars to their consideration:

"That money is already become very scarce in these colonies, and is still decreasing by the necessary exportation of specie from the continent for the discharge of our debts to British merchants.

THE DEPLORABLE STATE OF AMERICA, OR SC——H GOVERNMENT

Referring to the secret influence of the S[cottis]h Lord Bute over the British Ministry

From the collection of the New York Historical Society.

"That an immensely heavy debt is yet due from the colonies for British manufactures, and that they are still burdened with taxes to discharge the arrearages due for aids granted by them in the late war.

"That the balance of trade will ever be much against the colonies, and in favor of Great Britain, while we consume her manufactures, the demand for which must ever increase in proportion to the number of inhabitants settled here with the means of purchasing them. We therefore humbly conceive it to be the interest of Great Britain to increase, rather than diminish, these means, as the profits of all the trade of the colonies ultimately center there to pay for her manufactures, as we are not allowed to purchase elsewhere; and by the consumption of which, at the advanced prices the British taxes oblige the makers and venders to put on them, we eventually contribute very largely to the revenues of the crown.

"That from the nature of American business, the multiplicity of suits and papers used in matters of small value, in a country where freeholds are so minutely divided, and property so frequently transferred, a stamp duty must ever be very burdensome and unequal.

"That it is extremely improbable that the honorable House of Commons should, at any time, be thoroughly acquainted with our condition, and all facts requisite to a just and equal taxation of the colonies.

"It is also humbly submitted, whether there be not a material distinction in reason and sound policy, at least, between the necessary exercise of parliamentary jurisdiction in general acts, for the amendment of the common law, and the regulation of trade and commerce through the whole empire, and the exercise of that jurisdiction, by imposing taxes on the colonies."

With the exception of the foregoing petitions, address and general declaration of rights, little is known or has been collected with respect to the proceedings of this first American congress. But James Otis of Massachusetts is remembered to have been particularly distinguished for his eloquence and thorough knowledge of American rights. In the margin of Ramsay's "History of the American Revolution," Mr. Rodney, one of the commissioners from Delaware, made the following entry, "The historian passes by this congress in a very light manner. It was this congress in which James Otis, of Boston, displayed that light and knowledge of the interest of America, which, shining like a sun, lit up those stars which shone on this subject afterward."

This congress adjourned on the 25th of October, and their proceedings were approved by all the members except Mr. Ruggles of Massachusetts, and Mr. Ogden of New Jersey, both of whom left New York without signing the address and petitions. The commissioners from South Carolina and Connecticut were limited by their instructions to make report to their respective legislatures, and the committee of New York, who had been admitted as members, had authority to apply to the King or Parliament. The address and petitions were, therefore, signed by the commissioners from only six of the colonies. The proceedings of the congress, however, were afterward sanctioned and approved by the assemblies not only of South Carolina, Connecticut and New York, but of the colonies not therein represented.

PROTESTS OF COLONIAL LEGISLATURES

The subject of the stamp duties was not left with the congress alone; it was taken up by the colonial legislatures, either before or subsequent to the meeting of that body.

The Legislature of Connecticut, in their instructions to their agent at London, after declaring the act laying internal duties to be "an infringement of the essential liberties of the colonists," proceed to say, "we can by no means be content that you should give up the matter of *right,* but must beg you would on all proper occasions claim and firmly insist on the *exclusive right* of the colonies to tax themselves, and the privilege of trial by jury; and to maintain these principles in the most effectual manner possible as what we can *never recede from."*

Opposition to the stamp duties was not confined to legislative resolutions and declarations. Numerous individuals in every part of the country held meetings, and in bold and decided language expressed, not only their detestation of the act, but their unalterable determination that the same should never be carried into effect.

ADDRESS OF PLYMOUTH, MASS.

The instructions given to their representative in the assembly by the inhabitants of the town of Plymouth, the immediate descendants of the Pilgrims who first planted New England, will be read with peculiar interest.

After expressing their esteem for the British constitution, and stating their grievances, they say to their representative, Mr. Foster, "You, sir, represent a people who are not only descended from the first settlers of this country, but inhabit the very *spot* they first possessed. Here was first laid the foundation of the British empire in this part of America, which, from a very small beginning, has increased and spread in a manner very surprising, and almost incredible; especially when we consider that all this has been effected without the aid and assistance of any power on earth; that we have *defended, protected,* and *saved* ourselves against the incursions and cruelty of savages, and the subtilty and inhumanity of our inveterate and natural enemies the French; and all this without the appropriation of any tax by stamps, or stamp act laid upon our fellow subjects, in any part of the King's dominions, for defraying the expenses thereof.

"This place, sir, was at first the asylum of liberty, and, we hope, will ever be preserved sacred to it; though it was then no more than a forlorn wilderness, inhabited by savage men and beasts. To this place our fathers (whose memory be revered), possessed of the principles of liberty in their purity, disdaining slavery, fled to enjoy those privileges which they had an undoubted right to, but were deprived of by the hands of violence and oppression in their native country. We, sir, their posterity, the freeholders and other inhabitants of this town, legally assembled for that purpose, possessed of the same sentiments, and retaining the same ardor for liberty, think it our indispensable duty on this occasion to express to you these our sentiments of the Stamp Act and its fatal consequences to this country, and to enjoin upon you, as you regard not only the welfare, but the very being of this people, that you (consistent with our allegiance to the King and relation to the government of Great Britain), disregarding all proposals for that purpose, exert all your power and influence in relation to the Stamp Act, at least, until we hear the success of our petitions for relief. We likewise, to avoid disgracing our ancestors, as well as the reproaches of our own consciences, and the curses of posterity, recommend it to you to obtain, if possible, in the honorable House of Representatives of the people a full and explicit assertion of our rights, and to have the same entered on their public records that all generations yet to come may be convinced that we have not only a just sense of our liberties, but that we never (with submission to divine Providence) will be slaves to any power on earth; and, as we have at all times an abhorrence of tumults and disorders, we think ourselves happy in being at present under no apprehensions of any, and in having good and wholesome laws, sufficient to preserve the peace of the province in all future times, unless provoked by some imprudent measures; so we think it by no means advisable for you to interest yourself in the protection of stamp papers or stamp officers.''

Boycott of the Stamps

Many of the resolutions adopted at these meetings of the citizens were of an inflammatory character.

The following declaration of the freemen of the County of Essex, in New Jersey, and of Talbot County, in Maryland, will serve, among thousands of others of a similar cast, to show the spirit then universally prevailing in America against stamps and stamp officers.

After declaring the act itself unconstitutional, they add, "that they will detest, abhor, and hold in contempt all and every person or persons who shall merely accept of any employment or office relating to the said Stamp Act, or shall take any shelter or advantage of the same, and all and every stamp-pimp, informer, and encourager of the execution of said act; and that they will have no communication with any such persons, unless it be to inform them of their vileness."

The merchants of New York, on the 31st of October, nobly sacrificed their interest on this occasion by entering into an agreement or assocation to have no goods shipped from Great Britain, unless the Stamp Act should be repealed.

The merchants of Philadelphia and Boston soon after joined those of New York in similar associations.

Another association of a different and, indeed, of a novel character was in December entered into by some of the citizens of New York and Connecticut, who were called the "Sons of Liberty," the object of which association was in reality to prevent, by force if necessary, the execution of the act, under the pretence of maintaining unimpaired the principles of the British constitution, of which they declared the act to be a violation. In this association the act is thus noticed:

And whereas, a certain pamphlet has appeared in America in the form of an act of Parliament called and known by the name of the *Stamp Act*, but has never been *legally* published or introduced, neither can it, as it would immediately deprive them of the most invaluable part of the British constitution, viz. the trial by juries, and the most just mode of taxation in the world, that is of *taxing themselves;* rights that every British subject becomes heir to as soon as born. For the preservation of which and every part of the British constitution, they do reciprocally resolve and determine to march with the utmost dispatch, at their own proper cost and expense, on the first proper notice (which must be signified to them by at least six of the Sons of Liberty) *with their whole force,* if required and it can be spared, to the relief of those that shall, are, or may be in danger from the Stamp Act, or its aiders or abettors, or anything relative to it, on account of anything that may have been done in opposition to its obtaining; and they do mutually and most fervently recommend it to each other to be vigilant in watching all those who, from the nature of their offices, vocations, or dispositions, may be the most likely to introduce the use of stamped paper, to the total subversion of the British constitution and American liberty; and the same, when discovered, immediately to advise each other of, let them be of what rank or condition soever; and they also do agree that they will mutually, and to the utmost of their power, by all just ways and means, endeavor to bring all such betrayers of their country to the most condign punishment; and further they do mutually resolve to defend the liberty of the press in their respective colonies from all unlawful violations and impediments whatever on account of said act, as the only means (under divine Providence) of preserving their lives, liberties and fortunes, and the same, in regard to the judges, clerks, attorneys, etc., that shall proceed without any regard to the Stamp Act, from all pains, fines, mulcts, penalties, or any other molestation whatever; and, finally, that they will, to the utmost of their power, endeavor to bring about, accomplish, and perfect the like association with all the colonies on the continent, for the like salutary purposes and no other.

This singular association was afterward extended to some of the other colonies, and but for a repeal of the act would, no doubt, have been generally adopted.

These various associations and resolutions were encouraged and supported, and the spirit of the people kept alive, by the numerous publications in the newspapers in America, most of which were enlisted in favor of the colonists in this controversy.

The pens of American patriots in favor of liberty and in opposition to the claim of Parliament during the year 1765 were not confined to newspaper publications.

An "Essay on the Canon and Feudal Law," by John Adams; "Considerations on the Propriety of Imposing Taxes on the British Colonies, for the Purpose of Raising a Revenue by Act of Parliament," by Daniel Dulany of Maryland, and "An Enquiry into the Rights of the British Colonies," by Theodoric Bland of Virginia, are most notable.

"OUR BLOOD-BOUGHT LIBERTY"

JOHN ADAMS

"Be it remembered," says Mr. Adams, "that liberty must, at all hazards, be supported! We have a right to it, derived from our Maker! but, if we had not, our fathers have earned it and bought it for us, at the expense of their ease, their estates, their pleasure, and their blood. Is there not something extremely fallacious," he adds, "in the commonplace images of mother country and children colonies? Are we children of Great Britain, any more than the cities of London, Exeter, and Bath? Are we not brethren and fellow subjects with those in Britain, only under a somewhat different method of legislation, and a totally different method of taxation? But, admitting we are children, have not children a right to complain when their parents are attempting to break their limbs, to administer poison, or to sell them to enemies for slaves?"

"Let the pulpit," he concludes, "resound with the doctrines and sentiments of religious liberty. Let us hear the danger of thraldom to our consciences from ignorance, extreme poverty, and dependence, in short from civil and political slavery. Let us see delineated before us the true map of man. Let us hear the dignity of his nature, and the noble rank he holds among the works of God! that consenting to slavery is a sacrilegious breach of trust, is offensive in the sight of God as it is derogatory from our honor, our interest, or happiness; and that God Almighty has promulgated from heaven liberty, peace, and good will to man.

"Let the bar proclaim, 'the laws, the rights, the generous plan of power' delivered down from remote antiquity; inform the world of the mighty struggles and numberless sacrifices, made by our ancestors, in the defense of freedom. Let it be known that British liberties are not the grants of princes or parliaments, but original rights, conditions of original contracts, coequal with prerogative and coeval with government. That many of our rights are inherent and essential, agreed on as maxims, and established as preliminaries, even before a parliament existed: Let them search for the foundation of British laws and government in the frame of human nature, in the constitution of the intellectual and moral world. There let us see that truth, liberty, justice, and benevolence are its everlasting basis; and that, if these could be removed, the superstructure is overthrown of course.''

After stating that the ''encroachments upon liberty, in the reigns of James I and Charles I, first turned the attention of learned men to government, and produced the greatest number of statesmen ever seen in any age or nation,'' Mr. Adams says, ''the prospect now before us in America ought in the same manner to engage the attention of every man of learning to matters of power and right, that we may be neither led nor driven blindfolded to irretrievable destruction. Nothing less than this seems to have been meditated for us by somebody or other in Great Britain. There seems to be a direct and formal design on foot to enslave all America. This, however, must be done by degrees. The first step that is intended seems to be an entire subversion of the whole system of our fathers by the introduction of the canon and feudal law into America. The canon and feudal systems, though greatly mutilated in England, are not yet destroyed. Like the temples and palaces in which the great contrivers of them were once worshiped and inhabited, they exist in ruins; and much of the domineering spirit of them still remains. The designs and labor of a certain society to introduce the former of them into America have been well exposed to the public by a writer of great abilities; and the further attempts to the same purpose, that may be made by that society, or by the ministry or Parliament, I leave to the conjecture of the thoughtful. But it seems very manifest from the Stamp Act itself that a design is formed to strip us, in a great measure, of the means of knowledge, by loading the press, the colleges, and even an almanac and a newspaper, with restraints and duties; and to introduce the inequalities and dependencies of the feudal system by taking from the poorer sort of people all their little subsistence, and conferring it on a set of stamp officers, distributors and their deputies.''

DULANY ON THE ACT

Mr. Dulany and Mr. Bland were among the most distinguished lawyers and statesmen in America. The former not only proved the illegality of the Stamp Act, and the evils the Americans must experience from the new parliamentary regulations of the colonial trade, whereby they were rendered unable to pay for the large balances always due for English manufactures; but pointed out a remedy for these evils in future. The remedy suggested was domestic industry, which, he said, would render the American colonists less dependent on the mother country for articles either of necessity or luxury.

"Let the manufacture of America," says this enlightened statesman, "be the symbol of dignity, the badge of virtue, and it will soon break the fetters of distress. A garment of linsey-woolsey, when made the distinction of patriotism, is more honorable, and attractive of respect and veneration, than all the pageantry, and the robes, and the plumes, and the diadem of an emperor without it. Let the emulation be, not in the richness and variety of foreign productions, but in the improvement and perfection of our own—let it be demonstrated that the subjects of the British empire in *Europe and America* are the same, that the hardships of the latter will ever recoil on the former.

"In theory it is supposed that each is equally important to the other, that all partake of the adversity and depression of any. The theory is just, and time will certainly establish it; but if another principle should be hereafter adopted in practice, and a violation deliberate, cruel, ungrateful, and attended with every circumstance of provocation be offered to our fundamental rights, why should we leave it to the slow advances of time (which may be the great hope and reliance, probably, of the authors of the injury, whose view it may be to accomplish their selfish purposes in the interval) to prove what might be demonstrated immediately? Instead of moping, and puling, and whining, to excite compassion; in such a situation, we ought with spirit, and vigor, and alacrity to bid defiance to tyranny by exposing its impotence, by making it as contemptible as it would be detestable. By a vigorous application to manufactures, the consequence of oppression in the colonies to the inhabitants of Great Britain would strike home, and immediately. None could mistake it. Craft and subtilty would not be able to impose on the most ignorant and credulous; for, if any should be so weak of sight as not to see, they would not be so callous as not to feel it. Such conduct would be the most dutiful and beneficial to the mother country. It would point out the distemper when the remedy might be easy, and a cure at once effected by a simple alteration of regimen." [1]

Bland's book, published in 1766, was the first written on colonial rights. He was regarded as an authority on the subject, his knowledge of Virginia matters in particular gaining him the title of the "Virginia Antiquary."

A statement of the public sentiment and feeling in America, in relation to the Stamp Act, was, in a variety of ways, communicated to the ministry and people of Great Britain. A person high in office, in New York, in November of this year, writes to a nobleman in England, "Depend upon it, they will suffer no man to execute any law to raise *internal taxes,* unimposed by their own assemblies. None of the distributors durst act; and that man's heart must be fortified with tenfold steel who ventures to approve the doctrine that the Parliament hath a right to give away the estates of the colonists without their consent." [2]

Stamp Act Riots

The indignation of the people against the act, unfortunately, was not confined to resolutions and agreements; but in some of the colonies broke out into acts of violence and unjustifiable outrage against the persons and property of its supporters. These outrages were carried to the greatest length in Boston. The house of Chief-Justice Thomas Hutchinson was attacked in a riotous manner, his furniture and pictures destroyed, and his valuable library and manuscripts, in a wanton manner, either burnt or thrown into the street. Mr. Hutchinson was very obnoxious to the people of Massachusetts not only for favoring the execution of the Stamp Act, but because he was instrumental in enforcing the acts of trade. The houses of several revenue officers, among them that of Mr. Oliver, the distributor of stamps, were also injured. These riotous acts were, however,

[1] Nevertheless Dulany became a loyalist when the Revolution that he had prophesied might result from the Stamp Act finally came to pass.
[2] Adolphus's History of England; appendix 5.

disapproved by the great mass of the people of Boston, and of the province generally.

Such was the general determination of the people against the execution of the act that the distributors of the stamp paper who did not voluntarily resign were compelled so to do, either by threats or force. On the 1st of November, the day the act was to take effect, neither stamps nor stamp officers were to be found in the colonies. The courts of justice were for a time closed, vessels did not depart from American ports, and business of various kinds was interrupted. This state of things, however, remained for a short period only; business by general consent soon resumed its usual course without the aid of stamp paper.

CHAPTER II

THE SUPREMACY OF PARLIAMENT

[DEBATES IN PARLIAMENT]

Debate on the Right to Tax America between George Grenville and William Pitt. I.—Debate on the Resolution Declaring the Supremacy of Parliament: in favor, Gen. Henry Seymour Conway and the Marquis of Rockingham; opposed, Col. Isaac Barré and William Pitt—Examination of Dr. Benjamin Franklin—Debate on the Repeal of the Stamp Act: in favor, Gen. Conway, Mr. Pitt, and Col. Barré; opposed, Mr. Grenville— Debate in the House of Lords between Lords Camden and Mansfield on the Supremacy of Parliament—Stamp Act Repealed and Supremacy of Parliament Asserted.

WHILE this measure of the British Government was thus agitating the colonies a change took place in the British ministry. The immediate authors of the measure itself were removed from the councils of the King, and others, supposed more favorable to the American interest, came into office.

On the 14th of January, 1766, the American papers relating to the origin, progress, and tendency of the disturbances in the colonies were laid before the House of Commons. These papers the House determined to take into consideration on the 28th of the same month.

Upon the day of the submission of the American papers occurred the great debate between George Grenville and William Pitt on the right of Parliament to tax America.

Pitt's speeches were extemporaneous, and, since verbatim reporting was not practiced in his time, are not preserved in the exact form in which they were delivered. Of all his speeches, that on the Stamp Act, reported by Sir Robert Dean and Lord Charlemont, is said to be closest in verbiage to the actual oration, with perhaps the exception of his Address to the Throne concerning Affairs in America, reported by Hugh Boyd and corrected by Pitt.

THE RIGHT TO TAX AMERICA

PITT VS. GRENVILLE

Mr. PITT arose from his place in the House and said:

It is a long time, Mr. Speaker, since I have attended in Parliament. When the resolution was taken in this House to tax America I was ill in bed. If I could have endured to be carried in my bed—so great was the agitation of my mind for the consequences—I would have solicited some kind hand to have laid me down on this floor, to have borne my testimony against it! It is now an act that has passed. I would speak with decency of every act of this House; but I must beg the indulgence of the House to speak of it with freedom.

I hope a day may soon be appointed to consider the state of the nation with respect to America. I hope gentlemen will come to this debate with all the temper and impartiality that his Majesty recommends, and the importance of the subject requires; a subject of greater importance than ever engaged the attention of this House, that subject only excepted when, near a century ago, it was the question whether you yourselves were to be bond or free. In the meantime, as I cannot depend upon my health for any future day (such is the nature of my infirmities), I will beg to say a few words at present, leaving the justice, the equity, the policy, the expediency of the act to another time.

I will only speak to one point—a point which seems not to have been generally understood—I mean to the *right*. Some gentlemen [alluding to Mr. Nugent] seem to have considered it as a point of honor. If gentlemen consider it in that light, they leave all measures of right and wrong, to follow a delusion that may lead to destruction. It is my opinion that this kingdom has no right to lay a tax upon the colonies. At the same time, I assert the authority of this kingdom over the colonies to be sovereign and supreme, in every circumstance of government and legislation whatsoever. They are the subjects of this kingdom; equally entitled with yourselves to all the natural rights of mankind and the peculiar privileges of Englishmen; equally bound by its laws, and equally participating in the constitution of this free country. The Americans are the sons, not the bastards of England! Taxation is no part of the governing or legislative power. The taxes are a voluntary *gift* and *grant* of the Commons alone. In legislation the three estates of the realm are alike concerned; but the concurrence of the peers and the Crown to a tax is only necessary to clothe it with the form of a law. The gift and grant is of the Commons alone. In ancient days the Crown, the barons, and the clergy possessed the lands. In those days the barons and the clergy gave and granted to the Crown. They gave and granted what was their own! At present, since the discovery of America, and other circumstances permitting, the commons are become the proprietors of the land. The Church (God bless it!) has but a pittance. The property of the lords, compared with that of the commons, is as a drop of water in the ocean; and this House represents those commons, the proprietors of the lands; and those proprietors virtually represent the rest of the inhabitants. When, therefore, in this House, we give and grant, we give and grant what is our own. But in an American tax what do we do? "We, your Majesty's commons for Great Britain, give and grant to your Majesty"— what? Our own property! No! "We give and grant to your Majesty" the property of your Majesty's commons of America! It is an absurdity in terms.

The distinction between legislation and taxation is essentially necessary to liberty. The Crown and the peers are equally legislative powers with the Commons. If taxation be a part of simple legislation the Crown and the peers have rights in taxation as well as yourselves; rights which they will claim, which they will exercise, whenever the principle can be supported by power.

There is an idea in some that the colonies are *virtually* represented in the House. I would fain know by whom an American is represented here. Is he represented by any knight of the shire in any county in this kingdom? Would to God that respectable representation was augmented to a greater number! Or will you tell him that he is represented by any representative of a borough? a borough which, perhaps, its own representatives never saw! This is what is called the rotten part of the constitution. It cannot continue a century.[1] If it does not drop it must be amputated. The idea of a virtual representation of America in this House is the most contemptible idea that ever entered into the head of a man. It does not deserve a serious refutation.

[1] The "rotten boroughs" in England were abolished in 1832.

The commons of America, represented in their several assemblies, have ever been in possession of the exercise of this, their constitutional right, of giving and granting their own money. They would have been slaves if they had not enjoyed it! At the same time, this kingdom, as the supreme governing and legislative power, has always bound the colonies by her laws, by her regulations, and restrictions in trade, in navigation, in manufactures, in everything, except that of taking their money out of their pockets without their consent.

Here I would draw the line:

Quam ultra citraque neque consistere rectum.[1]

At the conclusion of Mr. Pitt's remarks, Mr. Grenville arose in behalf of the government. He began by severely censuring the ministry for not giving Parliament earlier notice of the disturbances in America. "They began," said he, "in July, and now we are in the middle of January; lately they were only occurrences; they are now grown to disturbances, to tumults and riots. I doubt they border on open rebellion; and, if the doctrine I have heard this day be confirmed, I fear they will lose that name to take that of revolution. The government over them being dissolved, a revolution will take place in America."

Then, applying himself to the issue of the debate, namely, the distinction between internal and external taxation, Mr. Grenville continued:

I cannot understand the difference between external and internal taxes. They are the same in effect, and differ only in name. That this kingdom has the sovereign, the supreme legislative power over America is granted; it cannot be denied; and taxation is a part of that sovereign power. It is one branch of the legislation. It is, it has been, exercised over those who are not, who were never, represented. It is exercised over the India Company, the merchants of London, the proprietors of the stocks, and over many great manufacturing towns. It was exercised over the county palatine of Chester, and the bishopric of Durham, before they sent any representatives to Parliament. I appeal for proof to the preambles of the acts which gave them representatives; one in the reign of Henry VIII, the other in that of Charles II. [Mr. Grenville then quoted the acts, and

[1] "Right lies wholly neither with one side nor the other."

desired that they might be read; which being done, he said]: When I proposed to tax America I asked the House if any gentleman would object to the right; I repeatedly asked it, and no man would attempt to deny it. Protection and obedience are reciprocal. Great Britain protects America; America is bound to yield obedience. If not, tell me when the Americans were emancipated? When they want the protection of this kingdom they are always very ready to ask it. That protection has always been afforded them in the most full and ample manner. The nation has run herself into an immense debt to give them their protection; and now, when they are called upon to contribute a small share toward the public expense—an expense arising from themselves—they renounce your authority, insult your officers, and break out, I might almost say, into open rebellion. The seditious spirit of the colonies owes its birth to the factions in this House. Gentlemen are careless of the consequences of what they say, provided it answers the purposes of opposition. We were told we trod on tender ground. We were bid to expect disobedience. What is this but telling the Americans to stand out against the law, to encourage their obstinacy with the expectation of support from hence? "Let us only hold out a little," they would say, "our friends will soon be in power." Ungrateful people of America! Bounties have been extended to them. When I had the honor of serving the Crown, while you yourselves were loaded with an enormous debt, you gave bounties on their lumber, on their iron, their hemp, and many other articles. You have relaxed in their favor the Act of Navigation, that palladium of the British commerce; and yet I have been abused in all the public papers as an enemy to the trade of America. I have been particularly charged with giving orders and instructions to prevent the Spanish trade, and thereby stopping the channel by which alone North America used to be supplied with cash for remittances to this country. I defy any man to produce any such orders or instructions. I discouraged no trade but what was illicit, what was prohibited by an act of Parliament. I desire a West India merchant [Mr. Long], well known in the city, a gentleman of character, may be examined. He will tell you that I offered to do every thing in my power to advance the trade of America. I was above giving an answer to anonymous calumnies; but in this place it becomes one to wipe off the aspersion.

Here Mr. Grenville ceased. Several members got up to speak, but Mr. Pitt seeming to rise, the House was so clamorous for Mr. *Pitt!* Mr. *Pitt!* that the speaker was obliged to call to order. Mr. Pitt said:

I do not apprehend I am speaking twice. I did expressly reserve a part of my subject, in order to save the time of this House; but I am compelled to proceed in it. I do not speak twice; I only finish what I designedly left imperfect. But if the House is of a different opinion, far be it from me to indulge a wish of transgression against order. I am content, if it be your pleasure, to be silent.

Here he paused. The House resounding with *Go on! go on!* he proceeded:

Gentlemen, sir, have been charged with giving birth to *sedition* in America. They have spoken their sentiments with freedom against this unhappy act, and that freedom has become their crime. Sorry I am to hear the liberty of speech in this House imputed as a crime. But the imputation shall not discourage me. It is a liberty I mean to exercise. No gentleman ought to be afraid to exercise it. It is a liberty by which the gentleman who calumniates it might have profited. He ought to have desisted from his project. The gentleman tells us America is obstinate; America is almost in open rebellion. I rejoice that America has resisted. Three millions of people, so dead to all the feelings of liberty as voluntarily to submit to be slaves, would have been fit instruments to make slaves of the rest. I come not here armed at all points, with law cases and acts of Parliament, with the statute book doubled down in dog's ears, to defend the cause of liberty. If I had, I myself would have cited the two cases of Chester and Durham. I would have cited them to show that, even under former arbitrary reigns, Parliaments were ashamed of taxing a people without their consent, and allowed them representatives. Why did the gentleman confine himself to Chester and Durham? He might have taken a higher example in Wales—Wales, that never was taxed by Parliament till it was incorporated.[1] I would not debate a particular point of law with the gentleman. I know his abilities. I have been obliged to his diligent researches. But, for the defence of liberty, upon a general principle, upon a constitutional principle, it is a ground on which I stand firm—on which I dare meet any man.

[1] The right of representation in Parliament was given to Wales, as well as to the adjoining counties of Chester and Monmouth, in the reign of Henry VIII, and to the county of Durham in 1673. Before this representation was accorded these districts were free from direct national taxation.

The gentleman tells us of many who are taxed, and are not represented—the India company, merchants, stockholders, manufacturers. Surely many of these are represented in other capacities, as owners of land, or as freemen of boroughs. It is a misfortune that more are not equally represented. But they are all inhabitants, and as such, are they not virtually represented? Many have it in their option to be actually represented. They have connections with those that elect, and they have influence over them. The gentleman mentioned the stockholders. I hope he does not reckon the debts of the nation as a part of the national estate.

Since the accession of King William, many ministers, some of great, others of more moderate abilities, have taken the lead of government. [Here Mr. Pitt went through the list of them, bringing it down till he came to himself, giving a short sketch of the characters of each, and then proceeded] : None of these thought, or even dreamed, of robbing the colonies of their constitutional rights. That was reserved to mark the era of the late administration. Not that there were wanting some, when I had the honor to serve His Majesty, to propose to me to burn my fingers with an American stamp act. With the enemy at their back, with our bayonets at their breasts, in the day of their distress, perhaps the Americans would have submitted to the imposition; but it would have been taking an ungenerous, an unjust advantage. The gentleman boasts of his bounties to America! Are not these bounties intended finally for the benefit of this kingdom? If they are not, he has misapplied the national treasures!

I am no courtier of America. I stand up for this kingdom. I maintain that the Parliament has a right to bind, to restrain America. Our legislative power over the colonies is sovereign and supreme. When it ceases to be sovereign and supreme I would advise every gentleman to sell his lands, if he can, and embark for that country. When two countries are connected together like England and her colonies, without being incorporated, the one must necessarily govern. The greater must rule the less. But she must so rule it as *not to contradict the fundamental principles that are common to both*.

If the gentleman does not understand the difference between external and internal taxes, I cannot help it. There is a plain distinction between taxes levied for the purposes of raising a revenue and duties imposed for the regulation of trade, for the accommodation of the subject; although, in the consequences, some revenue may incidentally arise from the latter.

The gentleman asks, When were the colonies emancipated?
I desire to know, when were they made slaves? But I dwell not
upon words. When I had the honor of serving His Majesty I
availed myself of the means of information which I derived from
my office. I speak, therefore, from knowledge. My materials
were good. I was at pains to collect, to digest, to consider them;
and I will be bold to affirm that the profit to Great Britain from
the trade of the colonies, through all its branches, is two millions
a year. This is the fund that carried you triumphantly through
the last war. The estates that were rented at two thousand
pounds a year, threescore years ago, are at three thousand at
present. Those estates sold then from fifteen to eighteen years
purchase; the same may now be sold for thirty. You owe this
to America. This is the price America pays you for her protection. And shall a miserable financier come with a boast that
he can bring "a pepper-corn" into the exchequer by the loss of
millions to the nation?[1] I dare not say how much higher these
profits may be augmented. Omitting the immense increase of
people, by natural population, in the northern colonies, and the
emigration from every part of Europe, I am convinced on other
grounds that the commercial system of America may be altered
to advantage. You have prohibited where you ought to have
encouraged. You have encouraged where you ought to have
prohibited. Improper restraints have been laid on the continent
in favor of the islands. You have but two nations to trade with
in America. Would you had twenty! Let acts of Parliament
in consequence of treaties remain; but let not an English minister become a custom-house officer for Spain, or for any foreign
power. Much is wrong! Much may be amended for the general
good of the whole!

Does the gentleman complain he has been misrepresented
in the public prints? It is a common misfortune. In the Spanish affair of the last war I was abused in all the newspapers for
having advised his Majesty to violate the laws of nations with
regard to Spain. The abuse was industriously circulated even
in hand-bills. If administration did not propagate the abuse
administration never contradicted it. I will not say what advice I did give the King. My advice is in writing, signed by myself, in the possession of the Crown. But I will say what advice
I did not give to the King. I did *not* advise him to violate any
of the laws of nations.

[1] This refers to a statement of Mr. Nugent, one of the debaters on the
side of the Administration, that, "a peppercorn [which is a British form of
purely nominal payment], in acknowledgment of the right to tax America,
is of more value than millions without it."

As to the report of the gentleman's preventing in some way the trade of bullion with the Spaniards, it was spoken of so confidently that I own I am one of those who did believe it to be true.

The gentleman must not wonder he was not contradicted when, as minister, he asserted the right of Parliament to tax America. I know not how it is, but there is a modesty in this House which does not choose to contradict a minister. Even your chair, sir, looks too often toward St. James'.[1] I wish gentlemen would get the better of this modesty. If they do not perhaps the collective body may begin to abate of its respect for the representative. Lord Bacon has told me that a great question would not fail of being agitated at one time or another. I was willing to agitate such a question at the proper season, viz., that of the German war—*my* German war, they called it! Every session I called out, Has anybody any objection to the German war? Nobody would object to it, one gentleman only excepted, since removed to the Upper House by succession to an ancient barony [Lord Le Despencer, formerly Sir Francis Dashwood]. He told me he did not like a German war. I honored the man for it, and was sorry when he was turned out of his post.

A great deal has been said without doors of the power, of the strength of America. It is a topic that ought to be cautiously meddled with. In a good cause, on a sound bottom, the force of this country can crush America to atoms. I know the valor of your troops. I know the skill of your officers. There is not a company of foot that has served in America out of which you may not pick a man of sufficient knowledge and experience to make a governor of a colony there. But on this ground, on the Stamp Act, which so many here will think a crying injustice, I am one who will lift up my hands against it.

In such a cause your success would be hazardous. America, if she fell, would fall like the strong man; she would embrace the pillars of the state, and pull down the constitution along with her. Is this your boasted peace—not to sheathe the sword in its scabbard, but to sheathe it in the bowels of your countrymen? Will you quarrel with yourselves, now the whole house of Bourbon is united against you; while France disturbs your fisheries in Newfoundland, embarrasses your slave trade to Africa, and withholds from your subjects in Canada their property stipulated by treaty; while the ransom for the Manillas is denied by Spain, and its gallant conqueror basely traduced into a mean

[1] The English royal court.

plunderer; a gentleman [Colonel Draper], whose noble and generous spirit would do honor to the proudest grandee of the country? The Americans have not acted in all things with prudence and temper: they have been wronged: they have been driven to madness by injustice. Will you punish them for the madness you have occasioned? Rather let prudence and temper come first from this side. I will undertake for America that she will follow the example. There are two lines in a ballad of Prior's, of a man's behavior to his wife, so applicable to you and your colonies, that I cannot help repeating them:

> "Be to her faults a little blind;
> Be to her virtues very kind."

Upon the whole, I will beg leave to tell the House what is my opinion. It is that the Stamp Act be repealed absolutely, totally, and immediately. That the reason for the repeal be assigned, viz., because it was founded on an erroneous principle. At the same time, let the sovereign authority of this country over the colonies be asserted in as strong terms as can be devised, and be made to extend to every point of legislation whatsoever; that we may bind their trade, confine their manufactures, and exercise every power whatsoever, except that of taking their money out of their pockets without their consent.

Debate on the Supremacy of Parliament

On the 27th of January, 1766, the petition of the American Congress was offered to the House of Commons. Several objections to receiving it were immediately made, such as that it came from an unauthorized and unconstitutional assembly; and that to receive a petition from persons thus assembled without any authority from the Crown would give countenance to such illegal meetings in future. Such meetings, it was said, were pregnant with danger to His Majesty's authority and government. Another strong objection to the reception of the memorial arose from the petitioners denying the right of Parliament to impose internal taxes, and questioning their right even to lay duties for the regulation of trade in the colonies. This, it was said, struck at the very vitals of legislative authority, and strongly pointed to a state independent of the mother country.

Finally, after an examination of the petition in com-

mittee of the whole, which lasted three or four days,
Secretary Henry Seymour Conway moved a resolution
declaring "that the King's Majesty, by and with the advice and consent of the Lords, spiritual anl temporal, and
Commons of Great Britain, in Parliament assembled,
had, hath, and, of right, ought to have full power and
authority to make laws and statutes of sufficient force
and validity to bind the colonies and people of America subjects of Great Britain, *in all cases* whatsoever.''

This resolution was followed by four others, declaring that the tumults and insurrections in the colonies
were in open defiance of His Majesty's government; and,
the same being encouraged by sundry votes and resolutions in the colonial assemblies, proper recompense must
be made to those who had suffered in their persons and
property.

The ministry had now determined to procure a repeal of the acts relating to stamps; and at the same time
to assert in the most unqualified manner the absolute
supremacy of Parliament over the colonies.

In introducing the first resolution, Gen. Conway and
the Marquis of Rockingham, chancellor of the exchequer,
said they were induced to offer the proposition in so
extensive a manner not only as necessary to meet the
resolutions and language of several of the colonies, but
because, upon the fullest enquiry into the constitution
of Great Britain, they were convinced that, in *point of
law,* the King, Lords, and Commons were undoubtedly
possessed of that power, though in point of *policy, justice, or equity,* it was a power they ought to exercise,
but in the *most extraordinary cases only.*

Col. Barré moved to strike out the words in the
declaratory resolution, ''in all cases whatsoever''; he
should then, he said, have no objection to it. He was
seconded by Mr. Pitt.

This brought up directly the great question of the
right of Parliament to tax the colonists, and the long
and animated debate which followed was principally
confined to this point alone.

Those in favor of the motion said, among other things, that the emigrants to the colonies carried with them every right the crown could grant, and every right of British subjects. That they carried with them the common law of the land; and that by this common law, and the spirit of the constitution, no man could be taxed without being represented—that the people of America could not, with the least propriety, be said to be represented in the Parliament of Great Britain; and it was representation alone which gave the right and power to the Commons of imposing taxes. This, they said, was the foundation of all the arguments and reasoning of Mr. Locke on the subject; and greater authority could not be produced. That the principles of *taxation* as distinguished from *legislation* were as distinct principles and powers as any two propositions under the sun; and had been so considered uniformly by their ancestors for many ages—that the counties palatine of Chester and Durham had always taxed themselves by writs of requisition, and on that account, when the grant of a charter was made out erecting Lancaster into a county palatine, there was an express reservation of the power of Parliament to impose taxes upon the people of that county; which would have been unnecessary if the power of Parliament was such as contended for.

That the clergy formerly taxed themselves; for, though the archbishops and others sat in Parliament, it was not as representatives of the clergy; the body of the clergy, therefore, separately and by themselves, granted subsidies to the Crown, and neither Lords nor Commons attempted to alter or vary them; and that this was a strong authority to show the difference between taxation and legislation.

That, by the principles of the constitution, the Commons alone made grants to the Crown—that all bills which passed both houses of Parliament remained in the Upper House for the fiat of the King, except bills of subsidy and taxes, which, when passed by the Lords, were again sent down to the Commons, and by the speaker presented to the sovereign as the free gift of the Commons; and of the Commons alone the King asks for a supply, and to them only he renders his thanks when granted. That by solemn compacts express powers had been granted to the colonists; powers repeatedly recognized by Parliament. It was evidently intended that the Americans should be as free as other British subjects: they have the power of raising and granting their money—a power which constitutes the essence of Parliament—if this is taken from them the very existence, the very essence, of assemblies is destroyed. The colonists, therefore, have a right to consider the Stamp Act as a grievance which should be removed. The justice of the claim upon the colonies for contribution, it was said, could not be denied; but the *mode* in which this contribution should be made was a distinct thing. That with respect to taxes Great Britain and the colonies might have opposing interests; and there was a possibility that the burdens of the one might be relieved at the expense and oppression of the other—that the circumstances and abilities of the colonists could never be so justly and truly known to the Commons of England as to their own Assemblies—there they can enjoy the exercise of that fundamental right of British subjects, to have some one to speak for them when their property is called for by way of taxes, and to represent their condition and abilities. This in Parliament is impracticable, and they are, thereby, deprived of a most important privilege. The supreme power, wherever lodged, must always be controlled by reason, by the principles of justice and humanity—the distance and situation of the colonists, however, were such that the greatest caution could not exempt them from oppression. A lenient, humane, and magnanimous conduct, it was said, did more to secure and preserve to Rome her distant colonies than all the legions she was ever mistress of, or could at any time command. Should the House, after all, be of opinion that Parliament possessed this *summum jus,* it should be remembered, they said, that *summa injuria* was its well-known offspring.

The opponents of the motion of Col. Barré rejoiced that the debate was now confined to the single question of *power* and *right* in Parliament to pass the law, so loudly complained of, without intermingling in the debate the *expediency* of its repeal; which would be a proper subject for consideration another day. In opposition to the motion it was observed that the establishment of the colonies was originally by license from the Crown —that, on account of the distance of the emigrants from the great executive power of the realm, the Crown granted them charters investing them with powers of government necessary for their protection, defence, and for the support of civil authority among them—that these powers were of the same nature with those granted to the East India company and to the great cities and corporations in England; each having power to raise money for their support, but neither, by any grant the King could make, could be exempted from the supreme authority of King, Lords, and Commons—that the Crown was but a part of the supreme power of the realm, and could not grant that which belonged to the supreme legislative power, which extended wheresoever the sovereignty of the Crown extended—that the colonists in their new settlements owed the same subjection and allegiance to the supreme power as when residing in Great Britain—that no time or distance could terminate this subjection and allegiance, and which, by the law of the land, must descend to their posterity. That no compact made between the Crown and his subjects upon their emigration could have destroyed their relation with this supreme sovereign power. That Parliament should have the power to alter or change their property, to enact laws for the punishment of great offences and, in particular, of high treason, by which they might be divested of their property, their inheritances taken away, without their immediate consent; and yet not have power to impose a tax upon that property seemed, they said, an extraordinary proposition. That, after the Revolution of 1688, upon an application to have the judgment reversed, which in 1684 had adjudged the charter of Massachusetts null and void, on a writ of quo warranto the agents urged the illegality of the proceedings, and insisted that the judgment should be reversed on that account, and their charter restored; yet Pollexfen and Holt were of opinion that, if the judgment should be reversed, and the charter restored, they must still expect to have it repealed, because in making the extensive grants contained in it the Crown had exceeded its authority. That in the year 1713, also, a bill was brought into Parliament for the purpose of raising a revenue in the province of New York which had been refused by the assembly there for the support of His Majesty's government; that this bill was prepared by Sir Edward Northey and Lord Raymond, who were not only able lawyers, but great supporters and defenders of the rights of the subjects. That in 1716 a bill was introduced into Parliament by the great Secretary Stanhope for resuming the powers granted in the colony charters; and that in this, and other similar cases, the power of Parliament to revoke these charters, or resume the powers therein granted, was not questioned. If Parliament, they said, could take away the charters themselves under which the colonists claimed the exclusive right of laying taxes it must have the power of taxation itself. As to representation, they said, whether actual or virtual, it was by no means the sole and ancient basis of the supreme power and authority of Parliament; the clergy, it was true, for a time taxed themselves, but not because they were unrepresented in Parliament. Gentlemen conversant with the true ancient history of Great Britain could not be ignorant, they said, of the former extensive power of the church in this kingdom; that among other exertions of this power the Pope, at the instance of the clergy, issued his mandate exempting their lands from taxation, because appropriated to the maintenance of holy church; but, not having exempted their chattels, Parliament afterward was about to tax these, when a compact was made between the Crown and the Pope (to whom the clergy had again complained) that the bill should be rescinded, and the clergy yield a contribution to government, provided it should be made by themselves separately. This, they said, was the foundation of the clergy's subsidizing their lands and property, separate and apart, an undoubted infraction of the constitution; and this power, in after and more enlightened days, was restored. The supreme power, they said, must be complete and entire in taxation as well as legislation; that indulgence had been given to some subordinate districts and governments to raise money by way of taxation for local purposes; yet that indulgence could not abridge the supreme legislature of any of its powers and authority. Upon this principle, they stated, the Parliament of Great Britain alone could, and actually did (Ireland having that indulgence granted), absolve the people of Ireland from duties due to the Crown imposed by acts passed in their own Parliament; on the same principle the Commons of England directed that the charge of the army, kept up for the security and defence of the kingdom, should be provided for by the people of Ireland; leaving such provision to be made by the Irish Parliament; which, if not complied with, would have been enforced by a law of Great Britain, and this was so understood at the time in both kingdoms. That all the ancient subsidy acts declared that the subsidies laid and imposed were to be paid by his Majesty's subjects within the realm and *in all the King's domains;* though particular parts and places were sometimes expressly excepted, as Wales constantly before the statute of Henry VIII, Ireland, the counties Palatine, upon whom the charge of defending the northern frontier was imposed by their charter, Calais, Guienne, Gascony, and particular corporations, for certain reasons; and that if those places had not been excepted they must have paid the subsidy, though not represented in Parliament. The strength of the empire in America itself, they also declared, depended on an exact and entire obedience to the supreme authority in Great Britain; that if this authority should be infringed in any instance confusion must inevitably follow; that cases might, and undoubtedly would, happen to puzzle the ablest lawyers, to distinguish the difference between *duties* and *taxation*, between the right of laying the one or the other; that this was settled and established to be one entire power lodged in the commons of England in the time of William III, between the House of Lords and Commons when the Lords were disposed to establish a difference between *duties* and *impositions* on merchandize, and the grant of *taxes* and *subsidies,* with a view to confirm the power of the Commons to the latter only; but the Commons, from the long and uniform usage of Parliament, claimed this power entire and in its full extent. It was for the welfare and happiness of the whole, as well as for the dignity and honor of Parliament, it was also said, that the power now questioned by the colonists should be supported with firmness and resolution. It was not a little extraordinary that it should be now disputed by the Americans. At so late as the year 1755 a general complaint was transmitted to Great Britain against the assembly of Pennsylvania for not making the necessary provision for the defence and protection of that colony; and, but for particular circumstances, Parliament would have then interfered. That in consequence of some provincial differences Maryland, as was said, did not contribute her proportion toward the general expense of the late war, and that the other colonies had contemplated sending a representation against that colony, praying the interposition of Parliament. The Americans must then have had different views of the power which they now deny. That government is founded in trust, and that this trust, wherever placed, was absolute and entire: that the *kingdom* and *colonies* composed one great political body; and, though the jealous language of liberty could not but be admired by all who loved the constitution, yet when that jealousy was carried so far as to tell the sovereign power we will not trust you unless you give up that power, it became alarming, and called for the exertion of wisdom and spirit. Ask France, they said, what occasion for your destruction she would wish; she will answer, *divisions* between you and your colonies; she would desire the diminution of your authority over the colonies as one of the surest means of accomplishing the great object of her ambition. To preserve this sovereignty entire is then so essentially necessary for the advantage and happiness of both America and Great Britain that, if once abridged, or the entire dependency of the colonies given up, your power and authority as a great and respected kingdom and empire are gone; no friend will trust you, no enemy will fear you.

This debate was considered so important and was of such absorbing interest that it did not end until four in the morning, when the motion of Col. Barré was negatived by a very large majority, few voices answering in the affirmative.[1]

EXAMINATION OF BENJAMIN FRANKLIN

The resolutions of General Conway were reported to the House on the 10th of February and agreed to; and the next day an inquiry began on the subject of repealing the law complained of. This inquiry and examination continued until the 18th of the same month. Dr. Benjamin Franklin among others was called before the House, and underwent a long examination. No person was better acquainted with the circumstances and internal concerns of the colonies, the temper and disposition of the colonists toward the parent country, or their feelings in relation to the late measures of Parliament. His answers to the numerous questions put to him in the course of this inquiry not only show his extensive acquaintance with the internal state of the colonies, but evince his sagacity as a statesman. To the question whether the Americans would submit to pay the stamp duty if the act were modified and the duty reduced to a small amount, he answered, "No, they never will submit to it." British statesmen were extremely desirous that the colonial assemblies should acknowledge the right of Parliament to tax them, and rescind and erase from their journals their resolutions on this subject. To a question, whether the American assemblies would do this, Dr. Franklin answered, "They never will do it, unless compelled by force of arms."

THE COMMONS REPEAL THE STAMP ACT

Soon after this examination was finished, Gen. Conway proposed a resolution to *repeal* the act imposing stamp duties in America. This produced another debate, and the same arguments were renewed. The sense of the house was first taken on a motion to strike out the word "repeal" and insert "explain and

[1] Charles Garth's MSS. Letters to South Carolina. This gentleman was a member of Parliament, and present at all the debates on American affairs.

amend"; this was negatived, 275 to 167, and decided the fate of the resolution. In this, as well as in the preceding debates on American affairs, Mr. Grenville and his adherents were opposed to the claims of the colonists, and strongly urged the execution of the Stamp Act at every hazard. Mr. Pitt, afterward Lord Chatham, and Col. Barré were the chief opponents of Mr. Grenville.

FUNERAL PROCESSION OF THE STAMP ACT
A cartoon circulated by the Sons of Liberty
From the collection in the New York Public Library

The bill repealing the Stamp Act was passed by the Commons, together with the declaration of the right of Parliament to tax America, and on March 5, 1766, both bills were sent to the House of Lords.

The declaration of the Supremacy of Parliament had already been debated in the House of Lords. On February 3 a motion was made declaring the right of Great Britain to tax America. In the debate which followed the American cause was supported by the powerful talents of Charles Pratt, Lord Camden. As a consequence of this generous advocacy the noble lord became very popular in the colonies, many towns and counties being named in his honor.

PARLIAMENT MAY NOT CONTRAVENE NATURAL RIGHTS

LORD CAMDEN

The noble lord denied the right of Parliament to tax America, because unrepresented, saying:

My position is this—I repeat it—I will maintain to the last hour taxation and representation are inseparably connected. God has joined them, no British Parliament can separate them; to endeavor to do so is to stab our vitals. This position is founded in the law of nature. It is more, it is in itself an eternal law of nature. For whatever is a man's own is absolutely his own. No man has a right to take it from him without his consent either expressed by himself or his representative. Whoever attempts to do this attempts an injury. Whoever does it commits a robbery.

Therefore, my Lords, in my opinion the Legislature have no right to make this law. The sovereign authority, the omnipotence of the Legislature, is a favorite doctrine; but there are some things which you cannot do. You cannot take away a man's property without making him a compensation. You have no right to condemn a man by bill of attainder without hearing him. But, though Parliament cannot take away a man's property, yet every subject must make contributions, and this he consents to do by his representative. Notwithstanding the King, Lords, and Commons could in ancient times tax other people, they could not tax the clergy.

Lord Camden then repeated Pitt's argument relative to Wales and other regions of the greater island that had not been taxed when unrepresented in Parliament, and added to these the case of Ireland, of which the same was true.

He was replied to by William Murray, Lord Mansfield, whose speech is by far the ablest presentation of the affirmative side of the supremacy of Parliament. It was really directed against Pitt, though formally against Camden, whose arguments were largely repetitions of Pitt's.

NECESSITY OF A SUPREME LEGISLATURE

LORD MANSFIELD

MY LORDS—I shall speak to the question strictly as a matter of right; for it is a proposition in its nature so perfectly distinct from the expediency of the tax, that it must necessarily be taken separate, if there is any true logic in the world; but of the expediency or inexpediency I will say nothing. It will be time enough to speak upon that subject when it comes to be a question.

I shall also speak to the distinctions which have been taken, without any real difference, as to the nature of the tax; and I shall point out, lastly, the necessity there will be of exerting the force of the superior authority of government, if opposed by the subordinate part of it.

I am extremely sorry that the question has ever become necessary to be agitated, and that there should be a decision upon it. No one in this House will live long enough to see an end put to the mischief which will be the result of the doctrine which has been inculcated; but the arrow is shot and the wound already given. I shall certainly avoid personal reflections. No one has had more cast upon him than myself; but I never was biased by any consideration of applause from without, in the discharge of my public duty; and, in giving my sentiments according to what I thought law, I have relied upon my own consciousness. It is with great pleasure I have heard the noble Lord who moved the resolution express himself in so manly and sensible a way when he recommended a dispassionate debate, while, at the same time, he urged the necessity of the House coming to such a resolution, with great dignity and propriety of argument.

I shall endeavor to clear away from the question all that mass of dissertation and learning displayed in arguments which have been fetched from speculative men who have written upon the subject of government, or from ancient records, as being little to the purpose. I shall insist that these records are no proofs of our present constitution. A noble Lord has taken up his argument from the settlement of the constitution at the Revolution [of 1688]; I shall take up my argument from the constitution as it now is. The constitution of this country has been always in a moving state, either gaining or losing something, and with respect to the modes of taxation, when we get beyond the reign of Edward I, or of King John, we are all in doubt and obscurity. The history of those times is full of uncertainties.

In regard to the writs upon record they were issued some of them according to law, and some not according to law; and such [*i. e.*, of the latter kind] were those concerning ship-money, to call assemblies to tax themselves, or to compel benevolences. Other taxes were raised from escuage, fees for knights' service, and by other means arising out of the feudal system. Benevolences are contrary to law; and it is well known how people resisted the demands of the Crown in the case of ship-money, and were persecuted by the Court; and if any set of men were to meet now to lend the King money it would be contrary to law, and a breach of the rights of Parliament.

I shall now answer the noble Lord particularly upon the cases he has quoted. With respect to the Marches of Wales, who were the borderers, privileged for assisting the King in his war against the Welsh in the mountains, their enjoying this privilege of taxing themselves was but of a short duration, and during the life of Edward the First, till the Prince of Wales came to be the King; and then they were annexed to the Crown, and became subject to taxes like the rest of the dominions of England; and from thence came the custom, though unnecessary, of naming Wales and the town of Monmouth in all proclamations and in acts of Parliament. Henry the Eighth was the first who issued writs for it to return two members to Parliament. The Crown exercised this right *ad libitum*, from whence arises the inequality of representation in our Constitution at this day. Henry VIII. issued a writ to Calais to send one burgess to Parliament. One of the counties palatine [I think he said Durham] was taxed fifty years to subsidies before it sent members to Parliament. The clergy were at no time unrepresented in Parliament. When they taxed themselves it was done with the concurrence and consent of Parliament, who permitted them to tax themselves upon their petition, the Convocation sitting at the same time with the Parliament. They had, too, their representatives always sitting in this House, bishops and abbots; and, in the other House, they were at no time without a right of voting singly for the election of members; so that the argument fetched from the case of the clergy is not an argument of any force, because they were at no time unrepresented here.

The reasoning about the colonies of Great Britain, drawn from the colonies of antiquity, is a mere useless display of learning; for the colonies of the Tyrians in Africa, and of the Greeks in Asia, were totally different from our system. No nation before ourselves formed any regular system of colonization but the Romans; and their system was a military one, and of garrisons placed in the principal towns of the conquered provinces. The states of Holland were not colonies of Spain; they were states dependent upon the house of Austria in a feudal dependence. Nothing could be more different from our colonies than that flock of men, as they have been called, who came from the North and poured into Europe. Those emigrants renounced all laws, all protection, all connection with their mother countries. They chose their leaders, and marched under their banners to seek their fortunes and establish new kingdoms upon the ruins of the Roman empire.

But our colonies, on the contrary, emigrated under the sanction of the Crown and Parliament. They were modeled gradually into their present forms, respectively, by charters, grants, and statutes; but they were never separated from the mother country, or so emancipated as to become *sui juris*. There are several sorts of colonies in British America. The charter colonies, the proprietary governments, and the King's colonies. The first colonies were the charter colonies, such as the Virginia Company; and these companies had among their directors members of the privy council and of both houses of Parliament; they were under the authority of the privy council, and had agents resident here, responsible for their proceedings. So much were they considered as belonging to the Crown, and not to the King personally (for there is a great difference, though few people attend to it), that when the two houses, in the time of Charles the First, were going to pass a bill concerning the colonies, a message was sent to them by the King that they were the King's colonies, and that the bill was unnecessary, for that the privy council would take order about them; and the bill never had the royal assent. The Commonwealth Parliament, as soon as it was settled, were very early jealous of the colonies separating themselves from them; and passed a resolution or act (and it is a question whether it is not in force now) to declare and establish the authority of England over its colonies.

But if there was no express law, or reason founded upon any necessary inference from an express law, yet the usage alone would be sufficient to support that authority; for have not the colonies submitted ever since their first establishment to the jurisdiction of the mother country? In all questions of property the appeals from the colonies have been to the privy council here; and such causes have been determined, not by the law of the colonies, but by the law of England. A very little while ago there was an appeal on a question of limitation in a devise of land with remainders; and, notwithstanding the intention of the testator appeared very clear, yet the case was determined contrary to it, and that the land should pass according to the law of England. A very little while ago there was an appeal on a question of limitation in a devise of land with remainders; and, notwithstanding the intention of the testator appeared very clear, yet the case was determined contrary to it, and that the land should pass according to the law of England. The colonies have been obliged to recur very frequently to the jurisdiction here, to settle the disputes among their own governments. I well remember several references on this head, when the late Lord Hardwicke was attorney general, and Sir Clement Wearg solicitor general. New Hampshire and Connecticut were in blood about their differences; Virginia and Maryland were in arms against each other. This shows the necessity of one superior decisive jurisdiction, to which all subordinate jurisdictions may recur. Nothing, my Lords, could be more fatal to the peace of the colonies at any time than the Parliament giving up its authority over them; for in such a case there must be an entire dissolution of government. Considering how the colonies are composed, it is easy to foresee there would be no end of feuds and factions among the several separate governments, when once there shall be no one government here or there of sufficient force or authority to decide their mutual differences; and, government being dissolved, nothing remains but that the colonies must either change their Constitution, and take some new form of government, or fall under some foreign power. At present the several forms of their Constitution are very various, having been produced, as all governments have been originally, by accident and circumstances. The forms of government in every colony were adopted, from time to time, according to the size of the colony; and so have been extended again, from time to time, as the numbers of their inhabitants and their commercial connections outgrew the first model. In some colonies at first there was only a governor assisted by two or three counsel; then more were added; afterward courts of justice were erected; then assemblies were created. Some things were done by instructions from the secretaries of state; other things were done by order of the King and council; and other things by commissions under the great seal. It is observable that in consequence of these establishments from time to time, and of the dependency of these governments upon the supreme Legislature at home, the lenity of each government in the colonies has been extreme toward the subject; and a great inducement has been created for people to come and settle in them. But, if all those governments which are now independent of each other should become independent of the mother country, I am afraid that the inhabitants of the colonies are very little aware of the consequences. They would feel in that case very soon the hand of power more heavy upon them in their own governments than they have yet done, or have ever imagined.

The constitutions of the different colonies are thus made up of different principles. They must remain dependent, from the necessity of things, and their relations to the jurisdiction of the mother country; or they must be totally dismembered from it, and form a league of union among themselves against it, which could not be effected without great violences. No one ever thought the contrary till the trumpet of sedition was blown. Acts of Parliament have been made, not only without a doubt of their legality, but with universal applause, the great object of which has been ultimately to fix the trade of the colonies, so as to center in the bosom of that country from whence they took their original. The Navigation Act shut up their intercourse with foreign countries. Their ports have been made subject to customs and regulations which have cramped and diminished their trade. And duties have been laid, affecting the very inmost parts of their commerce, and, among others, that of the post; yet all these have been submitted to peaceably, and no one ever thought till now of this doctrine, that the colonies are not to be taxed, regulated, or bound by Parliament. A few particular merchants were then, as now, displeased at restrictions which did not permit them to make the greatest possible advantages of their commerce in their own private and peculiar branches. But, though these few merchants might think themselves losers in articles which they had no right to gain, as being prejudicial to the general and national system, yet I must observe that the colonies, upon the whole, were benefited by these laws. For these restrictive laws, founded upon principles of the most solid policy, flung a great weight of naval force into the hands of the mother country, which was to protect its colonies. Without a union with her the colonies must have been entirely weak and defenceless, but they thus became relatively great, subordinately, and in proportion as the mother country advanced in superiority over the rest of the maritime powers in Europe, to which both mutually contributed, and of which both have reaped a benefit, equal to the natural and just relation in which they both stand reciprocally, of dependency on one side and protection on the other.

There can be no doubt, my Lords, but that the inhabitants of the colonies are as much represented in Parliament as the greatest part of the people of England are represented; among nine millions of whom there are eight which have no votes in electing members of Parliament. Every objection, therefore, to the dependency of the colonies upon Parliament, which arises to it upon the ground of representation, goes to the whole present Constitution of Great Britain; and I suppose it is not meant to new-model *that*, too. People may form speculative ideas of perfection, and indulge their own fancies or those of other men. Every man in this country has his particular notion of liberty; but perfection never did, and never can, exist in any human institution. To what purpose, then, are arguments drawn from a distinction—in which there is no real difference—of a virtual and actual representation? A member of Parliament, chosen for any borough, represents not only the constituents and inhabitants of that particular place, but he represents the inhabitants of every other borough in Great Britain. He represents the city of London, and all the other commons of this land, and the inhabitants of all the colonies and dominions of Great Britain; and is, in duty and conscience, bound to take care of their interests.

I have mentioned the customs and the post tax. This leads me to answer another distinction, as false as the above; the distinction of internal and external taxes. The noble Lord who quoted so much law, and denied upon those grounds the right of the Parliament of Great Britain to lay internal taxes upon the colonies, allowed at the same time that restrictions upon trade, and duties upon the ports, were legal. But I cannot see a real difference in this distinction; for I hold it to be true that a tax laid in any place is like a pebble falling into and making a circle in a lake, till one circle produces and gives motion to another, and the whole circumference is agitated from the center. For nothing can be more clear than that a tax of ten or twenty per cent. laid upon tobacco, either in the ports of Virginia or London, is a duty laid upon the inland plantations of Virginia, a hundred miles from the sea, wheresoever the tobacco grows.

I do not deny but that a tax may be laid injudiciously and injuriously, and that people in such a case may have a right to complain. But the nature of the tax is not now the question; whenever it comes to be one I am for lenity. I would have no blood drawn. There is, I am satisfied, no occasion for any to be drawn. A little time and experience of the inconveniences and miseries of anarchy may bring people to their senses.

With respect to what has been said or written upon this subject I differ from the noble Lord, who spoke of Mr. Otis and his book [1] with contempt, though he maintained the same doctrine in some points, while in others he carried it farther than Otis himself, who allows everywhere the supremacy of the Crown over the colonies. No man, on such a subject, is contemptible. Otis is a man of consequence among the people there. They have chosen him for one of their deputies at the Congress and general meeting from the respective governments. It was said the man is mad. What then? One madman often makes many. Masaniello [2] was mad. Nobody doubts it; yet, for all that, he overturned the government of Naples. Madness is catching in all popular assemblies and upon all popular matters. The book is full of wildness. I never read it till a few days ago, for I seldom look into such things. I never was actually acquainted with the contents of the Stamp Act till I sent for it on purpose to read it before the debate was expected. With respect to authorities in *another House,* I know nothing of them. I believe that I have not been in that House more than once since I had the honor to be called up to this; and, if I did know any thing that passed in the other House, I could not and would not mention it as an authority here. I ought not to mention any such authority. I should think it beneath my own and your Lordship's dignity to speak of it.

I am far from bearing any ill will to the Americans; they are a very good people, and I have long known them. I began life with them, and owe much to them, having been much concerned in the plantation causes before the privy council; and so I became a good deal acquainted with American affairs and people. I dare say their heat will soon be over, when they come to feel a little the consequences of their opposition to the Legislature. Anarchy always cures itself; but the ferment will continue so much the longer, while hot-headed men there find that there are persons of weight and character to support and justify them here.

Indeed, if the disturbances should continue for a great length of time force must be the consequence, an application adequate to the mischief, and arising out of the necessity of the case; for

[1] This may be "The Rights of the Colonies Asserted and Proved," published in 1764 in Boston, or "A Vindication of the Conduct of the House of Representatives of Massachusetts," published in 1762.

[2] Properly Tommaso Aniello, a fisherman who led a successful revolt in 1647 against the Duke of Arcos, Spanish viceroy of Naples, who had heavily taxed the people. Succeeding, his reason became impaired by the change of fortune, and, alienating his supporters by his arbitrary acts, he was assassinated by adherents of the viceroy.

force is only the difference between a superior and subordinate jurisdiction. In the former the whole force of the Legislature resides collectively, and when it ceases to reside the whole connection is dissolved. It will, indeed, be to very little purpose that we sit here enacting laws, and making resolutions, if the inferior will not obey them, or if we neither can nor dare enforce them; for then, and then, I say, of necessity, the matter comes to the sword. If the offspring are grown too big and too resolute to obey the parent you must try which is the strongest, and exert all the powers of the mother country to decide the contest.

I am satisfied, notwithstanding, that time and a wise and steady conduct may prevent those extremities which would be fatal to both. I remember well when it was the violent humor of the times to decry standing armies and garrisons as dangerous and incompatible with the liberty of the subject. Nothing would do but a regular militia. The militia are embodied; they march; and no sooner was the militia law thus put into execution, but it was then said to be an intolerable burden upon the subject, and that it would fall, sooner or later, into the hands of the Crown. That was the language, and many counties petitioned against it. This may be the case with the colonies. In many places they begin already to feel the effects of their resistance to government. Interest very soon divides mercantile people; and, although there may be some mad, enthusiastic, or ill-designing people in the colonies, yet I am convinced that the greatest bulk, who have understanding and property, are still well affected to the mother country. You have, my Lords, many friends still in the colonies; and take care that you do not, by abdicating your own authority, desert them and yourselves, and lose them forever.

In all popular tumults the worst men bear the sway at first. Moderate and good men are often silent for fear or modesty, who, in good time, may declare themselves. Those who have any property to lose are sufficiently alarmed already at the progress of these public violences and violations, to which every man's dwelling, person, and property are hourly exposed. Numbers of such valuable men and good subjects are ready and willing to declare themselves for the support of government in due time, if government does not fling away its own authority.

My Lords, the Parliament of Great Britain has its rights over the colonies; but it may abdicate its rights.

There was a thing which I forgot to mention. I mean, the manuscript quoted by the noble Lord. He tells you that it is there said that, if the act concerning Ireland had passed, the

Parliament might have abdicated its rights as to Ireland. In the first place, I heartily wish, my Lords, that Ireland had not been named, at a time when that country is of a temper and in a situation so difficult to be governed; and when we have already here so much weight upon our hands, encumbered with the extensiveness, variety, and importance of so many objects in a vast and too busy empire, and the national system shattered and exhausted by a long, bloody, and expensive war, but more so by our divisions at home, and a fluctuation of counsels. I wish Ireland, therefore, had never been named.

I pay as much respect as any man to the memory of Lord Chief Justice Hale; but I did not know that he had ever written upon the subject; and I differ very much from thinking, with the noble Lord, that this manuscript ought to be published. So far am I from it that I wish the manuscript had never been named; for Ireland is too tender a subject to be touched. The case of Ireland is as different as possible from that of our colonies. Ireland was a conquered country; it had its *pacta conventa* and its *regalia*. But to what purpose is it to mention the manuscript? It is but the opinion of one man. When it was written, or for what particular object it was written, does not appear. It might possibly be only a work of youth, or an exercise of the understanding, in sounding and trying a question problematically. All people, when they first enter professions, make their collections pretty early in life; and the manuscript may be of that sort. However, be it what it may, the opinion is but problematical; for the act to which the writer refers never passed, and Lord Hale only said that if it had passed the Parliament might have abdicated their right.

But, my Lords, I shall make this application of it. You may abdicate your right over the colonies. Take care, my Lords, how you do so, for such an act will be irrevocable. Proceed, then, my Lords, with spirit and firmness; and, when you shall have established your authority, it will then be a time to show your lenity. The Americans, as I said before, are a very good people, and I wish them exceedingly well; but they are heated and inflamed. The noble Lord who spoke before ended with a prayer. I cannot end better than by saying to it Amen; and in the words of Maurice, Prince of Orange, concerning the Hollanders: *"God bless this industrious, frugal, and well-meaning, but easily deluded people."*

The Stamp Act was repealed, and the Declaratory Act was passed, each by a large majority.

CHAPTER III

"No Taxation Without Representation"

[CONTROVERSY BETWEEN THE COLONIAL ASSEMBLIES AND PARLIAMENT]

The Townshend Taxes—John Dickinson [Pa.] and Josiah Quincy, Jr. [Mass.], oppose them—Declaration of the Massachusetts Assembly—Controversy between Lord Hillsborough and James Otis [Mass.]—Non-importation Agreement of Colonial Merchants—Royal Troops in the Colonies: Protest of Massachusetts Assembly—Parliament Demands Trial in England of Colonial Traitors: Protest of Virginia Assembly—"Appeal to the World" by Boston Citizens—All Taxes Repealed Save on Tea—The Boston Massacre—The Boston Tea Party—Speech of Josiah Quincy, Jr.: "Let Us Look to the End"—Parliament Closes Boston Port, and Dissolves Massachusetts Assembly: Protest of Col. Isaac Barré: "Olive Branch or Sword?"—Colonial Protests against the Bills—First Continental Congress Assembles: Its Addresses and Petitions—Eloquence of Patrick Henry [Va.]—Debate over Plan for Government of Colonies by Crown: in favor, Joseph Galloway [Pa.], John Jay [N. Y.], Edward Rutledge [S. C.]; opposed, Henry; it is defeated.

IN July, 1766, a new administration was formed in the British Government under the direction of William Pitt, who was made Earl of Chatham. Composed of men of different political parties, the Tory element was strong enough to revive the subject of taxing America. In May, 1767, Charles Townshend, chancellor of the exchequer, under the instigation of Ex-Minister George Grenville, submitted to the House of Commons a bill imposing duties on glass, paper, painters' materials, and tea, imported into the colonies, its preamble declaring that the impost was to defray the expenses of defending these provinces. Owing probably to Lord Chatham's absence from sickness, the bill passed both Houses without much opposition in June. Royal commissioners were appointed for the colonies

68

to superintend the execution of all the laws of Parliament relating to American trade.

These acts created a great stir in the colonies. John Dickinson of Pennsylvania wrote in a homely style, calculated to appeal to the common people, "Letters of a Pennsylvania Farmer," which presented the unconstitutionality as well as the injustice of the acts. They were universally read in America, and, translated into French, they greatly inclined the people of France toward the American cause.

Josiah Quincy, Jr., a young Boston lawyer, published in the Boston *Gazette* a series of extremely able articles against the "Townshend Acts," under the pen-name of "Hyperion."

The most eloquent of these articles was Quincy's "Appeal," which appeared in the Boston *Gazette* of October 3, 1768.

APPEAL TO AMERICANS

JOSIAH QUINCY, JR.

If ever there was a time, this is the hour for Americans to rouse themselves and exert every ability. Their all is at a hazard, and the die of fate spins doubtful! In vain do we talk of magnanimity and heroism; in vain do we trace a descent from the worthies of the earth, if we inherit not the spirit of our ancestors. Who is he who boasteth of his patriotism? Has he vanquished luxury, and subdued the worldly pride of his heart? Is he not yet drinking the poisonous draught and rolling the sweet morsel under his tongue? He who cannot conquer the little vanity of his heart, and deny the delicacy of a debauched palate, let him lay his hand upon his mouth, and his mouth in the dust.

Now is the time for this people to summon every aid, human and divine; to exhibit every moral virtue, and call forth every Christian grace. The wisdom of the serpent, the innocence of the dove, and the intrepidity of the lion, with the blessing of God, will yet save us from the jaws of destruction.

Where is the boasted liberty of Englishmen, if property may be disposed of, charters suspended, assemblies dissolved, and every valued right annihilated, at the uncontrollable will of an external power? Does not every man who feels one ethereal

spark yet glowing in his bosom find his indignation kindle at
the bare imagination of such wrongs? What would be our sentiments were this imagination realized?

Did the blood of the ancient Britons swell our veins, did the
spirit of our forefathers inhabit our breasts, should we hesitate
a moment in preferring death to a miserable existence in bondage? Did we reflect on their toils, their dangers, their fiery
trials, the thought would inspire unconquerable courage.

Who has the front to ask, "wherefore do you complain"?
Who dares assert everything worth living for is not lost when
a nation is enslaved? Are not pensioners, stipendiaries, and
salary men (unknown before) hourly multiplying on us, to riot
in the spoils of miserable America? Does not every eastern gale
waft us some new insect, even of that devouring kind which eat
up every green thing? Is not the bread taken out of the children's mouths, and given unto the dogs? Are not our estates
given to corrupt sycophants, without a design, or even a pretence, of soliciting our assent, and our lives put into the hands
of those whose tender mercies are cruelties? Has not an authority in a distant land, in the most public manner, proclaimed
a right of disposing of *the all* of Americans? In short, what
have we to lose—what have we to fear? Are not our distresses
more than we can bear; and, to finish all, are not our cities, in a
time of profound peace, filled with standing armies, to preclude
us from that last solace of the wretched—to open their mouths
in complaint, and send forth their cries in bitterness of heart?

But is there no ray of hope? Is not Great Britain inhabited
by the children of those renowned barons who waded through
seas of crimson gore to establish their liberty; and will they not
allow us, their fellow-men, to enjoy that freedom which we claim
from nature, which is confirmed by our constitution, and which
they pretend so highly to value? Were a tyrant to conquer us,
the chains of slavery, when opposition should become useless,
might be supportable; but to be shackled by Englishmen—by
our equals—is not to be borne!

By the sweat of our brow we earn the little we possess: from
nature we derive the common rights of man—and by charter we
claim the liberties of Britons? Shall we, dare we, pusillani-
mously surrender our birthright? Is the obligation to our
fathers discharged—is the debt we owe posterity paid? Answer
me, thou coward, who hidest thyself in the hour of trial. If
there is no reward in this life, no prize of glory in the next,
capable of animating thy dastard soul; think and tremble, thou
miscreant, at the whips and stripes thy master shall lash thee

with on earth—and the flames and scorpions thy second master shall torment thee with hereafter!

Oh, my countrymen! what will our children say, when they read the history of these times, should they find we tamely gave away, without one noble struggle, the most invaluable of earthly blessings? As they drag the galling chain, will they not execrate us? If we have any respect for things sacred; any regard to the dearest treasure on earth—if we have one tender sentiment for posterity; if we would not be despised by the whole world—let us, in the most open, solemn manner, and with determined fortitude, swear we will die, if we cannot live freemen!

Be not lulled, my countrymen, with vain imaginations, or idle fancies. To hope for the protection of heaven, without doing our duty, and exerting ourselves as becomes men, is to mock the Deity. Wherefore had man his reason, if it were not to direct him? Wherefore his strength, if it be not his protection? To banish folly and luxury, correct vice and immorality, and stand immovable in the freedom in which we are free indeed is eminently the duty of each individual, at this day. When this is done we may rationally hope for an answer to our prayers; for the whole counsel of God, and the invincible armor of the Almighty.

However righteous our cause we cannot, in this period of the world, expect a miraculous salvation. Heaven will undoubtedly assist us, if we act like men; but to expect protection from above, while we are enervated by luxury, and slothful in the exertion of those abilities with which we are endued, is an expectation vain and foolish. With the smiles of Heaven, virtue, unanimity, and firmness will ensue success. While we have equity, justice, and God on our side, tyranny, spiritual or temporal, shall never ride triumphant in a land inhabited by Englishmen.

The Massachusetts House of Representatives in January, 1768, protested to the King and the Ministry against the new taxes, on the ground that the colonies were not represented in the Parliament which enacted them. They said:

The original contract between the King and the first planters here was a royal promise in behalf of the nation, and which, till very lately, was never questioned, but the King had the power to make, namely, that "if the adventurers would, at their own cost and expense, and at the hazard of their lives, and everything dear to them, purchase a *new world*, subdue a wilderness, and thereby enlarge the King's dominions, they and their posterity should enjoy such rights and privileges as in their charter are expressed; which are, in general, all the rights, liberties, and privileges of His Majesty's natural born subjects, within the realm.''

The principal privileges implied, and in some of their charters expressed, is a freedom from all taxes but such as they shall consent to, in person, or by representatives of their own choice and election.

In reference to the appropriation of the new duties to the support of Crown officers and to the maintenance of troops in America the Assembly said:

Such a power under a corrupt administration, it is feared, would introduce an absolute government in America; at least, it would leave the people in a state of uncertainty of their security, which is far from being a state of civil liberty. The judges in the several colonies do not hold their commissions during good behavior. If, then, they are to have their salaries independent of the people, how easy it will be for a corrupt governor to have a set of judges to his mind, to deprive a bench of justice of its glory and the people of their security.

The House, during the same session, also addressed a circular letter to the colonies, stating the difficulties to be apprehended by the operation of the late acts of Parliament; and requesting their coöperation for redress.

The other colonies approved of the proceedings of Massachusetts, and joined in applying to the King for relief.

The Petitioners Rebuked

The circular letter of Massachusetts created no little alarm in the British cabinet. They viewed it as an attempt to convene another congress, to concert measures in opposition to the authority of Parliament. Union and concert among the colonies was a peculiar object of dread with the ministers; and they were determined, if possible, to prevent every measure leading to it. A letter from Lord Hillsborough, Secretary of State, was therefore addressed to the Governor of Massachusetts, directing him at the next meeting of the General Assembly of that colony "to require of the House of Representatives, in His Majesty's name, to *rescind* the resolution which gave birth to the circular letter of the speaker, and to declare their disapprobation of, and dissent to, that *rash* and *hasty* proceeding." If the House refused compliance, he was directed immediately to dissolve the Assembly, and to transmit their proceedings to the King, that measures might be taken to prevent for the future "a conduct of so extraordinary and unconstitutional a nature."

A circular letter was, at the same time, addressed to the governors of the other colonies declaring this measure of the people of Massachusetts "to be of a most *dangerous* and *factious* tendency, calculated to enflame the minds of His Majesty's good subjects in the colonies, to promote an unwarrantable *combination,* and to excite and encourage an open opposition to, and denial of, the authority of Parliament, and to subvert the true principles of the constitution"; directing them, also, to exert their utmost influence, to defeat "this flagitious attempt to disturb the public peace," by prevailing upon the assemblies to take no notice of it, and thereby treat it with the *contempt* it deserved.

REPLIES OF THE COLONIES

The House of Representatives of Massachusetts in June, 1768, peremptorily refused to rescind the proceedings of the preceding Assembly, declaring their right as British subjects in a respectful manner to petition the King and Parliament for a redress of grievances, and to request the other colonies to unite with them for the same purpose. They also addressed a letter to Lord Hillsborough, giving him a detailed account of the transaction, and repelling the suggestion made by him that the same was a *rash* and *flagitious attempt* to disturb the public peace. The House viewed the letter of Lord Hillsborough as an unwarrantable attempt on their rights; and, in their answer to the communication of the Governor on this subject, expressed themselves with no little warmth. "If the votes of the House were to be controlled by the *direction* of a minister," said these bold inheritors of the spirit of Pym and Hampden, "we have left us but a *shadow of liberty!*"

On the question to rescind, James Otis said: "When Lord Hillsborough knows that we will not rescind our acts, let him apply to Parliament to rescind theirs. Let Britain rescind their measures, or they are lost forever."

The ministerial mandate to the other colonies was equally disregarded.

NON-IMPORTATION AGREEMENT

During the summer of this year (1768), the merchants of Massachusetts, Connecticut, and New York, and, later, of Pennsylvania and other colonies, again had recourse to a non-importation agreement, particularly with respect to the articles on which duties were imposed. This was done, not only to obtain a repeal of the late revenue act, but with a view of encouraging *manufactures* in the colonies.

ROYAL TROOPS IN THE COLONIES

From 1765, when soldiers had been quartered on some of the colonies by act of Parliament, the provincial assemblies concerned had made repeated protests against their presence, and on constitutional grounds had refused to vote money for their maintenance. This greatly angered the British Government, and in July, 1767, Parliament inhibited the Massachusetts Assembly, which had been particularly obstinate, from passing any act whatever until it had voted supplies to the royal troops.

On the rumor that new troops were coming to Boston to enforce the acts of Parliament, a convention representing 96 Massachusetts towns met in Boston on September 22, 1768, and protested to the King against such coercion. They denied that they were inspired by a desire for independence.

"We clearly hold that the *sovereignty of His Sacred Majesty*, King George the Third, is entire in all parts of the British empire: God forbid that we should ever act or wish anything in oppugnation of the same. We appear as plain honest men, humbly soliciting peace and order. We wish ever to promote and cultivate a harmony and union between Great Britain and the colonies."

On the 15th of December, 1768, the House of Lords passed a number of resolutions severely censuring the conduct of the people of Massachusetts, and declaring in particular that the proceedings of Boston in calling a convention were subversive of His Majesty's Government and manifested a design to set up a new and unconstitutional authority independent of the Crown of Great Britain; and that the meeting of the convention was a daring insult offered to His Majesty's authority, and an audacious usurpation of the powers of government.

These resolutions were, about the first of February, agreed to by the House of Commons; and a joint address was at the time presented to the King, requesting him to direct the Governor of Massachusetts to transmit to the British Government full information "touching all *treasons*" in the province, in order that the accused parties might be tried *"within the realm,"* if His Majesty "saw sufficient ground for such a proceeding."

The King in answer to this address assured Parliament of his determination to give the necessary orders for bringing the authors of the unhappy disorders in Massachusetts to condign punishment.

Though these proceedings of Parliament pointed principally to Massachusetts, yet all the colonists considered themselves as deeply affected and were more firmly united than ever in opposition to this extraordinary claim of right to transport the colonists to England for trial for supposed offences committed in America.

The House of Burgesses in Virginia, early in May, 1769, declared that the sending of a colonist suspected of crime "beyond the seas to be tried is highly derogatory of the rights of British subjects, as thereby the inestimable privilege of trial by a jury from the vicinage, as well as the liberty of producing witnesses on such trial, will be taken away from the party accused.''

The House of Burgesses also prepared a petition to the King on this subject, couched in strong and feeling language.

DUTIES REMOVED SAVE ON TEA

The British Ministry, becoming alarmed at the spirit of resistance in the colonies, had promised, in a circular letter to the colonial governors, that, as a matter of pure commercial policy, Parliament would remove all taxes save on tea (which was retained to maintain the right of Parliament to tax America). The various assemblies repudiated this as not being a concession of the principle for which they contended.

On October 4, 1769, the people of Boston, in a town meeting, published ''An Appeal to the World,'' in which they not only vindicated themselves from the ''false, scandalous and infamous libels'' upon them, contained, as they said, in some of the letters of Governor Bernard and others laid before Parliament; but also declared ''that the taking off the duties on paper, glass and colors, merely on commercial principles, would not be satisfactory; that it would not relieve trade from its burdens, much less remove the grounds of discontent which prevailed through the continent, *upon higher principles.*''

''Their rights,'' they said, ''are invaded by those acts; therefore until they are all repealed the *cause* of their just complaints cannot be removed. In short, the grievances which lie heavily upon us we shall never think redressed till *every act* passed by the British Parliament for the express purpose of raising a revenue upon us without our consent is *repealed;* till the American board of commissioners of the customs is *dissolved,* the *troops recalled,* and things are restored to the state they were in before the late extraordinary measures of administration took place.''

The merchants of Philadelphia in November of this year, in a letter to the merchants of London, not only vindicated themselves and the colonists in general from aspersions cast upon them by Governor Bernard and others, but on the subject of the right of Parliament to impose taxes or duties upon them in any way expressed themselves in bold and determined language:

"Nothing short of a repeal of all the *revenue acts,* and putting things on the footing they were before the late innovations, can or will satisfy the minds of the people. Fleets and armies may overawe our towns, admiralty courts and boards of commissioners, with their swarms of underlings, may, by a vigorous execution of the same unconstitutional acts, ruin our commerce and render America of little use to the people of Britain; but while every *farmer is a freeholder* the spirit of liberty will prevail, and every attempt to divest them of their privileges of freemen must be attended with consequences injurious to the colonies and the mother country."

Repeal of All Taxes Save on Tea

Parliament again met on the 9th of January, 1770, and soon after the Duke of Grafton, First Lord of the Treasury, resigned, and the celebrated Lord North was appointed in his room. Though the speech from the throne declared that combinations still existed to destroy the commercial connection between Great Britain and her colonies, and though America was not yet "prostrate at the feet of the Ministry," Lord North himself, on the 5th of March, 1770, introduced a bill taking off the duties imposed by the act of 1767 on all the articles except tea. This partial repeal, which took place on the 12th of April, though not satisfactory, served in some measure to tranquilize the minds of the Americans. The insignificant duty on tea was continued for the purpose of maintaining the supremacy of Parliament, and, like a peppercorn rent, was reserved to show the tenure by which the colonists held their rights. The House of Burgesses in Virginia in a petition to the King declared that a partial suspension of the duties would not remove their too well grounded fears and apprehensions while that on tea was retained "for the avowed purpose of establishing a precedent against them."

THE BOSTON MASSACRE

As a result of the irritating presence of the royal troops in Boston a quarrel arose on March 5, 1770, between them and some of the citizens, in which eleven persons were either killed or wounded. Captain Preston and others of the soldiers were indicted for murder,

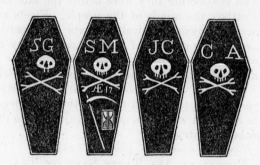

BOSTON MASSACRE COFFINS

The initials are for the slain Bostonians, *e. g.*, C A represents Crispus Attucks, the mulatto who led the mob

From the "American Historical Record"

but were acquitted largely owing to the eloquent defence made by their counsel, John Adams and Josiah Quincy, Jr. The anniversary of the event was observed annually for a number of years. The orations upon these occasions were wont to be inflammatory. Speeches by John Hancock and Dr. Joseph Warren were notably so.

THE BOSTON TEA-PARTY

The application by the colonists to the remaining tax, that on tea, caused the importation of the article into the colonies to cease, and the British Ministry began to devise means for forcing its introduction into America that the sovereignty of Parliament might be practically asserted.

In May, 1773, the Ministry procured an act of Parliament permitting the East India Company to export their teas to America, with a drawback of all the duties paid in England. By thus rendering the article cheaper in the colonies than in Great Britain it was supposed the Americans would be induced to pay the small duty upon it.

Concerning this act, a correspondence committee of Massachusetts, instituted for the purpose of fostering a common resistance among the colonies, wrote:

We cannot close without mentioning a fresh instance of the temper and design of the British ministry in allowing the East India Company, with a view of conciliating them, to ship their *teas* to America. It is easy to see how aptly this scheme will serve both to destroy the *trade* of the colonies and increase the *revenue*. How necessary, then, it is that each colony should take *effectual methods* to prevent this measure from having its designed effects.

In consequence of this act the company shipped large quantities of tea to different parts of the colonies, consigned to their particular friends or the friends of government, to be sold for their benefit. The shipments were principally made to Charleston, Philadelphia, New York and Boston. The colonists at once perceived that if the tea was permitted to be landed the duty must be paid, and that it would be difficult, if not impossible, to prevent its sale and consumption, and so they resolved that the tea should not be landed. On its arrival at Charleston it was indeed landed and put into stores, but the consignees were not permitted to offer it for sale. Such was the determined opposition at Philadelphia and New York that the consignees at these places declined taking charge of it, and the vessels with the tea on board returned to Great Britain without an entry at the custom house. The citizens of Boston held several town meetings at which they passed resolutions declaring that the tea should not be landed, or the duty paid, but be returned in the same vessels in which it came without an entry; they also declared they would support these resolutions at the risk of life and property, and they directed the captains of the vessels not to land the tea, but to apply for clearances without an entry of the vessels or cargoes. The collector, however, refused such applications, and the governor gave orders to Admiral Montague, then in the harbor of Boston, to guard all the passes out, and also directed the commander of the Castle to suffer no vessel except coasters to pass without a permit signed by himself. In the meantime the people of Boston for many nights kept watch at the wharves to prevent the landing of the tea. In this situation the leaders came to the bold resolution of destroying the tea itself.

On December 16 many thousands of the inhabitants of Boston and its vicinity met in the Old South Meeting-house and confirmed their former resolutions against the landing of the tea. During this meeting the captain of one of the vessels was sent, for the last time, to the governor, then at his seat at Milton, to request a passport.

The patriotic leaders, fully aware of the momentous consequences of the refusal of the Governor, had already anticipated them. During the absence of the messenger, and while the people assembled on the occasion were waiting his return with extreme solicitude, Josiah Quincy, Jr., addressed them.

Mr. Quincy began his speech by reminding his hearers of the consequences of the act which they were about to perform.

LET US LOOK TO THE END

JOSIAH QUINCY, JR.

It is not the spirit that vapors within these walls that must stand us in stead. The exertions of this day will *call forth events* which will make a very different spirit necessary for our salvation. Look to the end. Whoever supposes that shouts and hosannas will terminate the trials of the day entertains a childish fancy. We must be grossly ignorant of the importance and value of the prize for which we contend; we must be equally ignorant of the powers of those who have combined against us; we must be blind to that malice, inveteracy, and insatiable revenge which actuate our enemies, public and private, abroad and in our bosoms, to hope we shall end this controversy without the sharpest conflicts; to flatter ourselves that popular resolves, popular harangues, popular acclamations, and popular vapor will vanquish our fears. Let us consider the issue. Let us look to the end. Let us *weigh* and *consider* before we advance to those measures which must bring on the *most trying* and *terrible struggle* this country ever saw.

I see the clouds which now rise thick and fast on the horizon; the thunders roll, and the lightnings play, and to that God who rides on the whirlwind and directs the storm I commit my country.

When it was announced that the governor refused the passport Samuel Adams said, "This meeting can do nothing more to save the country." A war-whoop sounded from the gallery; the meeting was dissolved. Some one remarked, "Who knows how tea will mingle with salt-water?" and immediately after two or three different parties of men, previously selected, no doubt, some of them dressed in the habit of Indians, ran toward the wharves shouting, "To Griffin's wharf! Boston harbor a teapot to-night!" There the people repaired, and in three hours the tea was emptied from its 342 chests into the waters of the ocean in the presence of thousands of spectators. This being done, the people returned quietly to their dwellings. The next day Boston rang its bells, fired guns, and beat drums in celebration of the event. Samuel Adams said, "Oh, this is the most magnificent movement of all!" Lesser celebrations occurred in New York and Philadelphia and even in the Southern cities.

On the 7th of March, 1774, the papers relating to these transactions in America were laid before Parliament by the King. In his message to the two houses His Majesty said that he confided not only in their taking such measures as would "put an immediate stop to the present disorders," but also in their considering "what further provisions may be necessary to be established for securing the execution of the laws, and the just dependence of the colonies upon the Crown and Parliament of Great Britain."

THE BOSTON PORT BILL

Both houses in their answers assured His Majesty of their determination to make such provision as should secure the just dependence of the colonies and due obedience to the laws throughout all his dominions. On the 31st of March a bill which had passed both houses interdicting all commercial intercourse with the town of Boston, and, after the first of June following, prohibiting the landing or shipping any goods at that port, received the sanction of the King.

REGULATION OF MASSACHUSETTS GOVERNMENT

Soon after the passage of the "Boston Port Bill," as it was called, the Ministry presented a bill "for the better regulating the government of the province of Massachusetts Bay." This bill passed both houses by large majorities, and on the 20th of May became a law by the assent of the King.

By this act the people of Massachusetts were, without a hearing, deprived of some of the most important rights and privileges secured to them by their charter; rights which they had enjoyed from the first settlement of the colony.

The members of the council, heretofore under the charter chosen by the General Assembly, were now to be selected by the King; and the right of selecting jurors by the inhabitants of the several towns was taken from them. No part of this act, however, or, indeed, of any other act of the British Government, was more deeply felt by every freeholder in Massachusetts than that relating to town meetings. The liberty of convening at pleasure, which they considered as their sacred birthright, was taken from them, for, by this act, no town meeting could be called without leave of the governor, except the annual meeting in March or May.

To secure the due execution of the laws in the colonies some further provision was deemed necessary by Parliament. A third law therefore soon after passed, "for the impartial administration of justice in the cases of persons questioned, for any acts done by them, in the execution of the law, or for the suppression of riots and tumults in the province of Massachusetts Bay."

By this act persons informed against, or indicted for any act done, for the support of the laws of the *revenue,* or for the suppression of riots in Massachusetts, might, by the governor, with the advice of the council, be sent for trial to any other colony or to Great Britain.

These bills, however, did not pass without opposition in both houses. Col. Barré addressed the Ministry on the last bill in his bold and energetic language.

OLIVE BRANCH OR SWORD?

COL. ISAAC BARRÉ

"You have changed your ground. You are becoming the aggressors," he said, "and offering the last of human outrages to the people of America by subjecting them to military execution. Instead of sending them the olive branch you have sent the naked sword. By the olive branch I mean a repeal of all the late laws, fruitless to you and oppressive to them. Ask their aid in a constitutional manner and they will give it to the utmost of their ability. They never yet refused it when properly required. Your journals bear the recorded acknowledgments of the zeal with which they have contributed to the general necessities of the state. What madness is it that prompts you to attempt obtaining that by force which you may more certainly procure by requisition. They may be flattered into anything, but they are too much like yourselves to be driven. Have some indulgence for your own likeness; respect their sturdy English virtue; retract your odious exertions of authority; and remember that the first step toward making them contribute to your wants is to reconcile them to your government."

COLONIAL OPPOSITION TO THE PORT BILL

General Thomas Gage was appointed governor of Massachusetts. He arrived there about the middle of May, and was politely received by the inhabitants of Boston. The Port Bill came over at the same time, and a meeting of the people of Boston was immediately held to take it into consideration.

They resolved, among other things, "that the *impolicy, injustice, inhumanity,* and *cruelty* of the act exceed all their powers of expression; and therefore we leave it to the censure of others, and appeal to *God* and the *world.*"

They also declared it as their opinion that, "if the other colonies come into a joint resolution to stop all importation from, and exportation to, Great Britain and every part of the West Indies, till the act be repealed, the same would prove the salvation of North America and her liberties."

These resolutions, with the act itself, were immediately circulated through the colonies; and the severe interdict against the people of Boston excited universal indignation throughout America. In various ways the other colonies expressed their sympathies, sending their suffering neighbors provisions and money, and passing resolutions condemning their persecution.

The House of Burgesses in Virginia, being in session, appointed the first of June, the day the port of Boston was to be shut, as a day of "fasting, humiliation, and prayer, devoutly to implore the divine interposition for averting the heavy calamity which threatened destruction to their civil rights and the evils of a civil war; to give them *one heart and one mind* to oppose by all just and proper means every injury to American rights."

During an after-meeting of the Assembly, George Washington stated that he was ready at his own expense to raise one thousand men and march to the relief of Boston.

The Call for a Colonial Congress

The advantage of committees of correspondence was perceived on this occasion. The patriotic Virginians recommended to their committee to correspond with the committees of the other colonies on the expediency of appointing representatives from all the colonies to meet annually in a general congress to deliberate on those measures which the united interests of America might from time to time require.

The Assembly of Massachusetts met on the last of May, and the new governor, after negativing thirteen of the councillors, adjourned the assembly to meet at Salem on the 7th of June.

Soon after their meeting at this place the House of Representatives, on motion of Samuel Adams, resolved:

That a meeting of the committees from the several colonies on this continent is highly expedient and necessary to consult upon the present state of the colonies, and the miseries to which they are and must be reduced by the operation of certain acts of Parliament, respecting America; and to deliberate and determine upon proper measures, to be by them recommended to all the colonies, for the recovery and establishment of their just rights and liberties, civil and religious, and the restoration of that union and harmony, between Great Britain and the colonies, most ardently desired by all good men.

The house immediately appointed a committee of five, Thomas Cushing, Samuel Adams, Robert Treat Paine, James Bowdoin and John Adams, to meet similar delegates from the other colonies at Philadelphia, or any other suitable place, on the first of the succeeding September. The governor, having obtained information of what was going on in the house, sent his secretary to dissolve the assembly, but finding the doors closed he was obliged to read his proclamation on the steps leading to the chamber where the representatives were convened for the last time under royal authority. The members did not disperse until they had finished their important business.

The expediency and even the necessity of a general congress and a more intimate union of the colonies was perceived by all, and in the course of the summer delegates were appointed either by the regular assemblies or by conventions of the people in all the colonies except Georgia to attend a congress to be held in Philadelphia in September.

RESOLUTIONS OF VIRGINIA

The convention of Virginia, composed of deputies from all parts of the colony, met on the first of August. It not only appointed some of her distinguished citizens to attend this congress, but entered into a number of resolutions, and formed an association in which they engaged after the first day of November, 1774, that they would not import from Great Britain any goods whatever (medicines excepted) or from any other place any British manufactures, or any article which should have been brought into such place from Great Britain; and that if, before the 10th of August, 1775, American grievances should not be redressed, they would not after that day export tobacco or any other article to that country.

To this convention Thomas Jefferson submitted instructions to the delegates to the Continental Congress, maintaining that the Parliament of Virginia had as much right to pass laws for the government of England as the British Parliament had to pass laws for the government of Virginia. These instructions, though not adopted, were published in a pamphlet which Edmund Burke reprinted with amendments and additions of his own and circulated throughout England. They procured for Jefferson, to use his own words, "the honor of having his name inserted in a long list of proscriptions enrolled in a bill of attainder."

Though many influential colonists, among them John Dickinson, were still desirous of a reconciliation with the parent country on terms mutually advantageous, many of the leading and intelligent patriots of Massachusetts were now convinced that force must decide the contest. John Adams held this opinion. In conversing with Samuel Adams immediately after their appointment to the general congress he said:

"I suppose we must go to Philadelphia and enter into non-importation, non-consumption, and non-exportation agreements; but they will be of no avail; we shall have to resist by force."

While the people of Boston were suffering from the loss of their commerce the act depriving them of their charter rights arrived. To this act the people determined never to submit. As a result of their menacing attitude the royal councillors were obliged either to resign or seek protection in Boston. The grand and petit jurors, when summoned to attend the courts under the new order of things, refused to take the oaths required or to act. In some of the counties the people would not permit the courts to be held by unconstitutional judges. They assembled on the days of the session of the courts in such numbers as to fill the avenues to the court houses, and when the sheriffs commanded them to give place for the judges they refused, declaring "that they knew of no court, nor any other establish-

THE ABLE DOCTOR, OR AMERICA SWALLOWING THE BITTER DRAUGHT

ment, independent of the ancient laws and usages of their country, and to none other would they submit or give way on any account."

THE FIRST CONTINENTAL CONGRESS

On September 1, 1774, the delegates to the general congress convened at Philadelphia. A committee was appointed to state the rights of the colonies in general, the several instances in which those rights had been violated, and the means most proper to be pursued for obtaining a restoration of them. In regard to the action of General Gage in raising fortifications around Boston and in preventing a free communication with that town the congress not only addressed a letter to the general requesting him to discontinue such fortifications, but also passed a resolution approving of the opposition of the inhabitants of Massachusetts to the execution of the late acts of Parliament, and declaring that, "if the same shall be attempted to be carried into execution *by force,* in such case all America ought to support them in their opposition.''

On the 14th of October the members of this congress with unexampled unanimity declared:

That the inhabitants of the English colonies in North America, by the immutable laws of nature, the principles of the English constitution, and the several charters or compacts, have the following rights:

1.   That they are entitled to life, liberty, and property; and they have never ceded to any foreign power whatever a right to dispose of either without their consent.

2.   That our ancestors, who first settled these colonies, were, at the time of their emigration from the mother country, entitled to all the rights, liberties, and immunities of free and natural born subjects within the realm of England.

3.   That by such emigration they by no means forfeited, surrendered, or lost any of those rights, but that they were, and their descendants now are, entitled to the exercise and enjoyment of all such of them as their local and other circumstances enable them to exercise and enjoy.

4.   That the foundation of English liberty and of all free governments is a right in the people to participate in their legislative council; and, as the English colonists are not represented, and from their local and other circumstances cannot properly be represented in the British Parliament, they are entitled to a free and *exclusive power of legislation* in their several provincial legislatures, where their right of representation can alone be preserved in all cases of taxation and internal policy, subject only to the negative of their sovereign in such manner as has been heretofore used and accustomed.   But, from the necessity of the case and a regard to the mutual interest of both countries, we cheerfully consent to the operation of such acts of the British Parliament as are, *bona fide*, restrained to the regulation of our external commerce for the purpose of securing the commercial advantages of the whole empire to the mother country, and the commercial benefits of its respective members; excluding every idea of taxation internal or external for raising a *revenue* on the subjects in America without their consent.

5.   That the respective colonies are entitled to the common law of England, and, more especially, to the great and inestimable privilege of being tried by their peers of the vicinity according to the course of that law.

6.   That they are entitled to the benefit of such of the Eng-

lish statutes as existed at the time of their colonization; and which they have, by experience, respectively found to be applicable to their several local and other circumstances.

7. That these, His Majesty's colonies, are likewise entitled to all the immunities and privileges granted and confirmed to them by royal charters, or secured by their several codes of provincial laws.

8. That they have a right peaceably to assemble, consider of their grievances, and petition the King; and that all prosecutions, prohibitory proclamations, and commitments for the same are illegal.

9. That the keeping a standing army in these colonies in times of peace without the consent of the legislature of that colony in which such army is kept is against law.

10. It is indispensably necessary to good government, and rendered essential by the English constitution, that the constituent branches of the legislature be independent of each other; that, therefore, the exercise of legislative power in several colonies, by a council appointed during pleasure by the Crown, is unconstitutional, dangerous, and destructive to the freedom of American legislation.

All and each of which the aforesaid deputies, in behalf of themselves and their constituents, do claim, demand, and insist on as their indubitable rights and liberties; which cannot be legally taken from them, altered or abridged by any power whatever without their consent by their representatives in their several provincial legislatures.

Then after enumerating the various acts of Parliament which were violations of their rights they proceeded to say:

To these grievous acts and measures America cannot submit; but, in hopes their fellow subjects in Great Britain will on a revision of them restore us to that state in which both countries found happiness and prosperity, we have for the present only resolved to pursue the following peaceable measures: 1. To enter into a non-importation association. 2. To prepare an address to the people of Great Britain, and a memorial to the inhabitants of British America; and, 3. To prepare a loyal address to His Majesty, agreeably to resolutions already entered into.

The articles relating to American rights received the unanimous assent of Congress with the exception of the fourth.

This article produced no little debate, and on the last clause of it perfect unanimity did not prevail. The delegates from Massachusetts had been too much engaged in the controversy with Governor Hutchinson on the great question of parliamentary power to agree to this qualifying clause. This contest had satisfied them that it was difficult, if not impossible, to draw a satisfactory line between a duty laid for the regulation of commerce and for revenue.

A non-importation agreement was signed by all the members of this Congress including a pledge not to use any of the prohibited goods nor to consume any tea upon which duty had been paid.

In case the acts complained of should not be repealed by the 10th day of September, 1775, they agreed not to export to Great Britain, Ireland, or the West Indies any commodities or merchandise whatever, although they would continue sending rice to Europe.

The following was said in conclusion:

And we do solemnly bind ourselves and our constituents, under the ties aforesaid, to adhere to this association until such parts of the several acts of Parliament [objected to] are repealed. And we recommend it to the provincial conventions, and to the committees in the respective colonies, to establish such farther regulations as they may think proper for carrying into execution this association.

Lord Chatham, in referring to this celebrated convention, declared that though he had studied and admired the free states of antiquity, the master spirits of the world, "yet for solidity of reasoning, force of sagacity, and wisdom of conclusion, no body of men could stand in preference to this congress."

PATRICK HENRY'S ELOQUENCE

The loss of Patrick Henry's speech at the opening of the Congress is especially deplorable, as it was the one which gave him national reputation. An account of its deliverance however has fortunately been preserved.

"Mr. Henry rose slowly, as if borne down by the weight of the subject, and, after faltering, according to his habit, through a most impressive exordium, he launched gradually into a recital of the colonial wrongs. Rising, as he advanced, with the grandeur of his subject, and glowing at length with all the majesty and expectation of the occasion, his speech seemed more than that of mortal man. There was no rant, no rhapsody, no labor of the understanding, no straining of the voice, no confusion of the utterance. His countenance was erect, his eye steady, his action noble, his enunciation clear and firm, his mind poised on its center, his views of his subject comprehensive and great, and his imagination coruscating with a magnificence and a variety which struck even that assembly with amazement and awe. He sat down amid murmurs of astonishment and applause; and as he had been before proclaimed the greatest orator of Virginia, he was now, on every hand, admitted to be the first orator of America."

The speech was on the method of voting in the congress, whether it should be by colonies, by the poll of delegates, or by the various interests represented. The first method was adopted against the opposition of Henry. A fragment of his speech remains. It is the first breathing of the national spirit which would disregard State lines where national interests are at stake.

"Not a Virginian, But an American"

PATRICK HENRY

"Fleets and armies and the present state of things show that the government is dissolved. Where are your landmarks—your boundaries of colonies? We are in a state of nature! All distinctions are thrown down; all America is thrown into one mass. The distinctions between Virginians, Pennsylvanians, New Yorkers, and New Englanders are no more. I am not a Virginian, but an American."

Galloway's Plan of Union

Henry's vehement opposition later in the session to a plan of union of the colonies proposed by Joseph Galloway, a wealthy lawyer of Philadelphia, and advocated by John Jay, Edward Rutledge, and other conservatives, was probably instrumental in defeating it, as the vote was very close. The plan was similar to Franklin's Albany Plan of Union, proposed in 1754. It provided for a President-General, appointed by the Crown, and a grand council of representatives to be chosen by the colonial assemblies and to meet annually. The council was to have sole charge of internal colonial affairs, its other acts being subject to review by Parliament, although it in turn would have the right of veto over acts of Parliament relating to the colonies. Henry objected to the plan as a recognition of Parliament's right to rule the colonies, which he emphatically denied. Galloway afterwards justified the suspicion that he was secretly acting in the interests of Great Britain by turning Tory.

Address to the British People

In their address to the people of Great Britain, after enumerating the several acts of Parliament deemed violations of their rights, they appeal to the generosity, to the virtue, to the justice of the nation, for relief. They not only remind the people of the parent country of the immense benefits they had heretofore derived from a monopoly of colonial commerce, but call upon them to witness the loyalty and attachment of the colonists to the common interest of the empire.

"Did we not," they ask, "in the last war, add all the strength of this vast continent to the force which repelled our common enemy? Did we not leave our native shores and meet disease and death to promote the success of British arms in foreign climates? Did you not thank us for our zeal; and even reimburse us large sums of money, which, you confessed, we had advanced beyond our proportion, and far beyond our ability?"

After these appeals they repel the charges brought against them. "You have been told that we are seditious, impatient of government, and desirous of independency. Be assured," they said, "that these are not facts, but calumnies. Permit us to be as free as yourselves, and we shall ever esteem a union with you to be our greatest glory and our greatest happiness; we shall ever be ready to contribute all in our power to the welfare of the whole empire; we shall consider your enemies as our enemies, and your interest as our own."

In conclusion, referring to the ministerial proceedings toward the colonies, they say: "But if you are determined that your ministers shall wantonly sport with the rights of mankind— if neither the voice of justice, the dictates of the law, the principles of the constitution, nor the suggestions of humanity, can restrain your hands from shedding human blood in such an impious cause, we must then tell you that we will never submit to be hewers of wood or drawers of water for any ministry or nation in the world.

"Place us in the same situation that we were at the close of the late war and our former harmony will be restored.

"But, lest the same supineness, and the same inattention to our common interest which you have for several years shown should continue, we think it necessary to anticipate the consequences.

"By the destruction of the trade of Boston the ministry have endeavored to induce submission to their measures. The like fate may befall us all. We will endeavor, therefore, to live without trade, and recur for subsistence to the fertility and bounty of our native soil, which will afford us all the necessaries and some of the conveniences of life. We have suspended our importation from Great Britain and Ireland; and in less than a year's time, unless our grievances should be redressed, shall discontinue our exports to those kingdoms and the West Indies.

"It is with the utmost regret, however, that we find ourselves compelled, by the over-ruling principles of self-preservation, to adopt measures detrimental in their consequences to numbers of our fellow subjects in Great Britain and Ireland. But we hope the magnanimity and justice of the British nation will furnish a Parliament of such wisdom, independence, and public spirit as may save the violated rights of the whole empire from the devices of wicked ministers and evil counselors, whether in or out of office, and thereby restore that harmony, friendship, and fraternal affection between all the inhabitants of His Majesty's kingdoms and territories so ardently wished for by every true and honest American."

This address was prepared by John Jay of New York. Thomas Jefferson, while ignorant of the authorship of the address, said it was "a production certainly of the finest pen in America."

ADDRESS TO THE KING

The address to the King breathed a spirit of affection as well as loyalty. Nor did it contain the language of hypocrisy. They tell their sovereign their grievances and ask redress.

"Had our Creator," they say, "been pleased to give us existence in a land of slavery, the sense of our condition might have been mitigated by ignorance and habit. But, thanks be to His adorable goodness, we were born the heirs of freedom, and ever enjoyed our right under the auspices of your royal ancestors whose family was settled on the British throne to rescue and secure a pious and gallant nation from the popery and despotism of a superstitious and inexorable tyrant. Your Majesty, we are confident, justly rejoices that your title to the crown is thus founded on the title of your people to liberty; and, therefore, we doubt not but your royal wisdom must approve the sensibility that teaches your subjects anxiously to guard the blessing they received from divine Providence, and thereby to prove the performance of that compact which elevated the illustrious house of Brunswick to the imperial dignity it now possesses.

"The apprehension of being degraded into a state of servitude, from the preëminent rank of English freemen, while our minds retain the strongest love of liberty and clearly foresee the miseries preparing for us and our posterity, excites emotions in our breasts which, though we cannot describe, we should not wish to conceal. Feeling as men, and thinking as subjects, in the manner we do, silence would be disloyalty. By giving this faithful information we do all in our power to promote the great objects of your royal cares, the tranquillity of your government, and the welfare of your people.

"Duty to Your Majesty and regard for the preservation of ourselves and our posterity, the primary obligations of nature and society, command us to entreat your royal attention; and, as Your Majesty enjoys the signal distinction of reigning over freemen, we apprehend the language of freemen cannot be displeasing. Your royal indignation, we hope, will rather fall on those designing and dangerous men who, daringly interposing themselves between your royal person and your faithful subjects, and for several years past incessantly employed to dissolve the bonds of society by abusing Your Majesty's authority, misrepresenting your American subjects, and prosecuting the most desperate and irritating projects of oppression, have, at length, compelled us, by the force of accumulated injuries, too severe to be any longer tolerable, to disturb Your Majesty's repose by our complaints.

"These sentiments are extorted from hearts that much more willingly would bleed in Your Majesty's service. Yet so greatly have we been misrepresented that a necessity has been alleged of taking our property from us without our consent, 'to defray the charge of the administration of justice, the support of civil government, and the defence, protection, and security of the colonies.' But we beg leave to assure Your Majesty that such provision has been, and will be, made for defraying the two first articles as has been and shall be judged by the legislatures of the several colonies just and suitable to their respective circumstances: and for the defence, protection, and security of the colonies, their militia, if properly regulated, as they earnestly desire may immediately be done, would be fully sufficient, at least in time of peace; and, in case of war, your faithful colonists will be ready and willing, as they ever have been, when constitutionally required, to demonstrate their loyalty to Your Majesty by exerting their most strenuous efforts in granting supplies and raising forces. Yielding to no British subjects in affectionate attachment to Your Majesty's person, family, and government, we too dearly prize the privilege of expressing that attachment by those proofs that are honorable to the prince who receives them, and to the people who give them, ever to resign it to any body of men upon earth.

"Had we been permitted to enjoy in quiet the inheritance left us by our forefathers, we should at this time have been peaceably, cheerfully, and usefully employed in recommending ourselves, by every testimony of devotion, to Your Majesty, and of veneration to the state from which we derive our origin. But, though now exposed to unexpected and unnatural scenes of distress by a contention with that nation in whose parental guidance on all important affairs we have hitherto with filial reverence constantly trusted, and, therefore, can derive no instruction in our present unhappy and perplexing circumstances from any former experience, yet we doubt not the purity of our intention and the integrity of our conduct will justify us at that grand tribunal before which all mankind must submit to judgment.

"We ask but for peace, liberty, and safety. We wish not a diminution of the prerogative, nor do we solicit the grant of any new right in our favor. Your royal authority over us, and our connection with Great Britain we shall always carefully and zealously endeavor to support and maintain.

"Filled with sentiments of duty to Your Majesty, and of affection to our parent state, deeply impressed by our education and strongly confirmed by our reason, and anxious to evince the sincerity of these dispositions, we present this petition only to obtain redress of grievances and relief from fears and jealousies occasioned by the system of statutes and regulations adopted since the close of the late war, . . . by the abolition of which system the harmony between Great Britain and these colonies (so necessary to the happiness of both, and so ardently desired by the latter), and the usual intercourse will be immediately restored. In the magnanimity and justice of Your Majesty and Parliament we confide for a redress of our other grievances, trusting that, when the causes of our apprehensions are removed, our future conduct will prove us not unworthy of the regard we have been accustomed to enjoy. In appealing to that Being who searches thoroughly the hearts of His creatures, we solemnly profess that our councils have been influenced by no other motive than a dread of impending destruction.

"Permit us, then, most gracious sovereign, in the name of all your faithful people in America, with the utmost humility, to implore you, for the honor of Almighty God, whose pure religion our enemies are undermining; for your glory, which can be advanced only by rendering your subjects happy and keeping them united; for the interests of your family, depending on an adherence to the principles that enthroned it; for the safety and welfare of your kingdoms and dominions, threatened with almost unavoidable dangers and distresses, that Your Majesty, as the loving father of your whole people, connected by the same bonds of law, loyalty, faith, and blood, though dwelling in various countries, will not suffer the transcendant relation formed by these ties to be further violated, in uncertain expectations of effects that, if obtained, never can compensate for the calamities through which they must be gained.

"We, therefore, most earnestly beseech Your Majesty that your royal authority and interposition may be used for our relief, and that a gracious answer may be given to this petition.

"That Your Majesty may enjoy every felicity, through a long and glorious reign, over loyal and happy subjects, and that your descendants may inherit your prosperity and dominions till time shall be no more, is, and always will be, our sincere and fervent prayer."

The "Petition to the King" was written by John Dickinson. It was highly praised by Lord Chatham and others, one of whom said that "it will remain an imperishable monument to the glory of its author and of the assembly of which he was a member so long as fervid and manly eloquence and chaste and elegant composition shall be appreciated."

Congress also delivered an "Address to the Inhabitants of Quebec," in which they endeavored to convince them that a late act of Parliament respecting that province had deprived them of many of their rights and privileges, and to persuade them to unite in obtaining redress, and to join the confederacy.

After directing the Address to the King to be sent to the several colony agents in England to be presented to His Majesty, and recommending that another Congress be held on the 10th of May following, unless a redress of grievances should before that time be obtained, Congress, on the 26th of October, dissolved.

EFFECT OF THE CONGRESS

The proceedings of the Congress met with the almost unanimous approbation of the people of America. The non-importation agreement entered into by their delegates was adopted as their own. Committees of vigilance were appointed in all the towns and districts, and the names of those who disregarded it were published as the enemies of public liberty.

The various colonial assemblies and, where these could not convene owing to the opposition of the governors, special provincial conventions endorsed the proceedings of the general Congress. In Massachusetts such a provincial convention took measures to put the colony in a state of defence, and sent Josiah Quincy, Jr., to England to confer with the English Whigs.

A majority of the members of this Congress had little doubt that the measure taken by them, if supported by the American people, would produce a redress of grievances.

George Washington was of opinion that with the aid

of both the non-importation and non-exportation system America would prevail. Richard Henry Lee said to John Adams, "We shall undoubtedly carry all our points. You will be completely relieved; all the offensive acts will be repealed; the army and fleet will be recalled, and Britain will give up her foolish projects."

Adams, however, together with his cousin Samuel, and Patrick Henry were not so sanguine, believing that the contest must ultimately be decided by force. It was with this conviction that John Adams said to a friend, on being elected as a delegate to the Congress: "As to my fate the die is cast, the Rubicon is passed— and sink or swim, live or die, to survive or perish with my country is my unalterable resolution."[1]

[1] Compare the "Supposed Speech of John Adams," by Daniel Webster, on page 194.

CHAPTER IV

FORCE OR CONCILIATION?

Lord Chatham Moves That the Troops Be Withdrawn from Boston; His Speech on the Motion. He Is Supported by Lords Camden and Shelburne and the Marquis of Rockingham; the Measure Is Defeated—Chatham Presents a Plan of Conciliation: His Tilt with Lord Sandwich over the Character of Benjamin Franklin—British Petitions in Behalf of America Are "Shelved," and Acts to "Crush Rebellion" Are Adopted—Franklin's Proposals for Reconciliation—Conciliatory Plan of Lord North—Edmund Burke on "Conciliation with America"—His Resolutions Are Defeated—His Speech on "The Right to Tax America."

A NEW Parliament met on the 29th day of November, 1774. The King informed Parliament that a most daring resistance and disobedience to the law still prevailed in Massachusetts and had broken out in fresh violences; that these proceedings had been countenanced and encouraged in the other colonies, and that unwarrantable attempts had been made to obstruct the commerce of the kingdom by unlawful combinations, and he expressed his firm determination to withstand every attempt to weaken or impair the supreme authority of Parliament over all the dominions of the Crown.

Addresses in answer to the speech concurring in the sentiments expressed by the King were carried in both houses by large majorities. A committee was appointed to take the subject of colonial affairs into consideration.

Josiah Quincy, Jr., not long after his arrival in England, had an interview with Lord North as well as Lord Dartmouth at their special request.

The former, on the 19th of November, in conversation on the subject of American affairs, reminded Mr. Quincy of the *power* of Great Britain and that they were determined "to exert it to the utmost in order to effect the submission of the colonies."

99

"We must try," said he, "what we can do to support the authority we claim over America. If we are defective in power, we must sit down contented and make the best terms we can; and nobody can blame us after we have done our utmost; but till we have tried what we can do, we can never be justified in receding."

Mr. Quincy from this conversation with the Prime Minister, as well as information obtained from other sources, was convinced that the Americans had nothing to hope but from forcible resistance, and communicated this conviction to some of his particular friends in America.

In a letter to Joseph Reed of Philadelphia of the 17th of December he says:

"But by no means entertain an idea that commercial plans, founded on commercial principles, are to be engines of your freedom or the security of your felicity.

"Far different are the weapons with which oppression is repelled; far more noble the sentiments and actions which secure liberty and happiness to man.

"I cannot forbear telling you that I look to my countrymen with the feelings of one who verily believes they must yet seal their faith and constancy to their liberties *with blood.*"

Chatham's Motion to Remove the Troops

Parliament, after the holiday recess, convened on the 20th of January, and on the same day Lord Chatham took his seat in the House of Lords and immediately moved:

"That, in order to open the way toward our happy settlement of the dangerous troubles in America by beginning to allay ferments and soften animosities there, and, above all, for preventing in the meantime any sudden and fatal catastrophe at Boston, now suffering under daily irritation of an army before their eyes posted in their town, it may graciously please His Majesty that immediate orders may be dispatched to General Gage for removing His Majesty's forces from the town of Boston."

This motion was supported by one of the most eloquent and impressive speeches ever delivered by that distinguished statesman and orator.

On Removing the Troops from Boston

LORD CHATHAM

"My Lords, these papers from America, now laid by administration for the first time before your lordships, have been, to my knowledge, five or six weeks in the pocket of the minister. And, notwithstanding the fate of this kingdom hangs upon the event of this great controversy, we are but this moment called to a consideration of this important subject.

"My Lords, I do not wish to look into one of these papers. I know their contents well enough already. I know that there is not a member in this house but is acquainted with their purport, also. There ought, therefore, to be no delay in entering upon this matter. We ought to proceed to it immediately. We ought to seize the first moment to open the door of reconciliation. The Americans will never be in a temper or state to be reconciled— they ought not to be—till the troops are withdrawn. The troops are a perpetual irritation to those people; they are a bar to all confidence and all cordial reconcilement.

"The way must be immediately opened for reconciliation. It will soon be too late. I know not who advised the present measures; I know not who advises to a perseverance and enforcement of them; but this I will say, that whoever advises them ought to answer for it at his utmost peril. I know that no one will avow that he advised or that he was the author of these measures; every one shrinks from the charge. But somebody has advised His Majesty to these measures, and, if he continues to hear such evil counselors, His Majesty will be undone. His Majesty may indeed wear his crown, but, the American jewel out of it, it will not be worth the wearing. What more shall I say? I must not say the king is betrayed; but this I will say, the nation is ruined. What foundation have we for our claims over America? What is our right to persist in such cruel and vindictive measures against that loyal, respectable people?

"They say, you have no right to tax them without their consent. They say truly. Representation and taxation must go together; they are inseparable. Yet there is scarcely a man in our streets, though so poor as scarcely to be able to get his daily bread, but thinks he is the legislator of America. *'Our American subjects'* is a common phrase in the mouths of the lowest orders of our citizens; but property, my lords, is the sole and entire dominion of the owner: it excludes all the world besides the owner. None can intermeddle with it. It is an unity, a mathematical point. It is an atom; untangible by any but the proprietor. Touch it, and the owner loses his whole property. The touch contaminates the whole mass, the whole property vanishes. The touch of another annihilates it; for whatever is a man's own is absolutely and exclusively his own

After stating that the Americans had been abused, misrepresented and traduced in the most atrocious manner in order to give color to and urge on the most precipitate, unjust, cruel, and vindictive measures that ever disgraced a nation, he asks:

"But how have this respectable people behaved under their grievances? With unexampled patience, with unparalleled wisdom. They chose delegates by their free suffrages; no bribery, no corruption, no influence there, my Lords. Their representatives meet with the sentiments and temper and speak the sense of the continent. For genuine sagacity, for singular moderation, for solid wisdom, manly spirit, sublime sentiments, and simplicity of language, for everything respectable and honorable, the Congress of Philadelphia shine unrivaled. This wise people speak out. They do not hold the language of slaves; they tell you what they mean. They do not ask you to repeal your laws as a *favor;* they claim it as a *right*—they demand it. They tell you they will not submit to them; and I tell you, the acts must be repealed; they *will* be repealed; you cannot enforce them. The ministry are checkmated; they have a move to make on the board; yet not a move but they are ruined. Repeal, therefore, my Lords, I say. But bare repeal will not satisfy this enlightened and spirited people. What! repeal a bit of paper! repeal a piece of parchment! That alone will not do, my lords. You must go through the work—you must declare you have no right to tax—then they may trust you; then they will have some confidence in you."

After adverting to the distinction he had formerly made, in the debate on the repeal of the Stamp Act, between taxation and legislation (see page 41) Lord Chatham thus concludes:

"My Lords, deeply impressed with the importance of taking some healing measures at this most alarming, distracted state of our affairs, though bowed down with a cruel disease, I have crawled to this House to give you my best counsel and experience; and my advice is to beseech His Majesty to withdraw his troops. This is the best I can think of. It will convince America that you mean to try her cause in the spirit and by the laws of freedom and fair enquiry, and not by codes of blood. How can she now trust you with the bayonet at her breast? She has all the reason in the world now to believe you mean her death or bondage. Thus entered on the threshold of this business, I will knock at your gates for justice without ceasing, unless inveterate infirmities stay my hand. My Lords, I pledge myself never to leave this business. I will pursue it to the end in every shape. I will never fail of my attendance on it, at every step and period of this great matter, unless nailed down to my bed by the severity of disease. My Lords, there is no time to be lost; every moment is big with dangers. Nay, while I am now speaking the decisive blow may be struck and millions involved in the consequences. The very first drop of blood will make a wound that will not easily be skinned over. Years, perhaps ages, may not heal it. It will be *immedicabile vulnus:* a wound of that rancorous, malignant, corroding, festering nature which in all probability will mortify the whole body. Let us then, my Lords, set to this business in earnest! Not take it up by bits and scraps as formerly, just as exigencies pressed, without any regard to general relations, connections, and dependencies. I would not, by anything I have said, my lords, be thought to encourage America to proceed beyond the right line. I reprobate all acts of violence by her mobility.[1] But when her inherent constitutional rights are invaded, those rights she has an equitable claim to enjoy by the fundamental laws of the English constitution, and which are engrafted thereon by the unalterable laws of nature; then I own myself an American, and, feeling myself such, shall, to the verge of my life, vindicate those rights against all men who strive to trample upon or oppose them."

The motion of Lord Chatham, though supported by Lord Camden, Lord Shelburne, and the Marquis of Rockingham, was rejected by a large majority. The ministers, being now prepared to announce their determination to coerce obedience to the late acts of Par-

---

[1] *I. e.*, the common people; a word humorously coined from "mob" as an antonym for "nobility."

liament, refused to listen to the prophetic voice of this experienced statesman. This, however, did not prevent him from presenting to the House soon after a bill containing his favorite plan "for settling the troubles, and for asserting the supreme legislative authority and superintending power of Great Britain over the colonies."

CHATHAM'S PLAN OF CONCILIATION

The great outlines of this plan were in the first place a general declaration that the colonies of America were dependent on the imperial Crown of Great Britain and subordinate to the British Parliament, and that Parliament could make laws binding on them in all cases touching the general weal of the British empire; the bill then enacted that Parliament could lay no tax or tallage without common consent by an act of an American provincial assembly duly convened for that purpose.

It provided that a general congress be held in America to recognize such general *superintending authority* in Parliament; and that such congress be requested to take into consideration the making a free grant to the King, and his successors, of a certain *permanent revenue,* subject to the disposition of Parliament, to the alleviation of the national debt. That the same congress apportion the quotas of this revenue to each province. That the vice-admiralty courts be reduced to their ancient limits —that no person be sent to Great Britain for crimes committed in America—that the acts complained of, passed since 1763, be suspended—that the judges hold their offices during good behavior, and have their salaries from the Crown; and the bill also declared that the colonies were justly entitled to the privileges and franchises granted by their charters or constitutions, and that these charters could not be invaded or rescinded, unless for some legal ground of forfeiture. It asserted the right of the King to send a legal army to any part of his dominions; but that no military force could lawfully be used to destroy the just rights of the people.

Though this bill, as it contained a direct avowal of the *supreme authority* of Parliament over the colonies in all cases except that of taxation, could never have received the assent of the Americans, yet, as it ex-

Frontispiece in the "London Magazine."

CONCILIATION

BRITAIN, AMERICA, at length be Friends,
Accept the terms which CONCORD recommends!
Be ye but Steady to each other's Cause,
Protect, defend, and not infringe the Laws;
Ye may together—come the World in Arms,
Bear the brunt Shock of hostile, dire alarms.
'Tis Peace, Trade, Navigation, will support
The poor with bread—in Dignity the Court.
Rush to each other's Arms, be firm and true;
One Faith, one Fame, one Intrest, makes the Two.

105

pressly denied the parliamentary power of taxing the colonies without the consent of their assemblies, and made other concessions, it was rejected by a large majority on its first reading.

Lord Chatham had shown this bill to Dr. Benjamin Franklin before he submitted it to the House of Lords, but the latter had not an opportunity of proposing certain alterations which he had sketched. Dr. Franklin, however, at the special request of Lord Chatham, was present at the debates upon it.

Lord Dartmouth was at first disposed to have the bill lie upon the table, but Lord Sandwich opposed its being received and moved that it be immediately "rejected with the contempt it deserved. He could never believe," he said, "that it was the production of a British peer; that it appeared to him rather *the work of some American*." Turning his face toward Dr. Franklin, then standing at the bar, "he fancied," he said, "he had in his eye the person who drew it up, one of the bitterest and most mischievous enemies this country had ever known."

To this part of the speech of Lord Sandwich Chatham replied by saying "that it was entirely his own."

"This declaration," he said, "he thought himself the more obliged to make, as many of their lordships appeared to have so mean an opinion of it; for if it was so weak or so bad a thing, it was proper in him to take care that no other person should unjustly share in the censure it deserved. That it had been heretofore reckoned his vice not to be apt to take advice; but he made no scruple to declare that, if he were the first minister of this country, and had the care of settling this momentous business, he should not be ashamed of publicly calling to his assistance a person so perfectly acquainted with the whole of American affairs as the gentleman alluded to and so injuriously reflected on; one whom all Europe held in estimation for his knowledge and wisdom, and who ranked with our Boyles and Newtons; who was an honor, not to the English nation only, but to human nature."

Petitions in Favor of America Shelved

Soon after the meeting of Parliament in January petitions from the merchants of London and other trading towns in favor of America were presented to the House of Commons. These petitions, instead of being referred, as the petitioners expected, to the committee on American affairs, were, on motion of the minister, referred to another committee whose meeting was fixed at a more distant day. This was considered by the petitioners as very unfair treatment, and the committee to which their petitions were referred was called the *"committee of oblivion."* The petition of the American congress to the King had been sent to the house with other papers, but had been left entirely unnoticed. Dr. Franklin, Mr. Bollan, and Arthur Lee, colonial agents, to whom it had been entrusted, requested liberty to be heard upon it before the house. This, however, was refused, the ministers giving the old reason that it came from an illegal assembly. Thus the humble supplication of three millions of people could not be heard unless presented in a particular manner.

Acts to "Crush Rebellion"

Immediately after the rejection of Lord Chatham's bill the minister proposed in the House of Commons a joint address to the King on American affairs. In this address, which was carried by large majorities, Parliament declared that Massachusetts was in a state of rebellion, and that this colony had been supported by unlawful combinations and engagements entered into by several of the other colonies to the great injury and oppression of His Majesty's subjects in Great Britain. Assuring His Majesty of their determination never to relinquish the sovereign authority of the King and Parliament over the colonies, they requested him to take the most effectual measures to enforce obedience to that authority, and promised him their support at the hazard of their lives and property. In the long and pointed debates on this address it was declared by ministers and their supporters that the Americans had long wished to become independent, and only waited for ability and opportunity to accomplish their design. To prevent this, they said, and to crush the monster in its birth, was the duty of every Englishman, and this must be done at any price and at every hazard. In the course of the debates the Americans were branded with the epithets of cowards and paltroons, and some pretending to be well acquainted with their character declared them incapable of military discipline or exertion, and that a small force would reduce them to obedience.

Opposition to the address was made in both Houses, but in vain. The King in his answer assured Parliament of his firm determination in compliance with their request to enforce obedience to the laws and authority of the supreme legislature of the empire. His answer was followed by a message requesting an increase of his forces by sea and land. The restriction of the trade of the colonies and a prohibition of their use of the fisheries were also a part of the ministerial system of measures. The minister began this part of his system with Massachusetts, Connecticut, New Hampshire, and Rhode Island as being the most obstinate and refractory. On the 10th of February he presented a bill which soon became a law restricting the trade of these colonies to Great Britain, Ireland, and the British West Indies, and prohibiting their carrying on any fisheries on the banks of Newfoundland and other places for a limited time. The same restrictions were soon after extended to all the colonies represented in the Congress at Philadelphia, with the exception of New York and North Carolina. These bills were opposed by the minority in both houses as unjust and cruel toward the colonists, involving the innocent with the guilty; and unwise and impolitic in regard to the people of Great Britain. By the loss of their foreign trade and the fisheries the colonists, it was said, particularly those of New England, would be unable to pay the large balances due from them to the British merchants. But every argument, however just or reasonable, was urged in vain against the measures proposed by the minister. An idea prevailed in Great Britain that the people of New England were dependent on the fisheries for subsistence, and that, deprived of these, they would be starved into obedience and submission.

FRANKLIN'S PROPOSAL FOR RECONCILIATION

During this period Dr. Fothergill and Mr. Barclay, both friends to America, had frequent conversations with Dr. Franklin, earnestly soliciting him to suggest some plan of reconciliation which might be submitted to the consideration of the Ministry. They urged that this might be done immediately before the breach was irreparable, as additional measures against the people of New England were at that time in contemplation.

About the first of December Dr. Franklin sketched and presented to them a plan which he called "Hints for conversation upon the subject of terms that might probably produce a durable union between Great Britain and the colonies."

The "hints" included, among other propositions, that the tea duty act and all acts restraining manufactures in the colonies be repealed, the royal garrisons be removed, and the recent act in regard to Massachusetts and Quebec be revoked. In return, the Navigation Acts to be all reënacted in the colonies.

To some of Franklin's propositions Mr. Barclay and Dr. Fothergill made strong objections.

Restraining manufactures in the colonies, they said, was a favorite idea in Great Britain, and would not easily be relinquished. Dr. Franklin, however, insisted on the justice of allowing all subjects in every country to make the most of their natural advantages, but at their earnest request he consented to change the word *repealed* to *reconsidered*.

With respect to sending or quartering troops in the colonies, this, they observed, would never be granted, as all would be of opinion that the King, who was to defend all parts of his dominions, had a right of course to place his troops where they might best answer that purpose. Dr. Franklin in support of his proposition said that if the King could bring troops into the colonies without the consent of the colonial legislatures, he might also bring armies raised in America into England without consent of Parliament. If troops were necessary in America the consent of the local assemblies would no doubt always be obtained, and he refused to give up this article.

Strong objections, they said, would be made against repealing the late laws relating to Quebec and Massachusetts, the old colonists having nothing to do with Quebec, and the act altering the charter of Massachusetts being deemed by the Administration a valuable improvement in the government of that province. Dr. Franklin replied that the Americans had, at a great expense, assisted in the conquest of Canada, and therefore had a right to object to the establishment of an arbitrary government there.

"That as to amending the Massachusetts government," he told them, "though it might be shown that every one of these pretended amendments were real mischiefs, yet that charters being compacts between two parties, the King and the people, no alteration could be made in them, even for the better, but by the consent of both parties. That the Parliament's claim and exercise of a power to alter our charters, which had always been deemed inviolable but for forfeiture, and to alter laws made in pursuance of those charters which had received the royal approbation, and thenceforth were deemed fixed and unchangeable but by the powers that made them, had rendered all our constitutions uncertain, and set us quite afloat; that, as by claiming a right to tax us *ad libitum*, they deprived us of all property; so by this claim of altering our laws and charters at will they deprived us of all privilege and right whatever, but what we should hold at their pleasure; that this was a situation we could not be in, and must risk life and everything rather than submit to it."

The monopoly of the colonial commerce, it was said, could never be given up, and that any proposition of this kind would only give offence without producing any good. This article was therefore, at last, totally omitted.

The propositions were placed before the Ministry

and other gentlemen of influence in Parliament, and on the 4th of February, 1775, Dr. Fothergill and Mr. Barclay had an interview with Dr. Franklin on the subject. Mr. Barclay said there was a good disposition in the Administration toward the colonies, and hinted how much it was in the power of Dr. Franklin himself to promote an agreement, and that in such an event he might expect not only a restoration of his old place, but almost any other he might wish. To this Dr. Franklin replied that the Ministry, he was sure, would rather give him a *place* in a cart to Tyburn than any other place whatever.

The ministerial agents made counter propositions, to which Dr. Franklin replied that, as none of the late acts relating to the province of Massachusetts Bay were to be repealed, except the Boston Port Bill, "Massachusetts must suffer all the hazards and mischiefs of war rather than admit the alteration of their charters and laws by Parliament. They who can give up liberty to obtain a little temporary safety deserve neither liberty nor safety."

LORD NORTH'S PROPOSITION

Soon after the close of this negotiation and while Parliament were engaged in augmenting the military and naval force and declaring the colonists in a state of rebellion, Lord North, the Prime Minister, surprised both his political friends and enemies with a proposition called his *conciliatory plan* in relation to the colonies.

This proposition was submitted to the House of Commons by the minister on the 20th of February, 1775, and was finally adopted. It declared:

"That, when the Governor, Council and Assembly, or General Court of any of His Majesty's colonies in America shall propose to make provision, according to the condition, circumstances, and situation of such province or colony, for contributing their proportion for the common defence (such proportion to be raised under the authority of the General Court or Assembly of such colony and *disposable by Parliament*), and shall engage to make provision, also, for the support of the civil government and the administration of justice in such colony, it will be proper, if such proposal shall be *approved* by *His Majesty* and the two Houses of Parliament, and for so long as such provision shall be made accordingly, to *forbear* in respect to such colony to levy any duty, tax or assessment, except only such duties as it may be expedient to levy or impose for the regulation of commerce; the net proceeds of the duties last mentioned to be carried to the account of such colony respectively.''

This unexpected proposition was at first opposed by those who usually acted with the minister as totally inconsistent with the course of measures just adopted, and they would probably have voted against it had they not been quieted by explanations made by his particular friends as to its real object, which was to cause a division among the colonies; or, if this should not be the effect, and the reasonable terms offered should be rejected by them, to unite the people of England in strong coercive measures. The minister stated that it would be an infallible touch-stone to try the *sincerity* of the Americans. That he intended by it to separate the grain from the chaff. If rejected, ''we shall then,'' he observed, ''know how to act; after having shown our wisdom and our humanity by giving them an opportunity of redeeming their past faults, and holding out to them fitting terms of accommodation; if they reject them we shall stand justified in taking the most coercive measures, and they must be answerable to God and man for the consequences.''

The adoption of Lord North's conciliatory scheme did not prevent David Hartley and Edmund Burke from presenting to the House their respective plans of reconciliation.

HARTLEY'S AND BURKE'S PROPOSITIONS

Mr. Hartley proposed that at the request of Parliament the secretary of state should require a contribution from the colonies for the general expense of the empire, leaving the *amount* and *application* to the colonial assemblies.

Mr. Burke's proposition, founded on expediency, was to permit the colonies to tax themselves in their assemblies according to ancient usage and to repeal all acts of Parliament imposing duties in America.

These propositions, though supported by all the eloquence and powerful talents of Mr. Burke, were rejected by the usual ministerial majorities.

In presenting his proposition, Mr. Burke made what has been considered the greatest of all his speeches, and one to which there are few equals in forensic oratory, whether of ancient or of modern times.

ON CONCILIATION WITH AMERICA

EDMUND BURKE

Mr. Speaker: As I came into the House full of anxiety about the event of my motion, I found, to my infinite surprise, that the grand penal bill,[1] by which we had passed sentence on the trade and sustenance of America, is to be returned to us from the other House. I do confess I could not help looking on this event as a fortunate omen. I look upon it as a sort of providential favor by which we are put once more in possession of our deliberative capacity upon a business so very questionable in its nature, so very uncertain in its issue. By the return of this bill, which seemed to have taken its flight forever, we are at this very instant nearly as free to choose a plan for our American government as we were on the first day of the session. If, sir, we incline to the side of conciliation we are not at all embarrassed (unless we please to make ourselves so) by any incongruous mixture of coercion and restraint. We are, therefore, called upon, as it were by a superior warning voice, again to attend to America; to attend to the whole of it together; and to review the subject with an unusual degree of care and calmness.

Here the speaker told of the exhaustive research he had made in American affairs since the proposition of the Stamp Act.

[1] The act to confine the commerce of New England to Great Britain, Ireland and the British West Indies.

Sir, Parliament, having an enlarged view of objects, made during this interval more frequent changes in their sentiment and their conduct than could be justified in a particular person upon the contracted scale of private information. But, though I do not hazard anything approaching to a censure on the motives of former Parliaments to all those alterations, one fact is undoubted—that under them the state of America has been kept in continual agitation. Everything administered as remedy to the public complaint, if it did not produce, was at least followed by a heightening of the distemper; until, by a variety of experiments, that important country has been brought into her present situation—a situation which I will not miscall, which I dare not name, which I scarcely know how to comprehend in the terms of any description.

To restore order and repose to an empire so great and so distracted as ours is merely in the attempt an undertaking that would ennoble the flights of the highest genius, and obtain pardon for the efforts of the meanest understanding. Struggling a good while with these thoughts, by degrees I felt myself more firm. I derived, at length, some confidence from what in other circumstances usually produces timidity. I grew less anxious, even from the idea of my own insignificance. For, judging of what you are by what you ought to be, I persuaded myself that you would not reject a reasonable proposition because it had nothing but its reason to recommend it.

The *proposition* is peace. Not peace through the medium of war; not peace to be hunted through the labyrinth of intricate and endless negotiations; not peace to arise out of universal discord, fomented from principle, in all parts of the empire; not peace to depend on the juridical determination of perplexing questions, or the precise marking the shadowy boundaries of a complex government. It is simple peace, sought in its natural course and its ordinary haunts. It is peace sought in the spirit of peace, and laid in principles purely pacific. I propose, by removing the ground of the difference, and by restoring *the former unsuspecting confidence of the colonies in the mother country*,[1] to give permanent satisfaction to your people; and, far from a scheme of ruling by discord, to reconcile them to each other in the same act, and by the bond of the very same interest which reconciles them to British government.

My idea is nothing more. Refined policy ever has been the parent of confusion, and ever will be so as long as the world endures. Plain good intention, which is as easily discovered

[1] See declaration of the Congress at Philadelphia in 1774, on page 93.

at the first view as fraud is surely detected at last, is (let me say) of no mean force in the government of mankind. Genuine simplicity of heart is a healing and cementing principle. My plan, therefore, being formed upon the most simple grounds imaginable, may disappoint some people when they hear it. It has nothing to recommend it to the pruriency of curious ears. There is nothing at all new and captivating in it. It has nothing of the splendor of the project which has been lately laid upon your table by the noble Lord in the blue ribbon [Lord North]. It does not propose to fill your lobby with squabbling colony agents, who will require the interposition of your mace at every instant to keep the peace among them. It does not institute a magnificent auction of finance, where captivated provinces come to general ransom by bidding against each other until you knock down the hammer, and determine a proportion of payments beyond all the powers of algebra to equalize and settle.

The House has declared conciliation admissible *previous* to any submission on the part of America. It has even shot a good deal beyond that mark, and has admitted that the complaints of our former mode of exerting the right of taxation were not wholly unfounded.

The means proposed by the noble Lord for carrying his ideas into execution I think, indeed, are very indifferently suited to the end; and this I shall endeavor to show you before I sit down. But for the present I take my ground on the admitted *principle*. I mean to give peace. Peace implies reconciliation; and where there has been a material dispute reconciliation does in a manner always imply concession on the one part or on the other. In this state of things I make no difficulty in affirming that the proposal ought to originate from us. Great and acknowledged force is not impaired, either in effect or in opinion, by an unwillingness to exert itself. The superior power may offer peace with honor and with safety. Such an offer from such a power will be attributed to magnanimity. But the concessions of the weak are the concessions of fear. When such a one is disarmed, he is wholly at the mercy of his superior, and he loses forever that time and those chances which, as they happen to all men, are the strength and resources of all inferior power.

The capital leading questions on which you must this day decide are these two: *First, whether you ought to concede; and, secondly, what your concession ought to be.*

On the first of these questions we have gained, as I have

just taken the liberty of observing to you, some ground. But I am sensible that a good deal more is still to be done. Indeed, sir, to enable us to determine both on the one and the other of these great questions with a firm and precise judgment, I think it may be necessary to consider distinctly:

The true *nature* and the peculiar *circumstances* of the object which we have before us—because, after all our struggle, whether we will or not, we must govern America according to that nature and to those circumstances, and not according to our imaginations; not according to abstract ideas of right; by no means according to mere general theories of government, the resort to which appears to me, in our present situation, no better than arrant trifling. I shall therefore endeavor, with your leave, to lay before you some of the most material of these circumstances in as full and as clear a manner as I am able to state them.

Here the speaker discussed the *population* of the colonies, which he had found to be two million whites and five hundred thousand blacks, all increasing so fast that "while we spend our time in deliberating on the mode of governing two millions we shall find we have two millions more to manage." This fact, he said to the House, "will show that you ought not, in reason, to trifle with so large a mass of the interests and feelings of the human race. You could at no time do so without guilt, and, be assured, you will not be able to do it long with impunity."

But the population of this country, the great and growing population, though a very important consideration, will lose much of its weight if not combined with other circumstances. The *commerce* of your colonies is out of all proportion beyond the numbers of the people.

Examine this account:

The whole export trade of England, including that to the colonies, in 1704... £6,509,000
Exported to the colonies alone, in 1772..................... 6,024,000

Difference................................... £485,000

The trade with America alone is now within less than £500,000 of being equal to what this great commercial nation, England, carried on at the beginning of this century with the whole world!

But, it will be said, is not this American trade an unnatural protuberance that has drawn the juices from the rest of the body? The reverse. It is the very food that has nourished every other part into its present magnitude. Our general trade has been greatly augmented, and augmented more or less in almost every part to which it ever extended, but with this material difference, that, of the six millions which in the beginning of the century constituted the whole mass of our export commerce, the colony trade was but one twelfth part; it is now (as a part of sixteen millions) considerably more than a third of the whole. This is the relative proportion of the importance of the colonies of these two periods; and all reasoning concerning our mode of treating them must have this proportion as its basis, or it is a reasoning weak, rotten, and sophistical.

I pass to the colonies in another point of view—their *agriculture*. This they have prosecuted with such a spirit that, besides feeding plentifully their own growing multitude, their annual export of grain, comprehending rice, has, some years ago, exceeded a million in value. For some time past the old world has been fed from the new. The scarcity which you have felt would have been a desolating famine if this child of your old age, with a true filial piety, with a Roman charity, had not put the full breast of its youthful exuberance to the mouth of its exhausted parent.[1]

As to the wealth which the colonies have drawn from the sea by their *fisheries,* you had all that matter fully opened at your bar. You surely thought those acquisitions of value, for they seemed even to excite your envy; and yet the spirit by which that enterprising employment has been exercised ought rather, in my opinion, to have raised your esteem and admiration. And pray, sir, what in the world is equal to it? Pass by the other parts, and look at the manner in which the people of New England have of late carried on the whale fishery. While we follow them among the tumbling mountains of ice, and behold them penetrating into the deepest frozen recesses of Hudson's Bay and Davis' Straits—while we are looking for them beneath the arctic circle, we hear that they have pierced into the opposite region of polar cold—that they are at the antipodes, and engaged under the frozen Serpent of the south. Falkland Island, which seemed too remote and romantic an object for the grasp of national ambition, is but a stage and resting-place in the progress of their victorious industry. Nor is the equinoc-

[1] An allusion to the story of a Roman matron told in Valerius Maximus, V, 7, and Pliny, Nat. Hist., 7, 36.

tial heat more discouraging to them than the accumulated winter of both the poles. We know that, while some of them draw the line, and strike the harpoon on the coast of Africa, others run the longitude, and pursue their gigantic game along the coast of Brazil. No sea but what is vexed by their fisheries. No climate that is not witness to their toils. Neither the perseverance of Holland, nor the activity of France, nor the dexterous and firm sagacity of English enterprise, ever carried this most perilous mode of hardy industry to the extent to which it has been pushed by this recent people—a people who are still, as it were, but in the gristle, and not yet hardened into the bone of manhood. When I contemplate these things—when I know that the colonies in general owe little or nothing to any care of ours, and that they are not squeezed into this happy form by the constraints of watchful and suspicious government, but that, through a wise and salutary neglect, a generous nature has been suffered to take her own way to perfection—when I reflect upon these effects—when I see how profitable they have been to us, I feel all the pride of power sink, and all presumption in the wisdom of human contrivances melt and die away within me. My rigor relents. I pardon something to the spirit of liberty.

I am sensible, sir, that all which I have asserted in my detail is admitted in the gross; but that quite a different conclusion is drawn from it. America, gentlemen say, is a noble object. It is an object well worth fighting for. Certainly it is, if fighting a people be the best way of gaining them. Gentlemen in this respect will be led to their choice of means by their complexions and their habits. Those who understand the military art will, of course, have some predilection for it. Those who wield the thunder of the state may have more confidence in the efficacy of arms. But I confess, possibly for want of this knowledge, my opinion is much more in favor of prudent management than of force; considering force not as an odious, but a feeble, instrument for preserving a people so numerous, so active, so growing, so spirited as this in a profitable and subordinate connection with us.

First, sir, permit me to observe, that the use of force alone is but *temporary*. It may subdue for a moment, but it does not remove the necessity of subduing again; and a nation is not governed which is perpetually to be conquered.

My next objection is its *uncertainty*. Terror is not always the effect of force; and an armament is not a victory. If you do not succeed, you are without resource; for, conciliation fail-

ing, force remains; but, force failing, no farther hope of reconciliation is left. Power and authority are sometimes bought
by kindness, but they can never be begged as alms by an impoverished and defeated violence.

A farther objection to force is, that you *impair the object*
by your very endeavors to preserve it. The thing you fought
for is not the thing which you recover; but depreciated, sunk,
wasted, and consumed in the contest. Nothing less will content
me than *whole* America. I do not choose to consume its strength
along with our own, because in all parts it is the British strength
that I consume. I do not choose to be caught by a foreign
enemy at the end of this exhausting conflict, and still less in
the midst of it. I may escape; but I can make no insurance
against such an event. Let me add, that I do not choose wholly
to break the American spirit, because it is the spirit that has
made the country.

Lastly, we have no sort of *experience* in favor of force as an
instrument in the rule of our colonies. Their growth and their
utility have been owing to methods altogether different. Our
ancient indulgence has been said to be pursued to a fault.
It may be so; but we know, if feeling is evidence, that our fault
was more tolerable than our attempt to mend it; and our sin
far more salutary than our penitence.

These, sir, are my reasons for not entertaining that high
opinion of untried force by which many gentlemen, for whose
sentiments in other particulars I have great respect, seem to be
so greatly captivated.

But there is still behind a third consideration concerning
this object, which serves to determine my opinion on the sort
of policy which ought to be pursued in the management of America, even more than its population and its commerce—I mean
its temper and character. In this character of the Americans
a love of freedom is the predominating feature, which marks
and distinguishes the whole; and, as an ardent is always a jealous affection, your colonies become suspicious, restive, and un-
tractable, whenever they see the least attempt to wrest from
them by force, or shuffle from them by chicane, what they think
the only advantage worth living for. This fierce spirit of liberty is stronger in the English colonies, probably, than in any
other people of the earth, and this from a variety of powerful
causes, which, to understand the true temper of their minds,
and the direction which this spirit takes, it will not be amiss
to lay open somewhat more largely.

First, the people of the colonies are descendants of Englishmen. England, sir, is a nation which still, I hope, respects, and formerly adored, her freedom. The colonists emigrated from you when this part of your character was most predominant; and they took this bias and direction the moment they parted from your hands. They are, therefore, not only devoted to liberty, but to liberty according to English ideas and on English principles. Abstract liberty, like other mere abstractions, is not to be found. Liberty inheres in some sensible object; and every nation has formed to itself some favorite point which, by way of eminence, becomes the criterion of their happiness. It happened you know, sir, that the great contests for freedom in this country were, from the earliest times, chiefly upon the question of taxing. Most of the contests in the ancient commonwealths turned primarily on the right of election of magistrates, or on the balance among the several orders of the State. The question of money was not with them so immediate. But in England it was otherwise. On this point of taxes the ablest pens and most eloquent tongues have been exercised; the greatest spirits have acted and suffered. In order to give the fullest satisfaction concerning the importance of this point, it was not only necessary for those who, in argument, defended the excellence of the English constitution to insist on this privilege of granting money as a dry point of fact, and to prove that the right had been acknowledged in ancient parchments and blind usages to reside in a certain body called the House of Commons. They went much farther: they attempted to prove (and they succeeded) that in theory it ought to be so, from the particular nature of a House of Commons as an immediate representative of the people, whether the old records had delivered this oracle or not. They took infinite pains to inculcate as a fundamental principle that in all monarchies the people must, in effect, themselves, mediately or immediately, possess the power of granting their own money, or no shadow of liberty could subsist. The colonies draw from you, as with their life-blood, those ideas and principles. Their love of liberty, as with you, fixed and attached on this specific point of taxing. Liberty might be safe or might be endangered in twenty other particulars without their being much pleased or alarmed. Here they felt its pulse, and, as they found that beat, they thought themselves sick or sound. I do not say whether they were right or wrong in applying your general arguments to their own case. It is not easy, indeed, to make a monopoly of theorems and corollaries. The fact is, that they did thus apply those general arguments; and your mode of governing them, whether through lenity or indolence, through wisdom or mistake, confirmed them in the imagination that they, as well as you, had an interest in these common principles.

They were further confirmed in these pleasing errors by the form of their provincial legislative assemblies. Their governments are popular in a high degree; some are merely popular; in all, the popular representative is the most weighty; and this share of the people in their ordinary government never fails to inspire them with lofty sentiments, and with a strong aversion from whatever tends to deprive them of their chief importance.

If anything were wanting to this necessary operation of the form of government, *religion* would have given it a complete effect. Religion, always a principle of energy, in this new people is no way worn out or impaired; and their mode of professing it is also one main cause of this free spirit. The people are Protestants; and of that kind which is the most averse to all implicit submission of mind and opinion. This is a persuasion not only favorable to liberty, but built upon it. I do not think, sir, that the reason of this averseness in the dissenting churches from all that looks like absolute government is so much to be sought in their religious tenets as in their history. Every one knows that the Roman Catholic religion is at least coeval with most of the governments where it prevails; that it has generally gone hand in hand with them; and received great favor and every kind of support from authority. The Church of England, too, was formed from her cradle under the nursing care of regular government. But the dissenting interests have sprung up in direct opposition to all the ordinary powers of the world, and could justify that opposition only on a strong claim to natural liberty. Their very existence depended on the powerful and unremitted assertion of that claim. All Protestantism, even the most cold and passive, is a kind of dissent. But the religion most prevalent in our northern colonies is a refinement on the principle of resistance; it is the dissidence of dissent; and the Protestantism of the Protestant religion. This religion, under a variety of denominations, agreeing in nothing but in the communion of the spirit of liberty, is predominant in most of the northern provinces; where the Church of England, notwithstanding its legal rights, is in reality no more than a sort of private sect, not composing, most probably, the tenth of the people. The colonists left England when this spirit was high, and in the emigrants was the highest of all; and even that stream of foreigners which has been constantly flowing into these colonies has, for the greatest part, been composed of dissenters from the establishments of their several countries, and have brought with them a temper and character far from alien to that of the people with whom they mixed.

Sir, I can perceive by their manner that some gentlemen object to the latitude of this description, because in the southern colonies the Church of England forms a large body, and has a regular establishment. It is certainly true. There is, however, a circumstance attending these colonies, which, in my opinion, fully counterbalances this difference, and makes the spirit of liberty still more high and haughty than in those to the northward. It is that in Virginia and the Carolinas they have a vast multitude of *slaves*. Where this is the case in any part of the world, those who are free are by far the most proud and jealous of their freedom. Freedom is to them not only an enjoyment, but a kind of rank and privilege. Not seeing there that freedom, as in countries where it is a common blessing and as broad and general as the air, may be united with much abject toil, with great misery, with all the exterior of servitude, liberty looks among them like something that is more noble and liberal. I do not mean, sir, to commend the superior morality of this sentiment, which has at least as much pride as virtue in it; but I cannot alter the nature of man. The fact is so; and these people of the southern colonies are much more strongly, and with a higher and more stubborn spirit, attached to liberty than those to the northward. Such were all the ancient commonwealths; such were our Gothic ancestors; such, in our days, were the Poles, and such will be all masters of slaves who are not slaves themselves. In such a people the haughtiness of domination combines with the spirit of freedom, fortifies it, and renders it invincible.

Permit me, sir, to add another circumstance in our colonies which contributes no mean part toward the growth and effect of this intractable spirit—I mean their *education*. In no country perhaps in the world is the *law* so general a study. The profession itself is numerous and powerful; and in most provinces it takes the lead. The greater number of the deputies sent to Congress were lawyers. But all who read (and most do read) endeavor to obtain some smattering in that science. I have been told by an eminent bookseller that in no branch of his business, after tracts of popular devotion, were so many books as those on the law exported to the Plantations. The colonists have now fallen into the way of printing them for their own use. I hear that they have sold nearly as many of Blackstone's Commentaries in America as in England. General

Gage marks out this disposition very particularly in a letter on your table. He states that all the people in his government are lawyers, or smatterers in law; and that in Boston they have been enabled, by successful chicane, wholly to evade many parts of one of your capital penal constitutions.[1] The smartness of debate will say that this knowledge ought to teach them more clearly the rights of legislature, their obligations to obedience, and the penalties of rebellion. All this is mighty well. But my honorable and learned friend [the Attorney-General, afterward Lord Thurlow] on the floor, who condescends to mark what I say for animadversion, will disdain that ground. He has heard, as well as I, that when great honors and great emoluments do not win over this knowledge to the service of the state, it is a formidable adversary to government. If the spirit be not tamed and broken by these happy methods, it is stubborn and litigious. *Abeunt studia in mores.*[2] This study renders men acute, inquisitive, dexterous, prompt in attack, ready in defence, full of resources. In other countries, the people more simple and of a less mercurial cast, judge of an ill principle in government only by an actual grievance. Here they anticipate the evil, and judge of the pressure of the grievance by the badness of the principle. They augur misgovernment at a distance; and snuff the approach of tyranny in every tainted breeze.

The last cause of this disobedient spirit in the colonies is hardly less powerful than the rest, as it is not merely moral, but laid deep in the natural constitution of things. Three thousand miles of ocean lie between you and them. No contrivance can prevent the effect of this *distance* in weakening government. Seas roll and months pass between the order and the execution; and the want of a speedy explanation of a single point is enough to defeat the whole system. You have, indeed, "winged ministers" of vengeance, who carry your bolts in their pouches to the remotest verge of the sea.[3] But there a power steps in that limits the arrogance of raging passion and furious elements, and says: "So far shalt thou go, and no farther." Who are you, that should fret and rage, and bite the chains of nature? Nothing worse happens to you than does to all nations who have extensive empire; and it happens in all the forms into which empire can be thrown. In large bodies the circulation of power must be less vigorous at the extremities. Nature has said it.

[1] *I. e.*, that which prohibited the *calling* of town meetings (see page 82). This the colonists evaded by *adjourning* the meetings.
[2] "One's habitual pursuits pass over into character."
[3] "Winged minister of thunder."—*Horace.*

Here the speaker instanced the Turkish and Spanish empires as tolerant from necessity toward their distant provinces.

Then, sir, from these six capital sources of descent a fierce spirit of liberty has grown up. It has grown with the growth of the people in your colonies, and increased with the increase of their wealth; a spirit that, unhappily meeting with an exercise of power in England, which, however lawful, is not reconcilable to any ideas of liberty, much less with theirs, has kindled this flame that is ready to consume us.

I do not mean to commend either the spirit in this excess, or the moral causes which produce it. Perhaps a more smooth and accommodating spirit of freedom in them would be more acceptable to us. Perhaps ideas of liberty might be desired, more reconcilable with an arbitrary and boundless authority. Perhaps we might wish the colonists to be persuaded that their liberty is more secure when held in trust for them by us, as guardians during a perpetual minority, than with any part of it in their own hands. But the question is not whether their spirit deserves praise or blame. What, in the name of God, shall we do with it? You have before you the object, such as it is, with all its glories, with all its imperfections on its head. You see the magnitude, the importance, the temper, the habits, the disorders. By all these considerations we are strongly urged to determine something concerning it. We are called upon to fix some rule and line for our future conduct which may give a little stability to our politics, and prevent the return of such unhappy deliberations as the present. Every such return will bring the matter before us in a still more intractable form. For what astonishing and incredible things have we not seen already? What monsters have not been generated from this unnatural contention? While every principle of authority and resistance has been pushed upon both sides, as far as it would go, there is nothing so solid and certain, either in reasoning or in practice, that it has not been shaken. Until very lately, all authority in America seemed to be nothing but an emanation from yours. Even the popular part of the colony constitution derived all its activity, and its first vital movement, from the pleasure of the Crown. We thought, sir, that the utmost which the discontented colonists could do, was to disturb authority. We never dreamed they could of themselves supply it, knowing in general what an operose business it is to establish a government absolutely new. But having, for our purposes in this contention, resolved that none but an obedient assembly should sit, the humors of the

people there, finding all passage through the legal channel
stopped, with great violence broke out another way. Some provinces have tried their experiment as we have tried ours; and
theirs has succeeded. They have formed a government sufficient
for the purposes, without the bustle of a revolution or the trouble-
some formality of an election. Evident necessity and tacit consent have done the business in an instant. So well they have
done it, that Lord Dunmore (the account is among the fragments
on your table) tells you, that the new institution is infinitely
better obeyed than the ancient government ever was in its most
fortunate periods. Obedience is what makes government, and
not the names by which it is called; not the name of governor, as formerly, or committee, as at present. This new government has originated directly from the people, and was not
transmitted through any of the ordinary artificial media of a
positive constitution. It was not a manufacture ready formed
and transmitted to them in that condition from England. The
evil arising from hence is this: that, the colonists having once
found the possibility of enjoying the advantages of order in the
midst of a struggle for liberty, such struggles will not hencefor-
ward seem so terrible to the settled and sober part of mankind
as they had appeared before the trial.

Pursuing the same plan of punishing by the denial of the
exercise of government to still greater lengths, we wholly abro-
gated the ancient government of Massachusetts. We were confident that the first feeling, if not the very prospect of anarchy,
would instantly enforce a complete submission. The experiment
was tried. A new, strange, unexpected face of things appeared.
Anarchy is found tolerable. A vast province has now subsisted, and subsisted in a considerable degree of health and vigor,
for near a twelvemonth, without governor, without public council, without judges, without executive magistrates. How long
it will continue in this state, or what may arise out of this un-
heard-of situation, how can the wisest of us conjecture? Our
late experience has taught us that many of those fundamental
principles, formerly believed infallible, are either not of the
importance they were imagined to be, or that we have not at all
adverted to some other far more important and far more powerful principles which entirely overrule those we had considered
as omnipotent. I am much against any farther experiments
which tend to put to the proof any more of these allowed opinions which contribute so much to the public tranquillity. In
effect, we suffer as much at home by this loosening of all ties,
and this concussion of all established opinions, as we do abroad.

For, in order to prove that the Americans have no right to their liberties, we are every day endeavoring to subvert the maxims which preserve the whole spirit of our own. To prove that the Americans ought not to be free, we are obliged to depreciate the value of freedom itself; and we never seem to gain a paltry advantage over them in debate without attacking some of those principles, or deriding some of those feelings for which our ancestors have shed their blood.

Sir, I would state that, as far as I am capable of discerning, there are but three ways of proceeding relative to this stubborn spirit which prevails in your colonies and disturbs your government. These are, to change that spirit, as inconvenient, by removing the causes; to prosecute it as criminal; or to comply with it as necessary. I would not be guilty of an imperfect enumeration. I can think of but these three. Another has, indeed, been started—that of giving up the colonies; but it met so slight a reception that I do not think myself obliged to dwell a great while upon it. It is nothing but a little sally of anger, like the frowardness of peevish children, who, when they cannot get all they would have, are resolved to take nothing.

The *first* of these plans, to change the spirit as inconvenient by removing the causes, I think is the most like a systematic proceeding. It is radical in its principle, but it is attended with great difficulties, some of them little short, as I conceive, of impossibilities. This will appear by examining into the plans which have been proposed.

As the growing population of the colonies is evidently one cause of their resistance, it was last session mentioned in both Houses by men of weight, and received, not without applause, that, in order to check this evil, it would be proper for the Crown to make no farther grants of land.

But if you stopped your grants what would be the consequence? The people would occupy without grants. They have already so occupied in many places. You cannot station garrisons in every part of these deserts. If you drive the people from one place they will carry on their annual tillage, and remove with their flocks and herds to another. Many of the people in the back settlements are already little attached to particular situations. Already they have topped the Appalachian Mountains. From thence they behold before them an immense plain, one vast, rich, level meadow—a square of five hundred miles. Over this they would wander without a possibility of restraint. They would change their manners with the habits of their life; would soon forget a government by which they were disowned;

would become hordes of English Tartars; and, pouring down upon your unfortified frontiers a fierce and irresistible cavalry, become masters of your governors and your counselors, your collectors and controllers, and of all the slaves that adhered to them. Such would, and, in no long time, must, be the effect of attempting to forbid as a crime, and to suppress as an evil, the command and blessing of Providence, "Increase and multiply." Such would be the happy result of an endeavor to keep as a lair of wild beasts that earth which God by an express charter has given to the children of men. Far different, and surely much wiser, has been our policy hitherto. Hitherto we have invited our people, by every kind of bounty, to fixed establishments. We have invited the husbandman to look to authority for his title. We have taught him piously to believe in the mysterious virtue of wax and parchment. We have thrown each tract of land, as it was peopled, into districts, that the ruling power should never be wholly out of sight. We have settled all we could, and we have carefully attended every settlement with government.

Adhering, sir, as I do, to this policy, as well as for the reasons I have just given, I think this new project of hedging in population to be neither prudent nor practicable.

To impoverish the colonies in general, and in particular to arrest the noble course of their marine enterprises would be a more easy task. I freely confess it. We have shown a disposition to a system of this kind; a disposition even to continue the restraint after the offence, looking on ourselves as rivals to our colonies, and persuaded that of course we must gain all that they shall lose. Much mischief we may certainly do. The power inadequate to all other things is often more than sufficient for this. I do not look on the direct and immediate power of the colonies to resist our violence as very formidable. In this, however, I may be mistaken. But when I consider that we have colonies for no purpose but to be serviceable to us, it seems to my poor understanding a little preposterous to make them unserviceable in order to keep them obedient. It is, in truth, nothing more than the old and, as I thought, exploded problem of tyranny, which proposes to beggar its subject into submission. But remember, when you have completed your system of impoverishment, that nature still proceeds in her ordinary course; that discontent will increase with misery; and that there are critical moments in the fortunes of all states when they who are too weak to contribute to your prosperity may be strong enough to complete your ruin. *"Spoliatis arma supersunt."* [1]

[1] "To the despoiled arms still remain."

The temper and character which prevail in our colonies are, I am afraid, unalterable by any human art. We cannot, I fear, falsify the pedigree of this fierce people, and persuade them that they are not sprung from a nation in whose veins the blood of freedom circulates. The language in which they would hear you tell them this tale would detect the imposition. Your speech would betray you. An Englishman is the unfittest person on earth to argue another Englishman into slavery.

I think it is nearly as little in our power to change their republican religion as their free descent; or to substitute the Roman Catholic as a penalty, or the Church of England as an improvement. The mode of inquisition and dragooning is going out of fashion in the old world, and I should not confide much to their efficacy in the new. The education of the Americans is also on the same unalterable bottom with their religion. You cannot persuade them to burn their books of curious science; to banish their lawyers from their courts of law; or to quench the lights of their assemblies by refusing to choose those persons who are best read in their privileges. It would be no less impracticable to think of wholly annihilating the popular assemblies in which these lawyers sit. The army, by which we must govern in their place, would be far more chargeable to us; not quite so effectual; and perhaps, in the end, full as difficult to be kept in obedience.

With regard to the high aristocratic spirit of Virginia and the southern colonies, it has been proposed, I know, to reduce it, by declaring a general *enfranchisement of their slaves*. This project has had its advocates and panegyrists, yet I never could argue myself into an opinion of it. Slaves are often much attached to their masters. A general wild offer of liberty would not always be accepted. History furnishes few instances of it. It is sometimes as hard to persuade slaves to be free as it is to compel freemen to be slaves; and in this auspicious scheme we should have both these pleasing tasks on our hands at once. But when we talk of enfranchisement do we not perceive that the American master may enfranchise, too, and arm servile hands in defence of freedom? A measure to which other people have had recourse more than once, and not without success, in a desperate situation of their affairs.

Slaves as these unfortunate black people are, and dull as all men are from slavery, must they not a little suspect the offer of freedom from that very nation which has sold them to their present masters?—From that nation, one of whose causes of quarrel with those masters is their refusal to deal any more in that inhuman traffic? An offer of freedom from England would come rather oddly, shipped to them in an African vessel, which is refused an entry into the ports of Virginia or Carolina, with a cargo of three hundred Angola negroes. It would be curious to see the Guinea captain attempt at the same instant to publish his proclamation of liberty and to advertise the sale of slaves.

But let us suppose all these moral difficulties got over. The ocean remains. You cannot pump this dry; and as long as it continues in its present bed so long all the causes which weaken authority by distance will continue.

> "Ye gods! annihilate but space and time,
> And make two lovers happy!"

was a pious and passionate prayer, but just as reasonable as many of these serious wishes of very grave and solemn politicians.

If, then, sir, it seems almost desperate to think of any alternative course for changing the moral causes (and not quite easy to remove the natural) which produce the prejudices irreconcilable to the late exercise of our authority, but that the spirit infallibly will continue, and, continuing, will produce such effects as now embarrass us, the *second* mode under consideration is to prosecute that spirit in its overt acts as *criminal*.

At this proposition I must pause a moment. The thing seems a great deal too big for my ideas of jurisprudence. It should seem, to my way of conceiving such matters, that there is a very wide difference in reason and policy between the mode of proceeding on the irregular conduct of scattered individuals, or even of bands of men, who disturb order within the state, and the civil dissensions which may from time to time on great questions agitate the several communities which compose a great empire. It looks to me to be narrow and pedantic to apply the ordinary ideas of criminal justice to this great public contest. I do not know the method of drawing up an indictment against a whole people. I cannot insult and ridicule the feelings of millions of my fellow-creatures, as Sir Edward Coke insulted one excellent individual at the bar.[1] I am not ripe to pass sentence on the gravest public bodies, intrusted with magistracies of great authority and dignity, and charged with the safety of their fellow-citizens, upon the very same title that I am. I really think that, for wise men, this is not judicious; for sober

[1] Sir Walter Raleigh at his trial for treason. See Howell's "State Trials."

men, not decent; for minds tinctured with humanity, not mild and merciful.

Perhaps, sir, I am mistaken in my idea of an empire as distinguished from a single state or kingdom. But my idea of it is this: that an empire is the aggregate of many states under one common head whether this head be a monarch or a presiding republic. It does, in such constitutions, frequently happen (and nothing but the dismal, cold, dead uniformity of servitude can prevent its happening) that the subordinate parts have many local privileges and immunities. Between these privileges and the supreme common authority the line may be extremely nice. Of course disputes—often, too, very bitter disputes, and much ill blood, will arise. But, though every privilege is an exemption, in the case, from the ordinary exercise of the supreme authority, it is no denial of it. The claim of a privilege seems rather, *ex vi termini*,[1] to imply a superior power; for to talk of the privileges of a state or of a person who has no superior is hardly any better than speaking nonsense. Now, in such unfortunate quarrels among the component parts of a great political union of communities I can scarcely conceive anything more completely imprudent than for the head of the empire to insist that, if any privilege is pleaded against his will or his acts, his *whole* authority is denied; instantly to proclaim rebellion, to beat to arms, and to put the offending provinces under the ban. Will not this, sir, very soon teach the provinces to make no distinctions on their part? Will it not teach them that the government against which a claim of liberty is tantamount to high treason is a government to which submission is equivalent to slavery? It may not always be quite convenient to impress dependent communities with such an idea.

We are, indeed, in all disputes with the colonies, by the necessity of things, the judge. It is true, sir; but I confess that the character of judge in my own cause is a thing that frightens me. Instead of filling me with pride, I am exceedingly humbled by it. I cannot proceed with a stern, assured, judicial confidence until I find myself in something more like a judicial character. I must have these hesitations as long as I am compelled to recollect that, in my little reading upon such contests as these, the sense of mankind has at least as often decided against the superior as the subordinate power. Sir, let me add, too, that the opinion of my having some abstract right in my favor would not put me much at my ease in passing sentence, unless I could be sure that there were no rights which in their exercise under

---

[1] "From the force of the end."

certain circumstances were not the most odious of all wrongs, and the most vexatious of all injustice. Sir, these considerations have great weight with me when I find things so circumstanced that I see the same party at once a civil litigant against me in point of right and a culprit before me; while I sit as criminal judge on acts of his whose moral quality is to be decided on upon the merits of that very litigation. Men are every now and then put, by the complexity of human affairs, into strange situations; but justice is the same, let the judge be in what situation he will.

In this situation let us seriously and coolly ponder. What is it we have got by all our menaces, which have been many and ferocious? What advantage have we derived from the penal laws we have passed, and which, for the time, have been severe and numerous? What advances have we made toward our object by the sending of a force which, by land and sea, is no contemptible strength? Has the disorder abated? Nothing less. When I see things in this situation, after such confident hopes, bold promises, and active exertions, I cannot, for my life, avoid a suspicion that the plan itself is not correctly right,

If, then, the removal of the causes of this spirit of American liberty be, for the greater part, or rather entirely, impracticable; if the ideas of criminal process be inapplicable, or, if applicable, are in the highest degree inexpedient, what way yet remains? No way is open but the third and last—to comply with the American spirit as necessary, or, if you please, to submit to it as a necessary evil.

If we adopt this mode, if we mean to *conciliate and concede,* let us see of what nature the concessions ought to be. To ascertain the nature of our concession we must look at their complaint. The colonies complain that they have not the characteristic mark and seal of British freedom. They complain that they are taxed in Parliament in which they are not represented. If you mean to satisfy them at all you must satisfy them with regard to this complaint. If you mean to please any people you must give them the boon which they ask; not what you may think better for them, but of a kind totally different. Such an act may be a wise regulation, but it is no concession, whereas our present theme is the mode of giving satisfaction.

Sir, I think you must perceive that I am resolved this day to have nothing at all to do with the question of the right of taxation. Some gentlemen startle, but it is true. I put it totally out of the question. It is less than nothing in my consideration. I do not, indeed, wonder, nor will you, sir, that gentlemen of profound learning are fond of displaying it on this profound subject. But my consideration is narrow, confined, and wholly limited to the policy of the question. I do not examine whether the giving away a man's money be a power excepted and reserved out of the general trust of government, and how far all mankind, in all forms of polity, are entitled to an exercise of that right by the charter of nature; or whether, on the contrary, a right of taxation is necessarily involved in the general principle of legislation, and inseparable from the ordinary supreme power. These are deep questions, where great names militate against each other; where reason is perplexed; and an appeal to authorities only thickens the confusion; for high and reverend authorities lift up their heads on both sides, and there is no sure footing in the middle. The point is

> That Serbonian bog
> Betwixt Damieta and Mount Cassius old,
> Where armies whole have sunk.[1]

I do not intend to be overwhelmed in this bog, though in such respectable company. The question with me is, not whether you have a right to render your people miserable, but whether it is not your interest to make them happy. It is not what a lawyer tells me I *may* do, but what humanity, reason, and justice tell me I *ought* to do. Is a politic act the worse for being a generous one? Is no concession proper but that which is made from your want of right to keep what you grant? Or does it lessen the grace or dignity of relaxing in the exercise of an odious claim, because you have your evidence-room full of titles, and your magazines stuffed with arms to enforce them? What signify all those titles and all those arms? Of what avail are they when the reason of the thing tells me that the assertion of my title is the loss of my suit, and that I could do nothing but wound myself by the use of my own weapons?

I am not determining a point of law. I am restoring tranquillity, and the general character and situation of a people must determine what sort of government is fitted for them. That point nothing else can or ought to determine.

My idea, therefore, without considering whether we yield as matter of right, or grant as matter of favor, is *to admit the people of our colonies into an interest in the constitution*, and, by recording that admission in the journals of Parliament, to give them as strong an assurance as the nature of the thing will

[1] From Milton's "Paradise Lost." The elevated style of Milton appealed peculiarly to Burke, who was his immediate successor in the line of supreme masters of English.

admit that we mean forever to adhere to that solemn declaration of systematic indulgence.

Here the speaker showed the futility of taxation of the colonies, and answered the contention of those who wished to retain the taxes, since if these were abolished the colonists would instantly attack the Trade Laws.

These gentlemen are convinced that this was the intention from the beginning, and the quarrel of the Americans with taxation was no more than a cloak and cover to this design. I am, sir, not a little surprised at this kind of discourse, and I am the more surprised, on account of the arguments which I constantly find in company with it, and which are often urged from the same mouths and on the same day.

For instance, when we allege that it is against reason to tax a people under so many restraints in trade as the Americans, the noble lord in the blue ribbon [Lord North] shall tell you that the restraints on trade are futile and useless; of no advantage to us, and of no burden to those on whom they are imposed; that the trade of America is not secured by the acts of navigation, but by the natural and irresistible advantage of a commercial preference.

But when strong internal circumstances are urged against the taxes; when the scheme is dissected; when experience and the nature of things are brought to prove, and do prove, the utter impossibility of obtaining an effective revenue from the colonies; then, sir, the sleeping trade laws revive from their trance, and this useless taxation is to be kept sacred, not for its own sake, but as a counterguard and security of the laws of trade.

Then, sir, you keep up revenue laws which are mischievous in order to preserve trade laws that are useless. Such is the wisdom of our plan in both its members. They are separately given up as of no value, and yet one is always to be defended for the sake of the other. But I cannot agree with the noble lord, nor with the pamphlet from whence he seems to have borrowed these ideas, concerning the inutility of the trade laws [1]; for, without idolizing them, I am sure they are still, in many ways, of great use to us; and in former times they have been of the greatest.

One fact is clear and indisputable. The public and avowed origin of this quarrel was on taxation. This quarrel has, indeed,

[1] This was by Dean Tucker, an advocate of complete free trade with the colonies.

brought on new disputes on new questions, but certainly the least bitter, and the fewest of all, on the trade laws. To judge which of the two be the real radical cause of quarrel, we have to see whether the commercial dispute did, in order of time, precede the dispute on taxation. There is not a shadow of evidence for it. Next, to enable us to judge whether at this moment a dislike to the trade laws be the real cause of quarrel, it is absolutely necessary to put the taxes out of the question by a repeal. See how the Americans act in this position, and then you will be able to discern correctly what is the true object of the controversy, or whether any controversy at all will remain. Unless you consent to remove this cause of difference it is impossible, with decency, to assert that the dispute is not upon what it is avowed to be. And I would, sir, recommend to your serious consideration whether it be prudent to form a rule for punishing people, not on their own acts, but on your conjectures. Surely it is preposterous at the very best. It is not justifying your anger by their misconduct, but it is converting your ill will into their delinquency.

But the colonies will go farther. Alas! alas! when will this speculating against fact and reason end? What will quiet these panic fears which we entertain of the hostile effect of a conciliatory conduct? Is it true that no case can exist in which it is proper for the sovereign to accede to the desires of his discontented subjects? Is there anything peculiar in this case to make a rule for itself? Is all authority of course lost when it is not pushed to the extreme? Is it a certain maxim that the fewer causes of dissatisfaction are left by government the more the subject will be inclined to resist and rebel?

Here the speaker entered into the subject of the constitutional relations of England with Ireland, Wales, Chester and Durham.

England, at the conquest of Ireland, extended to that country English laws and liberties.

This benefit, I confess, was not at first extended to *all* Ireland. Mark the consequence. English authority and English liberty had exactly the same boundaries.[1] Your standard could never be advanced an inch before your privileges. Sir John Davis[2]

[1] *I. e.*, they were limited by "The Pale," or the district of English settlement.
[2] In his work "Discoverie of the True Causes Why Ireland Was Never Entirely Subdued until the Beginning of His Majesty's Happy Reign" (1612).

shows beyond a doubt that the refusal of a general communication of these rights was the true cause why Ireland was five hundred years in subduing; and, after the vain projects of a military government attempted in the reign of Queen Elizabeth, it was soon discovered that nothing could make that country English in civility and allegiance but your laws and your forms of legislature. It was not English arms, but the English constitution, that conquered Ireland. From that time Ireland has ever had a general Parliament, as she had before a partial Parliament. This has made Ireland the great and flourishing kingdom that it is; and, from a disgrace and a burden intolerable to this nation, has rendered her a principal part of our strength and ornament. This country cannot be said to have ever formally taxed her. Your Irish pensioners would starve if they had no other fund to live on than taxes granted by English authority. Turn your eyes to those popular grants from whence all your great supplies are come, and learn to respect that only source of public wealth in the British empire.

My next example is Wales. This country was said to be reduced by Henry the Third. It was said more truly to be so by Edward the First.

Parliament attempted to subdue the fierce spirit of the Welsh by all sorts of rigorous laws. They prohibited by statute the sending all sorts of arms into Wales, as you prohibit by proclamation (with something more of doubt on the legality) the sending arms to America. They disarmed the Welsh by statute, as you attempted (but still with more question on the legality) to disarm New England by an instruction. They made an act to drag offenders from Wales into England for trial, as you have done (but with more hardship) with regard to America. By another act, where one of the parties was an Englishman, they ordained that his trial should be always by English. They made acts to restrain trade, as you do; and they prevented the Welsh from the use of fairs and markets, as you do the Americans from fisheries and foreign ports.

Here we rub our hands—a fine body of precedents for the authority of Parliament and the use of it—I admit it fully; and pray add likewise to these precedents that all the while Wales rid this kingdom like an *incubus;* that it was an unprofitable and oppressive burden; and that an Englishman traveling in that country could not go six yards from the highroad without being murdered.

The march of the human mind is slow. Sir, it was not until **after** two hundred years discovered that, by an eternal law,

Providence had decreed vexation to violence, and poverty to rapine. Your ancestors did, however, at length open their eyes to the ill husbandry of injustice. They found that the tyranny of a free people could of all tyrannies the least be endured, and that laws made against a whole nation were not the most effectual methods for securing its obedience. Accordingly, in the twenty-seventh year of Henry VIII, the course was entirely altered. With a preamble stating the entire and perfect rights of the Crown of England, it gave to the Welsh all the rights and privileges of English subjects. A political order was established; the military power gave way to the civil; the marches were turned into counties. But that a nation should have a right to English liberties, and yet no share at all in the fundamental security of these liberties, the grant of their own property, seemed a thing so incongruous that eight years after, that is, in the thirty-fifth of that reign, a complete and not ill-proportioned representation by counties and boroughs was bestowed upon Wales by act of Parliament. From that moment, as by a charm, the tumults subsided; obedience was restored; peace, order, and civilization followed in the train of liberty. When the day-star of the English constitution had arisen in their hearts all was harmony within and without.[1]

The speaker followed with the cases of Chester and Durham (which at one time were counties palatine, or possessed of royal privileges), and deduced from them the same point.

Now, if the doctrines of policy contained in these preambles, and the force of these examples in the acts of Parliament, avail anything, what can be said against applying them with regard to America? Are not the people of America as much Englishmen as the Welsh? The preamble of the act of Henry VIII says, the Welsh speak a language no way resembling that of His Majesty's English subjects. Is America in rebellion? Wales was hardly ever free from it. Have you attempted to govern America by penal statutes? You made fifteen for Wales. But your legislative authority is perfect with regard to America. Was it less perfect in Wales, Chester, and Durham? But America is *virtually* represented. What! does the electric force of virtual representation more easily pass over the Atlantic than pervade Wales, which lies in your neighborhood; or than Ches-

[1] This is a reference to Castor and Pollux. "As soon as their white star shines forth for sailors, the dashing tide flows away from the rocks, the winds subside, the clouds flee, and the threatening surge (because they have so willed it) reclines upon the deep."—*Horace,* book i, ode xii.

ter and Durham, surrounded by abundance of representation that is actual and palpable? But, sir, your ancestors thought this sort of virtual representation, however ample, to be totally insufficient for the freedom of the inhabitants of territories that are so near, and comparatively so inconsiderable. How, then, can I think it sufficient for those which are infinitely greater and infinitely more remote?

You will now, sir, perhaps imagine that I am on the point of proposing to you a scheme for representation of the colonies in Parliament. Perhaps I might be inclined to entertain some such thought, but a great flood stops me in my course. *Opposuit natura*.[1] I cannot remove the eternal barriers of the creation. The thing in that mode I do not know to be possible. As I meddle with no theory, I do not absolutely assert the impracticability of such a representation; but I do not see my way to it; and those who have been more confident have not been more successful. However, the arm of public benevolence is not shortened, and there are often several means to the same end. What nature has disjoined in one way wisdom may unite in another. When we cannot give the benefit as we would wish let us not refuse it altogether. If we cannot give the principal let us find a substitute. But how? Where? What substitute?

Fortunately I am not obliged for the ways and means of this substitute to tax my own unproductive invention. I am not even obliged to go to the rich treasury of the fertile framers of imaginary commonwealths; not to the Republic of Plato, not to the Utopia of More, not to the Oceana of Harrington. It is before me. It is at my feet.

And the dull swain
Treads daily on it with his clouted shoon.[2]

I only wish you to recognize, for the theory, the ancient constitutional policy of this kingdom with regard to representation as that policy has been declared in acts of Parliament; and, as to the practice, to return to that mode which a uniform experience has marked out to you as best, and in which you walked with security, advantage, and honor, until the year 1763.

My resolutions, therefore, mean to establish the equity and justice of a taxation of America, by *grant* and not by imposition. To mark the *legal competency* of the colony assemblies for the support of their government in peace, and for public aids in time of war. To acknowledge that this legal competency has had a *dutiful and beneficial exercise;* and that experience has shown

[1] "Nature has opposed."
[2] From Milton's "Comus," slightly misquoted.

the *benefit of their grants,* and the *futility of parliamentary taxation as a method of supply.*

These solid truths compose six fundamental propositions. There are three more resolutions corollary to these. If you admit the first set, you can hardly reject the others. But if you admit the first, I shall be far from solicitous whether you accept or refuse the last. I think these six massive pillars will be of strength sufficient to support the temple of British concord. I have no more doubt than I entertain of my existence that, if you admitted these, you would command an immediate peace; and, with but tolerable future management, a lasting obedience in America. I am not arrogant in this confident assurance. The propositions are all mere matters of fact; and if they are such facts as draw irresistible conclusions even in the stating, this is the power of truth, and not any management of mine.

Here the speaker presented his propositions, which were to the effect:

1. That the colonies were not represented in Parliament;

2. That they were nevertheless taxed to the prejudice of their interests;

[This is inferentially admitted in Lord North's proposition.]

3. That from distance and other circumstances no plan has been devised for such representation;

4. That each of the colonies had a popular legislature with taxing power;

5. That these legislatures have responded to requests from the British Government for grants to the King's service, and the right to do so has been acknowledged by Parliament;

[Also, they have contributed voluntarily and to satiety men and money to the defence of the empire in the French and Indian wars, as acknowledged by Parliament.]

6. That grants of such a nature are more agreeable to the colonies than taxes.

The conclusion is irresistible. You cannot say that you were driven by any necessity to an exercise of the utmost rights of legislature. You cannot assert that you took on yourselves the task of imposing colony taxes from the want of another legal body that is competent to the purpose of supplying the exigencies of the state without wounding the prejudices of the people. Neither is it true that the body so qualified, and having that competence, had neglected the duty.

The question now on all this accumulated matter is—whether you will choose to abide by a profitable experience, or a mischievous theory; whether you choose to build on imagination or fact; whether you prefer enjoyment or hope; satisfaction in your subjects or discontent?

Therefore, proposed Burke, (1) all taxes and repressive acts growing out of the same, such as the Boston Port Bill, are repealed, and the Act for the Trial of Treason committed out of the King's dominions [35th year of Henry VIII] is amended, to confine it to its proper bounds and original intentions, i. e., expressly for trial of treasons in places where the jurisdiction of the Crown does not extend;

2. Judges, paid by the colonial legislatures, shall hold office during good behavior, and not be removed except on complaint of the legislatures and colonial officers;

3. Courts of Admiralty shall be made more commodious for suitors and sued, and the judges put on decent salaries.

These courts I do not wish to take away. They are in themselves proper establishments. This court is one of the capital securities of the Act of Navigation. But courts incommodiously situated in effect deny justice; and a court partaking in the fruits of its own condemnation is a robber. The Congress complain, and complain justly, of this grievance.

These are the three consequential propositions. I have thought of two or three more, but they come rather too near detail, and to the province of executive government, which I wish Parliament always to superintend, never to assume. If the first six are granted congruity will carry the latter three. If not, the things that remain unrepealed will be, I hope, rather unseemly encumbrances on the building than very materially detrimental to its strength and stability.

I do not know that the colonies have, in any general way or in any cool hour, gone much beyond the demand of immunity in relation to taxes. It is not fair to judge of the temper or dispositions of any man, or any set of men, when they are composed and at rest, from their conduct or their expressions in a state of disturbance and irritation. It is, besides, a very great mistake to imagine that mankind follow up practically any speculative principle, either of government or freedom, as far as it will go in argument and logical illation. We Englishmen stop very short of the principles upon which we support any given part of our constitution, or even the whole of it together. This is nothing but what is natural and proper. All government, indeed every human benefit and enjoyment, every virtue and every prudent act, is founded on compromise and barter. We balance inconveniences; we give and take; we remit some rights that we may enjoy others; and we choose rather to be happy citizens than subtle disputants. As we must give away some natural liberty to enjoy civil advantages, so we must sacrifice some civil liberties for the advantages to be derived from the communion and fellowship of a great empire. But in all fair dealings the thing bought must bear some proportion to the purchase paid. None will barter away "the immediate jewel of his soul."[1] Though a great house is apt to make slaves haughty, yet it is purchasing a part of the artificial importance of a great empire too dear to pay for it all essential rights and all the intrinsic dignity of human nature. None of us who would not risk his life rather than fall under a government purely arbitrary. But, although there are some among us who think our constitution wants many improvements to make it a complete system of liberty, perhaps none who are of that opinion would think it right to aim at such improvement by disturbing his country and risking every thing that is dear to him. In every arduous enterprise we consider what we are to lose as well as what we are to gain; and the more and better stake of liberty every people possess, the less they will hazard in a vain attempt to make it more. These are *the cords of man*.[2] Man acts from adequate motive relative to his interest, and not on metaphysical speculations. Aristotle, the great master of reasoning, cautions us, and with great weight and propriety, against this species of delusive geometrical accuracy in moral arguments as the most fallacious of all sophistry.[3]

The Americans will have no interest contrary to the grandeur and glory of England when they are not oppressed by the weight

[1] From Shakespeare's "Othello."
[2] *Hosea*, xi, 4.
[3] *Politics*.

of it; and they will rather be inclined to respect the acts of a superintending legislature when they see them the acts of that power which is itself the security, not the rival, of their secondary importance. In this assurance my mind most perfectly acquiesces, and I confess I feel not the least alarm from the discontents which are to arise from putting people at their ease; nor do I apprehend the destruction of this empire from giving, by an act of free grace and indulgence, to two millions of my fellow-citizens some share of those rights upon which I have always been taught to value myself.

It is said, indeed, that this power of granting, vested in American assemblies, would dissolve the unity of the empire, which was preserved entire, although Wales, and Chester, and Durham were added to it. Truly, Mr. Speaker, I do not know what this unity means, nor has it ever been heard of, that I know, in the constitutional policy of this country. The very idea of subordination of parts excludes this notion of simple and undivided unity. England is the head, but she is not the head and the members, too. Ireland has ever had from the beginning a separate, but not an independent, legislature, which, far from distracting, promoted the union of the whole. Everything was sweetly and harmoniously disposed through both islands for the conservation of English dominion and the communication of English liberties. I do not see that the same principles might not be carried into twenty islands, and with the same good effect. This is my model with regard to America, as far as the internal circumstances of the two countries are the same. I know no other unity of this empire than I can draw from its example during these periods, when it seemed to my poor understanding more united than it is now, or than it is likely to be by the present methods.

I promised, before I finished, to say something of the proposition of the noble lord [Lord North].

First, then, I cannot admit that proposition of a ransom by auction, because it is a mere project. It is a thing new; unheard of; supported by no experience; justified by no analogy; without example of our ancestors, or root in the constitution. It is neither regular parliamentary taxation nor colony grant. *"Experimentum in corpore vili"* [1] is a good rule, which will ever make me adverse to any trial of experiments on what is certainly the most valuable of all subjects, the peace of this empire.

Secondly, it is an experiment which must be fatal, in the end, to our constitution. For what is it but a scheme for taxing the

---

[1] "Experiment upon a worthless body."

colonies in the ante-chamber of the noble lord and his successors? To settle the quotas and proportions in this House is clearly impossible. You, sir, may flatter yourself you shall sit a state auctioneer with your hammer in your hand, and knock down to each colony as it bids. But to settle (on the plan laid down by the noble lord) the true proportional payment for four or five-and-twenty governments according to the absolute and the relative wealth of each, and according to the British proportion of wealth and burden, is a wild and chimerical notion. This new taxation must therefore come in by the back door of the constitution. Each quota must be brought to this House ready formed; you can neither add nor alter. You must register it. You can do nothing farther. For on what grounds can you deliberate, either before or after the proposition? You cannot hear the counsel for all these provinces, quarreling each on its own quantity of payment, and its proportion to others. If you should attempt it the committee of provincial ways and means, or by whatever other name it will delight to be called, must swallow up all the time of Parliament.

Thirdly, it does not give satisfaction to the complaint of the colonies. They complain that they are taxed without their consent; you answer that you will fix the sum at which they shall be taxed. That is, you give them the very grievance for the remedy. You tell them indeed, that you will leave the mode to themselves. I really beg pardon. It gives me pain to mention it; but you must be sensible that you will *not perform* this part of the contract. For, suppose the colonies were to lay the duties which furnished their contingent upon the importation of your manufactures, you know you would never suffer such a tax to be laid. You know, too, that you would not suffer many other modes of taxation; so that, when you come to explain yourself, it will be found that you will neither leave to themselves the quantum nor the mode, nor, indeed, any thing. The whole is delusion from one end to the other.

Fourthly, this method of ransom by auction, unless it be *universally* accepted, will plunge you into great and inextricable difficulties. In what year of our Lord are the proportions of payments to be settled, to say nothing of the impossibility that colony agents should have general powers of taxing the colonies at their discretion? Consider, I implore you, that the communication by special messages, and orders between these agents and their constituents on each variation of the case, when the parties come to contend together and to dispute on their relative proportions, will be a matter of delay, perplexity, and confusion that never can have an end.

If all the colonies do not appear at the outcry what is the condition of those assemblies who offer, by themselves or their agents, to tax themselves up to your ideas of their proportion? The refractory colonies who refuse all composition will remain taxed only to your old impositions, which, however grievous in principle, are trifling as to production. The obedient colonies in this scheme are heavily taxed; the refractory remain un-burdened. What will you do? Will you lay new and heavier taxes by Parliament on the disobedient? Pray consider in what way you can do it. You are perfectly convinced that in the way of taxing you can do nothing but at the ports. Now suppose it is Virginia that refuses to appear at your auction, while Maryland and North Carolina bid handsomely for their ransom, and are taxed to your quota. How will you put these colonies on a par? Will you tax the tobacco of Virginia? If you do you give its death wound to your English revenue at home, and to one of the very greatest articles of your own foreign trade. If you tax the import of that rebellious colony, what do you tax but your own manufactures, or the goods of some other obedient and already well-taxed colony? Who has said one word on this labyrinth of detail, which bewilders you more and more as you enter into it? Who has presented, who can present you with a clew to lead you out of it? I think, sir, it is impossible that you should not recollect that the colony bounds are so implicated in one another (you know it by your own experiments in the bill for prohibiting the New England fishery) that you can lay no possible restraints on almost any of them which may not be presently eluded if you do not confound the innocent with the guilty, and burden those whom, upon every principle, you ought to exonerate. He must be grossly ignorant of America who thinks that, without falling into this confusion of all rules of equity and policy, you can restrain any single colony, especially Virginia and Maryland, the central and most important of them all.

Let it also be considered that either in the present confusion you settle a permanent contingent which will and must be tri-fling, and then you have no effectual revenue, or you change the quota at every exigency, and then on every new repartition you will have a new quarrel.

Reflect, besides, that, when you have fixed a quota for every colony you have not provided for prompt and punctual payment. Suppose one, two, five, ten years arrears. You cannot issue a Treasury Extent [1] against the failing colony. You must make

_____
[1] A writ of commission for valuing real property to satisfy a Crown debt.

new Boston Port bills, new restraining laws, new acts for drag-
ging men to England for trial. You must send out new fleets,
new armies. All is to begin again. From this day forward the
empire is never to know an hour's tranquillity. An intestine fire
will be kept alive in the bowels of the colonies which one time
or another must consume this whole empire. I allow, indeed,
that the empire of Germany raises her revenue and her troops
by quotas and contingents; but the revenue of the empire, and
the army of the empire, is the worst revenue and the worst army
in the world.

Instead of a standing revenue you will therefore have a perpetual quarrel. Indeed, the noble lord who proposed this
project of a ransom by auction seemed himself to be of that
opinion. His project was rather designed for breaking the union
of the colonies than for establishing a revenue. He confessed
that he apprehended that his proposal would not be to *their
taste*. I say this scheme of disunion seems to be at the bottom
of the project; for I will not suspect that the noble lord meant
nothing but merely to delude the nation by an airy phantom
which he never intended to realize. But, whatever his views may
be, as I propose the peace and union of the colonies as the very
foundation of my plan, it cannot accord with one whose foundation is perpetual discord.

Compare the two. This I offer to give you is plain and simple. The other, full of perplexed and intricate mazes. This is
mild; that harsh. This is found by experience effectual for its
purposes; the other is a new project. This is universal; the
other calculated for certain colonies only. This is immediate
in its conciliatory operation; the other remote, contingent, full
of hazard. Mine is what becomes the dignity of a ruling people;
gratuitous, unconditional, and not held out as matter of bargain
and sale. I have done my duty in proposing it to you. I have
indeed tired you by a long discourse; but this is the misfortune
of those to whose influence nothing will be conceded, and who
must win every inch of their ground by argument. You have
heard me with goodness. May you decide with wisdom! For my
part, I feel my mind greatly disburdened by what I have done
to-day. I have been the less fearful of trying your patience
because on this subject I mean to spare it altogether in future.
I have this comfort that, in every stage of the American affairs,
I have steadily opposed the measures that have produced the
confusion and may bring on the destruction of this empire. I
now go so far as to risk a proposal of my own. If I cannot give
peace to my country, I give it to my conscience.

But what, says the financier, is peace to us without money? Your plan gives us no revenue. No! But it does—for it secures to the subject the power of REFUSAL—the first of all revenues. Experience is a cheat, and fact a liar, if this power in the subject of proportioning his grant, or of not granting at all, has not been found the richest mine of revenue ever discovered by the skill or by the fortune of man. It does not indeed vote you £152,750 11s. 2¾d., nor any other paltry limited sum, but it gives the strong box itself, the fund, the bank, from whence only revenues can arise among a people sensible of freedom: *Posita luditur arca.*[1]

Cannot you in England; cannot you at this time of day; cannot you—a House of Commons—trust to the principle which has raised so mighty a revenue, and accumulated a debt of near one hundred and forty millions in this country? Is this principle to be true in England and false everywhere else? Is it not true in Ireland? Has it not hitherto been true in the colonies? Why should you presume that, in any country, a body duly constituted for any functions will neglect to perform its duty, and abdicate its trust? Such a presumption would go against all government in all modes. But in truth this dread of penury of supply from a free assembly has no foundation in nature. For first observe that, besides the desire, which all men have naturally, of supporting the honor of their own government, that sense of dignity and that security of property which ever attends freedom have a tendency to increase the stock of the free community. Most may be taken where most is accumulated. And what is the soil or climate where experience has not uniformly proved that the voluntary flow of heaped-up plenty, bursting from the weight of its own rich luxuriance, has ever run with a more copious stream of revenue than could be squeezed from the dry husks of oppressed indigence by the straining of all the politic machinery in the world?

I, for one, protest against compounding our demands. I declare against compounding, for a poor limited sum, the immense ever-growing, eternal debt which is due to generous government from protected freedom. And so may I speed in the great object I propose to you, as I think it would not only be an act of injustice, but would be the worst economy in the world, to compel the colonies to a sum certain, either in the way of ransom or in the way of compulsory compact.

But to clear up my ideas on this subject; a revenue from America transmitted hither—do not delude yourselves—you

[1] "The strong-box is staked."—*Juvenal*, satire 1.

never can receive it—no, not a shilling. We have experienced that from remote countries it is not to be expected. If, when you attempted to extract revenue from Bengal, you were obliged to return in loan what you had taken in imposition, what can you expect from North America?—for certainly, if ever there was a country qualified to produce wealth, it is India; or an institution fit for the transmission, it is the East India Company. America has none of these aptitudes. If America gives you taxable objects on which you lay your duties *here*, and gives you at the same time a surplus by a foreign sale of her commodities to pay the duties on these objects which you tax at home, she has performed her part to the British revenue. But with regard to her own internal establishments she may, I doubt not she will, contribute in moderation; I say in moderation, for she ought not to be permitted to exhaust herself. She ought to be reserved to a war, the weight of which, with the enemies that we are most likely to have, must be considerable in her quarter of the globe. There she may serve you, and serve you essentially.

For that service, for all service, whether of revenue, trade, or empire, my trust is in her interest in the British constitution. My hold of the colonies is in the close affection which grows from common names, from kindred blood, from similar privileges, and equal protection. These are ties which, though light as air, are as strong as links of iron. Let the colonies always keep the idea of their civil rights associated with your government; they will cling and grapple to you, and no force under heaven will be of power to tear them from their allegiance. But let it be once understood that your government may be one thing, and their privileges another, that these two things may exist without any mutual relation, the cement is gone; the cohesion is loosened; and everything hastens to decay and dissolution. As long as you have the wisdom to keep the sovereign authority of this country as the sanctuary of liberty, the sacred temple consecrated to our common faith, wherever the chosen race and sons of England worship Freedom they will turn their faces toward you. The more they multiply the more friends you will have. The more ardently they love liberty the more perfect will be their obedience. Slavery they can have anywhere. It is a weed that grows in every soil. They may have it from Spain; they may have it from Prussia; but, until you become lost to all feeling of your true interest and your natural dignity, freedom they can have from none but you. This is the commodity of price of which you have the monopoly. This is the true Act of Navigation which binds to you the commerce of the colonies, and through them secures to you the wealth of the world. Deny them this participation of freedom and you break that sole bond which originally made, and must still preserve, the unity of the empire. Do not entertain so weak an imagination as that your registers and your bonds, your affidavits and your sufferances, your cockets and your clearances, are what form the great securities of your commerce. Do not dream that your letters of office, and your instructions, and your suspending clauses, are the things that hold together the great contexture of this mysterious whole. These things do not make your government. Dead instruments, passive tools as they are, it is the spirit of the English communion that gives all their life and efficacy to them. It is the spirit of the English constitution which, infused through the mighty mass, pervades, feeds, unites, invigorates, vivifies every part of the empire, even down to the minutest member.

All this, I know well enough, will sound wild and chimerical to the profane herd of those vulgar and mechanical politicians who think that nothing exists but what is gross and material, and who, therefore, far from being qualified to be directors of the great movement of empire, are not fit to turn a wheel in the machine. But to men truly initiated these master principles are, in truth, all in all. Magnanimity in politics is not seldom the truest wisdom; and a great empire and little minds go ill together.

If we are conscious of our situation, and glow with zeal to fill our place as becomes our station and ourselves, we ought to auspicate all our public proceeding on America with the old warning of the church, *sursum corda!* [1] We ought to elevate our minds to the greatness of that trust to which the order of Providence has called us. By adverting to the dignity of this high calling our ancestors have turned a savage wilderness into a glorious empire, and have made the most extensive and the only honorable conquests, not by destroying, but by promoting, the wealth, the number, the happiness of the human race. Let us get an American revenue as we have got an American empire. English privileges have made it all that it is; English privileges alone will make it all it can be.

In full confidence of this unalterable truth I now, *quod felix faustumque sit,*[2] lay the first stone in the temple of peace; and I move you the first of my propositions.

[1] "Lift up your hearts."
[2] "May it be happy and auspicious," the Roman invocation at the inauguration of new enterprises, such as the founding of a temple.

This was defeated, 270 votes to 78. The others were not put to vote, since it was apparent that Parliament was determined at all costs to assert supremacy over the colonies. Later, when the war that resulted from this determination had fully justified all his predictions of dishonor to British arms, Burke thus commented upon the disastrous obstinacy of the Government:

THE RIGHT TO TAX AMERICA

EDMUND BURKE

But, Mr. Speaker, "we have a right to tax America." Oh, inestimable right! Oh, wonderful, transcendent right! the assertion of which has cost this country thirteen provinces, six islands, one hundred thousand lives, and seventy millions of money. Oh, invaluable right! for the sake of which we have sacrificed our rank among nations, our importance abroad, and our happiness at home! Oh, right! more dear to us than our existence, which has already cost us so much, and which seems likely to cost us our all. Infatuated man! Miserable and undone country! not to know that the claim of right, without the power of enforcing it, is nugatory and idle. We have a right to tax America, the noble lord tells us, therefore we ought to tax America. This is the profound logic which comprises the whole chain of his reasoning.

Not inferior to this was the wisdom of him who resolved to shear the wolf. What, shear a wolf! Have you considered the resistance, the difficulty, the danger of the attempt? No, says the madman, I have considered nothing but the right. Man has a right of dominion over the beasts of the forest; and therefore I will shear the wolf.

How wonderful that a nation could be thus deluded! But the noble lord deals in cheats and delusions. They are the daily traffic of his invention; and he will continue to play off his cheats on this House, so long as he thinks them necessary to his purpose, and so long as he has money enough at command to bribe gentlemen to pretend that they believe him. But a black and bitter day of reckoning will surely come; and whenever the day comes I trust I shall be able, by a parliamentary impeachment, to bring upon the heads of the authors of our calamities the punishment they deserve.

PEACE

When fell Debate & civil Wars shall cease,
Commerce shall spread her Sails o'er all the Seas.
ENGLAND, unrivaled in the liberal Arts,
Shall bear her Genius to remotest Parts.
Take to thy Breast AMERICA again,
Thou may'st defy imperious FRANCE & SPAIN.

Frontispiece in the "London Magazine," 1775

CHAPTER V

COLONIES VS. PARLIAMENT

Speech of James Wilson: "In Vindication of the Colonies"—The Virginia
Convention; Resolutions of Patrick Henry to Adopt Defensive Measures:
they are opposed by Richard Bland, Benjamin Harrison, Robert Carter
Nicholas and Edmund Pendleton; they are supported by Henry in his
Speech "Liberty or Death!"—Preparations for Armed Defence—The
Battle of Lexington and Concord—"Appeal to the British People by the
Massachusetts Convention"—The Second Continental Congress—Address
to the British People (drafted by Richard Henry Lee)—Congress Rejects
Lord North's Plan of Conciliation—George Washington Appointed Com-
mander-in-Chief of the Army—Washington's Speech of Acceptance—
"Declaration to the World" by Congress (drafted by John Dickinson)—
Preparations for Defence—Repressive Acts of Parliament.

IN January, 1775, a convention of the province of
Pennsylvania met at Philadelphia to take action on
the King's speech at the opening of Parliament (see
page 99).

A prominent member of this convention was James
Wilson, a man to whom the country was afterwards to
be largely indebted for his influential part in the formation of its constitution.

He delivered the following speech before the convention:

IN VINDICATION OF THE COLONIES

JAMES WILSON

MR. CHAIRMAN—Whence, sir, proceeds all the invidious and
ill-grounded clamor against the colonists of America? Why are
they stigmatized in Britain, as licentious and ungovernable?
Why is their virtuous opposition to the illegal attempts of their
governors represented under the falsest colors, and placed in
the most ungracious point of view? This opposition, when exhibited in its true light, and when viewed, with unjaundiced
eyes, from a proper situation, and at a proper distance, stands

confessed the lovely offspring of freedom. It breathes the spirit of its parent. Of this ethereal spirit the whole conduct, and particularly the late conduct of the colonists, has shown them eminently possessed. It has animated and regulated every part of their proceedings. It has been recognized to be genuine by all those symptoms and effects by which it has been distinguished in other ages and other countries. It has been calm and regular: it has not acted without occasion: it has not acted disproportionably to the occasion. As the attempts, open or secret, to undermine or to destroy it have been repeated or enforced, in a just degree its vigilance and its vigor have been exerted to defeat or to disappoint them. As its exertions have been sufficient for those purposes hitherto let us hence draw a joyful prognostic that they will continue sufficient for those purposes hereafter. It is not yet exhausted; it will still operate irresistibly whenever a necessary occasion shall call forth its strength.

Permit me, sir, by appealing, in a few instances, to the spirit and conduct of the colonists, to evince that what I have said of them is just. Did they disclose any uneasiness at the proceedings and claims of the British Parliament, before those claims and proceedings afforded a reasonable cause for it? Did they even disclose any uneasiness when a reasonable cause for it was first given? Our rights were invaded by their regulations of our internal policy. We submitted to them: we were unwilling to oppose them. The spirit of liberty was slow to act. When those invasions were renewed; when the efficacy and malignancy of them were attempted to be redoubled by the Stamp Act; when chains were formed for us; and preparations were made for riveting them on our limbs, what measures did we pursue? The spirit of liberty found it necessary now to act: but she acted with the calmness and decent dignity suited to her character. Were we rash or seditious? Did we discover want of loyalty to our Sovereign? Did we betray want of affection to our brethren in Britain? Let our dutiful and reverential petitions to the Throne—let our respectful, though firm, remonstrances to the Parliament—let our warm and affectionate addresses to our brethren, and (we will still call them) our friends in Great Britain—let all those, transmitted from every part of the continent, testify the truth. By their testimony let our conduct be tried.

As our proceedings, during the existence and operation of the Stamp Act, prove fully and incontestably the painful sensations that tortured our breasts from the prospect of disunion with Britain; the peals of joy, which burst forth universally, upon the repeal of that odious statute, loudly proclaim the heart-felt delight produced in us by a reconciliation with her. Unsuspicious, because undesigning, we buried our complaints and the causes of them in oblivion, and returned, with eagerness, to our former unreserved confidence. Our connection with our parent country, and the reciprocal blessings resulting from it to her and to us, were the favorite and pleasing topics of our public discourses and our private conversations. Lulled in delightful security, we dreamed of nothing but increasing fondness and friendship, cemented and strengthened by a kind and perpetual communication of good offices. Soon, however, too soon, were we awakened from the soothing dreams! Our enemies renewed their designs against us, not with less malice, but with more art. Under the plausible pretence of regulating our trade, and, at the same time, of making provision for the administration of justice and the support of government, in some of the colonies, they pursued their scheme of depriving us of our property without our consent. As the attempts to distress us, and to degrade us to a rank inferior to that of freemen, appeared now to be reduced into a regular system, it became proper, on our part, to form a regular system for counteracting them. We ceased to import goods from Great Britain. Was this measure dictated by selfishness or by licentiousness? Did it not injure ourselves, while it injured the British merchants and manufacturers? Was it inconsistent with the peaceful demeanor of subjects to abstain from making purchases, when our freedom and our safety rendered it necessary for us to abstain from them? A regard for our freedom and our safety was our only motive; for no sooner had the Parliament, by repealing part of the revenue laws, inspired us with the flattering hopes that they had departed from their intentions of oppressing and of taxing us, than we forsook our plan for defeating those intentions, and began to import as formerly. Far from being peevish or captious, we took no public notice even of their declaratory law of dominion over us: our candor led us to consider it as a decent expedient of retreating from the actual exercise of that dominion.

But, alas! the root of bitterness still remained. The duty on tea was reserved to furnish occasion to the ministry for a new effort to enslave and to ruin us; and the East India Company were chosen, and consented to be the detested instruments of ministerial despotism and cruelty. A cargo of their tea arrived at Boston. By a low artifice of the governor, and by the wicked activity of the tools of government, it was rendered impossible to store it up, or to send it back, as was done at other places. A number of persons, unknown, destroyed it.

Let us here make a concession to our enemies: let us suppose that the transaction deserves all the dark and hideous colors in which they have painted it: let us even suppose (for our cause admits of an excess of candor) that all their exaggerated accounts of it were confined strictly to the truth: what will follow? Will it follow that every British colony in America, or even the colony of Massachusetts Bay, or even the town of Boston, in that colony, merits the imputation of being factious and seditious? Let the frequent mobs and riots that have happened in Great Britain upon much more trivial occasions shame our calumniators into silence. Will it follow, because the rules of order and regular government were, in that instance, violated by the offenders, that, for this reason, the principles of the constitution, and the maxims of justice, must be violated by their punishment? Will it follow, because those who were guilty could not be known, that, therefore, those who were known not to be guilty must suffer? Will it follow that even the guilty should be condemned without being heard—that they should be condemned upon partial testimony, upon the representations of their avowed and embittered enemies? Why were they not tried in courts of justice, known to their constitution, and by juries of their neighborhood? Their courts and their juries were not, in the case of Captain Preston,[1] transported beyond the bounds of justice by their resentment: why, then, should it be presumed that, in the case of those offenders, they would be prevented from doing justice by their affection? But the colonists, it seems, must be stripped of their judicial, as well as of their legislative, powers. They must be bound by a legislature, they must be tried by a jurisdiction, not their own. Their constitutions must be changed: their liberties must be abridged: and those who shall be most infamously active in changing their constitutions and abridging their liberties must, by an express provision, be exempted from punishment.

I do not exaggerate the matter, sir, when I extend these observations to all the colonists. The Parliament meant to extend the effects of their proceedings to all the colonists. The plan on which their proceedings are formed extends to them all. From an incident of no very uncommon or atrocious nature, which happened in one colony, in one town in that colony, and in which only a few of the inhabitants of that town took a part, an occasion has been taken by those who probably intended it,

[1] Charged with murder in the Boston "Massacre."

and who certainly prepared the way for it, to impose upon that colony, and to lay a foundation and a precedent for imposing upon all the rest, a system of statutes, arbitrary, unconstitutional, oppressive, in every view, and in every degree subversive of the rights, and inconsistent with even the name of freemen.

Were the colonists so blind as not to discern the consequences of these measures? Were they so supinely inactive as to take no steps for guarding against them? They were not. They ought not to have been so. We saw a breach made in those barriers which our ancestors, British and American, with so much care, with so much danger, with so much treasure, and with so much blood had erected, cemented, and established for the security of their liberties, and—with filial piety let us mention it—of ours. We saw the attack actually begun upon one part: ought we to have folded our hands in indolence, to have lulled our eyes in slumbers, till the attack was carried on, so as to become irresistible in every part? But still our measures have been such as the spirit of liberty and of loyalty directed; not such as a spirit of sedition or of disaffection would pursue. Our counsels have been conducted without rashness and faction: our resolutions have been taken without frenzy or fury.

That the sentiments of every individual concerning that important object, his liberty, might be known and regarded meetings have been held and deliberations carried on in every particular district. That the sentiments of all those individuals might gradually and regularly be collected into a single point, and the conduct of each inspired and directed by the result of the whole united; county committees, provincial conventions, a Continental Congress have been appointed, have met and resolved. By this means a chain—more inestimable, and, while the necessity for it continues, we hope, more indissoluble than one of gold—a chain of freedom has been formed, of which every individual in these colonies who is willing to preserve the greatest of human blessings, his liberty, has the pleasure of beholding himself a link.

Are these measures, sir, the brats of disloyalty, of disaffection? There are miscreants among us, wasps that suck poison from the most salubrious flowers, who tell us they are. They tell us that all those assemblies are unlawful, and unauthorized by our constitutions; and that all their deliberations and resolutions are so many transgressions of the duty of subjects. The utmost malice brooding over the utmost baseness, and nothing but such a hated commixture must have hatched this calumny. Do not those men know—would they have others not to know—

that it was impossible for the inhabitants of the same province, and for the legislatures of the different provinces, to communicate their sentiments to one another in the modes appointed for such purposes, by their different constitutions? Do not they know—would they have others not to know—that all this was rendered impossible by those very persons who now, or whose minions now, urge this objection against us? Do not they know —would they have others not to know—that the different assemblies, who could be dissolved by the governors, were, in consequence of ministerial mandates, dissolved by them whenever they attempted to turn their attention to the greatest objects which, as guardians of the liberty of their constituents, could be presented to their view? The arch enemy of the human race torments them only for those actions to which he has tempted, but to which he has not necessarily obliged them. Those men refine even upon infernal malice: they accuse, they threaten us (superlative impudence!) for taking those very steps which we were laid under the disagreeable necessity of taking by themselves, or by those in whose hateful service they are enlisted.

As the invasions of our rights have become more and more formidable our opposition to them has increased in firmness and vigor, in a just, and in no more than a just, proportion. We will not import goods from Great Britain or Ireland: in a little time we will suspend our exportations to them; and, if the same illiberal and destructive system of policy be still carried on against us, in a little time more we will not consume their manufactures. In that colony where the attacks have been most open, immediate, and direct some further steps have been taken, and those steps have met with the deserved approbation of the other provinces.

Is this scheme of conduct allied to rebellion? Those who would blend, and whose crimes have made it necessary for them to blend, the tyrannic acts of administration with the lawful measures of government, and to veil every flagitious procedure of the ministry under the venerable mantle of majesty, pretend to discover, and employ their emissaries to publish the pretended discovery of such symptoms. We are not, however, to be imposed upon by such shallow artifices. No! we have not violated the laws or the constitution; and, therefore, we are safe as long as the laws retain their force and the constitution its vigor.

But we behold, sir, with the deepest anguish that our opposition has not been as effectual as it has been constitutional. The hearts of our oppressors have not relented: our complaints have not been heard: our grievances have not been redressed: our rights are still invaded: and have we no cause to dread that the invasions of them will be enforced, in a manner against which all reason and argument, and all opposition, of every peaceful kind, will be vain? Our opposition has hitherto increased with our oppression: shall it, in the most desperate of all contingencies, observe the same proportion?

Let us pause, sir, before we give an answer to this question. The fate of us; the fate of millions now alive; the fate of millions yet unborn, depends upon the answer. Let it be the result of calmness and intrepidity; let it be dictated by the principles of loyalty, and the principles of liberty. Let it be such as never, in the worst events, to give us reason to reproach ourselves, or others reason to reproach us, for having done too much or too little.

Perhaps the following resolution may be found not altogether unbefitting our present situation. With the greatest deference I submit it to the mature consideration of this assembly:

"That the act of the British Parliament for altering the charter and constitution of the colony of Massachusetts Bay, and those 'for the impartial administration of justice' in that colony, for shutting the port of Boston, and for quartering soldiers on the inhabitants of the colonies, are unconstitutional and void; and can confer no authority upon those who act under color of them. That the Crown cannot, by its prerogative, alter the charter or constitution of that colony: that all attempts to alter the said charter or constitution, unless by the authority of the legislature of that colony, are manifest violations of the rights of that colony, and illegal: that all force employed to carry such unjust and illegal attempts into execution is force without authority: that it is the right of British subjects to resist such force: that this right is founded both upon the letter and the spirit of the British constitution."

Our claim rests upon plain and indubitable truths. We do not send members to the British Parliament: we have parliaments (it is immaterial what name they go by) of our own. That a void act can confer no authority upon those who proceed under color of it is a self-evident proposition.

We can be at no loss in resolving that the King cannot, by his prerogative, alter the charter or constitution of the colony of Massachusetts Bay. Upon what principle could such an exertion of prerogative be justified? On the acts of Parliament? They are already proved to be void. On the discretionary power which the King has of acting where the laws are silent? That power must be subservient to the interest and happiness of those concerning whom it operates. But I go further. Instead of being supported by law, or the principles of prerogative, such an alteration is totally and absolutely repugnant to both. It is contrary to express law. The charter and constitution we speak of are confirmed by the only legislative power capable of confirming them; and no other power but that which can ratify can destroy. If it is contrary to express law the consequence is necessary that it is contrary to the principles of prerogative; for prerogative can operate only when the law is silent.

In no view can this alteration be justified, or so much as excused. It cannot be justified or excused by the acts of Parliament; because the authority of Parliament does not extend to it: it cannot be justified or excused by the operation of prerogative; because this is none of the cases in which prerogative can operate: it cannot be justified or excused by the legislative authority of the colony; because that authority never has been, and, I presume, never will be, given for any such purpose.

I will now advance a step further and say that all attempts to alter the charter or constitution of any colony, unless by the authority of its own legislature, are violations of its rights, and illegal.

If such attempts are illegal, must not all force, employed to carry them into execution, be force employed against law, and without authority? The conclusion is unavoidable.

Have not British subjects, then, a right to resist such force—force acting with authority—force employed contrary to law—force employed to destroy the very existence of law and of liberty? They have, sir; and this right is secured to them both by the letter and the spirit of the British constitution, by which the measures and the conditions of their obedience are appointed. The British liberties, sir, and the means and the right of defending them, are not the grants of princes; and of what our princes never granted they surely can never deprive us.

"Id rex potest," says the law, *"quod de jure potest."* "The king's power is a power according to law." His commands, if the authority of Lord Chief Justice Hale may be depended upon, are under the directive power of the law; and consequently invalid, if unlawful. "Commissions," says my Lord Coke, "are legal, and are like the king's writs; and none are lawful but such as are allowed by the common law, or warranted by some act of Parliament."

Let us examine any commission expressly directing those to whom it is given to use military force for carrying into execution the alterations proposed to be made in the charter and con-

stitution of Massachusetts Bay by the foregoing maxims and
authorities; and what we have said concerning it will appear
obvious and conclusive. It is not warranted by any act of Parliament, because, as has been mentioned on this, and has been
proved on other occasions, any such act is void. It is not warranted, and I believe it will not be pretended that it is warranted, by the common law. It is not warranted by the royal
prerogative, because, as has already been fully shown, it is dia-
metrically opposite to the principles and the ends of prerogative.
Upon what foundation, then, can it lean and be supported?
Upon none. Like an enchanted castle, it may terrify those whose
eyes are affected by the magic influence of the sorcerers, despotism and slavery; but so soon as the charm is dissolved, and the
genuine rays of liberty and of the constitution dart in upon us,
the formidable appearance vanishes, and we discover that it was
the baseless fabric of a vision that never had any real existence.

And now, sir, let me appeal to the impartial tribunal of reason and truth; let me appeal to every unprejudiced and judicious observer of the laws of Britain and of the constitution
of the British government; let me appeal, I say, whether the
principles on which I argue, or the principles on which alone my
arguments can be opposed, are those which ought to be adhered
to and acted upon; which of them are most consonant to our laws
and liberties; which of them have the strongest, and are likely
to have the most effectual tendency to establish and secure the
royal power and dignity.

British Government Prohibits Second Congress

The New York Assembly met in January, 1775, and
endorsed the Bill of Rights adopted by the Congress at
Philadelphia, and prepared petitions to the King, Lords,
and Commons, disapproving ''of the violent measures
that had been pursued in some of the colonies,'' and
claiming an exemption from *internal taxation* and the
exclusive right of providing for the support of their
own civil government and the administration of justice
as their undoubted and inalienable rights as Englishmen.

When the petition of the Assembly was presented
to the House of Commons a hearing was refused it
because it denied or called in question the right of
Parliament to tax the colonies. A circular letter was

sent by the British Secretary of State to the colonial governors forbidding the election of delegates to the Congress in May, 1775, which had been determined upon by the Congress of 1774.

Notwithstanding this royal recommendation delegates were chosen from all the colonies to attend the Congress.

THE VIRGINIA CONVENTION

The leading spirit of the provincial convention of Virginia which met in Richmond March, 1775, to choose delegates to the May Congress was Patrick Henry.

His speech before the convention displayed an increase of his boldness of spirit. It is the most declamatory of all his orations, and therefore has become the most popular, being recited by generations of American schoolboys. It has been called "Patrick Henry's individual declaration of war against Great Britain." It was upon the following resolutions which he had proposed to the convention:

1. *Resolved:* That a well regulated militia, composed of gentlemen and yeomen, is the natural strength and only security of a free government; that such a militia in this colony would forever render it unnecessary for the mother country to keep among us, for the purpose of our defence, any standing army or mercenary forces, always subversive of the quiet and dangerous to the liberties of the people, and would obviate the pretext of taxing us for their support.

2. That such a militia is at this time especially necessary to protect our rights and liberties, which have been rendered insecure by the remissness of government in calling our Legislature together.

3. That this colony be immediately put into a posture of defence.

These resolutions precipitated an animated debate in which they were opposed as premature by Colonels Richard Bland and Benjamin Harrison, and Robert Carter Nicholas and Edmund Pendleton. Mr. Henry stood alone in their support.

The oration was delivered in the "Old Church" at

Richmond.   One who heard the speech thus describes the scene:

"Henry rose with an unearthly fire burning in his eye.   He commenced somewhat calmly, but the smothered excitement began more and more to play upon his features and thrill in the tones of his voice.   The tendons of his neck stood out white and rigid like whipcords.   His voice rose louder and louder, until the walls of the building, and all within them, seemed to shake and rock in its tremendous vibrations.   Finally his pale face and glaring eyes became terrible to look upon.   Men leaned forward in their seats, with their heads strained forward, their faces pale, and their eyes glaring like the speaker's.   His last exclamation, 'Give me liberty or give me death!' was like the shout of the leader which turns back the rout of battle."[1]

LIBERTY OR DEATH!

PATRICK HENRY

MR. PRESIDENT.—No man thinks more highly than I do of the patriotism, as well as abilities, of the very worthy gentlemen who have just addressed the House.   But different men often see the same subject in different lights; and, therefore, I hope that it will not be thought disrespectful to those gentlemen if, entertaining, as I do, opinions of a character very opposite to theirs, I shall speak forth my sentiments freely and without reserve.   This is no time for ceremony.   The question before the House is one of awful moment to this country.   For my own part I consider it as nothing less than a question of freedom or slavery; and in proportion to the magnitude of the subject ought to be the freedom of the debate.   It is only in this way that we can hope to arrive at truth, and fulfil the great responsibility which we hold to God and our country.   Should I keep back my opinions at such a time, through fear of giving offence, I should consider myself as guilty of treason toward my country, and of an act of disloyalty toward the majesty of heaven, which I revere above all earthly kings.

Mr. President, it is natural to man to indulge in the illusions of hope.   We are apt to shut our eyes against a painful truth, and listen to the song of that syren, till she transforms us into beasts.   Is this the part of wise men, engaged in a great and arduous struggle for liberty?   Are we disposed to be of the number of those who, having eyes, see not, and, having ears, hear

[1] From Tyler's "Life of Patrick Henry."

not, the things which so nearly concern their temporal salvation?
For my part, whatever anguish of spirit it may cost, I am willing
to know the whole truth; to know the worst and to provide for it.

I have but one lamp by which my feet are guided; and that is
the lamp of experience. I know of no way of judging of the
future but by the past. And, judging by the past, I wish to know
what there has been in the conduct of the British Ministry for
the last ten years to justify those hopes with which gentlemen
have been pleased to solace themselves and the House? Is it that
insidious smile with which our petition has been lately received?
Trust it not, sir; it will prove a snare to your feet. Suffer not
yourselves to be betrayed with a kiss. Ask yourselves how this
gracious reception of our petition comports with these warlike
preparations which cover our waters and darken our land. Are
fleets and armies necessary to a work of love and reconciliation?
Have we shown ourselves so unwilling to be reconciled that force
must be called in to win back our love? Let us not deceive ourselves, sir. These are the implements of war and subjugation;
the last arguments to which kings resort. I ask gentlemen, sir,
what means this martial array, if its purpose be not to force us
to submission? Can gentlemen assign any other possible motives for it? Has Great Britain any enemy in this quarter of
the world to call for all this accumulation of navies and armies?
No, sir, she has none. They are meant for us; they can be
meant for no other. They are sent over to bind and rivet upon
us those chains which the British Ministry have been so long
forging. And what have we to oppose to them? Shall we try
argument? Sir, we have been trying that for the last ten years.
Have we anything new to offer on the subject? Nothing. We
have held the subject up in every light of which it is capable;
but it has been all in vain. Shall we resort to entreaty and
humble supplication? What terms shall we find which have not
been already exhausted? Let us not, I beseech you, sir, deceive
ourselves longer. Sir, we have done everything that could be
done to avert the storm which is now coming on. We have petitioned; we have remonstrated; we have supplicated; we have
prostrated ourselves before the throne, and have implored its
interposition to arrest the tyrannical hands of the ministry and
Parliament. Our petitions have been slighted; our remonstrances have produced additional violence and insult; our sup-
plications have been disregarded; and we have been spurned,
with contempt, from the foot of the throne. In vain, after these
things, may we indulge the fond hope of peace and reconciliation. There is no longer any room for hope. If we wish to be

free—if we mean to preserve inviolate those inestimable privileges for which we have been so long contending—if we mean not basely to abandon the noble struggle in which we have been so long engaged, and which we have pledged ourselves never to abandon until the glorious object of our contest shall be obtained, we must fight! I repeat it, sir, we must fight! An appeal to arms and to the God of Hosts is all that is left us!

They tell us, sir, that we are weak; unable to cope with so formidable an adversary. But when shall we be stronger? Will it be the next week, or the next year? Will it be when we are totally disarmed, and when a British guard shall be stationed in every house? Shall we gather strength by irresolution and inaction? Shall we acquire the means of effectual resistance by lying supinely on our backs, and hugging the delusive phantom of hope, until our enemies shall have bound us hand and foot? Sir, we are not weak, if we make a proper use of the means which the God of nature hath placed in our power. Three millions of people, armed in the holy cause of liberty, and in such a country as that which we possess, are invincible by any force which our enemy can send against us. Besides, sir, we shall not fight our battles alone. There is a just God who presides over the destinies of nations; and who will raise up friends to fight our battles for us. The battle, sir, is not to the strong alone; it is to the vigilant, the active, the brave. Besides, sir, we have no election. If we were base enough to desire it, it is now too late to retire from the contest. There is no retreat but in submission and slavery! Our chains are forged! Their clanking may be heard on the plains of Boston! The war is inevitable—and let it come! I repeat it, sir, let it come!

It is in vain, sir, to extenuate the matter. Gentlemen may cry peace, peace—but there is no peace. The war is actually begun! The next gale that sweeps from the north will bring to our ears the clash of resounding arms! Our brethren are already in the field! Why stand we here idle? What is it that gentlemen wish? What would they have? Is life so dear, or peace so sweet, as to be purchased at the price of chains and slavery? Forbid it, Almighty God! I know not what course others may take; but, as for me, give me liberty, or give me death!

In pursuance of Henry's resolution a committee was appointed to present a plan of armed defence of Virginia. On it were appointed, among others, Henry, George Washington, Thomas Jefferson and Richard Henry Lee.

AMERICA IN FLAMES

The "next gale that swept from the North" did
indeed bear "the clash of resounding arms—the news
of Lexington and Concord (April 19).   Ere it reached
Virginia all New England was in arms, and thousands of
the patriots were moving toward the scene of action, led
by such veterans of the French War as Israel Putnam of
Connecticut.

The provincial Congress of Massachusetts immediately resolved that an army of thirteen thousand men
should be raised and the other New England colonies
were requested to furnish an additional number for the
defence of the country. The treasurer was directed to
borrow £100,000 for the use of the province, and they
declared that the citizens were no longer under any
obligations of obedience to Governor Gage.

The provincial Congress also sent at once to Dr.
Franklin, their agent in England, an address to the
people of Great Britain in which they gave an account
of the beginning of hostilities and added:

Appeal to the British People

by massachusetts

These, brethren, are marks of ministerial vengeance against
this colony for refusing, with her sister colonies, a submission to
slavery; but they have not yet detached us from our royal sovereign. We profess to be his loyal and dutiful subjects, and so
hardly dealt with as we have been are still ready with our lives
and fortunes to defend his person, family, crown, and dignity.
Nevertheless, to the persecution and tyranny of his cruel ministry we will not tamely submit; appealing to heaven for the
justice of our cause, we determine to die or be free.

We cannot think that the honor, wisdom, and valor of Britons will suffer them to be long inactive spectators of measures
in which they themselves are so deeply interested; measures pursued in opposition to the solemn protest of many noble lords
and expressed sense of conspicuous commoners, whose knowledge
and virtue have long characterized them as some of the greatest
men in the nation; measures executing contrary to the interest,
petitions, and resolves of many large, respectable, and opulent
counties, cities, and boroughs in Great Britain; measures highly
incompatible with justice, but still pursued with a specious pre-

tence of easing the nation of its burdens; measures which, if successful, must end in the ruin and slavery of Britain, as well as the persecuted American colonies.

We sincerely hope that the great sovereign of the Universe, who hath so often appeared for the English nation, will support you in every rational and manly exertion with these colonies for saving us from ruin; and that in a constitutional connection with the mother country we shall soon be altogether a free and happy people.

Second Continental Congress

The second Continental Congress convened according to arrangement on May 10, 1775. It met in the state house (now Independence Hall). Dr. Benjamin Franklin, who had returned from England, was added to the Pennsylvania delegation.

John Hancock, the proscribed patriot, was elected President on May 24, in place of Peyton Randolph, who had been obliged to return to Virginia by ill health.

The beginning of hostilities in Massachusetts received the immediate attention of Congress. They unanimously determined that the colonies be placed in a state of defence, so that Parliament might not carry their several unconstitutional and oppressive acts into execution by force of arms. But Congress still expressed an ardent wish for a restoration of former harmony, and accordingly resolved to present another petition to the King. This petition was written by John Dickinson, who had penned the one to His Majesty in the first Congress. This Congress also addressed the people of Great Britain and the province of Quebec, and it sent an address to the inhabitants of Ireland, and a letter to those of the island of Jamaica. The address to the British people was prepared by a committee which consisted of Richard Henry Lee, Robert R. Livingston, and Edmund Randolph. To Mr. Lee may be credited its language.

Address to the British People

The endearing appellation of "friends, countrymen, and brethren" was used toward the people of Great Britain, and they were entreated by these *ties* seriously to attend to the second attempt of Congress to prevent their dissolution.

After again recapitulating former injuries and stating the recent acts of hostility by the wanton destruction of their lives, as well as property, they seriously ask:

Whether the descendants of Britons could tamely submit to this? "No," they add, "we never will—while we revere the memory of our gallant and virtuous ancestors, we never can surrender those glorious privileges, for which they fought, bled, and conquered." "Admit," they tell them, "that your fleets and armies can destroy our towns, and ravage our coasts; these are inconsiderable objects, things of no moment to men whose bosoms glow with the ardor of liberty. We can retire beyond the reach of your navy and, without any sensible diminution of the necessaries of life, enjoy a luxury, which, from that period, you will want, the luxury of being free." They again repel the charge of aiming at independence.

"Our enemies charge us with sedition. In what does it consist? In our refusal to submit to unwarrantable acts of injustice and cruelty? If so, show us a period in your history in which you have not been equally seditious.

"We are accused of aiming at independence; but how is this accusation supported? By the allegations of your ministers, not by our actions. Abused, insulted, and contemned, what steps have we pursued to obtain redress? We have carried our dutiful petitions to the throne. We have applied to your justice for relief. We have retrenched our luxury, and withheld our trade.

"The advantages of our commerce were designed as a compensation for your protection: when you ceased to protect, for what were we to compensate?

"What has been the success of our endeavors? The clemency of our sovereign is unhappily diverted; our petitions are treated with indignity; our prayers answered by insults. Our application to you remains unnoticed, and leaves us the melancholy apprehension of your wanting either the will or the power to assist us.

"Even under these circumstances, what measures have we taken that betray a desire of independence? Have we called in the aid of those foreign powers who are the rivals of your grandeur? When your troops were few and defenceless, did we take advantage of their distress and expel them our towns? Or have we permitted them to fortify, to receive new aid, and to acquire additional strength?

"Let your enemies and ours persuade you that in this we were influenced by fear or any other unworthy motive. The lives of Britons are still dear to us. They are the children of our parents, and an uninterrupted intercourse of mutual benefits had knit the bonds of friendship. When hostilities were commenced, when, on a late occasion we were wantonly attacked by your troops, though we repelled their assaults and returned their blows, yet we lamented the wounds they obliged us to give; nor have we yet learned to rejoice at a victory over Englishmen.

"As we wish not to color our actions, or disguise our thoughts, we shall, in the simple language of truth, avow the measures we have pursued, the motives upon which we have acted, and our future designs.

"When our late petition to the throne produced no other effect than fresh injuries, and votes of your legislature, calculated to justify every severity; when your fleets and your armies were prepared to wrest from us our property, to rob us of our liberties or our lives; when the hostile attempts of General Gage evinced his designs, we levied armies for our security and defence. When the powers vested in the governor of Canada gave us reason to apprehend danger from that quarter; and we had frequent intimations that a cruel and savage enemy was to be let loose upon the defenceless inhabitants of our frontiers; we took such measures as prudence dictated, as necessity will justify. We possessed ourselves of Crown Point and Ticonderoga. Yet, give us leave most solemnly to assure you, that, we have not lost sight of the object we have ever had in view: a reconciliation with you on constitutional principles, and a restoration of that friendly intercourse which, to the advantage of both, we till lately maintained."

After reminding them that the loss of liberty in America would be only a prelude to its loss in Great Britain, they conclude: "a cloud hangs over your head and ours—ere this reaches you it may probably burst upon us; let us, then (before the remembrance of former kindness is obliterated), once more repeat these appellations, which are ever grateful to our ears; let us entreat heaven to avert our ruin and the destruction that threatens our friends, brethren, and countrymen on the other side of the Atlantic."

REJECTION OF LORD NORTH'S PLAN OF CONCILIATION

Congress referred the conciliatory plan of Lord North to a committee consisting of Dr. Franklin, Thomas

Jefferson, John Adams, and Richard Henry Lee, and in accordance with their report rejected the plan as unreasonable, insidious, and unsatisfactory.

Congress claimed the right of the colonies to give their own money to the empire, and to designate how it should be expended, and refused to accept the remission of taxes when this was conditioned upon contributions. They also objected to the proposal because it was "borne on the point of the bayonet by military plenipotentiaries." Besides, they said, the British monopolization of colonial trade already laid them "under heavy contribution."

Congress further objected to the "intermeddling" of Parliament with the civil government or administration of justice in the colonies.

They rejected the plan, also, because it gave no redress of the other grievances of the colonies as presented in the petition of the first Congress, and because Parliament was adding to these by prohibiting the New England fisheries, and by interdicting intercolonial as well as foreign trade.

They went so far as to question the good faith of the proposition, as intended "to lull into fatal security" the friends of the colonies in Great Britain, while the ministry prepared suddenly to reduce "the 'cowardly' sons of America to unreserved submission," as Lord North had presaged in a former speech, and as the actions of the British Government in Massachusetts and the preparations of armaments of the British Government in Massachusetts and the preparations of armaments for America indicated was the intention.

Therefore, said Congress, "when these things are laid together . . . can the world be deceived into an opinion that we are unreasonable, or can it hesitate to believe us, that nothing but our own exertions may defeat the ministerial sentence of death or abject submission?"

Congress then proceeded to organize an army for defence. George Washington was unanimously chosen commander-in-chief, which appointment he accepted with his characteristic modesty in the following address to the president:

"Though I am truly sensible of the high honor done me in this appointment, yet I feel great distress from a consciousness that my abilities and military experience may not be equal to the extensive and important trust. However, as the Congress desire it, I will enter upon the momentous duty and exert every power I possess in their service, and for the support of the glorious cause. I beg they will accept my most cordial thanks for this distinguished testimony of their approbation.

"But, lest some unlucky event should happen unfavorable to my reputation, I beg it may be remembered by every gentleman in the room that I this day declare with the utmost sincerity I do not think myself equal to the command I am honored with.

"As to pay, sir, I beg leave to assure the Congress that, as no pecuniary consideration could have tempted me to accept this arduous employment at the expense of my domestic ease and happiness, I do not wish to make any profit from it. I will keep an exact account of my expenses. These, I doubt not, they will discharge, and that is all I desire."

On the 6th of July Congress declared to the world the causes which led them to take up arms.

DECLARATION TO THE WORLD

BY CONGRESS

Having stated the various acts of the British Parliament in violation of their rights, and the hostile proceedings of the Administration to enforce them, they observed:

"We are reduced to the alternative of choosing between unconditional submission to the tyranny of irritated ministers or resistance by force. The latter is our choice. We have counted the cost of this contest, and find nothing so dreadful as voluntary slavery. Honor, justice, and humanity forbid us tamely to surrender that freedom which we received from our gallant ancestors; and which our innocent posterity have a right to receive from us. We cannot endure the infamy and guilt of resigning succeeding generations to that wretchedness which inevitably awaits them if we basely entail hereditary bondage upon them.

"Our cause is just—our union is perfect—our internal resources are great, and, if necessary, foreign assistance is undoubtedly attainable. We gratefully acknowledge, as signal instances of the divine favor toward us, that His providence would not permit us to be called into this severe controversy until we were grown to our present strength, had been previously exercised in warlike operations, and possessed of the means of defending ourselves. With hearts fortified with these animating reflections we most solemnly, before God and the world, declare that, exerting the utmost energy of those powers which the beneficent Creator hath graciously bestowed upon us, the arms we have been compelled by our enemies to assume, we will, in defiance of every hazard, with unabating firmness and perseverance, employ for the preservation of our liberties; being with one mind resolved to die freemen rather than to live slaves. Lest this declaration shall disquiet the minds of our friends and fellow subjects in any part of the empire, we assure them that we mean not to dissolve that union which has so long and so happily subsisted between us, and which we sincerely wish to see restored. Necessity has not yet driven us to that desperate measure, or induced us to excite any other nation to war against them. We have not raised armies with ambitious designs of separating from Great Britain and establishing independent states. We fight not for glory or for conquest. We exhibit to mankind the remarkable spectacle of a people attacked by unprovoked enemies without any imputation or even suspicion of offence. They boast of their privileges and civilization, and yet proffer no milder conditions than servitude or death. In our own native land, in defence of the freedom that is our birthright, and which we ever enjoyed till the late violation of it, for the protection of our property, acquired solely by the honest industry of our forefathers and ourselves, against violence actually offered we have taken up arms. We shall lay them down when hostilities shall cease on the part of the aggressors and all danger of their being renewed, and not before.

"With an humble confidence in the mercies of the supreme and impartial judge and ruler of the universe we most devoutly implore His divine goodness to protect us happily through this great conflict, to dispose our adversaries to reconciliation on reasonable terms and thereby relieve the empire from the calamities of civil war."

This was drawn by John Dickinson.

On the recommendation of the New York delegates, as instructed by their provincial convention, Congress issued paper currency to be discharged proportionately by the colonies, the united colonies to pay that part which any colony should fail to discharge.

On the first of August Congress adjourned to meet on the fifth of September.

The capture of Ticonderoga by Ethan Allen and Benedict Arnold early in May, 1775, the brave defence of Bunker (or Breed's) Hill by the raw New England militia in June, and the investment of the British troops in Boston by General Washington which followed, infused great hope in the patriots.

ACTS OF CONGRESS

At the next meeting of Congress in September delegates from Georgia were present, and the name of "The

JOIN or DIE

A common newspaper heading in 1776; devised by Franklin in May, 1754, at the beginning of the French War

Thirteen United Colonies" was chosen to designate the country. A national navy was established and authority given to private persons to capture ships of the enemy.

The first military movement decided upon was the conquest of Canada. The invading force under Richard Montgomery and Benedict Arnold was repulsed at Quebec with the death of Montgomery.

At the request of the people of New Hampshire, South Carolina, and Virginia, Congress advised them in the formation of provisional governments to be terminated when Great Britain and the colonies should be reconciled.

REPRESSIVE ACTS OF PARLIAMENT

In his speech at the opening of Parliament in October, 1775, the King ignored the petition to him by Congress, and advocated extensive military operations in which foreign as well as British troops were to be employed to put down the rebellion which he declared had been undertaken by the colonists for the purpose of establishing an *independent empire.*

While it was generally agreed by Parliament that the war should be prosecuted vigorously, a lively debate ensued over the employment of mercenaries to destroy people of their own blood. The proposition was carried.

The passage of an act to prohibit all trade with the colonies, containing a clause empowering British naval commanders to impress into the King's service captured American seamen and *other persons,* following as it did the employment of mercenary troops, shut and bolted the door on all prospect of reconciliation. The ablest men in America now began to advocate separation from Great Britain. Many colonials who had taken an active part in opposing the war left the country for Canada or England.

RECEPTION OF THE AMERICAN LOYALISTS BY GREAT BRITAIN
From the collection of the New York Historical Society

CHAPTER VI

COLONIES VS. THE CROWN

[SPEECHES AND DEBATES ON THE DECLARATION OF INDE- PENDENCE]

The Mecklenburgh [N. C.] Declaration of Independence—"Common Sense," by Thomas Paine [Pa.]—Judge William Henry Drayton's Charge to the Grand Jury of Charleston, S. C.: "America Created to Be Free"— Declaration of Rights by Virginia (drafted by George Mason)—Resolution of Independence Introduced in Congress by Richard Henry Lee [Va.]—Thomas Jefferson's Report of the Debate on Lee's Resolution: in favor, Lee, John Adams [Mass.], George Wythe [Va.]; opposed, James Wilson [Pa.], Robert R. Livingston [N. Y.], Edward Rutledge [S. C.], John Dickinson [Pa.]—Daniel Webster's Re-creation of the De- bate: Supposed Speeches of John Hancock [Mass.] and John Adams— Speech of Mr. Lee: "Independence a Solemn Duty"—The Declaration Is Passed.

A CONVENTION made up of two delegates from each militia company of Mecklenburgh county, N. C., met, on May 20, 1775, at Charlotte, the county seat, and passed certain resolutions which on their face seem to be a forecast not only of the declarations of the second Congress, then in session, but of the Declaration of Independence in July, 1776. A fierce controversy over the authenticity of these resolutions has been waged by American historians, owing to the fact that the original transcript was burned in 1800, and only what purports to be a copy has been preserved.

The two significant resolutions are:

"Resolved, That we, the citizens of Mecklenburgh county, do hereby dissolve the political bands which have connected us to our mother country and hereby absolve ourselves from all allegiance to the British Crown, and abjure all political connec- tion, contract, or association, with a nation which has wantonly trampled on our rights and liberties and inhumanly shed the innocent blood of American patriots at Lexington.

"Resolved, That we do hereby declare ourselves a free and independent people, are, and of right ought to be, a sovereign and self-governing association, under the control of no power other than that of God and the general Congress; to the maintenance of which independence we solemnly pledge to each other our mutual coöperation, our lives, our fortunes, and our most sacred honor."

Foremost among the writers who advocated independence at this time were Thomas Paine and William Henry Drayton.

Paine in January, 1776, at the suggestion of Dr. Benjamin Rush, published a pamphlet "Common Sense," addressed "to the inhabitants of America," and advocating complete independence of the country in a forcible popular style which at once made him a man of note throughout all the colonies. The book, says Dr. Rush, "burst forth with an effect that has rarely been produced by types and paper in any age or country."

In the second article of "Common Sense," entitled "Thoughts on the Present State of American Affairs," Paine says:

It is repugnant to reason, and the universal order of things, to all examples from former ages, to suppose that this continent can longer remain subject to any external power. The most sanguine in Britain do not think so. The utmost stretch of human wisdom cannot, at this time, compass a plan short of separation which can promise the continent even a year's security. Reconciliation is *now* a fallacious dream. Nature hath deserted the connection and art cannot supply her place. For, as Milton wisely expresses, "never can true reconcilement grow where wounds of deadly hate have pierced so deep."

Every quiet method for peace hath been ineffectual. Our prayers have been rejected with disdain, and only tended to convince us that nothing flatters vanity or confirms obstinacy in kings more than repeated petitioning. Wherefore, since nothing but blows will do, for God's sake let us come to a final separation, and not leave the next generation to be cutting throats under the violated unmeaning names of parent and child.

A government of our own is our natural right; and when a man seriously reflects on the precariousness of human affairs he will become convinced that it is infinitely wiser and safer to form a constitution of our own in a cool, deliberate manner, while we have it in our power, than to trust such an interesting event to time and chance. If we omit it now some Masaniello may hereafter arise, who, laying hold of popular disquietudes, may collect together the desperate and the discontented, and, by assuming to themselves the powers of government, finally sweep away the liberties of the continent like a deluge. Ye that oppose independence now, ye know not what ye do; ye are opening a door to eternal tyranny by keeping vacant the seat of government.

O ye that love mankind! Ye that dare oppose, not only the tyranny, but the tyrant, stand forth! Every spot of the old world is overrun with oppression. Freedom hath been hunted round the globe. Asia and Africa have long expelled her. Europe regards her like a stranger, and England hath given her warning to depart. Oh, receive the fugitive, and prepare in time an asylum for mankind.

In the last article of the pamphlet, "On The Present Ability of America," after discussing the military and financial power of the united colonies, Paine says in conclusion:

Youth is the seed-time of good habits, as well in nations as in individuals. It might be difficult, if not impossible, to form the continent into one government half a century hence. The vast variety of interests occasioned by an increase of trade and population would create confusion. Colony would be against colony. Each being able might scorn each other's assistance; and, while the proud and foolish gloried in their little distinctions, the wise would lament that the union had not been formed before. Wherefore the *present time* is the *true time* for establishing it. The intimacy which is contracted in infancy and the friendship which is formed in misfortune are, of all others, the most lasting and unalterable. Our present union is marked with both these characters: we are young, and we have been distressed; but our concord hath withstood our troubles and fixes a memorable era for posterity to glory in.

The present time, likewise, is that peculiar time which never happens to a nation but once, viz., the time of forming itself into a government. Most nations have let slip the opportunity, and, by that means, have been compelled to receive laws from their conquerors instead of making laws for themselves. First they had a king, and then a form of government; whereas the articles or charter of government should be formed first and men delegated to execute them afterward; but from the errors of other nations let us learn wisdom and lay hold of the present opportunity—*to begin government at the right end.*

In an appendix to the pamphlet Paine declares:

"He who takes nature for his guide is not easily beaten out of his argument, and on that ground I answer generally, *That* INDEPENDENCE *being a* SINGLE SIMPLE LINE, *contained within ourselves, and reconciliation a matter exceedingly perplexed and complicated, and in which a treacherous, capricious court is to interfere, gives the answer without a doubt.*"

"Wherefore," concludes Paine, "instead of gazing at each other with suspicious or doubtful curiosity, let each of us hold out to his neighbor the hearty hand of friendship, and unite in drawing a line which, like an act of oblivion, shall bury in forgetfulness every former dissension. Let the names of Whig and Tory be extinct, and let none other be heard among us than those of a *good citizen, an open and resolute friend,* and *a virtuous supporter of the* RIGHTS *of* MANKIND, *and of the* FREE AND INDEPENDENT States of America."

Another early advocate of entire separation from Great Britain was William Henry Drayton, Chief-Justice of South Carolina. On the 23rd of April, 1776, he delivered a notable address to the grand jury of Charleston upon the adoption of the new State Constitution, in which he foreshadowed the Declaration of Independence by his enumeration of the acts of the King and Parliament which justified the separation of the colonies from the British empire.

AMERICA CREATED TO BE FREE

JUDGE WILLIAM HENRY DRAYTON

Gentlemen of the Grand Jury: When, by evil machinations tending to nothing less than absolute tyranny, trials by jury have been discontinued, and juries, in discharge of their duty, have assembled, and, as soon as met, as silently and arbitrarily dismissed without being impaneled, whereby, in contempt of *Magna Charta*, justice has been delayed and denied; it cannot but afford to every good citizen the most sincere satisfaction once more to see juries, as they now are, legally impaneled, to the end that the laws may be duly administered—I do most heartily congratulate you upon so important an event.

In this court, where silence has but too long presided, with a direct purpose to loosen the bands of government that this country might be involved in anarchy and confusion, you are now met to regulate your verdicts under a new constitution of government independent of royal authority—a constitution which arose according to the great law of nature and of nations, and which was established in the late congress, on the 26th of March last.

After enumerating the various oppressive acts of Parliament which had led to the revolution of the colonial government, he continued:

These acts have, either immediately or in their evident consequences, deeply affected all the colonies: ruin stared them in the face. They united their counsels and laid their just complaints before the Throne, praying a redress of grievances. But, to their astonishment, their dutiful petition for peace and safety was answered *only* by an actual commencement of war and military destruction!

In the mean time the British troops that had been peaceably received by the devoted inhabitants of Boston, *as the troops of their sovereign, bound to protect them!* fortified that town, to imprison the inhabitants and to hold that capital against the people to whom it belonged! And the British rulers having determined to appeal from reason and justice to violence and arms, a select body of those troops being in the night suddenly and privately marched from Boston—at Lexington, on the 19th day of April, 1775, they, by surprise, drew the sword of civil war and plunged it into the breasts of the Americans! Against this horrid injustice the Almighty gave instant judgment: a handful of country militia, badly armed, suddenly collected, and, unconnectedly and irregularly brought up to repel the attack, discomfited the regular bands of the tyranny; they retreated, and night saved them from total slaughter.

Thus forced to take up arms in our own defence, America *yet again* most dutifully petitioned the King, that he would be pleased "to direct some mode by which the united applications of his faithful colonists to the throne, in presence of their common councils, might be improved into a happy and permanent reconciliation; and that, in the meantime, measures might be taken for preventing the further destruction of the lives of His Majesty's subjects.'' But it was in vain! The petition on the part of millions, *praying that the effusion of blood might be* STAYED, was not thought worthy of an answer! The nefarious war continued. The ruins of Charlestown, Falmouth, and Norfolk, towns not constructed for offence or defence, mark the *humane* progress of the royal arms: so the ruins of Carthage, Corinth, and Numantium proclaimed to the world that justice was expelled the Roman senate! On the other hand, the fortitude with which America has endured these civil and military outrages; the union of her people, as astonishing as unprecedented, when we consider their various manners and religious tenets; their distance from each other; their various and clashing local interests; their self-denial; and their *miraculous* success in the prosecution of the war: I say, these things all demonstrate that the Lord of Hosts is on our side! So it is apparent that the Almighty Constructor of the universe, having formed this continent of materials to compose a state preëminent in the world, is now making use of the tyranny of the British rulers, as an instrument to fashion and arrange those materials for the end for which, in His wisdom, he had formed them.

In this enlightened age humanity must be particularly shocked at a recital of such violences; and it is scarce to be believed, that the British tyranny could entertain an idea of proceeding against America by a train of more dishonorable machinations. But, nothing less *than absolute proof* has convinced us that, in carrying on the conspiracy against the rights of humanity, the tyranny is capable of attempting to perpetrate whatever is infamous.

For the little purpose of disarming the imprisoned inhabitants of Boston, the King's general, Gage, in the face of day, violated the public faith, *by himself plighted,* and, in concert with other governors, and with John Stuart,[1] he made every attempt *to instigate the savage nations to war upon the southern colonies,* indiscriminately to massacre man, woman, and child. The governors in general have demonstrated that truth is not in them; they have enveigled negroes from, and have armed them against, their masters; they have armed brother against brother—son against father! Oh! Almighty Director of the universe! what confidence can be put in a government ruling by

See Dr. David Ramsay's ''History of South Carolina.''

such engines, and upon such principles of *unnatural* destruction!
—a government that, upon the 21st day of December last, made
a law, *ex post facto,* to justify what had been done, not only
without law, but in its nature unjust!—a law to make prize of
all vessels trading in, to, or from the united colonies—a law to
make slaves of the crews of such vessels, and to compel them to
bear arms against their conscience, their fathers, their bleeding
country! The world, so old as it is, heretofore had never heard
of so atrocious a procedure: it has no parallel in the registers of
tyranny. . . .

For this only end the house of Brunswick was called to rule
over us. Oh! agonizing reflection! that house ruled us with
swords, fire, and bayonets! The British government operated
only to our destruction. Nature cried aloud, self-preservation is
the great law—we have but obeyed.

You have now a form of government in every respect preferable to the mode under the British authority: and this will
most clearly appear by contrasting the two forms of government.

Under the British authority governors were sent over to us
who were utterly unacquainted with our local interests, the
genius of the people, and our laws; generally, they were but too
much disposed to obey the mandates of an arbitrary ministry;
and, if the governor behaved ill, we could not by any peaceable
means procure redress. But, under our present happy constitution, our executive magistrate arises according to the spirit and
letter of holy writ—*"their governors shall proceed from the
midst of them."* Thus the people have an opportunity of choosing a man intimately acquainted with their true interests, their
genius, and their laws; a man perfectly disposed to defend them
against arbitrary ministers, and to promote the happiness of
that people from among whom he was elevated, and by whom,
without the least difficulty, he may be removed and blended in
the common mass.

Again, under the British authority it was in effect declared,
that we had no property; nay, that we could not possess any;
and that we had not any of the rights of humanity. For men
who knew us not, men who gained in proportion as we lost,
arrogated to themselves a right to BIND us in all cases whatsoever! But our constitution is calculated to FREE us from
foreign bondage; to secure to us our property; to maintain to
us the rights of humanity; and to defend us and our posterity
against British authority aiming to reduce us to the most abject
slavery!

Again, the British authority declared that we should not erect slitting mills; and to this unjust law we implicitly and respectfully submitted, so long as, with safety to our lives, we could yield obedience to such authority; but a resolution of congress now grants a premium to encourage the construction of such mills. The British authority discouraged our attempting to manufacture for our own consumption; but the new constitution, by authorizing the disbursement of large sums of money by way of loan or premium, encourages the making of iron, bar-steel, nail-rods, gun-locks, gun-barrels, sulphur, niter, gunpowder, lead, woolens, cottons, linens, paper, and salt.

Upon the whole, it has been the policy of the British authority to oblige us to supply our wants at their market, which is the *dearest* in the known world, and to cramp and confine our trade so as to be subservient to their commerce, our real interest being ever out of the question. On the other hand, the new constitution is wisely adapted to enable us to trade with foreign nations, and thereby to supply our wants at the *cheapest* markets in the universe; to extend our trade infinitely beyond what it has ever been known; to encourage manufactures among us; and it is peculiarly formed to promote the happiness of the people, from among whom, by virtue and merit, THE POOREST MAN may arrive at THE HIGHEST DIGNITY. Oh, Carolinians! happy would you be under this new constitution, if you knew your happy state.

Possessed of a constitution of government founded upon so generous, equal, and natural a principle—a government expressly calculated to make the people rich, powerful, virtuous and happy, who can wish to change it, to return under a royal government, the vital principles of which are the reverse in every particular! It was my duty to lay this happy constitution before you in its genuine light: it is your duty to understand, to instruct others, and to defend it.

I might here with propriety quit this truly important subject, but my anxiety for the public weal compels me yet to detain your attention, while I make an observation or two upon one particular part of the constitution.

When all the various attempts to enslave America by fraud, under guise of law; by military threats; by famine, massacre, breach of public faith, and open war are considered on the one hand, and, on the other, the constitution, expressing that some mode of government should be established ''until an accommodation of the unhappy differences between Great Britain and America can be obtained; an event which, though traduced and treated as rebels, we still ardently desire," I say, when these two points are contrasted, can we avoid revering the magnanimity of that great council of the state, who, after such injuries, could entertain such a principle! But the virtuous are ever generous. We do not wish revenge: we earnestly wish an accommodation of our unhappy disputes with Great Britain; for we prefer peace to war. Nay, there may be even such an accommodation as, excluding every idea of revenue by taxation or duty, or of legis-lation by act of Parliaments, may vest the king of Great Britain with such a limited dominion over us as may tend, *bona fide,* to promote our true commercial interests, and to secure our free-dom and safety—the only just ends of any dominion. But, while I declare thus much on the one side, on the other it is my duty also to declare that, in my opinion, our true commercial interests cannot be provided for but by such a material alteration of the British acts of navigation as, according to the resolve of the hon-orable the Continental Congress, will "secure the commercial advantages of the whole empire to the mother country, and the commercial benefits of its respective members." And that our liberties and safety cannot be depended upon, if the king of Great Britain should be allowed to hold our forts and cannon, or to have authority over a single regiment in America, or a sin-gle ship of war in our ports. For, if he holds our forts, *he may turn them against us,* as he did Boston against her proprietors; if he acquires our cannon *he will effectually disarm the colony;* if he has a command of troops among us, even if we raise and pay them, *shackles are fixed upon us*—witness Ireland and her national army. The most express act of Parliament cannot give us security, for acts of Parliament are as *easily* repealed as made. Royal proclamations are not to be depended upon, witness *the disappointments of the inhabitants of Quebec and St. Augustine.* Even a change of ministry will not avail us, because, notwith-standing the rapid succession of ministers for which the British court has been famous during the present reign, *yet the same ruinous policy ever continued to prevail against America.* In short, I think it my duty to declare, in the awful seat of justice and before Almighty God, that, in my opinion, the Americans can have no safety but by the Divine favor, their own virtue, and their being so prudent as NOT TO LEAVE IT IN THE POWER OF THE BRITISH RULERS TO INJURE THEM. Indeed, the ruinous and deadly injuries received on our side, and the jealousies enter-tained, and which, in the nature of things, must daily increase against us, on the other, demonstrate to a mind in the least given to reflection upon the rise and fall of empires, that true recon-

cilement never can exist between Great Britain and America,
the latter being in subjection to the former. The Almighty
created America to be independent of Britain. Let us beware
of the impiety of being backward to act as instruments in the
almighty hand, now extended to accomplish His purpose, and
by the completion of which alone America, in the nature of
human affairs, can be secure against the craft and insidious
designs of HER ENEMIES, WHO THINK HER PROSPERITY AND POWER
ALREADY BY FAR TOO GREAT. In a word, our piety and
political safety are so blended that, to refuse our labors in this
Divine work, is to refuse to be a great, a free, a pious, and a
happy people!

And now, having left the important alternative, political
happiness or wretchedness, under God, in a great degree in your
own hands, I pray the Supreme Arbiter of the affairs of men
so to direct your judgment, as that you may act agreeable to
what seems to be His will revealed in His miraculous works in
behalf of America, bleeding at the altar of liberty!

COLONIAL DECLARATIONS OF INDEPENDENCE

When the prohibitory act of Parliament reached
America, Congress, viewing it as a declaration of war,
directed that reprisals be made, both by public and
private armed vessels against the ships and goods of
the inhabitants of Great Britain found on the high seas,
and that American ports be opened to all the world
except the dominions of Great Britain. On May 10
Congress recommended to the assemblies, and where no
sufficient government had been established to the conventions of the colonies, "to adopt such government
as should, in the opinion of the representatives of the
people, best conduce to the happiness and safety of their
constituents in particular and America in general."

This was a preliminary step to a general declaration of independence.

Some of the colonial assemblies had already expressed their opinions on this question; the convention
of North Carolina having empowered their delegates in
Congress "to concur with those in the other colonies in
declaring independency." This was the first direct
public act of any colonial assembly or convention in

WAR

See the dread Harbinger of human Woe,
Approach BRITTANIA resolutely Slow.
The envied Bond that held the League is broke,
And gloomy vengeance has announc'd her stroke,
May desolation abdicate the plain,
And Peace & Harmony prevail again.

Frontispiece in the "London Magazine," 1776.

favor of the measure. On the 15th of May the convention of Virginia went still farther and unanimously *instructed* their delegates in the general Congress to propose independence.

On June 12, 1776, the Virginia convention, still in session, passed a Declaration of Rights, which anticipated the Declaration of Independence in its enunciation of natural rights and was even more explicit as to the principles of democratic government. It was drafted by George Mason.

VIRGINIA BILL OF RIGHTS

A declaration of rights made by the representatives of the good people of Virginia, assembled in full and free convention; which rights do pertain to them and their posterity as the basis and foundation of government.

Section 1. That all men are by nature equally free and independent, and have certain inherent rights, of which, when they enter into a state of society, they cannot, by any compact, deprive or divest their posterity; namely, the enjoyment of life and liberty, with the means of acquiring and possessing property, and pursuing and obtaining happiness and safety.

Sec. 2. That all power is vested in, and consequently derived from, the people; that magistrates are their trustees and servants, and at all times amenable to them.

Sec. 3. That government is, or ought to be, instituted for the common benefit, protection, and security of the people, nation, or community; of all the various modes and forms of government, that is best which is capable of producing the greatest degree of happiness and safety, and is most effectually secured against the danger of maladministration; and that, when any government shall be found inadequate or contrary to these purposes, a majority of the community hath an indubitable, inalienable, and indefensible right to reform, alter, or abolish it, in such manner as shall be judged most conducive to the public weal.

Sec. 4. That no man, or set of men, are entitled to exclusive or separate emoluments or privileges from the community, but in consideration of public services; which, not being descendible, neither ought the offices of magistrate, legislator, or judge to be hereditary.

Sec. 5: That the legislative and executive powers of the

State should be separate and distinct from the judiciary,[1] and that the members of the two first may be restrained from oppression, by feeling and participating the burdens of the people they should, at fixed periods, be reduced to a private station, return into that body from which they were originally taken, and the vacancies be supplied by frequent, certain, and regular elections, in which all or any part of the former members to be again eligible or ineligible, as the laws shall direct.

Sec. 6. That elections of members to serve as representatives of the people, in assembly, ought to be free; and that all men having sufficient evidence of permanent common interest with, and attachment to, the community have the right of suffrage, and cannot be taxed or deprived of their property for public uses, without their own consent or that of their representatives so elected, nor bound by any law to which they have not, in like manner, assented for the public good.

Sec. 7. That all power of suspending laws, or the execution of laws, by any authority without consent of the representatives of the people, is injurious to their rights and ought not to be exercised.

Sec. 8. That in all capital or criminal prosecutions a man hath a right to demand the cause and nature of his accusation, to be confronted with the accusers and witnesses, to call for evidence in his favor, and to a speedy trial by an impartial jury of twelve men of his vicinage, without whose unanimous consent he can not be found guilty; nor can he be compelled to give evidence against himself; that no man be deprived of his liberty, except by the law of the land or the judgment of his peers.

Sec. 9. That excessive bail ought not to be required, nor excessive fines imposed, nor cruel and unusual punishments inflicted.

Sec. 10. That general warrants, whereby an officer or messenger may be commanded to search suspected places without evidence of a fault committed, or to seize any person or persons not named, or whose offence is not particularly described and supported by evidence, are grievous and oppressive, and ought not to be granted.

---

[1] In the constitution adopted June 29, 1776, by the convention that issued this bill of rights, it is provided that ''The legislative, executive, and judiciary department shall be separate and distinct, so that neither exercise the powers properly belonging to the other.'' ''These,'' says Hannis Taylor, in his ''Origin and Growth of the American Constitution,'' ''are the first complete dogmatic statements as to the division of powers ever incorporated in a formal document.'' See Resolve 10 of the Declaration of Rights of the First Continental Congress on page 89.

Sec. 11.   That in controversies respecting property, and in suits between man and man, the ancient trial by jury is preferable to any other, and ought to be held sacred.

Sec. 12.   That freedom of the press is one of the great bulwarks of liberty, and can never be restrained but by despotic governments.

Sec. 13.   That a well-regulated militia, composed of the body of the people, trained to arms, is the proper, natural, and safe defence of a free state; that standing armies, in time of peace, should be avoided as dangerous to liberty; and that in all cases the military should be under strict subordination to, and governed by, the civil power.

Sec. 14.   That the people have a right to uniform government; and, therefore, that no government separate from, or independent of, the government of Virginia ought to be erected or established within the limits thereof.

Sec. 15.   That no free government, or the blessings of liberty, can be preserved to any people but by a firm adherence to justice, moderation, temperance, frugality, and virtue, and by frequent recurrence to fundamental principles.

Sec. 16.   That religion, or the duty which we owe to our Creator and the manner of discharging it, can be directed only by reason and conviction, not by force or violence; and, therefore, all men are equally entitled to the free exercise of religion according to the dictates of conscience; and that it is the mutual duty of all to practice Christian forbearance, love, and charity toward each other.

LEE'S RESOLUTION

The great question of independence was brought *directly* before Congress by Richard Henry Lee. On the 7th of June, 1776, he submitted the following resolutions:

Resolved, That these United Colonies are, and of right ought to be, free and independent States, that they are absolved from all allegiance to the British Crown, and that all political connection between them and the state of Great Britain is, and ought to be, totally dissolved.

That it is expedient forthwith to take the most effectual measures for forming foreign alliances.

That a plan of confederation be prepared and transmitted to the respective colonies for their consideration and approbation.

On the 8th these resolutions were debated in committee of the whole.

No question of greater magnitude was ever presented to the consideration of a deliberative body, or debated with more energy, eloquence, and ability.

DEBATE ON LEE'S RESOLUTION

Thomas Jefferson, in his "Writings" (Vol. I, page 10), has given an account of this debate.

SATURDAY, June 8.   They [Congress] proceeded to take it [Lee's resolution] into consideration, and referred it to a committee of the whole, into which they immediately resolved themselves, and passed that day and Monday, the 10th, in debating on the subject.

It was argued by [James] Wilson, Robert R. Livingston, E[dward] Rutledge, [John] Dickinson, and others,—

That, though they were friends to the measures themselves, and saw the impossibility that we should ever again be united with Great Britain, yet they were against adopting them at this time:

That the conduct we had formerly observed was wise and proper now, of deferring to take any capital step till the voice of the people drove us into it:

That they were our power, and without them our declarations could not be carried into effect:

That the people of the middle colonies (Maryland, Delaware, Pennsylvania, the Jerseys, and New York) were not yet ripe for bidding adieu to British connection, but that they were fast ripening, and, in a short time, would join in the general voice of America:

That the resolution entered by this House on the 15th of May, for suppressing the exercise of all powers derived from the Crown, had shown, by the ferment into which it had thrown these middle colonies, that they had not yet accommodated their minds to a separation from the mother country:

That some of them had expressly forbidden their delegates to consent to such a declaration, and others had given no instructions, and, consequently, no powers to give such consent:

That, if the delegates of any particular colony had no power to declare such colony independent, certain they were the others could not declare it for them; the colonies being as yet perfectly independent of each other:

That the Assembly of Pennsylvania was now sitting above stairs; their convention would sit within a few days; the convention of New York was now sitting; and those of the Jerseys and Delaware counties would meet on the Monday following; and it was probable these bodies would take up the question of independence, and would declare to their delegates the voice of their state:

That, if such a declaration should now be agreed to, these delegates must retire, and possibly their colonies might secede from the Union:

That such a secession would weaken us more than could be compensated by any foreign alliance:

That, in the event of such a division, foreign powers would either refuse to join themselves to our fortunes, or, having us so much in their power as that desperate declaration would place us, they would insist on terms proportionably more hard and prejudicial:

That we had little reason to expect an alliance with those to whom alone, as yet, we had cast our eyes:

That France and Spain had reason to be jealous of that rising power, which would one day certainly strip them of all their American possessions:

That it was more likely they should form a connection with the British court, who, if they should find themselves unable otherwise to extricate themselves from their difficulties, would agree to a partition of our territories, restoring Canada to France, and the Floridas to Spain, to accomplish for themselves a recovery of these colonies:

That it would not be long before we should receive certain information of the disposition of the French court, from the agent whom we had sent to Paris for that purpose:

That, if this disposition should be favorable, by waiting the event of the present campaign, which we all hoped would be successful, we should have reason to expect an alliance on better terms:

That this would, in fact, work no delay of any effectual aid from such ally, as, from the advance of the season and distance of our situation, it was impossible we could receive any assistance during this campaign:

That it was prudent to fix among ourselves the terms on which we would form an alliance, before we declared we would form one at all events.

And that, if these were agreed on, and our declaration of independence ready by the time our ambassador should be prepared to sail, it would be as well as to go into that declaration at this day.

On the other side it was argued by J[ohn] Adams, [Richard Henry] Lee, [George] Wythe, and others that no gentleman had argued against the policy or the right of separation from Britain, nor had supposed it possible we should ever renew our connection; that they had only opposed its being now declared:

That the question was not whether, by a declaration of independence, we should make ourselves what we are not; but whether we should declare a fact which already exists:

That, as to the people or Parliament of England, we had always been independent of them, their restraints on our trade deriving efficacy from our acquiescence only, and not from any rights they possessed of imposing them; and that, so far, our connection had been federal only, and was now dissolved by the commencement of hostilities:

That, as to the King, we had been bound to him by allegiance, but that this bond was now dissolved by his assent to the late act of Parliament, by which he declares us out of his protection, and by his levying war on us—a fact which had long ago proved us out of his protection, it being a certain position in law that allegiance and protection are reciprocal, the one ceasing when the other is withdrawn:

That James II. never declared the people of England out of his protection; yet his actions proved it, and the Parliament declared it:

No delegates, then, can be denied, or ever want, a power of declaring an existent truth:

That, the delegates from the Delaware counties having declared their constituents ready to join, there are only two colonies, Pennsylvania and Maryland, whose delegates are absolutely tied up; and that these had, by their instructions, only reserved a right of confirming or rejecting the measure:

That the instructions from Pennsylvania might be accounted for from the time in which they were drawn, near a twelvemonth ago, since which the face of affairs has totally changed:

That, within that time, it had become apparent that Britain was determined to accept nothing less than a *carte blanche,* and that the King's answer to the lord mayor, aldermen, and common council of London, which had come to hand four days ago, must have satisfied every one of this point:

That the people wait for us to lead the way:

That *they* are in favor of the measure, though the instructions given by some of their *representatives* are not:

That the voice of the representatives is not always consonant with the voice of the people, and that this is remarkably the case in these middle colonies:

That the effect of the resolution of the 15th of May has proved this, which, raising the murmurs of some in the colonies of Pennsylvania and Maryland, called forth the opposing voice of the freer part of the people, and proved them to be the majority even in these colonies:

That the backwardness of these two colonies might be ascribed, partly to the influence of proprietary power and connections, and partly to their having not yet been attacked by the enemy:

That these causes were not likely to be soon removed, as there seemed no probability that the enemy would make either of these the seat of this summer's war:

That it would be vain to wait either weeks or months for perfect unanimity, since it was impossible that all men should ever become of one sentiment on any question:

That the conduct of some colonies, from the beginning of this contest, had given reason to suspect it was their settled policy to keep in the rear of the confederacy, that their particular prospect might be better, even in the worst event:

That, therefore, it was necessary for those colonies who had thrown themselves forward and hazarded all from the beginning to come forward now, also, and put all again to their own hazard:

That the history of the Dutch Revolution, of whom three states only confederated at first, proved that a secession of some colonies would not be so dangerous as some apprehended:

That a *declaration of independence* alone could render it consistent with European delicacy for European powers to treat with us, or even to receive an ambassador from us:

That, till this, they would not receive our vessels into their ports, nor acknowledge the adjudications of our courts of admiralty to be legitimate, in cases of capture of British vessels:

That, though France and Spain may be jealous of our rising power, they must think it will be much more formidable with the addition of Great Britain, and will, therefore, see it their interest to prevent a coalition; but, should they refuse, we shall be but where we are; whereas, without trying, we shall never know whether they will aid us or not:

That the present campaign may be unsuccessful, and therefore we had better propose an alliance while our affairs wear a hopeful aspect:

That to wait the event of this campaign will certainly work delay, because, during this summer, France may assist us effectually by cutting off those supplies of provisions from England and Ireland on which the enemy's armies here are to depend; or by setting in motion the great power they have collected in the West Indies, and calling our enemy to the defence of the possessions they have there:

That it would be idle to lose time in settling the terms of alliance till we had first determined we would enter into alliance:

That it is necessary to lose no time in opening a trade for our people, who will want clothes, and will want money, too, for the payment of taxes:

And that the only misfortune is, that we did not enter into alliance with France six months sooner—as, besides opening her ports for the vent of our last year's produce, she might have marched an army into Germany and prevented the petty princes there from selling their unhappy subjects to subdue us.

On the 10th the resolution was adopted in committee by a bare majority of the colonies.

It appearing, in the course of the debates, that the colonies of New York, New Jersey, Pennsylvania, Delaware, Maryland, and South Carolina were not yet matured for falling from the parent stem, but that they were fast advancing to that state, it was thought most prudent to wait a while for them, and to postpone the final decision to July 1st; but, that this might occasion as little delay as possible, a committee was appointed to prepare a Declaration of Independence. The committee were John Adams, Dr. Franklin, Roger Sherman, Robert R. Livingston, and Thomas Jefferson.[1] Committees were also appointed, at the same time, to prepare a plan of confederation for the colonies, and to state the terms proper to be proposed for foreign alliance. The committee for drawing the Declaration of Independence desired T. Jefferson to do it. It was accordingly done, and, being approved by them, he reported it to the House on Friday, the 28th of June, when it was read, and ordered to lie on the table. On Monday, the 1st of July, the House resolved itself into a committee of the whole and resumed the consideration of the original motion made by the delegates of Virginia, which, being again debated through the day, was carried in the affirmative

[1] Mr. Lee would have been a member of this committee, and, indeed, as the mover of the resolutions, would undoubtedly have been made its chairman, had he not been called home by the illness of his wife.

by the votes of New Hampshire, Connecticut, Massachusetts, Rhode Island, New Jersey, Maryland, Virginia, North Carolina, and Georgia.[1] South Carolina and Pennsylvania voted against. it. Delaware had but two members present and they were divided. The delegates from New York declared they were for it themselves, and were assured their constituents were for it; but that their instructions having been drawn near a twelvemonth before, when reconciliation was still the general object, they were enjoined by them to do nothing which should impede that object. They therefore thought themselves not justifiable in voting on either side, and asked leave to withdraw from the question; which was given them. The committee rose and reported their resolution to the house. Mr. Edward Rutledge, of South Carolina, then requested the determination might be put off to the next day, as he believed his colleagues, though they disapproved of the resolution, would then join in it for the sake of unanimity. The ultimate question, whether the house would agree to the resolution of the committee, was accordingly postponed to the next day, when it was again moved, and South Carolina concurred in voting for it. In the meantime, a third member had come post from the Delaware counties, and turned the vote of that colony in favor of the resolution. Members of a different sentiment attending that morning from Pennsylvania also, her vote was changed, so that the whole twelve colonies, who were authorized to vote at all, gave their voices for it,[2] and, within a few days (July 9) the Convention of New York approved of it, and thus supplied the void occasioned by the withdrawing of her delegates from the vote.

Congress proceeded the same day to consider the Declaration of Independence, which had been reported, and laid on the table the Friday preceding, and on Monday referred to a committee of the whole. The pusillanimous idea that we had friends in England worth keeping terms with still haunted the minds of many. For this reason, those passages which conveyed censures on the people of England were struck out, lest they should give offence. The clause, too, reprobating the enslaving the inhabitants of Africa was struck out in complaisance to South Carolina and Georgia, who had never attempted to restrain the importa-

[1] In this debate, to use Jefferson's later phrase, John Adams was a "colossus" in defence of the resolution, "not graceful, not elegant, not always fluent in his public addresses, yet he came out with a power, both of thought and expression, that moved us from our seats."

[2] Thus July 2, 1776, and not July 4, was the real beginning of American independence.

Declaration of Independence.

tion of slaves, and who, on the contrary, still wished to continue it. Our northern brethren also, I believe, felt a little tender under those censures; for, though their people had very few slaves themselves, yet they had been pretty considerable carriers of them to others. The debates, having taken up the greater parts of the 2d, 3d, and 4th days of July, were, on the evening of the last, closed; the Declaration was reported by the committee, agreed to by the House, and signed by every member present, except Mr. Dickinson.

Unfortunately the speeches of Adams and others in the debate on Lee's resolution were not preserved. Therefore, Daniel Webster, in his memorial oration on "Adams and Jefferson," delivered in Faneuil Hall, Boston, August 2, 1826, following the precedent established by Thucydides, the Greek historian, imputed actual words to the orators, in order to present the scene vividly before all coming generations. In this reconstruction he used words uttered by the speakers on other occasions (see page 98).

The Debate on the Declaration

DANIEL WEBSTER

Let us, then, bring before us the assembly, which was about to decide a question thus big with the fate of empire. Let us open their doors and look in upon their deliberations. Let us survey the anxious and careworn countenances; let us hear the firm-toned voices of this band of patriots.

Hancock presides over the solemn sitting; and one of those not yet prepared to pronounce for absolute independence is on the floor, and is urging his reasons for dissenting from the Declaration.

"Let us pause! This step, once taken, cannot be retraced. This resolution, once passed, will cut off all hope of reconciliation. If success attend the arms of England, we shall then be no longer colonies, with charters and with privileges; these will all be forfeited by this act; and we shall be in the condition of other conquered people, at the mercy of the conquerors. For ourselves, we may be ready to run the hazard; but are we ready to carry the country to that length? Is success so probable as to justify it? Where is the military, where the naval power, by which we are to resist the whole strength of the arm of England—for she will exert that strength to the utmost? Can we rely on the constancy and perseverance of the people? or will they not act as the people of other countries have acted, and, wearied with a long war, submit, in the end, to a worse oppression? While we stand on our old ground, and insist on redress of grievances, we know we are right and are not answerable for consequences. Nothing, then, can be imputed to us. But if we now change our object, carry our pretensions farther, and set up for absolute independence, we shall lose the sympathy of mankind. We shall no longer be defending what we possess, but struggling for something which we never did possess, and which we have solemnly and uniformly disclaimed all intention of pursuing, from the very outset of the troubles. Abandoning thus our old ground, of resistance, only to arbitrary acts of oppression, the nations will believe the whole to have been mere pretence, and they will look on us, not as injured, but as ambitious subjects. I shudder before this responsibility. It will be on us, if, relinquishing the ground on which we have stood so long, and stood so safely, we now proclaim independence, and carry on the war for that object, while these cities burn, these pleasant fields whiten and bleach with the bones of their owners, and these streams run blood. It will be upon us, it will be upon us, if, failing to maintain this unreasonable and ill-judged declaration, a sterner despotism, maintained by military power, shall be established over our posterity, when we ourselves, given up by an exhausted, a harassed, a misled people, shall have expiated our rashness and atoned for our presumption on the scaffold.''

It was for MR. ADAMS to reply to arguments like these. We know his opinions, and we know his character. He would commence with his accustomed directness and earnestness.

''Sink or swim, live or die, survive or perish, I give my hand and my heart to this vote.[1] It is true, indeed, that in the beginning we aimed not at independence. But there's a Divinity which shapes our ends. The injustice of England has driven us to arms; and, blinded to her own interest for our good, she has obstinately persisted, till independence is now within our grasp. We have but to reach forth to it, and it is ours. Why, then, should we defer the Declaration? Is any man so weak as now to hope for a reconciliation with England, which shall leave either safety to the country and its liberties, or safety to his own life and his own honor? Are not you, sir, who sit in that chair—is not he our venerable colleague near you—are you not both already the proscribed and predestined objects of punishment and of vengeance? Cut off from all hope of royal clem-

[1] See page 98.

ency, what are you, what can you be, while the power of England remains, but outlaws? If we postpone independence, do we
mean to carry on or to give up the war? Do we mean to submit
to the measures of Parliament, Boston Port Bill and all? Do
we mean to submit and consent that we ourselves shall be ground
to powder, and our country and its rights trodden down in the
dust? I know we do not mean to submit. We never shall submit. Do we intend to violate that most solemn obligation ever
entered into by men, that plighting, before God, of our sacred
honor to Washington, when, putting him forth to incur the
dangers of war, as well as the political hazards of the times, we
promised to adhere to him, in every extremity, with our fortunes
and our lives? I know there is not a man here who would not
rather see a general conflagration sweep over the land, or an
earthquake sink it, than one jot or tittle of that plighted faith
fall to the ground. For myself, having, twelve months ago,
in this place, moved you that George Washington be appointed
commander of the forces raised, or to be raised, for defence of
American liberty,[1] may my right hand forget her cunning and
my tongue cleave to the roof of my mouth if I hesitate or waver
in the support I give him.

"The war, then, must go on. We must fight it through.
And if the war must go on, why put off longer the Declaration
of Independence? That measure will strengthen us. It will
give us character abroad. The nations will then treat with
us, which they never can do while we acknowledge ourselves
subjects in arms against our sovereign. Nay, I maintain that
England herself will sooner treat for peace with us on the footing of independence than consent, by repealing her acts, to acknowledge that her whole conduct toward us has been a course
of injustice and oppression. Her pride will be less wounded
by submitting to that course of things which now predestinates
our independence, than by yielding the points in controversy to
her rebellious subjects. The former she would regard as the
result of fortune; the latter she would feel as her own deep
disgrace. Why, then, why, then, sir, do we not, as soon as possible, change this from a civil to a national war? And since
we must fight it through why not put ourselves in a state to
enjoy all the benefits of victory if we gain the victory?

"If we fail, it can be no worse for us. But we shall not fail.
The cause will raise up armies; the cause will create navies.
The people, the people, if we are true to them, will carry us,
and will carry themselves, gloriously, through this struggle. I

[1] See Life and Works of John Adams, Vol. II, pp. 417 *et seq.*

care not how fickle other people have been found. I know the people of these colonies, and I know that resistance to British aggression is deep and settled in their hearts and cannot be eradicated. Every colony, indeed, has expressed its willingness to follow, if we but take the lead. Sir, the Declaration will inspire the people with increased courage. Instead of a long and bloody war for the restoration of privileges, for redress of grievances, for chartered immunities, held under a British king, set before them the glorious object of entire independence, and it will breathe into them anew the breath of life. Read this Declaration at the head of the army; every sword will be drawn from its scabbard and the solemn vow uttered to maintain it, or to perish on the bed of honor. Publish it from the pulpit; religion will approve it, and the love of religious liberty will cling round it, resolved to stand with it or fall with it. Send it to the public halls; proclaim it there; let them hear it who heard the first roar of the enemy's cannon; let them see it who saw their brothers and their sons fall on the field of Bunker Hill, and in the streets of Lexington and Concord, and the very walls will cry out in its support.

"Sir, I know the uncertainty of human affairs, but I see, I see clearly through this day's business. You and I, indeed, may rue it. We may not live to the time when this Declaration shall be made good. We may die; die colonists; die slaves; die, it may be, ignominiously and on the scaffold. Be it so. Be it so. If it be the pleasure of Heaven that my country shall require the poor offering of my life, the victim shall be ready at the appointed hour of sacrifice, come when that hour may. But while I do live, let me have a country, or at least the hope of a country, and that a free country.

"But, whatever may be our fate, be assured, be assured that this Declaration will stand. It may cost treasure, and it may cost blood; but it will stand, and it will richly compensate for both. Through the thick gloom of the present, I see the brightness of the future, as the sun in heaven. We shall make this a glorious, an immortal, day. When we are in our graves our children will honor it. They will celebrate it with thanksgiving, with festivity, with bonfires, and illuminations. On its annual return they will shed tears, copious, gushing tears, not of subjection and slavery, not of agony and distress, but of exultation, of gratitude, and of joy. Sir, before God, I believe the hour is come. My judgment approves this measure, and my whole heart is in it. All that I have, and all that I am, and all that I hope, in this life, I am now ready here to stake upon it; and I

leave off as I begun, that live or die, survive or perish, I am
for the Declaration. It is my living sentiment, and by the blessing of God it shall be my dying sentiment, Independence *now,*
and INDEPENDENCE FOR EVER.''[1]

The following speech of Richard Henry Lee was delivered while the Declaration of Independence was under consideration.

INDEPENDENCE A SOLEMN DUTY

BY RICHARD HENRY LEE

The time will certainly come when the fated separation between the mother country and these colonies must take place,
whether you will or no, for it is so decreed by the very nature
of things, by the progressive increase of our population, the
fertility of our soil, the extent of our territory, the industry of
our countrymen, and the immensity of the ocean which separates
the two countries. And, if this be true, as it is most true, who
does not see that the sooner it takes place the better?—that
it would be the height of folly not to seize the present occasion
when British injustice has filled all hearts with indignation, inspired all minds with courage, united all opinions in one, and
put arms in every hand? And how long must we traverse three
thousand miles of a stormy sea to solicit of arrogant and insolent men either counsel or commands to regulate our domestic
affairs? From what we have already achieved it is easy to
presume what we shall hereafter accomplish. Experience is the
source of sage counsels, and liberty is the mother of great men.
Have you not seen the enemy driven from Lexington by citizens
armed and assembled in one day? Already their most celebrated generals have yielded in Boston to the skill of ours.
Already their seamen, repulsed from our coasts, wander over
the ocean, the sport of tempests and the prey of famine. Let
us hail the favorable omen, and fight, not for the sake of know-

---

[1] In answer to an inquiry as to the sources of this supposed speech of
Adams, Webster wrote: ''The day after the Declaration was made, Mr.
Adams, in writing to a friend, declared the event to be one that 'ought to
be commemorated, as the day of deliverance, by solemn acts of devotion to
God Almighty. It ought to be solemnized with pomp and parade, with
shows, games, sports, guns, bells, bonfires, and illuminations, from one end
of this continent to the other, from this time forward, for evermore.' And
on the day of his death, hearing the noise of bells and cannon, he asked the
occasion. On being reminded that it was 'Independence Day,' he replied,
'Independence forever!' ''

ing on what terms we are to be the slaves of England, but to secure to ourselves a free existence, to found a just and independent government.

Why do we longer delay? why still deliberate? Let this most happy day give birth to the American republic. Let her arise, not to devastate and conquer, but to reëstablish the reign of peace and the laws. The eyes of Europe are fixed upon us; she demands of us a living example of freedom that may contrast, by the felicity of her citizens, with the ever-increasing tyranny which desolates her polluted shores. She invites us to prepare an asylum where the unhappy may find solace and the persecuted repose. She entreats us to cultivate a propitious soil, where that generous plant which first sprang up and grew in England, but is now withered by the poisonous blasts of Scottish tyranny, may revive and flourish, sheltering under its salubrious and interminable shade all the unfortunate of the human race. This is the end presaged by so many omens; by our first victories; by the present ardor and union; by the flight of Howe, and the pestilence which broke out among Dunmore's people; by the very winds which baffled the enemy's fleets and transports, and that terrible tempest which engulfed seven hundred vessels upon the coast of Newfoundland.

If we are not this day wanting in our duty to our country, the names of the American legislators will be placed, by posterity, at the side of those of Theseus, of Lycurgus, of Romulus, of Numa, of the three Williams of Nassau, and of all those whose memory has been and will be forever dear to virtuous men and good citizens.

On the 4th of July the Declaration of Independence reported by the special committee came before Congress for final decision, and, after amendments, received the vote of every colony, as Jefferson has narrated. It also received the vote of every delegate present except John Dickinson, and was signed by everyone but him. It is said that when John Hancock affixed his bold signature he said: "There! I think old Mother Britain can see that without her spectacles!"

The Declaration was published in the "Evening Post" of Philadelphia in the morning of July 8, and at noon was read to the public from a platform in the yard of the State-house by Joseph Nixon, a member of the Pennsylvania Council of Safety. At the close of his reading, the bell of the State-house (the present "Liberty Bell") was rung; and the people gave themselves over to joyful demonstrations. The Declaration was reprinted by papers throughout the thirteen colonies.

THE HORSE AMERICA THROWING HIS MASTER
A British cartoon in 1779
From the collection in the New York Public Library

CHAPTER VII

The Declaration of Independence

Thomas Jefferson [Va.] Drafts the Declaration—Eulogies of Jefferson as the Author of the Declaration by Daniel Webster and Edward Everett—Original Draft of the Declaration, with Corrections Showing the Final Draft—Signing and Promulgation of the Declaration—Speech of Samuel Adams [Mass.] on "American Independence."

TO Thomas Jefferson and John Adams had been delegated the drafting of the Declaration, and Adams, with rare modesty, left this honorable task to Jefferson, confining himself to suggestions.

And Jefferson acquitted himself so well that, had he never written another line, his fame would have been imperishable, not only in America, but throughout the world, to which the Declaration stands as the supreme expression of natural rights and popular liberty. Said Daniel Webster, in his commemorative oration on Adams and Jefferson (1826):

"The merit of this paper is Mr. Jefferson's. Some changes were made in it, on the suggestion of other members of the committee, and others by Congress while it was under discussion. But none of them altered the tone, the frame, the arrangement, or the general character of the instrument. As a composition, the Declaration is Mr. Jefferson's. It is the production of his mind, and the high honor of it belongs to him, clearly and absolutely. . . . To say that he performed his great work well would be doing him injustice. To say that he did excellently well, admirably well, would be inadequate and halting praise. Let us rather say that he so discharged the duty assigned him that all Americans may well rejoice that the work of drawing the title-deed of their liberties devolved on his hands."

And Edward Everett, in his eulogy of Adams and Jefferson in the same year, said:

200

"To have been the instrument of expressing, in one brief, decisive act, the concentrated will and resolution of a whole family of states, of unfolding, in one all-important manifesto, the causes, the motives, and the justification of this great movement in human affairs; to have been permitted to give the impress and peculiarity of his own mind to a charter of public right, destined —or, rather, let me say, already elevated—to an importance in the estimation of men equal to any thing human, ever borne on parchment or expressed in the visible signs of thought—this is the glory of Thomas Jefferson."

The following text is the draft as presented to Congress, and as preserved in manuscript by the Department of State at Washington. John Adams also left behind him a copy of the draft in shorter form. Later Jefferson prepared a number of copies for his friends. That in the Madison collection is called "MS. A," and that in the Emmet collection is called "MS. B." The words with a white line drawn through them were stricken out in committee. The words within brackets were stricken out by Congress.[1]

DECLARATION OF INDEPENDENCE

REPORTED DRAFT

A Declaration by the Representatives of the United States of America, in General [2] Congress assembled.[3]

When in the course of human events it becomes necessary for a one people to advance from that subordination in which they have hitherto remained, & to dissolve the political bands which have connected them with other another and to assume among the powers of the earth the equal & independent separate and equal station to which the laws of nature & of nature's god entitle them, a decent respect to the opinions of mankind requires that they should declare the causes which impel them to the change the separation.

We hold these truths to be sacred & undeniable self-evident;

[1] The text and accompanying annotations are reprinted from Vol. V of the "Journals of the Continental Congress," published by the Government Printing Office.

[2] In MS. A this word is in brackets.

[3] In the engrossed form signed on August 2, 1776, the heading was changed to "The unanimous Declaration of the thirteen United States of America."

that all men are created equal, & independent; that from that equal creation they derive in they are endowed by their creator with equal rights some of which are certain [inherent &] inalienable [1] rights; that among which these are the preservation of life, & liberty, & the pursuit of happiness; that to secure these ends rights, governments are instituted among men, deriving their just powers from the consent of the governed; that whenever any form of government shall becomes destructive of these ends, it is the right of the people to alter or to abolish it, & to institute new government, laying it's foundation on such principles & organising it's powers in such form, as to them shall seem most likely to effect their safety & happiness. prudence indeed will dictate that governments long established should not be changed for light & transient causes: and accordingly all experience hath shewn that mankind are more disposed to suffer while evils are sufferable, than to right themselves by abolishing the forms to which they are accustomed. but when a long train of abuses & usurpations, [begun at a distinguished period, &] pursuing invariably the same object, evinces a design to subject reduce them to arbitrary power, under absolute Despotism,[2] it is their right, it is their duty, to throw off such government & to provide new guards for their future security. such has been the patient sufferance of these colonies; & such is now the necessity which constrains them to [expunge] alter their former systems of government. the history of his the present Majesty King of Great Britain,[3] is a history of [unremitting] repeated injuries and usurpations, [among which no one fact stands single or solitary appears no solitary fact to contradict the uniform tenor of the rest, all of which [have] but] all having in direct object the establishment of an absolute tyranny over these states. to prove this let facts be submitted to a candid world, [for the truth of which we pledge a faith yet unsullied by falsehood.]

he has refused his assent to laws the most wholesome and necessary for the public good:

he has forbidden his governors to pass laws of immediate & pressing importance, unless suspended in their operation till his assent should be obtained; and when so suspended, he has utterly neglected utterly to attend to them.

he has refused to pass other laws for the accommodation of

---

[1] "Unalienable" in the engrossed form.

[2] Against these three words Jefferson has written "Dr. Franklin's hand writing," but the insertion appears to have been made by Jefferson himself.

[3] Against these four words Jefferson has written "Mr. Adams' hand writing."

large districts of people, unless those people would relinquish
the right of representation in the legislature, a right inestimable
to them, & formidable to tyrants only :

he has called together legislative bodies at places unusual,
uncomfortable, & distant from the depository of their public
records, for the sole purpose of fatiguing them into compliance
with his measures :

he has dissolved Representative houses repeatedly [& con-
tinually] for opposing with manly firmness his invasions on
the rights of the people :

when dissolved he has refused for a long space of time time
after such Dissolutions [1] to cause others to be elected, whereby
the legislative powers, incapable of annihilation, have returned to
the people at large for their exercise, the state remaining in
the mean time exposed to all the dangers of invasion from without, & convulsions within :

he has endeavored to prevent the population of these states;
for that purpose obstructing the laws for naturalization of foreigners; refusing to pass others to encourage their migrations
hither; & raising the conditions of new appropriations of lands :

he has [suffered] obstructed the administration of justice
[totally to cease in some of these colonies states,] by refusing
his assent to laws for establishing judiciary powers :

he has made [our] judges dependant on his will alone, for
the tenure of their offices, and the amount & payment [2] of their
salaries :

he has erected a multitude of new offices [by a self-assumed
power,] & sent hither swarms of [3] officers to harrass our people
& eat out their substance :

he has kept among us in times of peace although our Conduct [4] standing armies [& ships of war] without our the consent
of our Legislatures :

he has affected to render the military, independent of & superior to the civil power :

he has combined with others to subject us to a jurisdiction
foreign to our constitutions and unacknowledged by our laws;
giving his assent to their acts of pretended acts of legislation,
for quartering large bodies of armed troops among us;

for protecting them by a mock-trial from punishment for any
murders which they should commit on the inhabitants of these
states ;

[1] Against these four words Jefferson has written ''Mr. Adams.''
[2] Against these words Jefferson has written ''Dr. Franklin.''
[3] MS. A reads ''new officers.''
[4] These words were in the writing of John Adams.

for cutting off our trade with all parts of the world;

for imposing taxes on us without our consent;

for depriving us in many cases [1] of the benefits of trial by jury;

for transporting us beyond seas to be tried for pretended offences;

for abolishing the free system of English laws in a neighboring province, establishing therein an arbitrary government and enlarging it's boundaries so as to render it at once an example & fit instrument for introducing the same absolute rule into these colonies [states] colonies;

for taking away our charters, abolishing our most important valuable Laws,[2] and altering fundamentally the forms of our governments,

for suspending our own legislatures and declaring themselves invested with power to legislate for us in all cases whatsoever:

he has abdicated government here, [withdrawing his governors, & declaring us out of his allegiance & protection:] by declaring us out of his protection & waging war against us.[3]

he has plundered our seas, ravaged our coasts, burnt our towns & destroyed the lives of our people:

he is at this time transporting large armies of *Scotch and other* [4] foreign mercenaries to compleat the works of death desolation and tyranny already begun with circumstances of cruelty & perfidy scarcely paralleled in the most barbarous ages and totally unworthy the head of a civilized nation:

he has constrained &c.[5]

he has excited domestic insurrections amongst us and has endeavored to bring on the inhabitants of our frontiers the merciless Indian savages, whose known rule of warfare is an undistinguished destruction of all ages, sexes, & conditions [of existence:]

[he has incited treasonable insurrections of our fellow-citizens, with the allurements of forfeiture & confiscation of our property:]

He has constrained others,[6] falling into his hands taken cap-

---

[1] MS. B omits these three words.

[2] Against this phrase Jefferson has written ''Dr. Franklin.''

[3] MS. B omits the words ''and waging war against us.''

[4] Omitted in engrossed copy.

[5] Probably a note of insertion for locating in the final form the third paragraph below. MS. A gives the final order of paragraphs, while MS. B follows the earlier arrangement. In the engrossed copy the paragraph appears here, beginning: ''He has constrained our fellow citizens, taken captive,'' etc.

[6] MS. A reads ''our fellow citizens.''

tive on the high seas to bear arms against their country, & to
destroy & be destroyed by the brethren whom they love, to
become the executioners of their friends & brethren, or to fall
themselves by their hands:

[he has waged cruel war against human nature itself, violating it's most sacred rights of life & liberty in the persons of
a distant people, who never offended him, captivating & carrying them into slavery in another hemisphere, or to incur miserable death in their transportation thither. this piratical warfare, the opprobrium of *infidel* powers, is the warfare of the
Christian king of Great Britain determined to keep open a
market where MEN should be bought & sold, and he has pros-
tituted his negative for suppressing every legislative attempt to
prohibit or to restrain this execrable commerce determining to
keep open a market where MEN should be bought and sold: and
that this assemblage of horrors might want no fact of distinguished dye, he is now exciting those very people to rise in
arms among us, and to purchase that liberty of which *he* has
deprived them, by murdering the people upon whom *he* also
obtruded them: thus paying off former crimes committed against
the *liberties* of one people, with crimes which he urges them
to commit against the *lives* of another.][1]

in every stage of these oppressions we have petitioned for
redress in the most humble terms; our repeated petitions have
been answered only [2] by repeated injuries.[3]   a prince whose
character is thus marked by every act which may define a tyrant,
is unfit to be the ruler of a free people [who mean to be free.
future ages will scarce [4] believe that the hardiness audacity of
one man adventured within the short compass of twelve years
only, on so many acts of tyranny without a mask to lay build a
foundation, so broad & undisguised,[5] for tyranny over a people
fostered & fixed in principles of liberty freedom.]

Nor have we been wanting in attentions to our British brethren. we have warned them from time to time of attempts by

[1] Mr. Jefferson, in his "Autobiography," gives the following reason
for the omission of this passage: "The clause reprobating the enslaving
the inhabitants of Africa was struck out in complaisance to *South Carolina*
and *Georgia*, who had never attempted to restrain the importation of slaves,
and who, on the contrary, still wished to continue it. Our Northern brethren
also, I believe, felt a little tender under those censures; for, though their
people had very few slaves themselves, yet they had been pretty considerable
carriers of them to others."

[2] Against this word Jefferson has written "Dr. Franklin."

[3] MS. B reads "injury."

[4] MS. A reads "scarcely."

[5] MS. A reads "so undisguised."

their legislature to extend a [1] an unwarrantable jurisdiction over [these our states] us. we have reminded them of the circumstances of our emigration & settlement here, [no one of which could warrant so strange a pretension: that these were effected at the expence of our own blood & treasure, unassisted by the wealth or the strength of Great Britain: that in constituting indeed our several forms of government, we had adopted one common king, thereby laying a foundation for perpetual league & amity with them: but that submission to their parliament was no part of our constitution, nor ever in idea if history may be credited: and] we have appealed to their native justice & magnanimity, [as well as to] & we have conjured them by the ties of our common kindred to disavow these usurpations which [were likely to] would inevitably interrupt our connection & correspondence & connection. they too have been deaf to the voice of justice & of consanguinity, [& when occasions have been given them, by the regular course of their laws, of removing from their councils the disturbers of our harmony, they have by their free election reëstablished them in power. at this very time too they are permitting their chief magistrate to send over not only soldiers of our common blood, but Scotch & foreign mercenaries, to invade & deluge us in blood destroy us.[2] these facts have given the last stab to agonizing affection, and manly spirit bids us to renounce forever these unfeeling brethren. we must endeavor to forget our former love for them, and to hold them as we hold the rest of mankind, enemies in war, in peace friends. we might have been a free & a great people together; but a communication of grandeur & of freedom it seems is below their dignity. be it so since they will have it: the road to glory & happiness & to glory is open to us too; we will climb must tread it in a separately state apart from them, and] we must therefore acquiesce in the necessity which pro denounces our everlasting Adieu [eternal] separation, and hold them as we hold the rest of mankind enemies in war, in peace friends!

We therefore the representatives of the United States of America in General Congress assembled appealing to the supreme judge of the world for the rectitude of our intentions do in the name & by authority of the good people of these [states] colonies,[3] [reject and renounce all allegiance & subjection to the

---

[1] This word should have been stricken out.

[2] Against these two words Jefferson has written "Dr. Franklin."

[3] Against the following text Jefferson wrote "a different phraseology inserted." In the engrossed copy this text follows: "I solemnly PUBLISH and DECLARE, That these United Colonies are, and, of Right, ought to be, *Free and Independent States;* that they are Absolved from all Allegiance

kings of Great Britain & all others who may hereafter claim by, through, or under them; we utterly dissolve & break off all political connection which may have heretofore have subsisted between us & the people of parliament [1] of Great Britain; and finally we do assert and declare these colonies to be free and independent states, and that as free & independent states, they shall hereafter have full power to levy war, conclude peace, contract alliances, establish commerce, & to do all other acts and things which independent states may of right do. And for the support of this declaration] we mutually pledge to each other our lives, our fortunes, & our sacred honour.

This declaration was directed to be engrossed,[2] and on the 2nd of August, 1776, was signed by all the members then present, and by some who were not members on the 4th of July.

Copies of the declaration were immediately sent to all the States, and to the commander of the American troops, and was publicly proclaimed in each State, and at the head of the army. The great mass of the people were now prepared for this event, and the declaration was received with acclamation.

On the day before the engrossed copy of the Declaration was signed, Samuel Adams of Massachusetts delivered an address on "American Independence," which, as the only speech which has been preserved of this eloquent orator, is a memorable document in American history. In the conclusion of this address he said:

AMERICAN INDEPENDENCE

SAMUEL ADAMS

Countrymen, the men who now invite you to surrender your rights into their hands are the men who have let loose the merci-

to the British Crown, and that all political connexion between them and the State of Great Britain is, and ought to be, totally dissolved; and that, as FREE and INDEPENDENT STATES, they have full Power to levy War, conclude Peace, contract Alliances, establish Commerce, and to do all other Acts and Things which INDEPENDENT STATES may of right do. AND for the support of this Declaration, with a firm reliance on the protection of divine Providence, we mutually pledge to each other our Lives, our Fortunes, and our sacred Honour."

[1] MS. B reads "parliament or people."

[2] The verbal changes made in engrossing have been pointed out in annotations to the second draft. Besides these there were numerous changes in capitalization and punctuation.

less savages to riot in the blood of their brethren; who have dared to establish Popery triumphant in our land; who have taught treachery to your slaves, and courted them to assassinate your wives and children.

These are the men to whom we are exhorted to sacrifice the blessings which Providence holds out to us: the happiness, the dignity, of uncontrolled freedom and independence.

Let not your generous indignation be directed against any among us who may advise so absurd and maddening a measure. Their number is but few, and daily decreases; and the spirit which can render them patient of slavery will render them contemptible enemies.

Our union is now complete; our Constitution composed, established, and approved. You are now the guardians of your own liberties. We may justly address you, as the *decemviri* did the Romans, and say: "Nothing that we propose can pass into a law without your consent. Be yourselves, O Americans, the authors of those laws on which your happiness depends."

You have now in the field armies sufficient to repel the whole force of your enemies and their base and mercenary auxiliaries. The hearts of your soldiers beat high with the spirit of freedom; they are animated with the justice of their cause, and while they grasp their swords can look up to Heaven for assistance. Your adversaries are composed of wretches who laugh at the rights of humanity, who turn religion into derision, and would, for higher wages, direct their swords against their leaders or their country. Go on, then, in your generous enterprise, with gratitude to Heaven for past success, and confidence of it in the future. For my own part, I ask no greater blessing than to share with you the common danger and common glory. If I have a wish dearer to my soul than that my ashes may be mingled with those of a Warren and a Montgomery, it is that these American States may never cease to be free and independent.

CHAPTER VIII

Revolution or Rebellion?

Speech of Lord Chatham against the American War—The French Alliance—Speech of Charles James Fox on "Folly of the American War"—Speech of John Wilkes on "Revolution, not Rebellion"—Inspiriting Address of Congress (drafted by Samuel Chase): "Be Not Deceived"—Congress Rejects British Proposals—Triumph of American Arms—Debate in Parliament over Grant of Independence to America: Measure Opposed by the Earl of Shelburne—Letter of Thomas Paine to Shelburne: "The Setting Sun of England"—The Treaty of Peace.

THE march toward independence was not to be the triumphal progress which the sanguine Adams anticipated. A year followed of doubtful contest. Not until Burgoyne's defeat at Saratoga (October 17, 1777) did the tide turn in favor of America.

On November 18, 1777, after vague reports of Burgoyne's defeat had reached England, but before news of the completeness of the disaster was known, Lord Chatham arose in the House of Lords and delivered his last appeal to his country to desist from its vain attempt to subjugate America. The occasion was an address to the Throne congratulating the King, among other things, upon the progress of the American war. Although Chatham was in his seventieth year, the speech possessed all the fire of his youth, and indeed is reckoned by many to be the best of all his orations. It is certainly the most finished, as it is the only one which was corrected by him.

Against the American War

LORD CHATHAM

I rise, my Lords, to declare my sentiments on this most solemn and serious subject. It has imposed a load upon my mind, which, I fear, nothing can remove, but which impels me to endeavor its alleviation by a free and unreserved communication of my sentiments.

. . . . .

I will not join in congratulation on misfortune and disgrace. I cannot concur in a blind and servile address, which approves and endeavors to sanctify the monstrous measures which have heaped disgrace and misfortune upon us. This, my Lords, is a perilous and tremendous moment! It is not a time for adulation. The smoothness of flattery cannot now avail—cannot save us in this rugged and awful crisis. It is now necessary to instruct the Throne in the language of truth. We must dispel the illusion and the darkness which develop it, and display, in its full danger and true colors, the ruin that is brought to our doors.

This, my Lords, is our duty. It is the proper function of this noble assembly, sitting, as we do, upon our honors in this House, the hereditary council of the Crown. *Who* is the minister—*where* is the minister, that has dared to suggest to the Throne the contrary, unconstitutional language this day delivered from it? The accustomed language from the Throne has been application to Parliament for advice, and a reliance on its constitutional advice and assistance. As it is the right of Parliament to give, so it is the duty of the Crown to ask it. But on this day, and in this extreme momentous exigency, no reliance is reposed on our constitutional counsels! no advice is asked from the sober and enlightened care of Parliament! but the Crown, from itself and by itself, declares an unalterable determination to pursue measures—and what measures, my Lords? The measures that have produced the imminent perils that threaten us; the measures that have brought ruin to our doors.

Can the minister of the day now presume to expect a continuance of support in this ruinous infatuation? Can Parliament be so dead to its dignity and its duty as to be thus deluded into the loss of the one and the violation of the other? To give an unlimited credit and support for the steady perseverance in measures not proposed for our parliamentary advice, but dictated and forced upon us—in measures, I say, my Lords, which have reduced this late flourishing empire to ruin and contempt! "But yesterday, and England might have stood against the world: now none so poor to do her reverence." I use the words of a poet; but, though it be poetry, it is no fiction. It is a shameful truth, that not only the power and strength of this country are wasting away and expiring, but her well-earned glories, her true honor, and substantial dignity are sacrificed.

France, my Lords, has insulted you; she has encouraged and

sustained America; and, whether America be wrong or right, the dignity of this country ought to spurn at the officious insult of French interference. The ministers and embassadors of those who are called rebels and enemies are in Paris; in Paris they transact the reciprocal interests of America and France. Can there be a more mortifying insult? Can even our ministers sustain a more humiliating disgrace? Do they dare to resent it? Do they presume even to hint a vindication of their honor, and the dignity of the state, by requiring the dismission of the plenipotentiaries of America? Such is the degradation to which they have reduced the glories of England! The people whom they affect to call contemptible rebels, but whose growing power has at last obtained the name of enemies; the people with whom they have engaged this country in war, and against whom they now command our implicit support in every measure of desperate hostility—this people, despised as rebels, or acknowledged as enemies, are abetted against you, supplied with every military store, their interests consulted, and their embassadors entertained, by your inveterate enemy! and our ministers dare not interpose with dignity or effect. Is this the honor of a great kingdom? Is this the indignant spirit of England, who "but yesterday" gave law to the house of Bourbon? My Lords, the dignity of nations demands a decisive conduct in a situation like this. Even when the greatest prince that perhaps this country ever saw filled our Throne, the requisition of a Spanish general, on a similar subject, was attended to and complied with; for, on the spirited remonstrance of the Duke of Alva, Elizabeth found herself obliged to deny the Flemish exiles all countenance, support, or even entrance into her dominions; and the Count Le Marque, with his few desperate followers, were expelled the kingdom. Happening to arrive at the Brille, and finding it weak in defence, they made themselves masters of the place; and this was the foundation of the United Provinces.

My Lords, this ruinous and ignominious situation, where we cannot act with success, nor suffer with honor, calls upon us to remonstrate in the strongest and loudest language of truth, to rescue the ear of majesty from the delusions which surround it. The desperate state of our arms abroad is in part known. No man thinks more highly of them than I do. I love and honor the English troops. I know their virtues and their valor. I know they can achieve anything except impossibilities; and I know that the conquest of English America *is an impossibility*. You cannot, I venture to say it, *you cannot* conquer America. Your armies in the last war effected everything that could be effected;

and what was it? It cost a numerous army, under the command of a most able general [Lord Amherst], now a noble Lord in this House, a long and laborious campaign, to expel five thousand Frenchmen from French America. My Lords, *you cannot conquer America.* What is your present situation there? We do not know the worst; but we know that in three campaigns we have done nothing and suffered much. Besides the sufferings, perhaps *total loss* of the Northern force, the best appointed army that ever took the field, commanded by Sir William Howe, has retired from the American lines. *He was obliged* to relinquish his attempt, and with great delay and danger to adopt a new and distant plan of operations. We shall soon know, and in any event have reason to lament, what may have happened since. As to conquest, therefore, my Lords, I repeat, it is impossible. You may swell every expense and every effort still more extravagantly; pile and accumulate every assistance you can buy or borrow; traffic and barter with every little pitiful German prince that sells and sends his subjects to the shambles of a foreign prince; your efforts are forever vain and impotent—doubly so from this mercenary aid on which you rely; for it irritates, to an incurable resentment, the minds of your enemies, to overrun them with the mercenary sons of rapine and plunder, devoting them and their possessions to the rapacity of hireling cruelty! If I were an American, as I am an Englishman, while a foreign troop was landed in my country, I never would lay down my arms—never—never—never.

Your own army is infected with the contagion of these illiberal allies. The spirit of plunder and of rapine is gone forth among them. I know it; and, notwithstanding what the noble Earl [Lord Percy] who moved the address has given as his opinion of the American army, I know from authentic information, and the *most experienced officers,* that our discipline is deeply wounded. While this is notoriously our sinking situation, America grows and flourishes; while our strength and discipline are lowered, hers are rising and improving.

But, my Lords, who is the man that, in addition to these disgraces and mischiefs of our army, has dared to authorize and associate to our arms the tomahawk and scalping-knife of the savage? to call into civilized alliance the wild and inhuman savage of the woods; to delegate to the merciless Indian the defence of disputed rights, and to wage the horrors of his barbarous war against our brethren? My Lords, these enormities cry aloud for redress and punishment. Unless thoroughly done away, it will be a stain on the national character. It is a violation of the constitution. I believe it is against law. It is not the least of our national misfortunes that the strength and character of our army are thus impaired. Infected with the mercenary spirit of robbery and rapine; familiarized to the horrid scenes of savage cruelty, it can no longer boast of the noble and generous principles which dignify a soldier; no longer sympathize with the dignity of the royal banner, nor feel the pride, pomp, and circumstance of glorious war, "that make ambition virtue!" What makes ambition virtue?—the sense of honor. But is the sense of honor consistent with a spirit of plunder, or the practice of murder? Can it flow from mercenary motives, or can it prompt to cruel deeds? Besides these murderers and plunderers, let me ask our ministers, What other allies have they acquired? What *other powers* have they associated in their cause? Have they entered into alliance with the *king of the gipsies?* Nothing, my Lords, is too low or too ludicrous to be consistent with their counsels.

The independent views of America have been stated and asserted as the foundation of this address. My Lords, no man wishes for the due dependence of America on this country more than I do. To preserve it, and not confirm that state of independence into which *your measures* hitherto have *driven them,* is the object which we ought to unite in attaining. The Americans, contending for their rights against arbitrary exactions, I love and admire. It is the struggle of free and virtuous patriots. But, contending for independency and total disconnection from England, as an Englishman, I cannot wish them success; for in a due constitutional dependency, including the ancient supremacy of this country in regulating their commerce and navigation, consist the mutual happiness and prosperity both of England and America. She derived assistance and protection from us; and we reaped from her the most important advantages. She was, indeed, the fountain of our wealth, the nerve of our strength, the nursery and basis of our naval power. It is our duty, therefore, my Lords, if we wish to save our country, most seriously to endeavor the recovery of these most beneficial subjects; and in this perilous crisis, perhaps the present moment may be the only one in which we can hope for success. For in their negotiations with France they have, or think they have, reason to complain; though it be notorious that they have received from that power important supplies and assistance of various kinds, yet it is certain they expected it in a more decisive and immediate degree. America is in ill humor with France; on some points they have not entirely answered her expectations.

Let us wisely take advantage of every possible moment of reconciliation. Besides, the natural disposition of America herself still leans toward England; to the old habits of connection and mutual interest that united both countries. This *was* the established sentiment of all the Continent; and still, my Lords, in the great and principal part, the sound part of America, this wise and affectionate disposition prevails. And there is a very considerable part of America yet sound—the middle and the southern provinces. Some parts may be factious and blind to their true interests; but if we express a wise and benevolent disposition to communicate with them those immutable rights of nature and those constitutional liberties to which they are equally entitled with ourselves, by a conduct so just and humane we shall confirm the favorable and conciliate the adverse. I say, my Lords, the rights and liberties to which they are equally entitled with ourselves, *but no more.* I would participate to them every enjoyment and freedom which the colonizing subjects of a free state can possess, or wish to possess; and I do not see why they should not enjoy every fundamental right in their property, and every original substantial liberty, which Devonshire, or Surrey, or the county I live in, or any other county in England, can claim; reserving always, as the sacred right of the mother country, the due constitutional dependency of the colonies. The inherent supremacy of the state in regulating and protecting the navigation and commerce of all her subjects is necessary for the mutual benefit and preservation of every part, to constitute and preserve the prosperous arrangement of the whole empire.

The sound parts of America, of which I have spoken, must be sensible of these great truths and of their real interests. America is not in that state of desperate and contemptible rebellion which this country has been deluded to believe. It is not a wild and lawless banditti, who, having nothing to lose, might hope to snatch something from public convulsions. Many of their leaders and great men have a great stake in this great contest. The gentleman who conducts their armies, I am told, has an estate of four or five thousand pounds a year; and when I consider these things I cannot but lament the inconsiderate violence of our penal acts, our declaration of treason and rebellion, with all the fatal effects of attainder and confiscation.

As to the disposition of foreign powers which is asserted [in the King's speech] to be pacific and friendly, let us judge, my Lords, rather by their actions and the nature of things than by interested assertions. The uniform assistance supplied to America by France suggests a different conclusion. The most important interests of France in aggrandizing and enriching herself with what she most wants, supplies of every naval store from America, must inspire her with different sentiments. The extraordinary preparations of the House of Bourbon, by land and by sea, from Dunkirk to the Straits, equally ready and willing to overwhelm these defenceless islands, should rouse us to a sense of their real disposition and our own danger. Not five thousand troops in England! hardly three thousand in Ireland! What can we oppose to the combined force of our enemies? Scarcely twenty ships of the line so fully or sufficiently manned that any admiral's reputation would permit him to take the command of. The river of Lisbon in the possession of our enemies! The seas swept by American privateers! Our Channel trade torn to pieces by them! In this complicated crisis of danger, weakness at home, and calamity abroad, terrified and insulted by the neighboring powers, unable to act in America, or acting only to be destroyed, where is the man with the forehead to promise or hope for success in such a situation, or from perseverence in the measures that have driven us to it? Who has the forehead to do so? Where is that man? I should be glad to see his face.

You cannot *conciliate* America by your present measures. You cannot *subdue* her by your present or by any measures. What, then, can you do? You cannot conquer; you cannot gain; but you can *address;* you can lull the fears and anxieties of the moment into an ignorance of the danger that should produce them. But, my Lords, the time demands the language of truth. We must not now apply the flattering unction of servile compliance or blind complaisance. In a just and necessary war, to maintain the rights or honor of my country, I would strip the shirt from my back to support it. But in such a war as this, unjust in its principle, impracticable in its means, and ruinous in its consequences, I would not contribute a single effort nor a single shilling. I do not call for vengeance on the heads of those who have been guilty; I only recommend to them to make their retreat. Let them walk off; and let them make haste, or they may be assured that speedy and condign punishment will overtake them.

My Lords, I have submitted to you, with the freedom and truth which I think my duty, my sentiments on your present awful situation. I have laid before you the ruin of your power, the disgrace of your reputation, the pollution of your discipline, the contamination of your morals, the complication of calamities, foreign and domestic, that overwhelm your sinking country. Your dearest interests, your own liberties, the constitution itself, totters to the foundation. All this disgraceful danger, this multitude of misery, is the monstrous offspring of this unnatural war. We have been deceived and deluded too long. Let us now stop short. This is the crisis—the only crisis of time and situation, to give us a possibility of escape from the fatal effects of our delusions. But if, in an obstinate and infatuated perseverance in folly, we slavishly echo the peremptory words this day presented to us, nothing can save this devoted country from complete and final ruin. We madly rush into multiplied miseries, and "confusion worse confounded."

Is it possible, can it be believed, that ministers are yet blind to this impending destruction? I did hope that instead of this false and empty vanity, this overweening pride, engendering high conceits and presumptuous imaginations, ministers would have humbled themselves in their errors, would have confessed and retracted them, and, by an active, though a late, repentance, have endeavored to redeem them. But, my Lords, since they had neither sagacity to foresee, nor justice nor humanity to shun these oppressive calamities—since not even severe experience can make them feel, nor the imminent ruin of their country awaken them from their stupefaction, the guardian care of Parliament must interpose. I shall, therefore, my Lords, propose to you an amendment of the address to His Majesty, . . . to recommend an immediate cessation of hostilities, and the commencement of a treaty to restore peace and liberty to America, strength and happiness to England, security and permanent prosperity to both countries. This, my Lords, is yet in our power; and let not the wisdom and justice of your Lordships neglect the happy, and, perhaps, the only opportunity. By the establishment of irrevocable law, founded on mutual rights, and ascertained by treaty, these glorious enjoyments may be firmly perpetuated. And let me repeat to your Lordships, that the strong bias of America, at least of the wise and sounder parts of it, naturally inclines to this happy and constitutional reconnection with you. Notwithstanding the temporary intrigues with France, we may still be assured of their ancient and confirmed partiality to us. America and France cannot be congenial. There is something decisive and confirmed in the honest American that will not assimilate to the futility and levity of Frenchmen.

My Lords, to encourage and confirm that innate inclination to this country, founded on every principle of affection, as well as consideration of interest; to restore that favorable disposition into a permanent and powerful reunion with this country; to revive the mutual strength of the empire; again to awe the House of Bourbon, instead of meanly truckling, as our present calamities compel us, to every insult of French caprice and Spanish punctilio; to reëstablish our commerce; to reassert our rights and our honor; to confirm our interests, and renew our glories forever—a consummation most devoutly to be endeavored! and which, I trust, may yet arise from reconciliation with America— I have the honor of submitting to you the following amendment, which I move to be inserted after the two first paragraphs of the address:

"And that this House does most humbly advise and supplicate His Majesty to be pleased to cause the most speedy and effectual measures to be taken for restoring peace in America; and that no time may be lost in proposing an immediate opening of a treaty for the final settlement of the tranquillity of these invaluable provinces, by a removal of the unhappy causes of this ruinous civil war, and by a just and adequate security against the return of the like calamities in times to come. And this House desire to offer the most dutiful assurances to His Majesty that they will, in due time, cheerfully coöperate with the magnanimity and tender goodness of His Majesty for the preservation of his people, by such explicit and most solemn declarations and provisions of fundamental and irrevocable laws as may be judged necessary for the ascertaining and fixing forever the respective rights of Great Britain and her colonies."

In the course of this debate Lord Suffolk defended the employment of the Indians in the war, contending that, besides its *policy* and *necessity,* the measure was also allowable on *principle;* for that "it was perfectly justifiable to use all the means that *God and nature put into our hands!"*
Lord Chatham leaped up, exclaiming as he rose:

I am astonished—shocked! to hear such principles confessed —to hear them avowed in this House, or in this country; principles equally unconstitutional, inhuman, and unchristian!
My Lords, I did not intend to have encroached again upon your attention, but I cannot repress my indignation. I feel myself impelled by every duty. My Lords, we are called upon as members of this House, as men, as Christian men, to protest against such notions standing near the Throne, polluting the

ear of Majesty. "That God and nature put into our hands!"
I know not what ideas that Lord may entertain of God and nature, but I know that such abominable principles are equally abhorrent to religion and humanity. What! to attribute the sacred sanction of God and nature to the massacres of the Indian scalping-knife—to the cannibal savage, torturing, murdering, roasting, and eating—literally, my Lords, *eating* the mangled victims of his barbarous battles! Such horrible notions shock every precept of religion, divine or natural, and every generous feeling of humanity. And, my Lords, they shock every sentiment of honor; they shock me as a lover of honorable war, and a detester of murderous barbarity.

These abominable principles, and this more abominable avowal of them, demand the most decisive indignation. I call upon that right reverend bench, those holy ministers of the Gospel, and pious pastors of our Church—I conjure them to join in the holy work, and vindicate the religion of their God. I appeal to the wisdom and the law of this learned bench to defend and support the justice of their country. I call upon the bishops to interpose the unsullied sanctity of their lawn; upon the learned judges, to interpose the purity of their ermine, to save us from this pollution. I call upon the honor of your Lordships to reverence the dignity of your ancestors, and to maintain your own. I call upon the spirit and humanity of my country to vindicate the national character. I invoke the genius of the constitution. From the tapestry that adorns these walls, the immortal ancestor [1] of this noble Lord frowns with indignation at the disgrace of his country. In vain he led your victorious fleets against the boasted Armada of Spain; in vain he defended and established the honor, the liberties, the religion—the *Protestant religion*—of this country, against the arbitrary cruelties of popery and the Inquisition, if these more than popish cruelties and inquisitorial practices are let loose among us—to turn forth into our settlements, among our ancient connections, friends, and relations, the merciless cannibal, thirsting for the blood of man, woman, and child, to send forth the infidel savage —against whom? against your Protestant brethren; to lay waste their country, to desolate their dwellings, and extirpate their race and name with these horrible hell-hounds of savage war— *hell-hounds, I say, of savage war!* Spain armed herself with blood-hounds to extirpate the wretched natives of America, and we improve on the inhuman example even of Spanish cruelty; we turn loose these savage hell-hounds against our brethren and

[1] Lord Effingham Howard, who was commander of the fleet in the fight with the Spanish Armada, which battle was depicted on the tapestry.

countrymen in America, of the same language, laws, liberties, and religion, endeared to us by every tie that should sanctify humanity.

My Lords, this awful subject, so important to our honor, our constitution, and our religion, demands the most solemn and effectual inquiry. And I again call upon your Lordships, and the united powers of the state, to examine it thoroughly and decisively, and to stamp upon it an indelible stigma of the public abhorrence. And I again implore those holy prelates of our religion to do away these iniquities from among us. Let them perform a lustration; let them purify this House, and this country, from this sin.

My Lords, I am old and weak, and at present unable to say more; but my feelings and indignation were too strong to have said less. I could not have slept this night in my bed, nor reposed my head on my pillow, without giving this vent to my eternal abhorrence of such preposterous and enormous principles.

Chatham's amendment lost by a vote of 97 to 24, and the address was carried.

Chatham died in the May following the speech, being more thoroughly convinced than ever, by the signing of the treaty between France and America, which took place on February 6, 1778, that Great Britain would never conquer America, and that the attempt to

A PICTURESQUE VIEW OF THE STATE OF THE NATION
[For February, 1778.]

do so would result in the greatest humiliation of her history.

THE FRENCH ALLIANCE

The essential and direct end of the French-American alliance was "to maintain the liberty, sovereignty, and independence, absolute and unlimited, of the United States, as well in matters of government as of commerce."

To this treaty there was annexed a secret article, that the King of Spain (who was the uncle of Louis XVI, and had already secretly contributed supplies to America) might join the alliance at such time as he should judge it proper to do so.

Great Britain was greatly alarmed by the alliance between her ancient enemy France and the revolted colonies. Charles James Fox took this occasion to advocate coming to terms with America.

FOLLY OF THE AMERICAN WAR

CHARLES JAMES FOX

You have now two wars before you, of which you must choose one, for both you cannot support. The war against America has hitherto been carried on against her alone, unassisted by any ally whatever. Notwithstanding she stood alone, you have been obliged, uniformly, to increase your exertions and to push your efforts to the extent of your power without being able to bring it to an issue. You have exerted all your force hitherto without effect, and you cannot now divide a force found already inadequate to its object.

My opinion is for withdrawing your forces from America entirely, for a defensive war you can never think of there. A defensive war would ruin this nation at any time, and, in any circumstances, offensive war is pointed out as proper for this country. Our situation points it out, and the spirit of the nation impels us to attack rather than defend. Attack France, then, for she is our object. The nature of these wars is different. The war against America is against our own countrymen; you have stopped me from saying against your fellow-subjects. That against France is against an inveterate foe and rival. Every blow you strike in America is against yourselves. It is against all idea of reconciliation, and against your own interest, even though you should be able, as you never will be, to force them to submit. Every stroke against France is of advantage to you. America must be conquered in France. France never can be conquered in America.

The war of the Americans is a war of passion. It is of such a nature as to be supported by the most powerful virtues—love of liberty and love of country—and at the same time by those passions in the human heart which give courage, strength, and perseverance to man—the spirit of revenge for the injuries you have done them, of retaliation for the hardships you have inflicted on them, and of opposition to the unjust powers you have exercised over them. Everything combines to animate them to this war; and such a war is without end. Whether it be called obstinacy or enthusiasm, under the name of religion or liberty, the effects are the same. It inspires a spirit which is unconquerable, solicitous to undergo difficulty, danger, and hardship. So long as there is a man in America—a being formed as we are—so long will he present himself against you in the field.

What has become of the ancient spirit of this people? Where is the national spirit that ever did honor to this country?

In accordance with Fox's appeal, or perhaps notwithstanding it, for he had the faculty of arousing antagonism to his propositions, Parliament, on February 17, 1778, passed acts removing the tax on tea, restoring the charter of Massachusetts, and appointing a commission to "treat, consult, and agree upon the means of quieting the disorders" in the colonies, and to declare an armistice pending negotiations. These acts were transmitted to General Washington in April, and by him submitted to Congress. Congress referred them to a committee, and, in pursuance of its report, refused to consider them unless Great Britain either withdrew her fleets and armies, or recognized the independence of the United States.

At last the common people of Great Britain became thoroughly aroused against the further prosecution of the war with America. Their tribune, John Wilkes, voiced their sentiments in a speech on the King's Address at the opening of Parliament in 1780.

JOHN WILKES, ESQ.

Drawn by William Hogarth

Revolution, Not Rebellion

SPEECH OF JOHN WILKES ON THE AMERICAN WAR

Mr. Speaker—It ill becomes the duty and dignity of Parliament to lose itself in such a fulsome adulatory address to the throne as that now proposed. We ought rather to approach it with sound and wholesome advice, and even with remonstrances against the ministers who have precipitated the British nation into an unjust, ruinous, murderous, and felonious war. I call the war with our brethren in America an unjust and felonious war, because the primary cause and confessed origin of it is to attempt to take their money from them without their consent, contrary to the common rights of all mankind and to those great fundamental principles of the English constitution for which Hampden bled. I assert that it is a murderous war, because it is an effort to deprive men of their lives for standing up in the defence of their property and their clear rights. Such a war, I fear, will draw down the vengeance of heaven upon this kingdom.

Sir, is any minister weak enough to flatter himself with the conquest of America? You cannot, with all your allies, with all the mercenary ruffians of the North, you cannot effect so wicked a purpose! The Americans will dispute every inch of territory with you, every narrow pass, every strong defile, every Thermopylæ, every Bunker Hill! More than half the empire is already lost, and almost all the rest is in confusion and anarchy. We have appealed to the sword, and what have we gained? Are we to pay as dear for the rest of America? The idea of the conquest of that immense country is as romantic as it is unjust.

But "the Americans have been treated with lenity!" Will facts justify the assertion? Was your Boston "Port Bill" a measure of lenity? Was your Fishery Bill a measure of lenity? Was your bill for taking away the charter of Massachusetts a measure of lenity? I omit your many other gross provocations and insults by which the brave Americans have been driven to their present state. Whether that state is one of rebellion or of fit resistance to unlawful acts of power I shall not declare. This I know: a successful resistance is revolution, not a rebellion. Rebellion, indeed, appears on the back of a flying enemy, but revolution flames on the breastplate of the victorious warrior.

Who can tell whether, in consequence of this day's action, the scabbard may not be thrown away by them as well as by us, and, should success attend them, whether in a few years the independent American may not celebrate the glorious era of the Revolution of 1775 as we do that of 1688?

REJECTION OF BRITISH PROPOSALS

Congress presented an inspiriting address to the country, instancing the peace proposals of Great Britain as evidence of her despair, though also of her rage, and warning the people not to relax their efforts for independence. It was written by Samuel Chase:

"BE NOT DECEIVED"

Be not . . . deceived. You have still to expect one severe conflict. Your foreign alliances, though they secure your independence, cannot secure your country from desolation, your habitations from plunder, your wives from insult or violation, nor your children from butchery. Foiled in their principal design, you must expect to feel the rage of disappointed ambition. Arise, then! to your tents! and gird you for battle. It is time to turn the headlong current of vengeance upon the head of the destroyer. . . . They have filled up the measure of their abominations, and like ripe fruit must soon drop from the tree. Although much is done, yet much remains to do. Expect not peace, while any corner of America is in possession of your foes. You must drive them away from this land of promise, a land flowing indeed with milk and honey. . . . For surely there is no man so absurd as to suppose that the least shadow of liberty can be preserved in a dependent connection with Great Britain. From the nature of the thing it is evident that the only security you could obtain would be the justice and moderation of a Parliament who have sold the rights of their own constituents. And this slender security is still farther weakened by the consideration that it was pledged to rebels (as they unjustly call the good people of these States) with whom they think they are not bound to keep faith by any law whatsoever. Thus would you be cast bound among men, whose minds, by your virtuous resistance, have been sharpened to the keenest edge of revenge. Thus would your children and your children's children be by you forced to a participation of all their debts, their wars, their luxuries, and their crimes. And this mad, this impious system they would lead you to adopt, because of the derangement of your finances.

It becomes you deeply to reflect on this subject. Is there

a country upon earth which hath such resources for the payment of her debts as America? such an extensive territory? so fertile, so blessed in its climate and productions? surely there is none. Neither is there any, to which the wise Europeans will sooner confide their property. What, then, are the reasons that your money hath depreciated? because no taxes have been imposed to carry on the war. Because your commerce hath been interrupted by your enemy's fleets. Because their armies have ravaged and desolated a part of your country. Because their agents have villainously counterfeited your bills. Because extortioners among you, inflamed with the lust of gain, have added to the price of every article of life. And because weak men have been artfully led to believe that it is of no value. How is this dangerous disease to be remedied? let those among you who have leisure and opportunity collect the moneys which individuals in their neighborhood are desirous of placing in the public funds. Let the several legislatures sink their respective emissions, that so, there being but one kind of bills, there may be less danger of counterfeits. Refrain a little while from purchasing those things which are not absolutely necessary, that so those who have engrossed commodities may suffer (as they deservedly will) the loss of their ill-begotten hoards, by reason of the commerce with foreign nations, which the fleets will protect. Above all, bring forward your armies into the field. Trust not to appearances of peace or safety. Be assured that, unless you persevere, you will be exposed to every species of barbarity. But if you exert the means of defence which God and nature have given you, the time will soon arrive when every man shall sit under his own vine, and under his own fig-tree, and there shall be none to make him afraid.

The sweets of a free commerce with every part of the earth will soon reimburse you for all the losses you have sustained. The full tide of wealth will flow in upon your shores, free from the arbitrary impositions of those whose interest and whose declared policy it was to check your growth. Your interests will be fostered and nourished by governments that derive their power from your grant, and will therefore be obliged, by the influence of cogent necessity, to exert it in your favor. It is to obtain these things that we call your strenuous, unremitted exertions. Yet do not believe that you have been, or can be, saved merely by your own strength. No! it is by the assistance of heaven, and this you must assiduously cultivate, by acts which heaven approves. Thus shall the power and the happiness of these sovereign, free, and independent states, founded on the virtue of their citizens, increase, extend, and endure until the Almighty shall blot out all the empires of the earth.

The peace commissioners sent by Parliament to America could not believe that Congress had been sincere in its refusal even to consider their proposals, and so renewed them. When Congress adhered to its former conditions, the commissioners then addressed their proposals to the colonial assemblies and the "free inhabitants of this once happy empire"; and offered pardon to all who should, within forty days, desert the American cause. They circulated this offer among the soldiers by means of flags of truce.

Congress declared that these actions were violations of international law, and recommended the state authorities to seize the commissioners.

Triumph of American Arms

While General Nathaniel Greene was conducting his successful campaign in the South, the allied French and American forces under Washington and Rochambeau compelled the surrender of Lord Cornwallis at Yorktown on October 19, 1781. This brilliant achievement put an end to military operations in America.

Parliament's Peace Proposals

In the meantime a congress of the belligerent nations was to be held at Vienna to negotiate for the reëstablishment of peace. But the American minister, John Adams, utterly refused to appear at the congress except as the representative of an independent nation. In this position he was upheld by France, whereupon Great Britain, in September, 1781, refused to accept the mediation of the powers, and thus put an end to the proposal.

Parliament met on the 27th of November, 1781, and, though the speech from the throne still breathed a spirit of hostility, and answers from both Houses were procured, in accordance with it, yet not long after the recess, the ministers found themselves in a minority in the House of Commons. On the 22d of February, 1782, General Conway in the House moved an Address to the

King, praying "that the war on the continent of North America might no longer be pursued for the impracticable purpose of reducing that country to obedience by force," and expressing their hope, "that the earnest desire and diligent exertion to restore the public tranquillity, of which they had received His Majesty's most gracious assurances, might, by a happy reconciliation with the revolted colonies, be forwarded and made effectual; to which great end, His Majesty's faithful Commons would be ready to give their utmost assistance."

This motion, being lost by a single vote only, was five days after renewed, by the same gentleman in a somewhat different form, and carried, whereupon the ministry resigned, in accordance with that precedent of Parliament which demands a change of government when the ministry is defeated on an important measure.

In the new administration the Marquis of Rockingham was placed at the head of the treasury, and the Earl of Shelburne and Mr. Fox held the important places of secretaries of state. This administration entered into negotiations in regard to peace with the French court and Dr. Franklin. Franklin summoned to his aid John Jay from Madrid.

While the majority of the British cabinet, including the prime minister, were determined to "offer America unlimited, unconditional independence," the Earl of Shelburne was opposed to it as the last measure to which the King would assent. When, on the death of the Marquis of Rockingham, Lord Shelburne was appointed first lord of the treasury, there was an open rupture in the cabinet, Fox and others resigning.

William Jones (afterward Sir William Jones) was sent to Paris to sound Franklin on securing peace short of an express acknowledgment of American independence. On his return he confessed himself defeated in this purpose. "The sturdy trans-atlantic yeomanry," he said, "will neither be *dragooned* nor *bamboozled* out of their liberty."

In regard to the policy of Lord Shelburne, Thomas Paine wrote the fourteenth of his papers in "The Crisis."

WHA WANTS ME?

"I am Ready & Willing to offer my Services to any Nation or People under heaven who are Desirous of Liberty & Equality."
—Vide Paine's Letter to the [French] Convention

A British cartoon published December 26, 1792

"THE SETTING SUN OF ENGLAND"

LETTER TO THE EARL OF SHELBURNE BY THOMAS PAINE

MY LORD—A speech, which has been printed in several of the British and New York newspapers as coming from Your Lordship, in answer to one from the Duke of Richmond of the tenth of July last, contains expressions and opinions so new and singular, and so enveloped in mysterious reasoning, that I address this publication to you for the purpose of giving them a free and candid examination. The speech that I allude to is in these words:

"His Lordship said it had been mentioned in another place that he had been guilty of inconsistency. To clear himself of this he asserted that he still held the same principles in respect to American independence which he at first imbibed. He had been, and yet was, of opinion that whenever the Parliament of Great Britain acknowledges that point, the sun of England's glory is set forever. Such were the sentiments he possessed on a former day, and such the sentiments he continued to hold at this hour. It was the opinion of Lord Chatham, as well as many other able statesmen.

"Other notable Lords, however, think differently; and, as the majority of the cabinet support them, he acquiesced in the measure, dissenting from the idea; and the point is settled for bringing the matter into the full discussion of Parliament, where it will be candidly, fairly, and impartially debated. The independence of America would end in the ruin of England; and that a peace patched up with France would give that proud enemy the means of yet trampling on this country.

"The sun of England's glory he wished not to see set forever; he looked for a spark at least to be left, which might in time light us up to a new day. But if independence was to be granted, if Parliament deemed that measure prudent, he foresaw, in his own mind, that England was undone. He wished to God that he had been deputed to Congress, that he might plead the cause of that country as well as of this, and that he might exercise whatever powers he possessed as an orator to save both from ruin, by striving to convince Congress that if their independence was signed their liberties were gone forever.

"Peace, His Lordship added, was a desirable object, but it must be an honorable peace and not a humiliating one, dictated by France or insisted on by America. It was very true that this kingdom was not in a flourishing state; it was impoverished by war. But if we were not rich, it was evident that France was poor. If we were straitened in our finances, the enemy were exhausted in their resources

"This was a great empire; it abounded with brave men who were able and willing to fight in a common cause; the language of humiliation should not, therefore, be the language of Great Britain. His Lordship said that he was not afraid nor ashamed of those expressions going to America. There were numbers, great numbers, there who were of the same way of thinking in respect to that country being dependent on this and who, with His Lordship, perceived ruin and independence linked together.''

Thus far the speech; on which I remark: That His Lordship is a total stranger to the mind and sentiments of America; that he has wrapped himself up in a fond delusion that something less than independence may, under his administration, be accepted; and he wishes himself sent to Congress to prove the most extraordinary of all doctrines, which is, that *independence,* the sublimest of all human conditions, is loss of liberty.

In answer to which we may say that, in order to know what the contrary word *dependence* means, we have only to look back to those years of severe humiliation, when the mildest of all petitions could obtain no other notice than the haughtiest of all insults; and when the base terms of unconditional submission were demanded, or undistinguishable destruction threatened.

It is nothing to us that the ministry have been changed, for they may be changed again. The guilt of a government is the crime of a whole country; and the nation that can, though but for a moment, think and act as England has done can never afterward be believed or trusted. There are cases in which it is as impossible to restore character to life as it is to recover the dead. It is a phœnix that can expire but once, and from whose ashes there is no resurrection.

Some offenses are of such a slight composition that they reach no further than the temper, and are created or cured by a thought.

But the sin of England has struck the heart of America, and nature has not left it in our power to say we can forgive.

Your Lordship wishes for an opportunity to plead before Congress *the cause of England and America, and to save,* as you say, *both from ruin.*

That the country which, for more than seven years, has sought our destruction should now cringe to solicit our protection is adding the wretchedness of disgrace to the misery of disappointment; and if England has the least spark of supposed honor left that spark must be darkened by asking, and extinguished by receiving, the smallest favor from America; for the criminal who owes his life to the grace and mercy of the injured is more executed by living that he who dies.

But a thousand pleadings, even from Your Lordship, can have no effect. Honor, interest, and every sensation of the heart would plead against you. We are a people who think not as you think; and, what is equally true, you cannot feel as we feel. The situations of the two countries are exceedingly different.

Ours has been the seat of war; yours has seen nothing of it. The most wanton destruction has been committed in our sight; the most insolent barbarity has been acted on our feelings. We can look round and see the remains of burned and destroyed houses, once the fair fruit of hard industry, and now the striking monuments of British brutality. We walk over the dead whom we loved, in every part of America, and remember by whom they fell.

There is scarcely a village but brings to life some melancholy thought, and reminds us of what we have suffered, and those we have lost by the inhumanity of Britain. A thousand images arise to us, which, from situation, you cannot see, and are accompanied by as many ideas which you cannot know; and therefore your supposed system of reasoning would apply to nothing, and all your expectations die of themselves.

The question whether England shall accede to the independence of America, and which Your Lordship says is to undergo a Parliamentary discussion, is so very simple, and composed of so few cases, that it scarcely needs a debate.

It is the only way out of an expensive and ruinous war, which has no object, and without which acknowledgment there can be no peace.

But Your Lordship says, *"the sun of Great Britain will set whenever she acknowledges the independence of America"*— whereas the metaphor would have been strictly just to have left the sun wholly out of the figure, and have ascribed her not acknowledging it to the influence of the moon.

But the expression, if true, is the greatest confession of disgrace that could be made, and furnishes America with the highest notions of sovereign independent importance.

Mr. Wedderburne, about the year 1776, made use of an idea of much the same kind—*"Relinquish America!"* says he— *"What is it but to desire a giant to shrink spontaneously into a dwarf."*

Alas! are those people, who call themselves Englishmen, of so little internal consequence that when America is gone or shuts her eyes upon them, their sun is set, they can shine no more, but grope about in obscurity, and contract into insignificant animals? Was America, then, the giant of the empire, and England only her dwarf in waiting?

Is the case so extremely altered that those who once thought we could not live without them are now brought to declare that they cannot exist without us?

Will they tell to the world, and that from their first minister

of state, that America is their all in all; that it is by her importance only they can live, and breathe, and have a being? Will
they, who long since threatened to bring us to their feet, bow
themselves at ours, and own that without us they are not a
nation? Are they become so unqualified to debate on independence that they have lost all idea of it themselves, and are calling
to the rocks and mountains of America to cover their insignificance?

Or, if America is lost, is it manly to sob over it like a child
for its rattle, and invite the laughter of the world by declarations of disgrace? Surely the more consistent conduct would be
to bear it without complaint; and to show that England, without
America, can preserve her independence and a suitable rank with
other European powers. You were not contented while you had
her, and to weep for her now is childish.

But Lord Shelburne thinks something may yet be done.
What that something is, or how it is to be accomplished, is a
matter in obscurity. By arms there is no hope. The experience
of nearly eight years, with the expense of £100,000,000 sterling
and the loss of two armies, must positively decide that point.

Besides, the British have lost their interest in America with
the disaffected. Every part of it has been tried. There is no
new scene left for delusion; and the thousands who have been
ruined by adhering to them, and have now to quit the settlements
they had acquired, and be conveyed like transports to cultivate
the deserts of Augustine and Nova Scotia, has put an end to all
further expectations of aid.

If you cast your eyes on the people of England, what have
they to console themselves with for the millions expended? Or
what encouragement is there left to continue throwing good
money after bad? America can carry on the war for ten years
longer, and all the charges of government included, for less than
you can defray the charges of war and government for one year.
And I, who know both countries, know well that the people of
America can afford to pay their share of the expense much better
than the people of England can.

Besides, it is their own estates and property, their own rights,
liberties, and government they are defending.

The British army in America care not how long the war lasts.
They enjoy an easy and indolent life. They fatten on the folly
of one country and the spoils of another; and, between their
plunder and their pay, may go home rich.

But the case is very different with the laboring farmer, the
working tradesman, and the necessitous poor in England, the

sweat of whose brow goes day after day to feed, in prodigality and sloth, the army that is robbing both them and us. Removed from the eye of the country that supports them, and distant from the government that employs them, they cut and carve for themselves, and there is none to call them to account.

But England will be ruined, says Lord Shelburne, if America is independent.

Then, I say, is England already ruined, for America is already independent; and if Lord Shelburne will not allow this, he immediately denies the fact which he infers. Besides, to make England the mere creature of America is paying too great a compliment to us, and too little to himself.

But the declaration is a rhapsody of inconsistency. For to say, as Lord Shelburne has numberless times said, that the war against America is ruinous, and yet to continue the prosecution of that ruinous war for the purpose of avoiding ruin, is a language which cannot be understood.

Neither is it possible to see how the independence of America is to accomplish the ruin of England after the war is over, and yet not effect it before. America cannot be more independent of her, nor a greater enemy to her, hereafter, than she now is; nor can England derive less advantages from her than at present. Why, then, is ruin to follow in the best state of the case, and not in the worst? And, if not in the worst, why is it to follow at all?

That a nation is to be ruined by peace and commerce, and fourteen or fifteen millions a year less expenses than before, is a new doctrine in politics. We have heard much clamor of national savings and economy; but surely the true economy would be to save the whole charge of a silly, foolish, and headstrong war; because, compared with this, all other retrenchments are baubles and trifles.

But is it possible that Lord Shelburne can be serious in supposing the least advantage can be obtained by arms, or that any advantage can be equal to the expense or the danger of attempting it?

Will not the capture of one army after another satisfy him; must all become prisoners? Must England ever be the sport of hope and the victim of delusion? Sometimes our currency was to fail; another time our army was to disband; then whole provinces were to revolt. And thus, from year to year, has every straw been catched at, and every will-with-a-wisp led them a new dance.

This year a still new folly is to take place. Lord Shelburne wishes to be sent to Congress, and he thinks that something may be done.

Are not the repeated declarations of Congress, and which all America supports, that they will not even hear any proposals whatever until the unconditional and unequivocal independence of America is recognized; are not, I say, these declarations answer enough?

But for England to receive anything from America now, after so many insults, injuries, and outrages acted toward us, would show such a spirit of meanness in her that we could not but despise her for accepting it. And so far from Lord Shelburne coming here to solicit it, it would be the greatest disgrace we could do them to offer it.

England would appear a wretch indeed, at this time of day, to ask or owe anything to the bounty of America. Has not the name of Englishman blots enough upon it without inventing more? Even Lucifer would scorn to reign in heaven by permission, and yet an Englishman can creep for only an entrance into America. Or, has a land of liberty so many charms that to be a doorkeeper in it is better than to be an English minister of state?

But what can this expected something be? Or, if obtained, what can it amount to but new disgraces, contentions, and quarrels?

The people of America have for years accustomed themselves to think and speak freely and contemptuously of English authority, and the inveteracy is so deeply rooted that a person invested with any authority from that country and attempting to exercise it here would have the life of a toad under a harrow.

They would look upon him as an interloper to whom their compassion permitted a residence. He would be no more than the Mungo of a farce; and, if he disliked that, he must set off. It would be a station of degradation, debased by our pity and despised by our pride, and would place England in a more contemptible situation than any she has yet suffered by the war.

We have too high an opinion of ourselves ever to think of yielding again the least obedience to outlandish authority; and, for a thousand reasons, England would be the last country in the world to yield it to. She has been treacherous, and we know it. Her character is gone, and we have seen the funeral.

Surely she loves to fish in troubled waters and drink the cup of contention, or she would not now think of mingling her affairs with those of America. It would be like a foolish dotard taking to his arms the bride that despises him, or who placed on his head the ensigns of her disgust. It is kissing the hand that boxes his ears and proposes to renew the exchange.

The thought is as servile as the war is wicked and shows the last scene of the drama as inconsistent as the first.

As America is gone, the only act of manhood is to *let her go*. Your Lordship had no hand in the separation and you will gain no honor by temporizing politics. Besides, there is something so exceedingly whimsical, unsteady, and even insincere in the present conduct of England that she exhibits herself in the most dishonorable colors.

On the second of August last General Carlton and Admiral Digby wrote to General Washington in these words:

"The resolution of the House of Commons of the twenty-seventh of February last has been placed in Your Excellency's hands, and intimations given at the same time that further pacific measures were likely to follow. Since which, until the present time, we have had no direct communications from England; but a mail is now arrived which brings us very important information. We are acquainted, sir, *by authority*, that negotiations for a general peace have already commenced at Paris, and that Mr. Grenville is invested with full powers to treat with all the parties at war, and is now at Paris in the execution of his commission.

"And we are further, sir, made acquainted *that His Majesty, in order to remove any obstacles to that peace which he so ardently wishes to restore, has commanded his ministers to direct Mr. Grenville that the independence of the Thirteen United Provinces should be proposed by him in the first instance, instead of making it a condition of a general treaty.*"

Now, taking your present measures into view and comparing them with the declaration in this letter, pray, what is the word of your King, or his ministers, or the Parliament good for? Must we not look upon you as a confederate body of faithless, treacherous men, whose assurances were fraud and their language deceit? What opinion can we possibly form of you, but that you are a lost, abandoned, profligate nation, who sport even with your own character, and to be held by nothing but the bayonet or the halter?

To say, after this, *that the sun of Great Britain will be set whenever she acknowledges the independence of America*, when the not doing it is the unqualified lie of government, can be no other than the language of ridicule, the jargon of inconsistency. There were thousands in America who predicted the delusion, and looked upon it as a trick of treachery, to take us from our guard, and draw off our attention from the only system of finance by which we can be called, or deserve to be called, a sovereign, independent people. The fraud, on your part, might be worth attempting, but the sacrifice to obtain it is too high.

There are others who credited the assurance because they thought it impossible that men who had their characters to establish would begin it with a lie. The prosecution of the war by the former ministry was savage and horrid, since which it has been mean, trickish, and delusive. The one went greedily into the passion of revenge, the other into the subtleties of low contrivances; till, between the crimes of both, there is scarcely left a man in America, be he Whig or Tory, who does not despise or detest the conduct of Britain.

The management of Lord Shelburne, whatever may be his views, is a caution to us, and must be to the world, never to regard British assurances. A perfidy so notorious cannot be hid. It stands, even in the public papers of New York, with the names of Carlton and Digby affixed to it. It is a proclamation that the King of England is not to be believed; that the spirit of lying is the governing principle of the ministry. It is holding up the character of the House of Commons to public infamy, and warning all men not to credit them. Such are the consequences which Lord Shelburne's management has brought upon his country.

After the authorized declarations contained in Carlton and Digby's letter you ought, from every motive of honor, policy, and prudence, to have fulfilled them, whatever might have been the event. It was the least atonement you could possibly make to America, and the greatest kindness you could do to yourselves; for you will save millions by a general peace, and you will lose as many by continuing the war.

COMMON SENSE.

Philadelphia, October 29, 1782.

PARLIAMENT'S ACKNOWLEDGMENT OF AMERICAN INDE-
PENDENCE

At last the ministry and the King realized that independence would have to be explicitly granted, and so agreed to a provisional treaty which should do this.

Preliminary treaties between Great Britain and France and Spain were also signed (on January 20, 1783). These and the American treaty were laid before

Parliament in February and precipitated a violent debate, which resulted in forcing Shelburne to resign, and, indeed, a new ministry to be appointed, the Duke of Portland becoming prime minister, and Lord North and Mr. Fox, by an extraordinary coalition, secretaries of state. In April the new administration sent David Hartley to Paris to complete the treaty. On the 15th of the same month the American Congress ratified the terms. The definitive treaty, differing little from the provisional, was signed at Paris on September 3, 1783, and was ratified by Congress on January 14, 1784.

MAGNA BRITTANNIA; HER COLONIES REDUCED
From the collection in the New York Public Library

CHAPTER IX

The Confederation

[INCLUDING TEXT OF THE ARTICLES OF CONFEDERATION]

Proposed Articles of Confederation by Dr. Benjamin Franklin [Pa.]—Report of Committee on the Confederation—Thomas Jefferson's Notes on the Debate on the Committee's Articles: Principal Speakers, Samuel Chase [Md.], John Adams [Mass.], Benjamin Harrison [Va.], James Wilson [Pa.], Dr. John Witherspoon [N. J.], Dr. Franklin, Dr. Benjamin Rush [Pa.], and Stephen Hopkins [R. I.]—The Adoption of the Articles—Text of the Articles—Speech of Dr. David Ramsay [S. C.] on "Our Independent Constitutions"—Proposal for National Revenue— Oliver Ellsworth [Ct.], James Madison [Va.], and Alexander Hamilton [N. Y.] Frame an Address on Public Revenue: "An Appeal to National Honor"—Gen. Washington's Address to the States on a Stable Government—Failure of the Plan—Congress Proposes a Commercial Treaty with Great Britain—Lord Sheffield's Speech in Opposition to Treaty: "Observations on the Commerce of the American States"—Rejection of Proposal—Ordinance of 1787 Organizing the Northwest Territory— Financial Distress of the States—George Washington on the Failure of the Confederacy.

THE need of a definite form of union was early felt, but, owing to the prevalent idea of primary allegiance to the States, was not easily agreed upon. Even before the Declaration of Independence was adopted, Dr. Franklin had, on July 21, 1775, presented to Congress a draft of Articles of Confederation as a plan of colonial union. Though not copied in the Journal of Congress, they remained on file in his handwriting, and had a considerable influence in the formation of the Articles of Confederation which were afterward adopted.

As Jefferson has stated (page 191), on June 11, 1776, Congress appointed a committee to prepare the form of a confederation to be entered into between the colonies. On July 12 the committee made its report.

In the debate which ensued upon the report the principal speakers were: Samuel Chase [Md.], John Adams [Mass.], Benjamin Harrison [Va.], James Wilson [Pa.], Dr. John Witherspoon [N. J.], Dr. Benjamin Franklin [Pa.], Dr. Benjamin Rush [Pa.], and Stephen Hopkins [R. I.].

Jefferson has given the following notes of the debate upon the proposed Articles of Confederation:

DEBATE ON THE CONFEDERATION

NOTES OF THOMAS JEFFERSON

On Friday, July 12, the committee appointed to draw the Articles of Confederation reported them, and on the 22d the House resolved themselves into a committee to take them into consideration. On the 30th and 31st of that month and 1st of the ensuing those articles were debated which determined the proportion, or quota, of money which each State should furnish to the common treasury, and the manner of voting in Congress. The first of these articles was expressed in the original draft in these words:

"Art. XI. All charges of war, and all other expenses that shall be incurred for the common defence or general welfare and allowed by the United States assembled, shall be defrayed out of a common treasury, which shall be supplied by the several colonies in proportion to the number of inhabitants of every age, sex, and quality, except Indians not paying taxes, in each colony—a true account of which, distinguishing the white inhabitants, shall be triennially taken and transmitted to the Assembly of the United States."

MR. CHASE moved that the quotas should be fixed, not by the number of inhabitants of every condition, but by that of the "white inhabitants." He admitted that taxation should be always in proportion to property; that this was, in theory, the true rule; but that, from a variety of difficulties, it was a rule which could never be adopted in practice. The value of the property in every State could never be estimated justly and equally. Some other measures for the wealth of the State must therefore be devised, some standard referred to, which would be more simple. He considered the number of inhabitants as a tolerably good criterion of property, and that this might always be obtained. He therefore thought it the best mode which we could adopt, with one exception only: he observed that negroes are property, and, as such, cannot be distinguished from the lands or personalties held in those States where there are few slaves; that the surplus of profit which a northern farmer is able to lay by, he invests in cattle, horses, etc., whereas a southern farmer lays out the same surplus in slaves. There is no more reason, therefore, for taxing the southern States on the farmer's head, and on his slave's head, than the northern ones on their farmers' heads and the heads of their cattle; that the method proposed would, therefore, tax the southern States according to their numbers and their wealth conjunctly, while the northern would be taxed on numbers only; that negroes, in fact, should not be considered as members of the State, more than cattle, and that they have no more interest in it.

MR. JOHN ADAMS observed that the numbers of people are taken, by this article, as an index of the wealth of the State, and not as subjects of taxation; that, as to this matter, it was of no consequence by what name you called your people, whether by that of *freemen* or of *slaves;* that, in some countries, the laboring poor are called *freemen,* in others they were called *slaves;* but that the difference as to the State was imaginary only. What matters it whether a landlord, employing ten laborers on his farm, give them annually as much money as will buy them the necessaries of life or give them those necessaries at short hand? The ten laborers add as much wealth to the State, increase its exports as much in the one case as the other. Certainly five hundred freemen produce no more profits, no greater surplus for the payment of taxes than five hundred slaves. Therefore the State in which are the laborers called *freemen* should be taxed no more than that in which are those called *slaves.* Suppose, by an extraordinary operation of nature or of law, one-half the laborers of a State could, in the course of one night, be transformed into slaves; would the State be made the poorer, or the less able to pay taxes? That the condition of the laboring poor in most countries—that of the fishermen particularly of the northern States—is as abject as that of slaves. It is the number of laborers which produces the surplus for taxation; and numbers, therefore, indiscriminately, are the fair index to wealth; that it is the use of the word "property" here, and its application to some of the people of the State, which produce the fallacy. How does the southern farmer procure slaves? Either by importation or by purchase from his neighbor. If he imports a slave he adds one to the number of laborers in his country, and, proportionately, to its profits and ability to pay taxes. If he buys from his neighbor it is only a transfer of a laborer from one farm to another, which does not change the annual produce of the State and therefore should not change its tax; that if a northern farmer works ten laborers on his farm he can, it is true, invest the surplus of ten men's labor in cattle; but so may the southern farmer working ten slaves; that a State of one hundred thousand freemen can maintain no more cattle than one of one hundred thousand slaves. Therefore they have no more of that kind of property. That a slave may, indeed, from the custom of speech, be more properly called the wealth of his master than the free laborer might be called the wealth of his employer; but, as to the state, both were equally its wealth and should therefore equally add to the quota of its tax.

MR. HARRISON proposed, as a compromise, that two slaves should be counted as one freeman. He affirmed that slaves did not do as much work as freemen and doubted if two effected more than one; that this was proved by the price of labor—the hire of a laborer in the southern colonies being from £8 to £12, while in the northern it was generally £24.

MR. WILSON said that, if this amendment should take place, the southern colonies would have all the benefit of slaves, while the northern ones would bear the burden; that slaves increase the profits of a State, which the southern States mean to take to themselves; that they also increase the burden of defence, which would, of course, fall so much the heavier on the northern; that slaves occupy the places of freemen and eat their food. Dismiss your slaves and freemen will take their places. It is our duty to lay every discouragement on the importation of slaves; but this amendment would give the *jus trium liberorum* to him who would import slaves; that other kinds of property were pretty equally distributed through all the colonies—there were as many cattle, horses, and sheep in the north as the south, and south as the north, but not so as to slaves—that experience has shown that those colonies have been always able to pay most which have the most inhabitants, whether they be black or white; and the practice of the southern colonies has always been to make every farmer pay poll taxes upon all his laborers, whether they be black or white. He acknowledges, indeed, that freemen work the most; but they consume the most also. They do not produce a greater surplus for taxation. The slave is neither fed nor clothed so expensively as a freeman. Again, white women are exempted from labor generally, but negro women are not. In this, then, the southern States have an advantage as the article now stands. It has sometimes been said that slavery is necessary, because the commodities they raise would be too dear for market if cultivated by freemen; but now it is said that the labor of the slave is the dearest.

MR. PAYNE urged the original resolution of Congress to proportion the quotas of the States to the number of souls.

DR. WITHERSPOON was of opinion that the value of lands and houses was the best estimate of the wealth of a nation, and that it was practicable to obtain such a valuation. This is the true barometer of wealth. The one now proposed is imperfect in itself and unequal between the States. It has been objected that negroes eat the food of freemen and therefore should be taxed: horses also eat the food of freemen; therefore they also should be taxed. It has been said, too, that, in carrying slaves into the estimate of the taxes the State is to pay, we do no more than those States themselves do who always take slaves into the estimate of the taxes the individual is to pay. But the cases are not parallel. In the southern colonies slaves pervade the whole colony; but they do not pervade the whole continent. That, as to the original resolution of Congress, to proportion the quotas according to the souls it was temporary only and related to the moneys heretofore emitted; whereas we are now entering into a new compact and therefore stand on original ground.

The question being put on August 1, the amendment proposed was rejected by the votes of New Hampshire, Massachusetts, Rhode Island, Connecticut, New York, New Jersey, and Pennsylvania, against those of Delaware, Maryland, Virginia, North and South Carolina. Georgia was divided.

The other article was in these words: "Art. XVII: In determining questions, each colony shall have one vote."

July 30, 31, August 1.—Present forty-one members. MR. CHASE observed that this article was the most likely to divide us of any one proposed in the draft then under consideration. That the larger colonies had threatened they would not confederate at all if their weight in Congress should not be equal to the numbers of people they added to the confederacy; while the smaller ones declared against a union if they did not retain an equal vote for the protection of their rights. That it was of the utmost consequence to bring the parties together, as, should we sever from each other, either no foreign power will ally with us at all or the different States will form different alliances and thus increase the horrors of those scenes of civil war and bloodshed which, in such a state of separation and independence, would render us a miserable people. That our importance, our interests, our peace, required that we should confederate, and that mutual sacrifices should be made to effect a compromise of this difficult question. He was of opinion the smaller colonies would lose their rights if they were not in some instances allowed an equal vote, and, therefore, that a discrimination should take place among the questions which would come before Congress. That the smaller States should be secured in all questions concerning life or liberty, and the greater ones in all respecting property. He therefore proposed that, in votes relating to money, the voice of each colony should be proportioned to the number of its inhabitants.

Dr. Franklin thought that the votes should be so proportioned in all cases. He took notice that the Delaware counties had bound up their delegates to disagree to this article. He thought it very extraordinary language to be held by any State that they would not confederate with us unless we would let them dispose of our money. Certainly, if we vote equally, we ought to pay equally; but the smaller States will hardly purchase the privilege at this price. That, had he lived in a State where the representation, originally equal, had become unequal by time and accident, he might have submitted rather than disturb government; but that we should be very wrong to set out in this practice when it is in our power to establish what is right. That at the time of the union between England and Scotland the latter had made the objection which the smaller States now do, but experience had proved that no unfairness had ever been shown them; that their advocates had prognosticated that it would again happen, as in times of old, that the whale would swallow Jonah; but he thought the prediction reversed in event and that Jonah had swallowed the whale; for the Scotch had, in fact, got possession of the government and gave laws to the English. He reprobated the original agreement of Congress to vote by colonies, and, therefore, was for their voting, in all cases, according to the number of taxables.

Dr. Witherspoon opposed every alteration of the article. All men admit that a confederacy is necessary. Should the idea get abroad that there is likely to be no union among us it will damp the minds of the people, diminish the glory of our struggle, and lessen its importance; because it will open to our view future prospects of war and dissension among ourselves. If an equal vote be refused the smaller States will become vassals to the larger, and all experience has shown that the vassals and subjects of free states are the most enslaved. He instanced the helots of Sparta and the provinces of Rome. He observed that foreign powers, discovering this blemish, would make it a handle for disengaging the smaller States from so unequal a confederacy. That the colonies should, in fact, be considered as individuals; and that, as such, in all disputes they should have an equal vote; that they are now collected as individuals making a bargain with each other, and, of course, had a right to vote as individuals. That in the East India Company they voted by persons and not by their proportion of stock. That the Belgic confederacy voted by provinces. That in questions of war the smaller States were as much interested as the larger and therefore should vote equally; and, indeed, that the larger States were more likely to bring war on the confederacy in proportion as their frontier was more extensive. He admitted that equality of representation was an excellent principle, but then it must be of things which are coördinate, that is, of things similar and of the same nature; that nothing relating to individuals could ever come before Congress; nothing but what would respect colonies. He distinguished between an incorporating and a federal union. The union of England was an incorporating one; yet Scotland had suffered by that union: for that its inhabitants were drawn from it by the hopes of places and employments; nor was it an instance of equality of representation, because, while Scotland was allowed nearly a thirteenth of representation, they were to pay only one-fortieth of the land tax. He expressed his hopes that in the present enlightened state of men's minds we might expect a lasting confederacy if it was founded on fair principles.

JOHN ADAMS advocated the voting in proportion to numbers. He said that we stand here as the representatives of the people; that in some States the people are many, in others they are few; that, therefore, their vote here should be proportioned to the numbers from whom it comes. Reason, justice, and equity never had weight enough on the face of the earth to govern the councils of men. It is interest alone which does it and it is interest alone which can be trusted; that, therefore, the interests within doors should be the mathematical representatives of the interests without doors; that the individuality of the colonies is a mere sound. Does the individuality of a colony increase its wealth or numbers? If it does, pay equally. If it does not add weight in the scale of the confederacy, it cannot add to their rights nor weigh in argument. A has £50, B £500, C £1,000 in partnership. Is it just they should equally dispose of the moneys of the partnership? It has been said we are independent individuals making a bargain together. The question is not what we are now, but what we ought to be when our bargain shall be made. The confederacy is to make us one individual only; it is to form us, like separate parcels of metal, into one common mass. We shall no longer retain our separate individuality, but become a single individual as to all questions submitted to the confederacy. Therefore all those reasons which prove the justice and expediency of equal representation in other assemblies hold good here. It has been objected that a proportional vote will endanger the smaller States. We answer that an equal vote will endanger the larger. Virginia, Pennsylvania, and Massachusetts are the three greater colonies. Consider their distance, their difference of produce, of interests, and of manners, and it is apparent they can never have an interest or inclination to combine for the oppression of the smaller; that the smaller will naturally divide on all questions with the larger. Rhode Island, from its relation, similarity, and intercourse, will generally pursue the same objects with Massachusetts; Jersey, Delaware, and Maryland, with Pennsylvania.

DR. RUSH took notice that the decay of the liberties of the Dutch republic proceeded from three causes: 1. the perfect unanimity requisite on all occasions; 2. their obligation to consult their constituents; 3. their voting by provinces. This last destroyed the equality of representation; and the liberties of Great Britain, also, are sinking from the same defect. That a part of our rights is deposited in the hands of our legislatures. There, it was admitted, there should be an equality of representation. Another part of our rights is deposited in the hands of Congress. Why is it not equally necessary there should be an equal representation there? Were it possible to collect the whole body of the people together they would determine the questions submitted to them by their majority. Why should not the same majority decide when voting here by their representatives? The larger colonies are so providentially divided in situation as to render every fear of their combining visionary. Their interests are different and their circumstances dissimilar. It is more probable they will become rivals and leave it in the power of the smaller States to give preponderance to any scale they please. The voting by the number of free inhabitants will have one excellent effect—that of inducing the colonies to discourage slavery and to encourage the increase of their free inhabitants.

MR. HOPKINS observed there were four larger, four smaller, and four middle sized colonies. That the four largest would contain more than half the inhabitants of the confederating States, and, therefore, would govern the others as they should please. That history affords no instance of such a thing as equal representation. The Germanic body votes by states; the Helvetic body does the same; and so does the Belgic confederacy. That too little is known of the ancient confederations to say what was their practice.

MR. WILSON thought that taxation should be in proportion to wealth, but that representation should accord with the number of freemen. That government is a collection or result of the wills of all; that if any government could speak the will of all it would be perfect; and that, so far as it departs from this, it becomes imperfect. It has been said that Congress is a representation of States, not of individuals. I say that the objects of its care are all the individuals of the States. It is strange that annexing the name of "state" to ten thousand men should give them an equal right with forty thousand. This must be the effect of magic not of reason. As to those matters which are referred to Congress, we are not so many States; we are one large state. We lay aside our individuality whenever we come here. The Germanic body is a burlesque on government, and their practice on any point is a sufficient authority and proof that it is wrong. The greatest imperfection in the constitution of the Belgic confederacy is their voting by provinces. The interest of the whole is constantly sacrificed to that of the small states. The history of the war in the reign of Queen Anne sufficiently proves this. It is asked: Shall nine colonies put it into the power of four to govern them as they please? I invert the question and ask: Shall two millions of people put it into the power of one million to govern them as they please? It is pretended, too, that the smaller colonies will be in danger from the greater. Speak in honest language and say: the minority will be in danger from the majority. And is there an assembly on earth where this danger may not be equally pretended? The truth is that our proceedings will then be consentaneous with the interests of the majority, and so they ought to be. The probability is much greater that the larger States will disagree than that they will combine. I defy the wit of man to invent a possible case, or to suggest any one thing on earth, which shall be for the interests of Virginia, Pennsylvania, and Massachusetts, and which will not also be for the interests of the other States.

The Articles of Confederation were debated from day to day, and time to time, for two years. On November 17, 1777, Congress, then in session at York, Pa., sent copies of the plan of Confederation to the legislatures of the States, and urged their early action upon it, saying:

"More than any other consideration it will confound our foreign enemies, defeat the flagitious practices of the disaffected, strengthen and confirm our friends, support our public credit, restore the value of our money, enable us to maintain our fleets and armies, and add weight and respect to our councils at home and to our treaties abroad.

"In short, this salutary measure can no longer be deferred. It seems essential to our very existence as a free people; and, without it, we may soon be constrained to bid adieu to independence, to liberty, and safety—blessings which, from the justice of our cause, and the favor of our Almighty Creator visibly manifested in our protection, we have reason to expect, if, in an humble dependence on His divine providence, we strenuously exert the means which are placed in our power.'

The Articles were ratified on July 9, 1778, by eight States; but the ratifications were not completed until January 30, 1781, when Maryland, the last State to give her assent, empowered her delegates to subscribe and ratify the Articles. Congress assembled on the 2d of March under the new powers.

The following is the text of the Articles:

THE ARTICLES OF CONFEDERATION

TO ALL TO WHOM THESE PRESENTS SHALL COME,

We, the undersigned, Delegates of the States affixed to our names, send greeting:

WHEREAS the delegates of the United States of America in Congress assembled, did, on the fifteenth day of November, in the year of our Lord one thousand seven hundred and seventy-seven, and in the second year of the Independence of America, agree to certain Articles of Confederation and Perpetual Union, between the States[1] of New Hampshire, Massachusetts Bay, Rhode Island, and Providence Plantations, Connecticut, New York, New Jersey, Pennsylvania, Delaware, Maryland, Virginia, North Carolina, South Carolina, and Georgia, in the words following, viz.:

[1] The initial of "States" is not capitalized anywhere in the original.

*Articles of Confederation and Perpetual Union, between the
States of New Hampshire, Massachusetts Bay, Rhode Is-
land, and Providence Plantations, Connecticut, New York,
New Jersey, Pennsylvania, Delaware, Maryland, Virginia,
North Carolina, South Carolina, and Georgia.*

Article 1.   The style of this confederacy shall be, "The
United States of America."

Art. 2.   Each State retains its sovereignty, freedom, and independence, and every power, jurisdiction, and right, which is
not by this Confederation expressly delegated to the United
States in Congress assembled.

Art. 3.   The said States hereby severally enter into a firm
league of friendship with each other for their common defence,
the security of their liberties, and their mutual and general welfare; binding themselves to assist each other against all force
offered to, or attacks made upon, them, or any of them, on account of religion, sovereignty, trade, or any other pretence
whatever.

Art. 4.   The better to secure and perpetuate mutual friendship and intercourse among the people of the different States in
this Union, the free inhabitants of each of these States—paupers,
vagabonds, and fugitives from justice, excepted—shall be entitled to all privileges and immunities of free citizens in the several States; and the people of each State shall have free ingress
and regress to and from any other State, and shall enjoy therein
all the privileges of trade and commerce, subject to the same
duties, impositions, and restrictions as the inhabitants thereof,
respectively, provided that such restrictions shall not extend
so far as to prevent the removal of property imported into any
State from any other State, of which the owner is an inhabitant;
provided, also, that no imposition, duty, or restriction shall be
laid by any State on the property of the United States, or either
of them.

If any person guilty of, or charged with, treason, felony, or
other high misdemeanor in any State shall flee from justice and
be found in any of the United States, he shall, upon demand of
the governor or executive power of the State from which he
fled, be delivered up and removed to the State having jurisdiction of his offence.

Full faith and credit shall be given in each of these States to
the records, acts, and judicial proceedings of the courts and magistrates of every other State.

Art. 5.   For the more convenient management of the general
interests of the United States, delegates shall be annually ap-

pointed in such manner as the legislature of each State shall direct, to meet in Congress on the first Monday in November, in every year, with a power reserved to each State to recall its delegates, or any of them, at any time within the year, and to send others in their stead for the remainder of the year.

No State shall be represented in Congress by less than two, nor by more than seven members; and no person shall be capable of being a delegate for more than three years in any term of six years; nor shall any person, being a delegate, be capable of holding any office under the United States, for which he, or another for his benefit, receives any salary, fees, or emolument of any kind.

Each State shall maintain its own delegates in a meeting of the States, and while they act as members of the committee of the States.

In determining questions in the United States in Congress assembled, each State shall have one vote.

Freedom of speech and debate in Congress shall not be impeached or questioned in any court or place out of Congress; and the members of Congress shall be protected in their persons from arrests and imprisonments during the time of their going to and from, and attendance on, Congress, except for treason, felony, or breach of the peace.

Art. 6.   No State, without the consent of the United States in Congress assembled, shall send any embassy to, or receive any embassy from, or enter into any conference, agreement, alliance, or treaty, with any king, prince, or state; nor shall any person holding any office of profit or trust under the United States, or any of them, accept of any present, emolument, office, or title, of any kind whatever, from any king, prince, or foreign state; nor shall the United States in Congress assembled, or any of them, grant any title of nobility.

No two or more States shall enter into any treaty, confederation, or alliance whatever between them without consent of the United States in Congress assembled, specifying accurately the purposes for which the same is to be entered into, and how long it shall continue.

No State shall lay any imposts or duties which may interfere with any stipulations in treaties entered into by the United States in Congress assembled with any king, prince, or state, in pursuance of any treaties already proposed by Congress to the courts of France and Spain.

No vessel of war shall be kept up in time of peace by any State, except such number only as shall be deemed necessary by the United States in Congress assembled for the defence of such State, or its trade; nor shall any body of forces be kept up by any State in time of peace, except such number only as, in the judgment of the United States in Congress assembled, shall be deemed requisite to garrison the forts necessary for the defence of such State; but every State shall always keep up a well-regulated and disciplined militia, sufficiently armed and accoutred, and shall provide and have constantly ready for use in public stores a due number of field-pieces and tents and a proper quantity of arms, ammunition, and camp equipage.

No State shall engage in any war without the consent of the United States in Congress assembled, unless such State be actually invaded by enemies, or shall have received certain advice of a resolution being formed by some nation of Indians to invade such State, and the danger is so imminent as not to admit of a delay till the United States in Congress assembled can be consulted;; nor shall any State grant commissions to any ships or vessels of war, nor letters of marque or reprisal, except it be after a declaration of war by the United States in Congress assembled, and then only against the kingdom or state, and the subjects thereof, against which war has been so declared, and under such regulations as shall be established by the United States in Congress assembled, unless such State be infested by pirates; in which case, vessels of war may be fitted out for that occasion and kept so long as the danger shall continue, or until the United States in Congress assembled shall determine otherwise.

Art. 7. When land forces are raised by any State for the common defence, all officers of or under the rank of colonel shall be appointed by the legislature of each State, respectively, by whom such forces shall be raised, or in such manner as such State shall direct; and all vacancies shall be filled up by the State which first made the appointment.

Art. 8. All charges of war, and all other expenses that shall be incurred for the common defence or general warfare, and allowed by the United States in Congress assembled, shall be defrayed out of a common treasury, which shall be supplied by the several States, in proportion to the value of all land within each State, granted to or surveyed for any person, as such land, and the buildings and improvements thereon, shall be estimated, according to such mode as the United States in Congress assembled shall, from time to time, direct and appoint.

The taxes for paying that proportion shall be laid and levied by the authority and direction of the legislatures of the several

States within the time agreed upon by the United States in Congress assembled.

Art. 9. The United States in Congress assembled shall have the sole and exclusive right and power of determining on peace and war, except in the cases mentioned in the sixth article—of sending and receiving ambassadors—entering into treaties and alliances; provided that no treaty of commerce shall be made whereby the legislative power of the respective States shall be restrained from imposing such imposts and duties on foreigners as their own people are subjected to, or from prohibiting the exportation or importation of any species of goods or commodities whatsoever—of establishing rules for deciding, in all cases, what captures, on land or water, shall be legal, and in what manner prizes taken by land or naval forces in the service of the United States shall be divided or appropriated—of granting letters of marque and reprisal in times of peace—appointing courts for the trial of piracies and felonies committed on the high seas, and establishing courts for receiving and determining finally appeals in all cases of capture; provided that no member of Congress shall be appointed a judge of any of the said courts.

The United States in Congress assembled shall also be the last resort on appeal in all disputes and differences now subsisting, or that hereafter may arise, between two or more States concerning boundary, jurisdiction, or any other cause whatever; which authority shall always be exercised in the manner following: Whenever the legislative or executive authority, or lawful agent, of any State in controversy with another shall present a petition to Congress stating the matter in question and praying for a hearing, notice thereof shall be given by order of Congress to the legislative or executive authority of the other State in controversy, and a day assigned for the appearance of the parties by their lawful agents, who shall then be directed to appoint, by joint consent, commissioners or judges to constitute a court for hearing and determining the matter in question; but if they cannot agree Congress shall name three persons out of each of the United States, and from the list of such persons each party shall alternately strike out one, the petitioners beginning, until the number shall be reduced to thirteen; and from that number not less than seven nor more than nine names, as Congress shall direct, shall, in the presence of Congress, be drawn out by lot; and the persons whose names shall be so drawn, or any five of them, shall be commissioners or judges, to hear and finally determine the controversy, so always as a major part of the judges, who shall hear the cause, shall agree in the determination; and, if either party shall neglect to attend at the day appointed, without showing reason which Congress shall judge sufficient, or, being present, shall refuse to strike, the Congress shall proceed to nominate three persons out of each State, and the secretary of Congress shall strike in behalf of such party absent or refusing; and the judgment and sentence of the court, to be appointed in the manner before prescribed, shall be final and conclusive; and, if any of the parties shall refuse to submit to the authority of such court, or to appear or defend their claim or cause, the court shall nevertheless proceed to pronounce sentence or judgment, which shall, in like manner, be final and decisive—the judgment or sentence, and other proceedings, being in either case transmitted to Congress, and lodged among the acts of Congress for the security of the parties concerned; provided that every commissioner, before he sits in judgment, shall take an oath, to be administered by one of the judges of the supreme or superior court of the State where the cause shall be tried, *"well and truly to hear and determine the matter in question, according to the best of his judgment, without favor, affection, or hope of reward"*: provided, also, that no State shall be deprived of territory for the benefit of the United States.

All controversies concerning the private right of soil, claimed under different grants of two or more States, whose jurisdiction, as they may respect such lands, and the States which passed such grants, are adjusted, the said grants, or either of them, being at the same time claimed to have originated antecedent to such settlement of jurisdiction, shall, on the petition of either party to the Congress of the United States, be finally determined, as near as may be, in the same manner as is before prescribed for deciding disputes respecting territorial jurisdiction between different States.

The United States in Congress assembled shall also have the sole and exclusive right and power of regulating the alloy and value of coin struck by their own authority, or by that of the respective States; fixing the standard of weights and measures throughout the United States; regulating the trade and managing all affairs with the Indians not members of any of the States, provided that the legislative right of any State within its own limits be not infringed or violated; establishing and regulating post-offices from one State to another throughout all the United States, and exacting such postage on the papers passing through the same as may be requisite to defray the expenses of the said office; appointing all officers of the land forces in the service of the United States, excepting regimental officers; appointing all the officers of the naval forces, and commissioning all officers whatever in the service of the United States; making rules for the government and regulation of the said land and naval forces, and directing their operations.

The United States in Congress assembled shall have authority to appoint a committee to sit in the recess of Congress, to be denominated "a committee of the States," and to consist of one delegate from each State; and to appoint such other committees and civil officers as may be necessary for managing the general affairs of the United States under their direction—to appoint one of their number to preside, provided that no person be allowed to serve in the office of president more than one year in any term of three years—to ascertain the necessary sums of money to be raised for the service of the United States, and to appropriate and apply the same for defraying the public expenses—to borrow money or emit bills on the credit of the United States, transmitting, every half year, to the respective States an account of the sums of money so borrowed or emitted—to build and equip a navy—to agree upon the number of land forces, and to make requisition from each State for its quota, in proportion to the number of white inhabitants in such State; which requisitions shall be binding; and thereupon the legislature of each State shall appoint the regimental officers, raise the men, and clothe, arm, and equip them in a soldier-like manner, at the expense of the United States; and the officers and men so clothed, armed, and equipped shall march to the place appointed, and within the time agreed on by the United States in Congress assembled: but, if the United States in Congress assembled shall, on consideration of circumstances, judge proper that any State should not raise men, or should raise a smaller number than its quota, and that any other State should raise a greater number of men than the quota thereof, such extra number shall be raised, officered, clothed, armed, and equipped in the same manner as the quota of such State, unless the legislature of such State shall judge that such extra number cannot be safely spared out of the same; in which case they shall raise, officer, clothe, arm, and equip as many of such extra number as they judge can be safely spared. And the officers and men so clothed, armed, and equipped shall march to the place appointed and within the time agreed on by the United States in Congress assembled.

The United States in Congress assembled shall never engage in a war; nor grant letters of marque and reprisal in time of peace; nor enter into any treaties or alliances; nor coin money; nor regulate the value thereof; nor ascertain the sums and expenses necessary for the defence and welfare of the United States, or any of them; nor emit bills; nor borrow money on the credit of the United States; nor appropriate money; nor agree upon the number of vessels of war to be built or purchased, or the number of land or sea forces to be raised; nor appoint a commander-in-chief of the army or navy—unless nine States assent to the same; nor shall a question on any other point, except for adjourning from day to day, be determined unless by the votes of a majority of the United States in Congress assembled.

The Congress of the United States shall have power to adjourn to any time within the year, and to any place within the United States, so that no period of adjournment be for a longer duration than the space of six months; and shall publish the journal of their proceedings monthly, except such parts thereof relating to treaties, alliances, or military operations as, in their judgment, require secrecy; and the yeas and nays of the delegates of each State on any question shall be entered on the journal when it is desired by any delegate; and the delegates of a State, or any of them, at his or their request, shall be furnished with a transcript of the said journal, except such parts as are above excepted, to lay before the legislatures of the several States.

Art. 10. The committee of the States, or any nine of them, shall be authorized to execute, in the recess of Congress, such of the powers of Congress as the United States in Congress assembled, by the consent of nine States, shall, from time to time, think expedient to vest them with, provided that no power be delegated to the said committee for the exercise of which, by the Articles of Confederation, the voice of nine States in the Congress of the United States assembled is requisite.

Art. 11. Canada, acceding to this Confederation, and joining in the measures of the United States, shall be admitted into, and entitled to, all the advantages of this union; but no other colony shall be admitted into the same unless such admission be agreed to by nine States.

Art. 12. All bills of credit emitted, moneys borrowed, and debts contracted, by or under the authority of Congress, before the assembling of the United States in pursuance of the present Confederation, shall be deemed and considered as a charge against the United States, for payment and satisfaction whereof the said United States, and the public faith, are hereby solemnly pledged.

Art. 13. Every State shall abide by the determination of the United States in Congress assembled, on all questions which, by this Confederation, are submitted to them. And the articles of this Confederation shall be inviolably observed by every State, and the union shall be perpetual; nor shall any alteration at any time hereafter be made in any of them, unless such alteration be agreed to in a Congress of the United States, and be afterward confirmed by the legislature of every State.

RATIFICATION.

And whereas it has pleased the Great Governor of the world to incline the hearts of the legislatures we respectively represent in Congress to approve of and to authorize us to ratify the said Articles of Confederation and Perpetual Union: *Know ye,* That we, the undersigned delegates, by virtue of the power and authority to us given for that purpose, do, by these presents, in the name and in behalf of our respective constituents, fully and entirely ratify and confirm each and every of the said Articles of Confederation and Perpetual Union, and all and singular the matters and things therein contained; and we do further solemnly plight and engage the faith of our respective constituents that they shall abide by the determinations of the United States in Congress assembled on all questions which by the said Confederation are submitted to them, and that the articles thereof shall be inviolably observed by the States we respectively represent; and that the union shall be perpetual.

In witness whereof, we have hereunto set our hands, in Congress. Done at Philadelphia, in the State of Pennsylvania, the ninth day of July, in the year of our Lord one thousand seven hundred and seventy-eight, and in the third year of the Independence of America.

On July 4, 1778, Dr. David Ramsay delivered at Charleston, S. C., an eloquent and scholarly oration, in which he dwelt particularly upon the advantages which would result to the States from their recent adoption of new constitutions, and the confederacy which they had adopted to maintain their common independence. It was afterward published with a dedication to Governor Christopher Gadsden as one who, "fearless of danger, undaunted by opposition, uninfluenced by the hope of reward, in the worst of times, has stood among the foremost, an early, active, zealous, disinterested champion in the cause of American Liberty and Independence."

Owing to its revelation of the light in which the question of sovereignty was viewed by one who was born and educated in the North, where also he was engaged in his profession, and who had entered into both professional and political activities in the South, the oration is a most significant document in its bearing upon the State Rights issue.

The following text of the speech is but a small portion of the address, since only those extracts are presented which bear upon constitutional matters.

Our Independent Constitutions

DR. DAVID RAMSAY

We are the first people in the world who have had it in their power to choose their own form of government. Constitutions were forced on all other nations by the will of their conquerors, or they were formed by accident, caprice, or the overbearing influence of prevailing parties or particular persons. But, happily for us, the bands of British Government were dissolved at a time when no rank above that of freemen existed among us, and when we were in a capacity to choose for ourselves among the various forms of government, and to adopt that which best suited our country and people. Our deliberations on this occasion were not directed by the overgrown authority of a conquering general, or the ambition of an aspiring nobility, but by the pole star of public good, inducing us to prefer those forms that would most effectually secure the greatest portion of political happiness to the greatest number of people. We had the example of all ages for our instruction, and many among us were well acquainted with the causes of prosperity and misery in other governments.

In times of public tranquillity, the mighty have been too apt to encroach on the rights of the many, but it is the great happiness of America that her independent constitutions were agreed upon by common consent at a time when her leading men needed the utmost support of the multitude, and therefore could have no other object in view but the formation of such constitutions as would best suit the people at large, and unite them most heartily in repelling common dangers.

As the strength of a people consists in their numbers, our separate States, sensible of their weakness, were actually excited by self-interest to form such free governments as would encourage the greatest influx of inhabitants. In this manner an emulation has virtually taken place in all the thirteen States, each contending with the others who should form the freest constitution. Thus independence has been the fruitful parent of governments formed on equal principles, more favorable to the liberty and happiness of the governed than any that have yet been recorded in the annals of history.

. . . .

Our independent constitutions, formed on the justest principles, promise fair to give the most perfect protection to life, liberty, and property, equally to the poor and the rich. As at the conflagration of Corinth, the various melted metals running together formed a new one called Corinthian brass, which was superior to any of its component parts; in like manner, perhaps, it is the will of Heaven that a new empire should be here formed of the different nations of the old world which will rise superior to all that have gone before it and extend human happiness to its utmost possible limits. None can tell to what perfection the arts of government may be brought. May we not therefore expect great things from the patriots of this generation, jointly coöperating to make the new-born Republic of America as complete as possible? Is it not to be hoped that human nature will here receive her most finished touches? That the arts and sciences will be extended and improved? That religion, learning, and liberty will be diffused over this continent? and, in short, that the American editions of the human mind will be more perfect than any that have yet appeared? Great things have been achieved in the infancy of states; and the ardor of a new people rising to empire and renown with prospects that tend to elevate the human soul encourages these flattering expectations.

Should any puny politician object that all these prospects are visionary, till we are certain of independence, I reply that we have been in possession of it for two years and are daily more able to support it, and our enemies less able to overset it. When we first dared to contend with Britain we were a loose, disjointed people under no other government but that of a well-regulated mob. If, in these circumstances we were able to defend ourselves, what may we not expect when we can draw forth our whole strength in a regular constitutional manner? If the maiden courage of our new levies has successfully withstood the well-trained bands of our enemies, can we distrust when three campaigns have made them equal in

· discipline with those with whom they are to contend? Such is the situation of Britain that, were we only able to keep up the appearance of an army, she could not afford to protract the war. But, instead of this, our troops are more numerous, better disciplined, clothed, and armed than they ever were. The most timid may dismiss all their doubts since Louis XVI of France, that illustrious protector of the rights of human nature, with a magnanimity worthy of himself, has guaranteed to us our independence. If Britain could not subdue America when she stood single and alone, how abortive must all her attempts prove when we are aided by the power of the greatest European monarch?

The special interposition of Providence in our behalf makes it impious to disbelieve the final establishment of our heaven-protected independence. Can any one seriously review the beginning, progress, and present state of the war and not see indisputable evidence of an overruling influence on the minds of men preparing the way for the accomplishment of this great event?

As all the tops of corn in a waving field are inclined in one direction by a gust of wind, in like manner the Governor of the World has given one and the same universal bent of inclination to the whole body of our people. Is it a work of man that thirteen States, frequently quarreling about boundaries, clashing in interests, differing in policy, manners, customs, forms of government, and religion, scattered over an extensive continent, under the influence of a variety of local prejudices, jealousies, and aversions, should all harmoniously agree, as if one mighty mind inspired the whole?

Our enemies seemed confident of the impossibility of our union; our friends doubted it, and all indifferent persons who judged of things present by what has heretofore happened considered the expectation thereof as romantic; but He who sitteth at the helm of the universe, and who boweth the hearts of a whole nation as the heart of one man, for the accomplishment of His own purposes, has effected that which to human wisdom and foresight seemed impossible. A review of the history of America, from its first discovery to the present day, forces upon us a belief that greater blessings are reserved for this continent than she ever could have possessed while lying low at the foot of an European island.

· · · · · · · · · · · ·

We have laid the foundations of a new empire which promises to enlarge itself to vast dimensions and to give happiness to a great continent. It is now our turn to figure on the face of the earth and in the annals of the world. The arts and sciences are planted among us, and, fostered by the auspicious influence of equal governments, are growing up to maturity, while truth and freedom flourish by their sides. Liberty, both civil and religious, in her noontide blaze shines forth with unclouded luster on all ranks and denominations of men.

Ever since the Flood true religion, literature, arts, empire, and riches have taken a slow and gradual course from east to west, and are now about fixing their long and favorite abode in this new western world. Our sun of political happiness is already risen, and hath lifted its head over the mountains, illuminating our hemisphere with liberty, light, and polished life. Our independence will redeem one-quarter of the globe from tyranny and oppression and consecrate it to the chosen seat of truth, justice, freedom, learning, and religion. We are laying the foundation of happiness for countless millions. Generations yet unborn will bless us for the blood-bought inheritance we are about to bequeath them. Oh happy times! Oh glorious days! Oh kind, indulgent, bountiful Providence, that we live in this highly favored period, and have the honor of helping forward these great events, and of suffering in a cause of such infinite importance!

PROPOSAL FOR NATIONAL REVENUE

One of the first matters which claimed the attention of Congress after the treaty of peace was the restoration of public credit and the establishment of funds for the payment of the debts incurred by the war.

Congress turned to customs duties as the most available means of securing funds to care for these obligations. It had, however, no power to levy a tariff without the assent of all the States.

After much debate, on the 18th of April, 1783, it recommended to the States to vest Congress with power to levy certain specified duties on spirits, wines, teas, pepper, sugar, molasses, cocoa, and coffee, and a flat duty of five per cent. *ad valorem* on all other imported goods.

These duties were to be applied solely to the payment of the interest and principal of the public debt, and for that purpose they were to continue twenty-five years; the collectors to be chosen by the States, but to be removable by Congress.

The States were also required to establish for the same time, and for the same object, substantial and effectual revenues of such nature as they should judge convenient; the proportion of each State to be fixed according to the number of white and other free citizens, including those bound to servitude for a term of years, and three-fifths of all other persons.

This system was not to take effect until acceded to by every State, and when adopted by all to be a mutual compact among the States, and irrevocable by anyone without the consent of the whole or of a majority of the United States in Congress.

To enforce the importance and necessity of adopting and carrying into effect this system of finance, Congress presented an address to the States. This was prepared by a committee consisting of Oliver Ellsworth, James Madison, and Alexander Hamilton.

AN APPEAL TO NATIONAL HONOR

BY CONGRESS

After explaining the system itself, the address prepared for Congress by Ellsworth, Madison, and Hamilton appealed to the gratitude and pride, as well as justice and plighted faith of the nation. It urged particularly the propriety of the provision recommended for the payment of the national debt. "If other motives than that of justice," it said, "could be requisite, on this occasion, no nation could ever feel stronger; for to whom are the debts to be paid?

To an ally, in the first place, who, to the exertion of his armies in support of our cause, has added the succors of his treasure; who, to his important loans, has added liberal donations; and whose loans themselves carry the impression of his magnanimity and friendship.

To individuals in a foreign country, in the next place, who were the first to give so precious a token of their confidence in our justice, and of their friendship for our cause, and who are members of a republic which was second in espousing our rank among nations.

Another class of creditors is that illustrious and patriotic band of fellow citizens, whose blood and whose bravery have defended the liberties of their country, who have patiently borne, among other distresses, the privation of their stipends, while the distresses of their country disabled it from bestowing them, and who even now ask for no more than such a portion of their dues as will enable them to retire from the field of glory into the bosom of peace and private citizenship, and for such effectual security for the residue of their claims as their country is now unquestionably able to provide.

The remaining class of creditors is composed partly of such of our fellow citizens as originally lent to the public the use of their funds, or have since manifested most confidence in their country by receiving transfers from the lenders, and partly of those whose property has been either advanced or assumed for the public service. To discriminate the merits of these several descriptions of creditors would be a task equally unnecessary and invidious. If the voice of humanity plead more loudly in favor of some than of others, the voice of policy, no less than justice, pleads in favor of all. A wise nation will never permit those who relieve the wants of their country, or who rely most on its faith, its firmness, and its resources, when either of them is distrusted, to suffer by the event.

Let it be remembered finally that it has ever been the pride and boast of America that the rights for which she contended were the rights of human nature. By the blessing of the author of these rights, or the means exerted for their defence, they have prevailed against all opposition, and form the basis of thirteen independent States. No instance has heretofore occurred, nor can any instance be expected hereafter to occur, in which the unadulterated forms of republican government can pretend to so fair an opportunity of justifying themselves by their fruits. In this view the citizens of the United States are responsible for the greatest trust ever confided to a political society.

If justice, good faith, honor, gratitude, and all other qualities which ennoble the character of a nation and fulfill the ends of government be the fruits of our establishments, the cause of liberty will acquire a dignity and luster which it has never yet enjoyed, and an example will be set which cannot but have the most favorable influence on the rights of mankind.

If, on the other side, our government should be unfortunately blotted with the reverse of these cardinal and essential virtues, the great cause which we have engaged to vindicate will be dishonored and betrayed; the last and fairest experiment in favor of the rights of human nature will be turned against them, and their patrons and friends exposed to be insulted and silenced by the votaries of tyranny and usurpation.

WASHINGTON ON A STABLE GOVERNMENT

' The propriety and necessity of adopting this system were strongly pressed upon the States by General Washington in a circular letter dated June 8, 1783, giving notice of his intended resignation, and congratulating the States on the happy termination of the war, and on the numerous advantages and blessings which, as a free and independent nation, they had now a right to expect. Having in the course of the war experienced, and at times too fatally experienced, the evils arising from a failure, on the part of the States, to comply with the requisitions of Congress, he reminded them that whether these advantages and blessings would be realized depended, in a great measure, on themselves, on their prompt and mutual coöperation in promoting the great interests of the Union. He considered four things as essentially necessary to the existence of the United States as an independent power.

1. An indissoluble union of the States under one federal head.

2. A sacred regard to justice.

3. The adoption of a proper peace establishment.

4. The prevalence of that pacific and friendly disposition, among the people of the United States, which would induce them to forget their local prejudices and policies, to make those mutual concessions which were requisite to the general prosperity; and, in some instances, to sacrifice their individual advantages to the interest of the community.

Failure of the Plan

This plan, however, though thus ably supported and recommended, was never accepted by the States in such a manner as to go into operation. The pressure of common danger being removed, the bond of federal union became weak and feeble, and the inefficiency of the national government more apparent. A jealousy between the State and general governments began to exist; and State interests predominated. The importing States levied contributions on their neighbors for their own benefit, and some of them would not relinquish the advantages of their local situation. Congress, indeed, had power to make treaties with foreign nations, but none to enforce the observance of them; they had power to contract debts, but were unable to enforce the collection of money for the payment of them. For this they were dependent on the will of thirteen distinct legislative bodies.

That part of the financial plan which required from the States a pledge of internal revenues for twenty-five years met with the greatest opposition. Congress was at length satisfied that a general compliance with this part of the system was not to be expected, and confined its requests to that relating to duties on imports. In 1786 all the States except New York had complied with this part of the system. The operation of the acts passed by some of the States, however, depended on similar acts from the others. The State of New York, instead of vesting Congress with the power of levying the duties, reserved this right to itself agreeably to a law passed in 1784; and also refused to make the collectors amenable to and removable by Congress.

While this system of revenue was under the consideration of the States, Congress could do nothing more than make requisitions, and, as these were not complied with, the interest of the domestic debt remained unpaid; and the money borrowed in Europe was applied to the payment of interest on foreign loans. In this situation the domestic debt was deemed of little value, and was sold for about one-tenth of its nominal amount.

Commercial Negotiations with Great Britain

Soon after the ratification of the treaty with Great Britain, Congress turned their attention to the subject of commercial intercourse with that nation.

But Great Britain refused to enter into a commercial treaty. Her statesmen could not be persuaded that the Americans would ever be united among themselves, or be able to form any lasting or beneficial engagements with other nations, not only for want of union, but from opposing interests, and from the imperfect powers of their general government. On this subject Lord Sheffield no doubt spoke the language of Englishmen in general when he said, in his "Observations on the Commerce of the American States":

It will not be an easy matter to bring the American States to act as a nation; *they are not to be feared as such by us.* . . . Their climate, their staples, their manners are different; their interests opposite, and that which is beneficial to one is destructive to the other. . . . In short, every circumstance proves that it will be extreme folly to enter into any engagements *by which we may not wish to be bound hereafter.* . . . No treaty can be made with the American States that can be binding on the whole of them. The act of confederation does not enable Congress to form more than *general treaties*—at the moment of the highest authority of Congress the power in question was withheld by the several States. No treaty that could be made could suit the different interests. When treaties are necessary, they must be made with the States respectively. Each State has reserved every power relative to imports, exports, prohibitions, duties, etc., to itself. But no treaty at present is necessary. We trade with several very considerable nations without commercial treaties.

In accordance with this policy, in July, 1783, the British Government issued orders in council for regulating the trade between the United States and the British dominions. American vessels thereby were entirely excluded from the British West Indies; and certain articles from the States such as fish, beef, pork, etc., were not allowed to be carried there, even in British bottoms. This prohibition was continued by temporary acts until

1788, when it was permanently established by act of Parliament.

Difficulties with Great Britain were not confined to regulations respecting commerce. Serious disputes soon arose concerning the execution of the treaty of peace; and each nation complained of infractions by the other.

Congress, in order to remove the difficulties complained of, in March, 1787, unanimously declared that all the acts, or parts of acts, existing in any of the States, repugnant to the treaty of peace, ought to be repealed; and they recommended to the States to make such repeal by a general law. They at the same time unanimously resolved "that the legislatures of the several States cannot of right pass any act or acts for interpreting, explaining, or construing a national treaty or any part or clause of it; nor for restraining, limiting, or in any manner impeding, retarding, or contracting the operation and execution of the same; for that, on being constitutionally made, ratified, and published, they become, in virtue of the Confederation, part of the law of the land, and are not only independent of the will and power of such legislatures, but also binding and obligatory on them."

In consequence of these declarations the States having laws against the treaty abolished these, save Virginia, which did so provisionally upon Great Britain fulfilling her obligations, and South Carolina, which observed that the subjects of Great Britain had encountered no other difficulties, or impediments, in the recovery of their debts, than had the citizens of America; that such was the situation of the State the legislature had conceived it necessary to pass laws tantamount to shutting the courts.

The British court was not yet disposed to enter into any commercial treaty with the United States, the ministers being, no doubt, satisfied that the advantages they enjoyed under their own regulations were greater than could be obtained by any treaty they could make with America.

Organization of the North-West Territory

The people of the United States had viewed the Western lands as a fund to aid in the payment of the national debt. Congress, therefore, in April, 1783, called upon those States who had not yet complied with their former requests on this subject to make liberal cessions of their territorial claims.

After a great deal of controversy the States claiming Western lands ceded these to the Federal Government; and Congress, in July, 1787, organized the North-West Territory, composed of the region now occupied by the States of Ohio, Indiana, Illinois, Michigan, and Wisconsin, establishing an ordinance for its government. This ordinance remains the basis of the governments established by Congress in all the Territories of the United States. By it Congress established certain articles of *compact,* between the original States and the people in the territory, and which were to remain unalterable, unless by common consent. By these no person in the territory was ever to be molested on account of his mode of worship or religious sentiments; and every person was entitled to the benefits of the writ of habeas corpus, trial by jury, and all those other fundamental rights usually inserted in American bills of rights. Schools and the means of education were forever to be encouraged, and the utmost good faith to be observed toward the Indians; particularly their lands and property were never to be taken from them without their consent. The territory, and the States that might be formed therein, were forever to remain a part of the American confederacy; but not less than three nor more than five States were to be established.

It was also provided that, whenever in any of those States there should be sixty thousand free inhabitants, such State was to be admitted into the Union, on the same footing with the original States in all respects whatever; and be at liberty to form a permanent constitution and State government; such constitution and government, however, was to be republican and conformable to the principles of the articles. If consistent with the general interest of the confederation, such State, however, might be admitted as a member of the Union with a less number than sixty thousand free inhabitants.

By the last article it was provided there should be neither slavery nor involuntary servitude in the Territory otherwise than in the punishment of crimes, of which the party should have been duly convicted.[1]

Financial Distress of the States

While Congress was thus forming a government for the Territory and laying the foundation of future new States at the west, it had lost all authority over the old States at the east. Many causes combined, at this period, to produce great distress, discontent, and disaffection in different parts of the Union. The General Government, as before stated, was totally inefficient, and the authority of the State governments greatly weakened, and in some instances almost destroyed.

In addition to the debts of the Union, the States individually had also incurred large debts during the war, for the payment of which they were called upon by their creditors. Immediately after peace, in consequence of large importations of foreign goods, particularly from Great Britain, large debts were contracted by individuals, and which, from the want of internal as well as external resources, they were unable to pay. The people were pressed at the same time for the payment of the debts of the Union, of the individual States, and of their own private debts. The courts of justice, which had been shut during the war, were filled with private suits. Under these circumstances, some of the States had recourse to the desperate expedient of paper money; others made personal property a tender, at an appraised value, in satisfaction of debts; and, in Massachusetts, not only were the judges in several counties prevented from holding courts, but the Government itself, in other respects, was set at defiance by an open and formidable insurrection of the people (Shay's Rebellion).

[1] Nathan Dane, of Massachusetts, was the author of this article.

Washington on Failure of the Confederacy

The enemies of the Revolution, who had predicted that the Americans, when separated from their parent country, would be unable to govern themselves, but fall into confusion, now secretly rejoiced at the verification of their predictions. Its friends began almost to despair of the commonwealth, and at times were led to doubt whether the people of America were indeed capable of self-government. Some, indeed, suggested that it might be necessary for the country to adopt a monarchical form of government. In reference to this suggestion General Washington said in a letter to John Jay:

What astonishing changes a few years are capable of producing! I am told that even respectable characters speak of a monarchical form of government without horror. From thinking proceeds speaking, thence to acting is often but a single step. But how irrevocable and tremendous! What a triumph for our enemies to verify their predictions! What a triumph for the advocates of despotism to find that we are incapable of governing ourselves, and that systems founded on the basis of equal liberty are merely ideal and fallacious! Would to God that wise measures may be taken in time to avert the consequences we have but too much reason to apprehend.

CHAPTER X

THE CONSTITUTIONAL CONVENTION

[PLANS OF GOVERNMENT]

First Proposal of the Constitution—Pelatiah Webster [Pa.] on Defects of
the Confederation—Webster's Comparison of the Adopted Constitution
with That Which He Had Proposed—George Washington on the Necessary Change in the Federal Government—Resolutions of Virginia—Suggestion of John Jay to Call a Convention to Revise the Articles of Confederation—The Annapolis Convention—It Issues Call for a Constitutional Convention—New York Legislature Votes upon Alexander Hamilton's Resolution to Give Congress Power to Levy Federal Duties on
Imports—His Speech: ''On Granting Taxing Powers to Congress''—
Resolve of Constitutional Convention to Form an Entirely New Government—Plans of Government by Edmund Randolph and Charles Pinckney—Letter of James Madison to Randolph—The Plans Are Referred to
a Committee—Its Resolutions—Plan of William Paterson.

THE Articles of Confederation were the result of an
old order of what might be called colonial statesmanship that was admirably adapted to secure
the *independence* of the several States, but was woefully
inadequate for the still greater task of welding them into
a nation. To save the country from the anarchy into
which it had fallen required a new order of what might
be called national statesmanship in which the lead was
taken by young men and those older persons whose
political activities had begun with the movement for
national independence. Of the younger men of this order, James Madison, Alexander Hamilton, and Charles
Pinckney were the most influential in devising plans of
government in which the principle of federation was subordinated to that of nationality. Of the older representatives, the most influential was a man with a type of mind
new to the country, the politico-economic as distinguished
from the purely political, and whose genius, therefore,

269

was little appreciated and correspondingly unrecognized up to this period—and, indeed, not adequately so until 1911, when probably more than justice was done him by the Hon. Hannis Taylor in his "The Origin and Growth of the American Constitution." This was Pelatiah Webster, to whom Mr. Taylor ascribes the entire merit of "inventing" the plan of the Constitution, and whose book presenting the invention he styles "the epoch-making achievement," which "must forever stand forth as a beacon light in the world's political history."

In October, 1776, Webster published an essay, in which he strongly urged the laying of a tax to provide for the speedy redemption of the continental bills of credit—a plan, however, which could not be followed owing to the fact that the powers of Congress were only advisory, and not mandatory upon the States. Undoubtedly the failure to adopt his plan, and the consequent disaster to the country, directed Webster's attention to the need of recognizing the Federal Government so that it should have the supreme essential of sovereignty— independent power. Though his succeeding work was in the field of economics—"Essays on Free Trade and Finance"—in one of the seven essays contained in this work he proposed the calling of a "Constitutional Convention" for making an entirely new Constitution. This essay was published in May, 1781. Two years later (in February, 1783) Webster "humbly offered to the public" an anonymous "Dissertation on the Political Union and Constitution of the Thirteen United States of North America Which Is Necessary to Their Preservation and Happiness," by "a Citizen of Philadelphia."

The view of Taylor that the American Constitution was an "invention" is held by many other writers, native and foreign, on the subject.

Alexis de Tocqueville, in his book "On Democracy in America" (1835), says of the Constitution that it was based "upon a wholly novel theory which may be considered a great discovery in modern political science. . . . The American States, which combined in 1789, agreed that the Federal Government should not only dictate, but should execute its own enactments. In both cases the right is the same, but the exercise of the right is different; and this difference produced the most momentous consequences.''

And William E. Gladstone said in the same tenor: ''As the British Constitution is the most subtile organism which has proceeded from progressive history, so the American Constitution is the most wonderful work ever struck off at a given time by the brain and purpose of a man.''

Other American historians and students of the origin of the Constitution do not view the plan of the Constitution so much of an ''invention'' as an almost necessary and even obvious development of the conditions of the time, one which arose naturally in the minds of all the constructive (as opposed to initiative) minds which set themselves freshly at work upon the problem. Thus George Ticknor Curtis, in his ''History of the Origin, Formation, and Adoption of the Constitution'' (1854), says: ''The Constitution of the United States was eminently the creature of circumstances—not of circumstances blindly leading the blind to an unconscious submission to an accident, but of circumstances which offered an intelligent choice of the means of happiness, and opened, from the experience of the past, the plain path of duty and success stretching onward to the future.''

According to this view Webster's plan of the Constitution was simply a formulation of the ideas which were ''in the air'' during the period, being generated all over the country by the formation of the State constitutions and applied from these to the obviously needed new Federal Constitution by such constructive minds as James Madison of Virginia, Charles Pinckney of South Carolina, and Alexander Hamilton of New York. Nevertheless Webster is certainly entitled to the credit of presenting the plan first, and in a thoroughly elaborated form.

In a note upon his ''Dissertation,'' published in his collected writings (1791), Webster tells how he came to write the work. It was, he said, because of the failure of the Confederation.

DEFECTS OF THE CONFEDERATION

PELATIAH WEBSTER

Forming a plan of confederation or a system of general government of the United States engrossed the attention of Congress from the Declaration of Independence, July 4, 1776, till the same was completed by Congress, July 9, 1778, and recommended to the several States for ratification, which finally took place March 1, 1781, from which time the said confederation was considered as the grand constitution of the general government, and the whole administration was conformed to it.

And as it had stood the test of discussion in Congress for two years before they completed and adopted it, and in all the States for three years more before it was finally ratified one would have thought that it must have been a very finished and perfect plan of government.

But on trial of it in practice it was found to be extremely weak, defective, totally inefficient, and altogether inadequate to its great ends and purposes, for

1. It blended the legislative and executive powers together in one body.

2. This body, viz.: Congress, consisted of but one house, without any check upon their resolutions.

3. The powers of Congress in very few instances were definite and final; in the most important articles of government they could do no more than recommend to the several States, the consent of every one of which was necessary to give legal sanction to any act so recommended.

4. They could assess and levy no taxes.

5. They could institute and execute no punishments except in the military department.

6. They had no power of deciding or controlling the contentions and disputes of different States with each other.

7. They could not regulate the general trade; or,

8. Even make laws to secure either public treaties with foreign states, or the persons of public ambassadors, or to punish violations or injuries done to either of them.

9. They could institute no general judiciary powers.

10. They could regulate no public roads, canals, or inland navigation, etc., etc., etc.

And what caps all the rest was that (while under such an inefficient political constitution the only chance we had of any tolerable administration lay wholly in the prudence and wisdom of the men who happened to take the lead in our public councils) it was fatally provided by the absurd doctrine of rotation that if any member of Congress by three years' experience and application had qualified himself to manage our public affairs with consistency and fitness, that he should be constitutionally and absolutely rendered incapable of serving any longer, till by three years' discontinuance he had pretty well lost the cue or train of the public counsels and forgot the ideas and plans which made his service useful and important, and in the meantime his place should be supplied by a fresh man who had the whole matter to learn, and when he had learned it was to give place to another fresh man, and so on to the end of the chapter.

The sensible mind of the United States by long experience of the fatal mischief of anarchy, or (which is about the same thing) of this ridiculous inefficient form of government, began to apprehend that there was something wrong in our policy which ought to be redressed and mended, but nobody undertook to delineate the necessary amendments.

I was then pretty much at leisure, and was fully of opinion (though the sentiment at that time would not very well bear) that it would be ten times easier to form a new Constitution than to mend the old one. I therefore sat myself down to sketch out the leading principles of that political constitution which I thought necessary to the preservation and happiness of the United States of America, which are comprised in this Dissertation.

I hope the reader will please consider that these are the original thoughts of a private individual, dictated by the nature of the subject only, long before the important theme became the great object of discussion in the most dignified and important assembly which ever sat or decided in America.

The "Dissertation" is a treatise on the nature of government so sound and searching that, while many of its propositions were not embodied in the Constitution, they all, in one form or another, have arisen as political issues in our national history. Besides the strictly Constitutional proposals there may be mentioned the following subjects of interest and importance to the student of politics:

Trade a chief concern of Government.

Supreme importance of the taxing power.

Retention of efficient officers in the public service

vs. rotation in office (a point in the discussion of Civil Service).

Frequent elections as a check on inefficiency and misconduct of public officers (a point in the discussion of the Recall).

The value of land, being created by population, as a natural and just standard of determining contributions to public revenue (a point in the discussion of the "Single Tax").

Unsettled lands the common property of the nation.

Open and thorough discussions in legislative bodies as a check on the election of knavish wire-pulling politicians, and upon hasty and ill-advised legislation.

Advantages of two chambers in legislative bodies over one in the above respect.

Departments of investigation to give information to Congress as an important feature of government.

Amendment, repeal, and new legislation as the proper cure for bad laws (a point in the discussion of the Initiative and Referendum).

A Chamber of Commerce as an advisory board and bureau of commercial information for the benefit of Congress (a point in the discussion of matters relative to the Departments of Commerce and Labor, the Consular Service, etc.).

Advantages of a dictatorship during war (a point in the discussion of the Suspension of Habeas Corpus Act, and similar issues of Lincoln's administration).

Complete control of the purse by the Legislature.

Executive departments to be directed by a Council of State.

All laws to carry power of enforcing them (Supremacy of Federal Legislation over State).

Coercion of a State by the Federal Government for the national welfare (a point in the discussion of Secession).

The strictly constitutional propositions of Webster may be inferred from a comparison which he instituted between them and the Constitution which was adopted. This he published in 1791 in his complete works. For the full text of the "Dissertation" see Appendix XI in

Hannis Taylor's "Origin and Growth of the American Constitution."

COMPARISON OF THE ADOPTED CONSTITUTION WITH THAT PROPOSED BY WEBSTER

At the time when this Dissertation was written (February 16, 1783) the defects and insufficiency of the Old Federal Constitution were universally felt and acknowledged. It was manifest, not only that the internal policy, justice, security, and peace of the States could never be preserved under it, but the finances and public credit would necessarily become so embarrassed, precarious, and void of support that no public movement which depended on the revenue could be managed with any effectual certainty; but though the public mind was under full conviction of all these mischiefs and was contemplating a remedy, yet the public ideas were not at all concentrated, much less arranged into any new system or form of government which would obviate these evils. Under these circumstances I offered this Dissertation to the public. How far the principles of it were adopted or rejected in the new Constitution, which was four years afterwards (September 17, 1787) formed by the general convention and since ratified by all the States, is obvious to every one.

I wish here to remark the great particulars of my plan which were rejected by the convention.

1. My plan was to keep the legislative and executive departments entirely distinct; the one to consist of the two Houses of Congress, the other to rest entirely in the Grand Council of State.

2. I proposed to introduce a Chamber of Commerce, to consist of merchants who should be consulted by the legislature in all matters of trade and revenue, and which should have the conducting the revenue committed to them.

The first of these the convention qualified; the second they say nothing of, i. e., take no notice of it.

3. I proposed that the great officers of state should have the perusal of all bills before they were enacted into laws, and should be required to give their opinion of them as far as they affected the public interest in their several departments, which report of them Congress should cause to be read in their respective Houses and entered on their minutes. This is passed over without notice.

4. I proposed that all public officers appointed by the

executive authority should be amenable both to them and to the legislative power, and removable for just cause by either of them. This is qualified by the convention.

And inasmuch as my sentiments in these respects were either qualified or totally neglected by the convention, I suppose they were wrong. However, the whole matter is submitted to the politicians of the present age and to our posterity in future.

In sundry other things the convention have gone into minutes, *e. g.,* respecting elections of presidents, senators and representatives in Congress, etc., which I proposed to leave at large to the wisdom and discretion of Congress and of the several States.

Great reasons may doubtless be assigned for their decision, and perhaps some little ones for mine. Time, the great arbiter of all human plans, may, after a while, give his decision; but neither the convention nor myself will probably live to feel either the exultation or mortification of his approbation or disapprobation of either of our plans.

But if any of these questions should in future time become objects of discussion, neither the vast dignity of the convention, nor the low, unnoticed state of myself, will be at all considered in the debates; the merits of the matter and the interests connected with or rising out of it will alone dictate the decision.

THE CALL FOR A CONVENTION

In 1780, one year before Webster's first proposal of an entirely new Constitution, Alexander Hamilton, then twenty-three years of age, proposed in a letter to James Duane a convention of all the States to revise the Articles of Confederation. In 1782 the legislature of his State, New York, recommended such a convention, and, in 1784, Gen. Washington, in a letter to the Governor of Virginia, urged that a radical change in the Federal Government was necessary. He said:

The disinclination of the individual States to yield competent powers to Congress for the Federal Government, their unreasonable jealousy of that body, and of one another, and the disposition which seems to pervade each, of being all-wise and all-powerful within itself, will, if there is not a change in the system, be our downfall as a nation. This is as clear to me as A, B, C, and I think we have opposed Great Britain, and have arrived at the present state of peace and independency to very little purpose if we cannot conquer our own prejudices. The powers of Europe begin to see this, and our newly acquired friends, the British, are already acting upon this ground; and wisely, too, if we are determined in our folly. They know that individual opposition to their measures is futile, and *boast* that we are not sufficiently united as a nation to give a general one! Is not the indignity alone of this declaration, while we are in the act of peace-making and reconciliation, sufficient to stimulate us to vest more extensive and adequate powers in the sovereigns of these United States?

In 1785 the legislature of Massachusetts passed resolutions similar to those of New York. Congress, however, whose adoption of the acts of the convention would be necessary to put them into effect, failed to approve of these recommendations, and the proposals came to nothing.

The meeting of such a convention was destined to develop in a fashion less formal and more natural, and therefore all the more effective in showing the proper relations of the Federal Government to the States. The legislatures of Virginia and Maryland were forced by the demands of commerce to adopt inter-State rules for the navigation of the Potomac River and Chesapeake Bay, which formed the common boundary of the States. Washington was consulted in the matter, and probably by his suggestion the appointment of a joint commission for framing the regulations led to the call by the Virginia legislature in January, 1786, of a convention of *all* the States:

To take into consideration the *trade* and *commerce* of the United States; to consider how far an uniform system, in their commercial intercourse and regulations, might be necessary to their common interest and permanent harmony, and to report to the several States such an act relative to this great object, as when unanimously ratified by them, would enable the United States, in Congress assembled, effectually to provide for the same.

It was afterward agreed that this meeting should be held at Annapolis, Md., in September of the same year.

Letters of Jay to Washington

In a letter to General Washington, written in February, John Jay observed:

Experience has pointed out errors in our National Government which call for correction, and which threaten to blast the fruit we expected from our tree of liberty. The convention proposed by Virginia may do some good, and would perhaps do more if it comprehended more objects. An opinion begins to prevail that a general convention for revising the Articles of Confederation would be expedient. Whether the people are yet ripe for such a measure, or whether the system proposed to be obtained by it is only to be expected from calamity and commotion, is difficult to ascertain.

In a second letter to General Washington, in June of the same year, Jay thus expressed his feelings and views:

Our affairs seem to lead to some crisis, some revolution, something that I cannot foresee or conjecture. I am uneasy and apprehensive, more so than during the war. Then we had a fixed object, and though the means and time of obtaining it were often problematical, yet I did firmly believe that justice was with us. The case is now altered. We are going and doing wrong, and therefore I look forward to evils and calamities, but without being able to guess at the instrument, nature, or measure of them. That we shall again recover, and things again go well, I have no doubt. Such a variety of circumstances would not, almost miraculously, have combined to liberate and make us a nation for transient and unimportant purposes. I therefore believe we are yet to become a great and respectable people, but *when* and *how* only the spirit of prophecy can discern.

What I most fear is that the better kind of people (by which I mean the people who are orderly and industrious, who are content with their situation, and not uneasy in their circumstances) will be led by the insecurity of property, the loss of confidence in their rulers, and the want of public faith and rectitude to consider the claims of liberty as imaginary and delusive. This state of uncertainty and fluctuation must disgust and alarm such men and prepare their minds for almost any change that may promise them quiet and security.

General Washington replied, heartily endorsing Jay's views.

THE ANNAPOLIS CONVENTION

At the convention only the States of Virginia, Delaware, Pennsylvania, New Jersey, and New York were represented. Delegates were appointed by New Hampshire, Massachusetts, Rhode Island, and North Carolina, but did not attend. In consequence of such a partial representation of the States, the commissioners present thought it improper to proceed on the important business with which they were intrusted. They were now, more than ever, sensible of the necessity of a general convention of all the States, and were also satisfied that the powers of this convention should extend to other objects than merely the regulation of trade and commerce. They therefore drew up a report and address to the States, in which, after stating the defects of the Federal Government and that the situation of the United States "was delicate and critical, calling for an exertion of the virtue and wisdom of all the members of the Confederacy," they recommended to all the States to concur "in the appointment of commissioners, to meet at Philadelphia, on the second Monday in May, 1787, to take into consideration the situation of the United States, to devise such further provisions as should appear to them necessary to render the Constitution of the Federal Government adequate to the exigencies of the Union." This address was sent to Congress as well as to the several States.

The Virginia legislature first appointed delegates, according to the recommendation of the meeting at Annapolis. Other States soon after followed the example of Virginia. In February, 1787, Congress indorsed the Convention, and this hastened the appointment of delegates from all the States except Rhode Island.

HAMILTON'S PLEA FOR A NATIONAL REVENUE

During this period the proposition to confer on Congress the power of levying imports as a means of obtaining national revenue again came before the legislature of New York, and, though it was supported by the eloquence of Hamilton, was defeated by a majority of fifteen. Nevertheless the legislature agreed to send representatives to the Constitutional Convention in Philadelphia, and appointed Hamilton, with Robert Yates and John Lansing, Jr., as the delegates.

The following is an abridgment of Hamilton's speech before the legislature. It was delivered on February 18, 1787.

ON GRANTING TAXING POWER TO CONGRESS

ALEXANDER HAMILTON

In the interpretation of laws it is admitted to be a good rule to resort to the coexisting circumstances, and collect from thence the intention of the framers of the law. Let us apply this rule to the present case.

In the commencement of the Revolution, delegates were sent to meet in Congress with large discretionary powers. In short, generally speaking, with full power "to take care of the republic." In the whole of this transaction the idea of an union of the colonies was carefully held up. It pervaded all our public acts.

In the Declaration of Independence we find it continued and confirmed. . . . "These United Colonies, . . . as free and independent States, have full power to levy war, conclude peace, contract alliances, establish commerce, and do all other acts and things that independent States may of right do."

Hence we see that the union and independence of these States are blended and incorporated in one and the same act, which, taken together, clearly imports that the United States had in their origin full power to do all acts and things which independent States may of right do, or, in other words, full power of sovereignty.

Accordingly we find that, upon the authority of that act only approved by the several States, they did levy war, contract alliances, and exercise other high powers of sovereignty, even to the appointment of a dictator, prior to the present confederation.

In this situation and with this plenitude of power, our Constitution knows and acknowledges the United States in

Congress assembled, and provides for the annual appointment of delegates to represent this State in that body, which, in substance, amounts to a constitutional recognition of the union with complete sovereignty.

A government may exist without any formal organization or precise definition of its powers. However improper it might have been that the Federal Government should have continued to exist with such absolute and undefined authority, this does not militate against the position that it did possess such authority. It only proves the propriety of a more regular formation to ascertain its limits. This was the object of the present confederation, which is in fact an abridgment of the original sovereignty of the union.

It may be said (for it has been said upon other occasions) that though the Constitution did consider the United States in the light I have described, and left the legislature at liberty in the first instance to have organized the Federal Government in such a manner as they thought proper, yet that liberty ceased with the establishment of the present confederacy. The discretion of the legislature was then determined.

This, upon the face of it, is a subtility uncountenanced by a single principle of government or a single expression of the Constitution. It is saying that a general authority given to the legislature for the permanent preservation and good of the community has been exhausted and spent by the exercise of a part of that authority. The position is the more destitute of color because the confederation, by the express terms of the compact, preserves and continues this power. The last clause of it authorizes Congress to propose, and the States to agree to, such alterations as might be afterwards found necessary or expedient.

We see, therefore, that the Constitution knows and acknowledges the United States in Congress; that it provides for the annual appointment of delegates to *represent this State* in that body without prescribing the objects or limits of that representation; that at the time our Constitution was framed the Union existed with full sovereignty, and that therefore the idea of sovereignty in the Union is not incompatible with it. We see further that the doctrine contained in the objection against granting legislative power would equally operate against granting executive power, would prove that the powers already vested in the Union are illegal and unconstitutional, would render a confederacy of the States in any form impracticable, and would defeat all those provisions of our own

Constitution which relate to the United States. I submit it
to the committee, whether a doctrine pregnant with such consequences can be true; whether it is not as opposite to our
Constitution as to the principles of national safety and prosperity, and whether it would not be lamentable if the zeal
of opposition to a particular measure should carry us to the
extreme of imposing upon the Constitution a sense foreign to
it, which must embarrass the national councils upon future
occasions when all might agree in the utility and necessity of
a different construction.

I return to the examination of the question: How far the
power proposed to be conferred upon Congress would be
dangerous to the liberty of the people? And here I ask:

Whence can this danger arise? The members of Congress
are annually chosen by the members of the several legislatures.
They come together with different habits, prejudices and
interests. They are in fact continually changing. How is it
possible for a body so composed to be formidable to the liberties
of States—several of which are largely empires in themselves?

In a contest of this kind the body of the people will always
be on the side of the State governments. This will not only
result from their love of liberty and regard to their own
safety, but from other strong principles of human nature.
The State governments operate upon those immediate familiar
personal concerns to which the sensibility of individuals is
awake. The distribution of private justice belonging to them,
they must always appear to the senses of the people as the
immediate guardians of their rights. They will, of course,
have the strongest hold on their attachment, respect, and
obedience.

What is to be feared from the efforts of Congress to establish
a tyranny with the great body of the people, under the direction
of their State governments, combined in opposition to their
views?

The causes taken notice of as securing the attachment of
the people to their local governments present us with another
important truth—the natural imbecility of Federal governments, and the danger that they will never be able to exercise
power enough to manage the general affairs of the Union,
though the States will have a common interest, yet they will
also have a particular interest. For example, as a part of
the Union, it will be the interest of every State to pay as
little itself, and to let its neighbors pay as much as possible.
Particular interests have always more influence upon men than

general. The Federal States, therefore, consulting their immediate advantage, may be considered as so many eccentric powers tending in a contrary direction to the government of the Union, and, as they will generally carry the people along with them, the confederacy will be in continual danger of dissolution. This, Mr. Chairman, is the real rock upon which the happiness of this country is likely to split. This is the point to which our fears and cares should be directed—to guard against this, and not to terrify ourselves with imaginary dangers from the specter of power in Congress, will be our true wisdom.

It is no objection to say that a great part of this fund will be dedicated to the use of the United States. Their exigencies must be supplied in some way or other. The more is done toward it by means of the impost, the less will be to be done in other modes. If we do not employ that resource to the best account, we must find others in *direct* taxation. And to this are opposed all the habits and prejudices of the community. There is not a farmer in the State who would not pay a shilling in the voluntary consumption of articles on which a duty is paid rather than a penny imposed immediately on his house and land.

Having now shown, Mr. Chairman, that there is no constitutional impediment to the adoption of the bill; that there is no danger to be apprehended to the public liberty from giving the power in question to the United States; that in the view of revenue the measure under consideration is not only expedient, but necessary—let us turn our attention to the other side of this important subject. Let us ask ourselves what will be the consequence of rejecting the bill. What will be the situation of our national affairs if they are left much longer to float in the chaos in which they are now involved?

Can our national character be preserved without paying our debts? Can the Union subsist without revenue? Have we realized the consequences which would attend its dissolution?

If these States are not united under a Federal Government, they will infallibly have wars with each other, and their divisions will subject them to all the mischiefs of foreign influence and intrigue. The human passions will never want objects of hostility. The Western Territory is an obvious and fruitful source of contest.

Wars with each other would beget standing armies—a source of more real danger to our liberties than all the powers that could be conferred upon the representatives of the Union.

And wars with each other would lead to opposite alliances with foreign powers and plunge us into all the labyrinths of European politics.

The Romans, in their progress to universal dominion, when they conceived the project of subduing the refractory spirit of the Grecian republics, which composed the famous Achaian League, began by sowing dissensions among them and instilling jealousies of each other, and of the common head, and finished by making them a province of the Roman empire.

The application is easy: if there are any foreign enemies, if there are any domestic foes to this country, all their arts and artifices will be employed to effect a dissolution of the Union. This cannot be better done than by sowing jealousies of the Federal head, and cultivating in each State an undue attachment to its own power.

The Constitutional Convention

The convention met as appointed (in Philadelphia in May, 1787).

Rhode Island, which had positively refused to pay her quota of national expenses, was not represented in the convention, and the delegation from New Hampshire, for whom the State legislature had failed to provide expenses, did not appear until late in the proceedings, when this failure had been remedied.

The delegates, while recognizing the greatness of the task before them, were determined to do their utmost to accomplish it. Thus the delegates of North Carolina said in a report to the governor of their State:

A very large field presents to our view without a single straight or eligible road that has been trodden by the feet of nations. An union of sovereign States, preserving their civil liberties and connected together by such ties as to preserve permanent and effective governments is a system not described, it is a circumstance that has not occurred in the history of men; if we shall be so fortunate as to find this in descript our time will have been well spent. Several members of the convention have their wives here and other gentlemen have sent for theirs. This seems to promise a summer's campaign. Such of us as can remain here from the inevitable avocation of private business are resolved to continue whilst there is any prospect of being able to serve the State and Union.

George Washington was unanimously elected as the chairman of the convention. Deputies from seven States were accounted a quorum, and a majority of fully represented States was to decide questions. The proceedings were to be secret (except where special leave was granted to the contrary) in order, as James Madison wrote to Thomas Jefferson in Paris on June 6, "to secure unbiased discussion within doors, and to prevent misconceptions and misconstructions without." In reference to this Jefferson wrote to John Adams on August 30:

I am sorry they began their deliberations by so abominable a precedent as that of tying up the tongues of their members. Nothing can justify this example but the innocence of their intentions and ignorance of the value of public discussions. I have no doubt that all their other measures will be good and wise. It is really an assembly of demigods.

This secrecy has been especially deplored by historians because the literal text of almost all the speeches made in the convention was lost, and many interesting incidents, referred to obscurely in the diaries and letters of the time, consigned to oblivion. James Madison, in his "Papers," left an admirable digest of the proceedings of the convention, to which the reader is referred (see Volume V of "Elliott's Debates").

The first question among the members of this assembly was whether they should amend the old government or form a new system. By the resolve of Congress, as well as the instructions of some of the States, they were met "for the sole and express purpose of revising the Articles of Confederation." Such, however, were the radical defects of the old government, that a majority determined to form an entire new one.

On the 29th of May, Edmund Randolph, of Virginia, submitted to the convention fifteen resolutions as the basis of a new constitution.

RANDOLPH'S PLAN

The points of this plan were:

1. Correction and enlargement of the Articles of Confederation better to promote common defence, security of liberty, and general welfare.

2. Suffrage in Congress to be proportioned to quotas of contribution or number of free inhabitants.

3. Congress to consist of two branches.

4. Congressmen to be elected at stated times by the people; to be above a fixed age; to be paid; to be ineligible for other offices during time of service, and for a fixed time thereafter; to be incapable of reëlection until after a fixed time; and to be subject to recall.

5. Second branch to be elected by first, from nominees by the State legislatures; to be above a fixed age; to hold office for a sufficient time to insure their independency; to be paid; to be ineligible for other offices during time of service, and for a fixed time thereafter.

6. Each branch to originate acts; Congress to possess its present powers, and in addition to legislate in all cases where the separate States are incompetent, or where the harmony of the United States may be interrupted by individual State legislation; Congress to negative such interrupting acts of the States, and to employ the force of the Union against any State failing to fulfill its duty under the Constitution.

7. A national executive to be instituted, chosen by Congress, for a fixed term, paid by a fixed sum which is not to be changed during the term, and ineligible for reëlection.

8. The executive and a convenient number of the national judiciary to compose a council of revision of legislative acts before their promulgation, their veto, however, to be overridden by a fixed proportion of the members of each legislative branch.

9. A national judiciary to be established to hold office during good behavior, to be paid on conditions prevailing with the executive; its lower tribunals to pass with final force on international and Federal questions.

10. New States to be formed from the territory within the limits of the United States by a fixed proportion of the votes of the States (not necessarily unanimous).

11. A republican form of government to be guaranteed to each State, except in case of voluntary junction of government and territory.

12. Provision to be made for continuance of a Congress until the Union is completely formed.

13. Articles of Union to be subject to amendment without assent of the national legislature.

14. The legislative, executive, and judiciary powers of the separate States to be sworn to support the Articles of Union.

15. The amendments to the Articles of Confederation to be submitted to conventions chosen by the States to consider them and decide thereon.

Madison's Letter to Randolph

In forming this plan, Governor Randolph had been aided by correspondence with James Madison. In a letter to Randolph on April 8, 1787, Madison wrote:

I think with you that it will be well to retain as much as possible of the old Confederation, though I doubt whether it may not be best to work the valuable articles into the new system, instead of engrafting the latter on the former. I am also perfectly of your opinion that in framing a system no material sacrifices ought to be made to local or temporary prejudices. . . . In truth my ideas of a reform strike so deeply at the old Confederation, and lead to such a systematic change, that they scarcely admit of the expedient.

I hold it for a fundamental point that an individual independence of the States is utterly irreconcilable with the idea of an aggregate sovereignty. I think at the same time that consolidation of the States into one simple republic is not less unattainable than it would be inexpedient. Let it be tried, then, whether any middle ground can be taken, which will at once support a due supremacy of the national authority and leave in force the local authorities so far as they can be subordinately useful.

The first step to be taken is, I think, a change in the principle of representation. According to the present form of the Union an equality of suffrage, if not just toward the larger members of it, is at least safe to them, as the liberty they exercise of rejecting or executing the acts of Congress is uncontrollable by the nominal sovereignty of Congress. Under a system which would operate without the intervention of the States, the case would be materially altered. A vote from Delaware would have the same effect as one from Massachusetts or Virginia.

Let the National Government be armed with a positive and complete authority in all cases where uniform measures are necessary, as in trade, etc., etc. Let it also retain the powers which it now possesses.

Let it have a negative in all cases whatsoever on the legislative acts of the States, as the King of Great Britain heretofore had. This I conceive to be essential and the least possible abridgment of the State sovereignties. Without such a defensive power, every positive power that can be given on paper will be unavailing. It will also give internal stability to the States. There has been no moment since the peace at which the Federal assent would have been given to paper money—etc., etc.

Let this national supremacy be extended also to the Judiciary Department. If the judges in the last resort depend on the States, and are bound by their oaths to them, and not to the Union, the intention of the law and the interests of the nation may be defeated by the obsequiousness of the tribunals to the policy or prejudices of the States. It seems at least essential that an appeal should lie to some national tribunals in all cases which concern foreigners or inhabitants of other States. The admiralty jurisdiction may be fully submitted to the National Government.

A government formed of such extensive powers ought to be well organized. The legislative department may be divided into two branches. One of them to be chosen every ——— years by the legislatures or the people at large; the other to consist of a more select number, holding their appointments for a longer term, and going out in rotation. Perhaps the negative on the State laws may be most conveniently lodged in this branch. A council of revision may be superadded, including the great ministerial officers.

A national executive will also be necessary. I have scarcely ventured to form my opinion yet, either of the manner in which it ought to be constituted, or of the authorities with which it ought to be clothed.

An article ought to be inserted expressly guaranteeing the tranquility of the States against internal as well as external dangers.

To give the new system its proper energy, it will be desirable to have it ratified by the authority of the people, and not merely by that of the legislatures.

I am afraid you will think this project, if not extravagant, absolutely unattainable and unworthy of being attempted. Conceiving it myself to go no further than is essential, the objections drawn from this source are to be laid aside. I flatter myself, however, that they may be less formidable on trial than in contemplation. The change in the principle of representation will be relinquished by a majority of the States, and those too of most influence. The Northern States will be reconciled to it by the *actual* superiority of their populousness; the Southern by their *expected* superiority on this point. This principle established, the repugnance of the large States to part with power will in a great degree subside, and the smaller States must ultimately yield to the predominant will. It is also already seen by many, and must by degrees be seen by all, that, unless the Union be organized efficiently on republican principles, innovation of a much more objectionable form may be obtruded; or, in the most favorable event, the partition of the Empire into rival and hostile confederacies will ensue.

One week later, April 16, 1787, Madison amplified his ideas in a letter to Washington. Hannis Taylor, in his "Origin and Growth of the American Constitution," contends that Madison had drafted the plan, but for policy's sake, since he had political opponents in his State, persuaded Governor Randolph, the head of Virginia, as well as of the Virginia delegation to the convention, to father it. Taylor draws this conclusion from his letters to Randolph and Washington, as well as from the circumstances that Madison had been engaged for a year previously in preparing himself for the Constitutional Convention, and that Randolph said, in his speech supporting the plan, not that he had *written* it, but *proposed* it at the instigation of his colleagues, and also from the fact that the plan is spread upon the journal of the Congress in Madison's hand.

Taylor also infers from the presence in Philadelphia of Madison at the time when Pelatiah Webster published his "Dissertation on the Constitution" that he got his essential ideas from this pamphlet.

On the same day on which the Randolph resolutions were presented, Charles Pinckney of South Carolina laid before the convention his draft of a proposed Federal Government.

The Pinckney Plan

The articles proposed were as follows. The substances of Articles II to V is given, and the text of the others.

Article I. The style of this government shall be: "The United States of America," and the government shall consist of supreme legislative, executive, and judicial powers.

Article II. There shall be two chambers of legislation, the House of Delegates and the Senate; these shall meet annually at a fixed time.

Article III. Delegates to be chosen by the people of the States; each to be a resident of the State he is chosen for; number of delegates from each State to be proportioned on population. All money bills to originate in House of Delegates, and not be altered by the Senate. House of Delegates to possess exclusive power of impeachment, and to choose its own officers; any vacancy in its membership to be supplied by the executive of the State represented.

Article IV. House of Delegates to elect Senators, a fixed number in each case from those citizens of each State who are above a fixed age. The Senators from New England to form class one, from the Middle States (New York to Delaware inclusive) class two, and from the Southern States (Maryland to Georgia inclusive) class three; terms of service of each class to be a fixed period, differing in duration from the other periods, and determined by lot. House of Delegates to supply vacancies. Senate to choose its own officers.

Article V. House of Delegates to be judges of the elections and qualifications of its members. Majority in each house to be a quorum. Freedom of debate; no speaker to be impeached for his words by an outside authority; members to be free of arrest while in attendance, except for treason, felony, or breach of the peace. Both houses to keep journals, and publish them, except on secret occasions. Yeas and Nays to be entered on them at request of a member. No adjournments to another place, or for more than a fixed time, to take place without consent of the other House. Members of each House not to hold other offices during service, and Senators not for one year after service. Members to be paid by the States which they represent. Bills to be approved by the President, or passed by a two-thirds majority over his veto or his failure to sign after a fixed number of days while Congress is in session.

Article VI. The Legislature of the United States shall have the power to lay and to collect taxes, duties, imposts, and excises;

To regulate commerce with all nations, and among the several States;

To borrow money and emit bills of credit;

To establish postoffices;

To raise armies;

To build and equip fleets;

To pass laws for arming, organizing, and disciplining the militia of the United States;

To subdue a rebellion in any State on application of its legislature;

To coin money and regulate the value of all coins, and to fix the standard of weights and measures;

To provide such dockyards and arsenals and erect such fortifications as may be necessary for the United States, and to exercise exclusive jurisdiction therein;

To appoint a Treasurer, by ballot;

To constitute tribunals inferior to the Supreme Court;

To establish post and military roads;

To establish and provide for a national university at the seat of government of the United States;

To establish uniform rules of naturalization;

To provide for the establishment of a seat of government for the United States not exceeding ———— miles square, in which they shall have exclusive jurisdiction;

To make rules concerning captures from an enemy;

To declare the law and punishment of piracies and felonies at sea, and of counterfeiting coin, and of all offences against the laws of nations;

To call forth the aid of the militia to execute the laws of the Union, enforce treaties, suppress insurrections, and repel invasions;

And to make all laws for carrying the foregoing powers into execution.

The legislature of the United States shall have the power to declare the punishment of treason, which shall consist only in levying war against the United States, or any of them, or in adhering to their enemies. No person shall be convicted of treason but by the testimony of two witnesses.

The proportion of direct taxation shall be regulated by the whole number of inhabitants of every description, which number shall, within ———— years after the first meeting of the legislature, and within the term of every ———— year after, be taken in the manner to be prescribed by the legislature.

No tax shall be laid on articles exported from the States; nor capitation tax, but in proportion to the census before directed.

All laws regulating commerce shall require the assent of two-thirds of the members present in each house. The United States shall not grant any title of nobility. The legislature of the United States shall pass no law on the subject of religion, nor touching or abridging the liberty of the press, nor shall the privilege of the writ of habeas corpus ever be suspended, except in case of rebellion or invasion.

All acts made by the legislature of the United States, pursuant to this Constitution, and all treaties made under the authority of the United States, shall be the supreme law of the land, and all judges shall be bound to consider them as such in their decisions.

Article VII. The Senate shall have the sole and exclusive power to declare war, and to make treaties, and to appoint ambassadors and other ministers to foreign nations, and judges of the Supreme Court.

They shall have the exclusive power to regulate the manner of deciding all disputes and controversies now existing, or which may arise between the States respecting jurisdiction or territory.

Article VIII. The executive power of the United States shall be vested in a President of the United States of America, which shall be his style; and his title shall be His Excellency. He shall be elected for ———— years, and shall be reëligible. He shall from time to time give information to the legislature of the state of the Union and recommend to their consideration the measures he may think necessary. He shall take care that the laws of the United States be duly executed. He shall commission all the officers of the United States; and, except as to ambassadors, other ministers, and judges of the Supreme Court, he shall nominate, and, with the consent of the Senate, appoint, all other officers of the United States. He shall receive public ministers from foreign nations, and may correspond with the executives of the different States. He shall have power to grant pardons and reprieves, except in impeachments. He shall be Commander-in-Chief of the army and navy of the United States, and of the militia of the several States; and shall receive a compensation which shall not be increased or diminished during his continuance in office. At entering on the duties of his office, he shall take an oath faithfully to execute the duties of a President of the United States. He shall be removed from his office on impeachment by the House of Delegates, and conviction in the Supreme Court of treason, bribery, or corruption. In case of his removal, death, resignation, or disability, the President of the Senate shall exercise the duties of his office until another President be chosen. And in case of the death of the President of the Senate, the Speaker of the House of Delegates shall do so.

Article IX. The legislature of the United States shall have the power, and it shall be their duty, to establish such courts of law, equity, and admiralty as shall be necessary.

The judges of the courts shall hold their offices during good behavior, and receive a compensation which shall not be increased or diminished during their continuance in office. One of these courts shall be termed the Supreme Court, whose jurisdiction shall extend to all cases arising under the laws of the United States, or affecting ambassadors, other public ministers and consuls, to the trial of impeachment of officers of the United States, to all cases of admiralty and maritime jurisdiction. In cases of impeachment affecting ambassadors and other public ministers this jurisdiction shall be original, and in all other cases appellate.

All criminal offences, except in cases of impeachment, shall be tried in the State where they shall be committed. The trials shall be open and public, and shall be by jury.

Article X. Immediately after the first census of the people of the United States, the House of Delegates shall apportion the Senate by electing for each State, out of the citizens resident therein, one Senator for every ———— members each State shall have in the House of Delegates. Each State shall be entitled to have at least one member in the Senate.

Article XI. No State shall grant letters of marque and reprisal, or enter into a treaty, or alliance, or confederation; nor grant any title of nobility; nor, without the consent of the legislature of the United States, lay any impost on imports; nor keep troops or ships of war in time of peace; nor enter into compacts with other States or foreign powers; nor emit bills of credit; nor make anything but gold, silver, or copper a tender in payment of debts; nor engage in war except for self-defence when actually invaded, or the danger of invasion be so great as not to admit of a delay until the Government of the United States can be informed thereof. And, to render these prohibitions effectual, the legislature of the United

States shall have the power to revise the laws of the several States that may be supposed to infringe the powers exclusively delegated by this Constitution to Congress, and to negative and annul such as do.

Article XII. The citizens of each State shall be entitled to all privileges and immunities of citizens in the several States. Any person charged with crimes in any State, fleeing from justice to another, shall, on demand of the executive of the State from which he fled, be delivered up, and removed to the State having jurisdiction of the offence.

Article XIII. Full faith shall be given in each State to the acts of the legislature, and to the records and judicial proceedings of the courts and magistrates of every State.

Article XIV. The Legislature shall have power to admit new States into the Union on the same terms with the original States, provided two-thirds of the members present in both Houses agree.

Article XV. On the application of the legislature of a State, the United States shall protect it against domestic insurrection.

Article XVI. If two-thirds of the legislatures of the States apply for the same, the legislature of the United States shall call a convention for the purpose of amending the Constitution, or, should Congress, with the consent of two-thirds of each House, propose to the States amendments to the same, agreement of two-thirds of the legislatures of the States shall be sufficient to make the said amendments parts of the Constitution.

The ratification of the ——— conventions of ——— States shall be sufficient for organizing this Constitution.

Some time before October 14, 1787, Mr. Pinckney published a pamphlet containing his "Observations on the Plan of Government Submitted to the Federal Convention Delivered at Different Times in the Course of Their Discussions." The text of this is found in Professor Farrand's "Records of the Federal Convention," Vol. III, page 106.

The plans of Randolph and Pinckney were referred to a committee of the whole, which debated the resolutions from day to day until June 13, when the committee reported to the convention nineteen resolutions founded on those proposed by Randolph.

RESOLUTIONS OF THE COMMITTEE OF THE WHOLE

1. *Resolved,* That it is the opinion of this committee that a national government ought to be established, consisting of a supreme legislative, judiciary, and executive.

2. *Resolved,* That the national legislature ought to consist of two branches.

3. *Resolved,* That the members of the first branch of the national legislature ought to be elected by the people of the several States for the term of three years, to receive fixed stipends, by which they may be compensated for the devotion of their time to public service to be paid out of the national treasury; to be ineligible to any office established by a particular State, or under the authority of the United States (except those peculiarly belonging to the functions of the first branch) during the term of service, and under the national government, for the space of one year after its expiration.

4. *Resolved,* That the members of the second branch of the national legislature ought to be chosen by the individual legislatures; to be of the age of thirty years at least; to hold their offices for a term sufficient to insure their independency— namely, seven years; to receive fixed stipends, by which they may be compensated for the devotion of their time to public service, to be paid out of the national treasury; to be ineligible to any office established by a particular State, or under the authority of the United States (except those peculiarly belonging to the functions of the second branch) during the term of service, and under the national government, for the space of one year after its expiration.

5. *Resolved,* That each branch ought to possess the right of originating acts.

6. *Resolved,* That the national legislature ought to be empowered to enjoy the legislative rights vested in Congress by the Confederation; and, moreover, to legislate in all cases to which the separate States are incompetent, or in which the harmony of the United States may be interrupted by the exercise of individual legislation; to negative all laws passed by the several States contravening, in the opinion of the national legislature, the Articles of Union, or any treaties subsisting under the authority of the Union.

7. *Resolved,* That the right of suffrage in the first branch

of the national legislature ought not to be according to the rule established in the Articles of Confederation, but according to some equitable ratio of representation, namely, in proportion to the whole number of white and other free citizens, and inhabitants of every age, sex, and condition, including those bound to servitude for a term of years, and three-fifths of all other persons not comprehended in the foregoing description, except Indians not paying taxes, in each State.

8. *Resolved,* That the rights of suffrage in the second branch of the national legislature ought to be according to the rule established for the first.

9. *Resolved,* That a national executive be instituted, to consist of a single person; to be chosen by the national legislature, for the term of seven years; with power to carry into execution the national laws; to appoint to offices in cases not otherwise provided for; to be ineligible a second time; and to be removable on impeachment and conviction of malpractice, or neglect of duty; to receive a fixed stipend, by which he may be compensated for the devotion of his time to public service, to be paid out of the national treasury.

10. *Resolved,* That the national executive shall have a right to negative any legislative act, which shall not be afterwards passed unless by two-third parts of each branch of the national legislature.

11. *Resolved,* That a national judiciary be established, to consist of one supreme tribunal; the judges of which to be appointed by the second branch of the national legislature; to hold their offices during good behavior; to receive punctually, at stated times, a fixed compensation for their services, in which no increase or diminution shall be made, so as to affect the persons actually in office at the time of such increase or diminution.

12. *Resolved,* That the national legislature be empowered to appoint inferior tribunals.

13. *Resolved,* That the jurisdiction of the national judiciary shall extend to cases which respect the collection of the national revenue, impeachment of any national officers, and questions which involve the national peace and harmony.

14. *Resolved,* That provision ought to be made for the admission of States, lawfully arising within the limits of the United States, whether from a voluntary junction of government and territory, or otherwise, with the consent of a number of voices in the national legislature less than the whole.

15. *Resolved,* That provision ought to be made for the

continuance of Congress and their authorities until a given day after the reform of the Articles of Union shall be adopted, and for the completion of all their engagements.

16. *Resolved,* That a republican constitution, and its existing laws, ought to be guaranteed to each State by the United States.

17. *Resolved,* That provision ought to be made for the amendment of the Articles of Union whensoever it shall seem necessary.

18. *Resolved,* That the legislative, executive, and judiciary powers within the several States ought to be bound by oath to support the Articles of Union.

19. *Resolved,* That the amendments which shall be offered to the Confederation by the convention ought, at a proper time or times after the approbation of Congress, to be submitted to an assembly, or assemblies of representatives, recommended by the several legislatures to be expressly chosen by the people to consider and decide thereon.

On the 15th of June William Paterson of New Jersey presented a plan of the Constitution.

PATERSON'S PLAN

This plan was a revision of the Articles of Confederation, giving Congress power to impose customs duties, stamps on paper, and postage for Federal revenue; to regulate foreign and interstate commerce, fines, etc., to be adjudicated by the judiciaries of the State where offences were committed, with appeal to the Federal judiciary, and to make requisitions of funds upon the States in proportion to the number of free citizens in each when a fixed proportion of States should authorize the requisitions.

A Federal executive of a fixed number of persons was to be appointed by Congress to serve for a fixed term; to be paid a fixed sum out of the Federal treasury with no change in the same during service; to be ineligible to hold other offices during service, and for a fixed time thereafter, and to be impeachable by a majority of State executives—which Federal executive was empowered to execute Federal acts, appoint Federal officers not otherwise chosen, and direct military operations, though not in person.

A Federal judiciary was to be appointed by Congress to hold office during good behavior; to be paid under the conditions of the executive salaries; to adjudicate impeachments of

Federal officers, and finally decide on all cases concerned with foreign affairs and Federal revenue.

State legislatures, executives, and judiciaries were to swear to support the Articles of Union.

Federal acts, above authorized, to be supreme over State acts on the subjects, and the Federal Government to be empowered to call on as many as necessary of the State governments to enforce them.

Provisions to be made for admission of new States and for adjudicating territorial disputes between the States.

Uniform rules of naturalization to be adopted by the States.

A citizen of one State committing an offence in another to be punished according to the law of his own State.

CHAPTER XI

People or States?

[DEBATE IN THE CONSTITUTIONAL CONVENTION ON THE BASIS OF REPRESENTATION]

Debate on the ''Jersey Plan'' of Equal Representation of States in Congress: in favor, John Lansing, Jr. [N. Y.], William Paterson [N. J.], Judge Oliver Ellsworth [Ct.]; opposed, James Wilson [Pa.], Gen. Charles Cotesworth Pinckney [S. C.], Gov. Edmund Randolph [Va.], Alexander Hamilton [N. Y.], James Madison [Va.]; the Plan Is Rejected.

THE great issue of the Convention was now fairly before it. The Virginia plan, presented by the committee of the whole, was not a mere revision of the Articles of the Confederation, but an entirely new national system, a government in which the people of the entire Union were proportionately represented, and which possessed supremacy in national affairs over the governments of the several States. The Jersey plan (as it was afterward called), presented by Mr. Paterson, was little more than a revision of the Articles of Confederation, enlarging the powers of Congress, it is true, but keeping it still in subordination to the State governments as far as was possible with this enlargement, and continuing the feature of equal representation of the States. Representatives of the more populous States were naturally in favor of the Virginia plan, and those from the less populous States of the Jersey plan.

Alexander Hamilton was not in accord with either plan, and suggested that both be committed to the committee of the whole, in order that a comparative estimate might be had of the two. Thereupon it was agreed that the convention resolve itself into a committee of the whole to discuss both propositions on the following day.

On the morrow (June 16) began the great debate in the convention between the large and the small States (in respect to population) over the two plans.

From this point on the account of the debates is taken from the minutes made privately by Judge Robert Yates, delegate from New York. In all the votes taken during the proceedings reported by him only eleven States were represented [see page 284].

The leading speakers in this debate were: John Lansing, Jr. [N. Y.], William Paterson [N. J.], James Wilson [Pa.], Charles Cotesworth Pinckney [S. C.], Oliver Ellsworth [Conn.], Edmund Randolph [Va.], Alexander Hamilton [N. Y.], and James Madison [Va.].

NATION OR FEDERATION?

CONSTITUTIONAL CONVENTION, JUNE 16-19, 1787

MR. LANSING observed that both plans were fairly contrasted —the one federal and the other national. In the first (the Jersey plan) the powers are exercised as flowing from the respective State governments, the second deriving its authority from the people of the respective States, which latter must ultimately destroy or annihilate the State governments. To determine the powers on these grand objects with which we are invested, he said, let us recur to the credentials of the respective States and see what the views were of those who sent us. The language is there expressive—it is upon the revision of the present Confederation—to alter and amend such parts as may appear defective, so as to give additional strength to the Union. And he would venture to assert that, had the legislature of the State of New York apprehended that their powers would have been construed to extend to the formation of a national government, to the extinguishment of their independency, no delegates would have here appeared on the part of that State. This sentiment must have had its weight on a former occasion, even in this house, for when the second resolution of Virginia declared, in substance, that a federal government could not be amended for the good of the whole, the remark of an honorable member of South Carolina (Pinckney) that, by determining this question in the affirmative, their deliberative powers were at an end induced this house to waive the resolution.

It is in vain to adopt a mode of government which we have reason to believe the people gave us no power to recommend, as they will consider themselves, on this ground, authorized to reject it. See the danger of exceeding your powers by the example which the requisition of Congress of 1783 afforded. They required an impost on all imported articles, to which, on federal grounds, they had no right unless voluntarily granted. What was the consequence? Some who had least to give granted it, and others, under various restrictions and modifications, so that it could not be symtematized. If we form a government, let us do it on principles which are likely to meet the approbation of the States. Great changes can only be gradually introduced. The States will never sacrifice their essential rights to a national government. New plans annihilating the rights of the States (unless upon evident necessity) can never be approved. I may venture to assert that the prevalent opinion of America is that granting additional powers to Congress would answer their views, and every power recommended for their approbation exceeding this idea will be fruitless.

MR. PATERSON.—As I had the honor of proposing a new system of government for the Union [see page 297], it will be expected that I should explain its principles.

First. The plan accords with our own powers.

Second. It accords with the sentiments of the people.

But if the subsisting Confederation is so radically defective as not to admit of amendment, let us say so and report its insufficiency and wait for enlarged powers. We must, in the present case, pursue our powers if we expect the approbation of the people. I am not here to pursue my own sentiments of government, but of those who have sent me, and I believe that a little practical virtue is to be preferred to the finest theoretical principles which cannot be carried into effect. Can we, as representatives of independent States, annihilate the essential powers of independency? Are not the votes of this convention taken, on every question, under the idea of independency? Let us turn to the fifth article of Confederation. In this it is mutually agreed that each State should have one vote; it is a fundamental principle, arising from confederated governments. The thirteenth article provides for amendments, but they must be agreed to by every State; the dissent of one renders every proposal null. The Confederation is in the nature of a compact, and can any State, unless by the consent of the whole, either in politics or law, withdraw their powers? Let it be said by Pennsylvania, and the other large States, that they, for the sake of peace, assented to the Confederation; can she now resume her original right without the consent of the donee?

And although it is now asserted that the larger States reluctantly agreed to that part of the Confederation which secures an equal suffrage to each, yet let it be remembered that the smaller States were the last who approved the Confederation.

On this ground representation must be drawn from the States to maintain their independency, and not from the people composing those States.

The doctrine advanced by a learned gentleman from Pennsylvania that all power is derived from the people, and that in proportion to their numbers they ought to participate equally in the benefits and rights of government, is right in principle, but, unfortunately for him, wrong in the application to the question now in debate.

When independent societies confederate for mutual defence, they do so in their collective capacity, and then each State, for those purposes, must be considered as *one* of the contracting parties. Destroy this balance of equality, and you endanger the rights of the *lesser* societies by the danger of usurpation in the greater.

Let us test the government intended to be made by the Virginia plan on these principles. The representatives in the national legislature are to be in proportion to the number of inhabitants in each State. So far, it is right upon these principles of equality, when State distinctions are done away, but those to certain purposes still exist. Will the government of Pennsylvania admit a participation of their common stock of land to the citizens of New Jersey? I fancy not. It therefore follows that a national government upon the present plan is unjust and destructive of the common principles of reciprocity. Much has been said that this government is to operate on persons, not on States. This, upon examination, will be found equally fallacious, for the fact is it will, in the quotas of revenue, be proportioned among the States, as States, and in this business Georgia will have one vote and Virginia sixteen. The truth is, both plans may be considered to compel individuals to a compliance with their requisitions, although the requisition is made on the States.

Much has been said in commendation of two branches in a legislature, and of the advantages resulting from their being checks to each other. This may be true when applied to the State governments, but will not equally apply to a national legislature, whose legislative objects are few and simple.

Whatever may be said of Congress, or their conduct on particular occasions, the people in general are pleased with such a body, and in general wish an increase of their powers for the good government of the Union. Let us now see the plan of the national government on the score of expense. The least the second branch of the legislature can consist of is ninety members; the first branch of at least 270. How are they to be paid in our present impoverished situation? Let us therefore fairly try whether the Confederation cannot be mended, and, if it can, we shall do our duty, and I believe the people will be satisfied.

MR. WILSON first stated the difference between the two plans.

Virginia plan proposes two branches in the legislature.

Jersey, a single legislative body.

Virginia, the legislative powers derived from the people.

Jersey, from the States.

Virginia, a single executive.

Jersey, more than one.

Virginia, a majority of the legislature can act.

Jersey, a small majority can control.

Virginia, the legislature can legislate on all national concerns.

Jersey, only on limited objects.

Virginia, legislature to negative all State laws.

Jersey, giving power to the executive to compel obedience by force.

Virginia, to remove the executive by impeachment.

Jersey, on application of a majority of the States.

Virginia, for the establishment of inferior judiciary tribunals.

Jersey, no provision.

It is said, and insisted on, that the Jersey plan accords with our powers. As for myself, I consider my powers to extend to everything or nothing; and therefore that I have a right and am at liberty to agree to either plan or none. The people expect relief from their present embarrassed situation, and look up for it to this national convention, and it follows that they expect a national government; and therefore the plan from Virginia has the preference to the other. I would with a reluctant hand add any powers to Congress, because they are not a body chosen by the people, and consist only of one branch, and each State in it has one vote. Inequality in representation poisons every government.

The English courts are hitherto pure, just, and incorrupt, while their legislature are base and venal. The one arises from unjust representation, the other from their independency of the legislature.

Lord Chesterfield remarks that one of the States of the United Netherlands withheld its assent to a proposition until a major of their State was provided for. He needed not have added (for the conclusion was self-evident) that it was one of the lesser States. I mean no reflection, but I leave it to gentlemen to consider whether this has not also been the case in Congress. The argument in favor of the Jersey plan goes too far, as it cannot be completed unless Rhode Island assents. A single legislature is very dangerous; despotism may present itself in various shapes. May there not be legislative despotism if, in the exercise of their power, they are unchecked or unrestrained by another branch? On the contrary an executive, to be restrained, must be an individual. The first triumvirate of Rome, combined, without law, was fatal to its liberties, and the second, by the usurpation of Augustus, ended in despotism. The two kings of Sparta, and the consuls of Rome, by sharing the executive, distracted their governments.

Mr. C. C. PINCKNEY supposed that if New Jersey was indulged with one vote out of thirteen she would have no objection to a national government. He supposed that the convention have already determined virtually that the Federal Government cannot be made efficient. A national government being therefore the object, this plan must be pursued, as our business is not to conclude, but to recommend.

JUDGE ELLSWORTH was of opinion that the first question on the new plan will decide nothing materially on principle, and therefore moved the postponement thereof in order to bring on the second.

GOVERNOR RANDOLPH.—The question now is which of the two plans is to be preferred. If the vote on the first resolve will determine it, and it is so generally understood I have no objection that it be put. The resolutions from Virginia must have been adopted on the supposition that a federal government was impracticable. And it is said that power is wanting to institute such a government, but when our all is at stake I will consent to any mode that will preserve us. View our present deplorable situation. France, to whom we are indebted

in every motive of gratitude and honor, is left unpaid the
large sums she has supplied us with in the day of our necessity. Our officers and soldiers, who have successfully fought
our battles, and the loaners of money to the public, look up
to you for relief.

The bravery of our troops is degraded by the weakness
of our government.

It has been contended that the 5th article of the Confederation cannot be repealed under the powers to new-modify
the Confederation by the 13th article. This surely is false
reasoning; since the whole of the Confederation, upon revision,
is subject to *amendment and alteration;* besides, our business
consists in recommending a system of government, not in making it. There are great reasons when persons with limited
powers are justified in exceeding them, and a person would be
contemptible not to risk it. Originally, our Confederation was
founded on the weakness of each State to repel a foreign enemy; and we have found that the powers granted to Congress
are insufficient. The body of Congress is ineffectual to carry
the great objects of safety and protection into execution. What
would their powers be over the commander of the military
but for the virtue of the commander? As the State assemblies
are constantly encroaching on the powers of Congress, the
Jersey plan would rather encourage such encroachment than
be a check to it; and, from the nature of the institution, Congress would never be governed by cabal and intrigue. They
are, besides, too numerous for an executive; nor can any additional powers be sufficient to enable them to protect us against
foreign invasion. Among other things, Congress was intended
to be a body to preserve peace among the States; and, in the
rebellion of Massachusetts, it was found they were not authorized to use the troops of the Confederation to quell it. Every
one is impressed with the idea of a general regulation of trade
and commerce. Can Congress do this, when, from the nature
of their institution, they are so subject to cabal and intrigue?
And would it not be dangerous to intrust such a body with
the power, when they are dreaded on these grounds? I am
certain that a national government must be established, and
this is the only moment when it can be done; and let me conclude by observing that the best exercise of power is to exert
it for the public good.

On June 18 Colonel Alexander Hamilton reopened
the debate with a powerful speech of five hours' dura-

tion, in the course of which he presented a plan of government differing widely from both of those before the convention.

Mr. Hamilton.—To deliver my sentiments on so important a subject, when the first characters of the Union have gone before me, inspires me with the greatest diffidence, especially when my own ideas are so materially dissimilar to the plans now before the committee. My situation is disagreeable; but it would be criminal not to come forward on a question of such magnitude. I have well considered the subject, and am convinced that no amendment of the Confederation can answer the purpose of a good government so long as the State sovereignties do, in any shape, exist; and I have great doubts whether a national government on the Virginia plan can be made effectual. What is federal? An association of several independent states into one. How or in what manner this association is formed is not so clearly distinguishable. We find the Diet of Germany has, in some instances, the power of legislation on individuals. We find the United States of America have it in an extensive degree in the case of piracies.

Let us now review the powers with which we are invested. We are appointed for the sole and express purpose of revising the Confederation, and to alter or amend it, so as to render it effectual for the purposes of a good government. Those who suppose it to be federal lay great stress on the terms *sole* and *express,* as if these words intended a confinement to a federal government; when the manifest import is no more than that the institution of a good government must be the *sole* and *express* object of your deliberations. Nor can we suppose an annihilation of our powers by forming a national government, as many of the States have made, in their constitutions, no provision for any alteration; and thus much I can say for the State I have the honor to represent, that, when our credentials were under consideration in the Senate, some members were for inserting a restriction in the powers, to prevent an encroachment on the Constitution: it was answered by others, and thereupon the resolve carried on the credentials, that it might abridge the constitutional powers of the State, and that possibly, in the formation of a new union, it would be found necessary. This appears reasonable, and therefore leaves us at liberty to form such a national government as we think best adapted for the good of the whole. I have, therefore, no difficulty as to the extent of our powers, nor do I feel myself restrained in the exercise of my judgment under them. We can only propose and recommend;—the power of ratifying or rejecting is still in the States. But on this great question I am still greatly embarrassed. I have before observed my apprehension of the inefficacy of either plan, and I have great doubts whether a more energetic government can pervade this wide and extensive country. I shall now show that both plans are materially defective.

1. A good government ought to be constant, and ought to contain an active principle. 2. Utility and necessity. 3. An habitual sense of obligation. 4. Force. 5. Influence.

I hold it that different societies have all different views and interests to pursue, and always prefer local to general concerns. For example: the New York legislature made an external compliance lately to a requisition of Congress; but do they not, at the same time, counteract their compliance by gratifying the local objects of the State, so as to defeat their concession? And this will ever be the case. Men always love power, and States will prefer their particular concerns to the general welfare; and as the States become large and important, will they not be less attentive to the general government? What, in the process of time, will Virginia be? She contains now half a million inhabitants: in twenty-five years she will double the number. Feeling her own weight and importance, must she not become indifferent to the concerns of the Union? And where, in such a situation, will be found national attachment to the general government?

By *force* I mean the *coercion* of law and the coercion of arms. Will this remark apply to the power intended to be vested in the government to be instituted by their plan? A delinquent must be compelled to obedience by force of arms. How is this to be done? If you are unsuccessful a dissolution of your government must be the consequence; and, in that case, the individual legislatures will reassume their powers; nay, will not the interests of the States be thrown into the State governments?

By *influence,* I mean the regular weight and support it will receive from those who find it their interest to support a government intended to preserve the peace and happiness of the community on the whole. The State governments, by either plan, will exert the means to counteract it. They have their State judges and militia all combined to support their State interests; and these will be influenced to oppose a national government. Either plan is therefore precarious. The national government cannot long exist when opposed by such a weighty rival. The experience of ancient and modern confederacies evinces this point, and throws considerable light on the subject. The Amphictyonic council of Greece had a right to require of its members troops, money, and the force of the country. Were they obeyed in the exercise of those powers? Could they preserve the peace of the greater states and republics? or where were they obeyed? History shows that their decrees were disregarded, and that the stronger States, regardless of their power, gave law to the lesser.

Let us examine the federal institution of Germany. It was instituted upon the laudable principle of securing the independency of the several states of which it was composed, and to protect them against foreign invasion. Has it answered these good intentions? Do we not see that their councils are weak and distracted, and that it cannot prevent the wars and confusions which the respective electors carry on against each other? The Swiss cantons, or the Helvetic union, are equally inefficient.

Such are the lessons which the experience of others affords us, and from whence results the evident conclusion that all federal governments are weak and distracted. To avoid the evils deducible from these observations, we must establish a general and national government, completely sovereign, and annihilate the State distinctions and State operations; and unless we do this no good purpose can be answered. What does the Jersey plan propose? It surely has not this for its object. By this we grant the regulation of trade and a more effectual collection of the revenue and some partial duties. These, at five or ten per cent., would only perhaps amount to a fund to discharge the debt of the corporation.

Let us take a review of the variety of important objects which must necessarily engage the attention of a national government. You have to protect your rights against Canada on the north, Spain on the south, and your western frontier against the savages. You have to adopt necessary plans for the settlement of your frontiers, and to institute the mode in which settlements and good governments are to be made.

How is the expense of supporting and regulating these important matters to be defrayed? By requisition on the States, according to the Jersey plan? Will this do it? We have already found it ineffectual. Let one State prove delinquent and it will encourage others to follow the example and thus the whole will fail. And what is the standard to quota among the States their respective proportions? Can lands be the standard? How would that apply between Russia and Holland? Compare Pennsylvania with North Carolina, or Connecticut with New York. Does not commerce or industry in the one or other make a great disparity between these different countries, and may not the comparative value of the States, from these circumstances, make an unequal disproportion when the data are numbers? I therefore conclude that either system would ultimately destroy the Confederation, or any other government which is established on such fallacious principles. Perhaps imposts—taxes on specific articles—would produce a more equal system of drawing a revenue.

Another objection against the Jersey plan is the unequal representation. Can the great States consent to this? If they did it would eventually work its own destruction. How are forces to be raised by the Jersey plan? By quotas? Will the States comply with the requisition? As much as they will with the taxes.

Examine the present Confederation and it is evident they can raise no troops nor equip vessels before war is actually declared. They cannot, therefore, take any preparatory measure before an enemy is at your door. How unwise and inadequate their powers! and this must ever be the case when you attempt to define powers: something will always be wanting. Congress, by being annually elected and subject to recall, will ever come with the prejudices of their States rather than the good of the Union. Add, therefore, additional powers to a body thus organized and you establish a *sovereignty* of the worst kind, consisting of a single body. Where are the checks? None. They must either prevail over the State governments, or the prevalence of the State governments must end in their dissolution. This is a conclusive objection to the Jersey plan.

Such are the insuperable objections to both plans: and what is to be done on this occasion? I confess I am at a loss. I foresee the difficulty, on a consolidated plan, of drawing a representation from so extensive a continent to one place. What can be the inducements for gentlemen to come six hundred miles to a national legislature? The expense would at least amount to a hundred thousand pounds. This, however, can be no conclusive objection, if it eventuates in an extinction of State governments. The burden of the latter would be saved and the expense, then, would not be great. State distinctions would be found unnecessary; and yet, I confess, to carry government to the extremities, the State governments, reduced to corporations, and with very limited powers, might be necessary, and the expense of the national government become less burdensome.

Yet, I confess, I see great difficulty of drawing forth a good representation. What, for example, will be the inducements for gentlemen of fortune and abilities to leave their houses and business to attend annually and long? It cannot be the wages: for these, I presume, must be small. Will not the power, therefore, be thrown into the hands of the demagogue, or middling politician—who, for the sake of a small stipend, and the hopes of advancement, will offer himself as a candidate, and the real men of weight and influence, by remaining at home, add strength to the State governments? I am at a loss to know what must be done. I despair that a republican form of government can remove the difficulties. Whatever may be my opinion, I would hold it, however, unwise to change that form of government. I believe the British government forms the best model the world ever produced; and such has been its progress in the minds of the many that the truth gradually gains ground this government has for its object *public strength* and *individual security*. It is said with us to be unattainable. If it was once formed it would maintain itself. All communities divide themselves into the few and the many. The first are the rich and well born, the other the mass of the people. The voice of the people has been said to be the voice of God; and, however generally this maxim has been quoted and believed, it is not true in fact. The people are turbulent and changing; they seldom judge or determine right. Give, therefore, to the first class a distinct, permanent share in the government. They will check the unsteadiness of the second; and, as they cannot receive any advantage by a change, they therefore will ever maintain good government. Can a democratic assembly, who annually revolve in the mass of the people, be supposed steadily to pursue the public good? Nothing but a permanent body can check the imprudence of democracy. Their turbulent and uncontrollable disposition requires checks. The Senate of New York, although chosen for four years, we have found to be inefficient. Will, on the Virginia plan, a continuance of seven years do it? It is admitted that you cannot have a good executive upon a democratic plan. See the excellency of the British executive. He is placed above temptation—he can have no distinct interests from the public welfare. Nothing short of such an executive can be efficient. The weak side of a republican government is the danger of foreign influence. This is unavoidable, unless it is so constructed

as to bring forward its first characters in its support. **I am,**
therefore, for a general government, yet would wish **to go the**
full length of republican principles.

Let one body of the legislature be constituted during good
behavior or life.

Let one executive be appointed who dares execute his powers.
It may be asked: Is this a republican system? It is strictly
so, as long as they remain elective.

And let me observe that an executive is less dangerous to
the liberties of the people when in office during life than for
seven years.

It may be said this constitutes an elective monarchy. Pray
what is a monarchy? May not the governors of the respective
States be considered in that light? But by making the executive subject to impeachment the term *monarchy* cannot apply.
These elective monarchs have produced tumults in Rome, and
are equally dangerous to peace in Poland; but this cannot apply
to the mode in which I propose the election. Let electors be appointed in each of the States to elect the legislature (*here Mr. H.
produced his plan*) to consist of two branches and I would give
them the unlimited power of passing *all laws* without exception.
The Assembly to be elected for three years by the people, in districts; the Senate to be elected by electors to be chosen for that
purpose by the people, and to remain in office during life. The
executive to have the power of negativing all laws; to make war
or peace, with the advice of the Senate; to make treaties with
their advice, but to have the sole direction of all military operations; and to send ambassadors, and appoint all military officers,
and to pardon all offenders, treason excepted, unless by advice
of the Senate. On his death or removal, the president of the
Senate to officiate, with the same powers, until another is elected.
Supreme judicial officers to be appointed by the executive and
the Senate. The legislature to appoint courts in each State, so
as to make the State governments unnecessary to it.

All State laws to be absolutely void which contravene the
general laws. An officer to be appointed in each State to have
a negative on all State laws. All the militia and the appointment
of officers to be under the national government.

I confess that this plan, and that from Virginia, are very
remote from the idea of the people. Perhaps the Jersey plan
is nearest their expectation. But the people are gradually ripening in their opinions of government. They begin to be tired of
an excess of democracy. And what, even, is the Virginia plan
but *pork still, with a little change of the sauce?*

HAMILTON'S PLAN

1. The supreme legislative power of the United States of America to be vested in two distinct bodies of men, the one to be called the Assembly, the other the Senate, who, together, shall form the legislature of the United States, with power to pass all laws whatsoever, subject to the negative hereafter mentioned.

2. The Assembly to consist of persons elected by the people, to serve for three years.

3. The Senate to consist of persons elected to serve during good behavior; their election to be made by electors chosen for that purpose by the people. In order to this, the States to be divided into election districts. On the death, removal, or resignation of any Senator his place to be filled out of the district from which he came.

4. The supreme executive authority of the United States to be vested in a governor, to be elected to serve during good behavior. His election to be made by electors, chosen by electors, chosen by the people in the election districts aforesaid. His authorities and functions to be as follows:

To have a negative upon all laws about to be passed, and the execution of all laws passed; to have the entire direction of war, when authorized or begun; to have, with the advice and approbation of the Senate, the power of making all treaties; to have the sole appointment of the heads or chief officers of the departments of Finance, War, and Foreign Affairs; to have the nomination of all other officers (ambassadors of foreign nations included), subject to the approbation or rejection of the Senate; to have the power of pardoning all offences except treason, which he shall not pardon without the approbation of the Senate.

5. On the death, resignation, or removal of the governor, his authorities to be exercised by the president of the Senate, until a successor be appointed.

6. The Senate to have the sole power of declaring war; the power of advising and approving all treaties; the power of approving or rejecting all appointments of officers, except the heads or chiefs of the departments of Finance, War, and Foreign Affairs.

7. The supreme judicial authority of the United States to be vested in   judges, to hold their offices during good behavior, with adequate and permanent salaries. This court to have original jurisdiction in all causes of capture; and an appellate jurisdiction in all causes in which the revenues of the general government, or the citizens of foreign nations, are concerned.

8.   The legislature of the United States to have power to institute courts in each State, for the determination of all matters of general concern.

9.   The Governors, Senators, and all officers of the United States to be liable to impeachment for mal- and corrupt conduct; and, upon conviction, to be removed from office, and disqualified for holding any place of trust or profit.   All impeachments to be tried by a court, to consist of the chief or senior judge of the superior court of law in each State; provided that such judge hold his place during good behavior and have a permanent salary.

10.   All laws of the particular States, contrary to the Constitution or laws of the United States, to be utterly void.   And the better to prevent such laws being passed, the governor or president of each State shall be appointed by the general government, and shall have a negative upon the laws about to be passed in the State of which he is governor or president.

11.   No State to have any forces, land or naval, and the militia of all the States to be under the sole and exclusive direction of the United States, the officers of which to be appointed and commissioned by them.

Judge Yates remarked that "Hamilton was praised by everybody, but supported by none."   His plan was not even referred to the "committee of detail" on July 26.   Hamilton was severely censured throughout his carreer for his undemocratic propositions in the convention, and so, in 1803, he wrote a letter to Col. Timothy Pickering explaining and justifying them.

HAMILTON'S LETTER TO PICKERING

The highest toned propositions which I made in the convention were for a President, Senate, and judges during good behavior—a House of Representatives for three years.   Though I would have enlarged the legislative power of the general Government, yet I never contemplated the abolition of the State governments; but, on the contrary, they were, in some particulars, constituent parts of my plan.

This plan was, in my conception, conformable with the strict theory of a government purely republican; the essential criteria of which are that the principal organs of the executive and legislative departments be elected by the people and hold their offices by a *responsible* and temporary or *defeasible* tenure.

A vote was taken on the proposition respecting the executive. Five States were in favor of it, among these Virginia; and, though, from the manner of voting by delegations, individuals were not distinguished, it was morally certain, from the known situation of the Virginia members (six in number, two of them, Mason and Randolph, professing popular doctrines), that Madison must have concurred in the vote of Virginia. Thus, if I sinned against republicanism, Mr. Madison was not less guilty.

I may truly then say that I never proposed either a President or Senate for life; and that I neither recommended nor meditated the annihilation of the State governments.

And I may add that, in the course of the discussions in the convention, neither the propositions thrown out for debate, nor even those voted in the earlier stages of deliberation, were considered as evidences of a definitive opinion in the proposer or voter. It appeared to me to be in some sort understood that, with a view to free investigation, experimental propositions might be made, which were to be received merely as suggestions for consideration.

Accordingly, it is a fact that my final opinion was against an executive during good behavior, on account of the increased danger to the public tranquillity incident to the election of a magistrate of this degree of permanency. In the plan of a constitution which I drew up while the convention was sitting, and which I communicated to Mr. Madison about the close of it, perhaps a day or two after, the office of President has no greater duration than for three years.

This plan was predicted upon these bases: 1. That the political principles of the people of this country would endure nothing but republican governments. 2. That, in the actual situation of the country, it was in itself right and proper that the republican theory should have a fair and full trial. 3. That to such a trial it was essential that the government should be so constructed as to give it all the energy and stability reconcilable with the principles of that theory.

These were the genuine sentiments of my heart, and upon them I acted.

I sincerely hope that it may not hereafter be discovered that, through want of sufficient attention to the last idea, the experiment of republican government, even in this country, has not been as complete, as satisfactory, and as decisive as could be wished.

On June 19 Mr. Madison made the closing argument against the Jersey plan.

MR. MADISON.—Many persons scruple the powers of the convention. If this remark had any weight it is equally applicable to the adoption of either plan. The difference of drawing the powers in the one from the people and in the other from the States does not affect the powers. There are two States in the Union where the members of Congress are chosen by the people. A new government must be made. Our all is depending on it; and, if we have but a clause that the people will adopt, there is then a chance for our preservation. Although all the States have assented to the Confederation, an infraction of any one article by one of the States is a dissolution of the whole. This is the doctrine of the civil law on treaties.

Jersey pointedly refused complying with a requisition of Congress and was guilty of this infraction, although she afterward rescinded her non-complying resolve. What is the object of a confederation? It is twofold: first, to maintain the union; secondly, good government. Will the Jersey plan secure these points? No; it is still in the power of the confederated States to violate treaties. Has not Georgia, in direct violation of the Confederation, made war with the Indians, and concluded treaties? Have not Virginia and Maryland entered into a partial compact? Have not Pennsylvania and Jersey regulated the bounds of the Delaware? Has not the State of Massachusetts at this time a considerable body of troops in pay? Has not Congress been obliged to pass a conciliatory act in support of a decision of their federal court, between Connecticut and Pennsylvania, instead of having the power of carrying into effect the judgment of their own court? Nor does the Jersey plan provide for a ratification, by the respective States, of the powers intended to be vested. It is also defective in the establishment of the judiciary, granting only an appellate jurisdiction, without providing for a second trial; and, in case the executive of a State should pardon an offender, how will it affect the definite judgment on appeal? It is evident, if we do not *radically* depart from a federal plan, we shall share the fate of ancient and modern confederacies. The Amphictyonic council, like the American Congress, had the power of judging, in the *last resort,* in war and peace— to call out forces—send ambassadors. What was its fate or continuance? Philip of Macedon with little difficulty destroyed every appearance of it. The Athenian had nearly the same fate. The Helvetic confederacy is rather a league. In the German confederacy the parts are too strong for the whole. The Dutch are in a most wretched situation—weak in all its parts, and only supported by surrounding contending powers.

The rights of individuals are infringed by many of the State laws—such as issuing paper money and instituting a mode to discharge debts differing from the form of the contract. Has the Jersey plan any checks to prevent the mischief? Does it in any instance secure internal tranquillity? Right and force, in a system like this, are synonymous terms. When force is employed to support the system, and men obtain military habits, is there no danger they may turn their arms against their employers? Will the Jersey plan prevent foreign influence? Did not Persia and Macedon distract the councils of Greece by acts of corruption? And are not Jersey and Holland at this day subject to the same distractions? Will not the plan be burdensome to the smaller States, if they have an equal representation? But how is military coercion to enforce government? True, a smaller State may be brought to obedience, or crushed; but what if one of the larger States should prove disobedient—are you sure you can, by force, effect a submission? Suppose we cannot agree on any plan; what will be the condition of the smaller States? Will Delaware and Jersey be safe against Pennsylvania, or Rhode Island against Massachusetts? And how will the smaller States be situated in case of partial confederacies? Will they not be obliged to make larger concessions to the greater States? The point of representation is the great point of difference, and which the greater States cannot give up; and, although there was an equalization of States, State distinctions would still exist. But this is totally impracticable; and what would be the effect of the Jersey plan if ten or twelve new States were added?

At the conclusion of Mr. Madison's remarks the Convention in committee of the whole reported the Jersey plan as inadmissible.

CHAPTER XII

STRONG OR WEAK GOVERNMENT?

[DEBATE IN THE CONSTITUTIONAL CONVENTION ON BASIS OF
REPRESENTATION]

Debate on the Virginia Plan of Representation of States in Congress According to Population: in favor (in the main), James Wilson [Pa.], James Madison [Va.], Charles Pinckney [S. C.], Alexander Hamilton [N. Y.], Hugh Williamson [N. C.], Elbridge Gerry [Mass.], Rufus King [Mass.], Gov. Edmund Randolph [Va.]; opposed (in the main), John Lansing, Jr. [N. Y.], George Mason [Va.], Dr. William Samuel Johnson [Ct.], Judge Oliver Ellsworth [Ct.], Luther Martin [Md.], Gov. Benjamin Franklin [Pa.], George Read [Del.], Abraham Baldwin [Ga.], Gunning S. Bedford, Jr. [Del.], Gouverneur Morris [Pa.], Robert Yates and Lansing, of New York, Leave the Convention—Their Report to Gov. George Clinton—George Washington's Despairing Letter to Hamilton.

IN the debate which ensued on the adoption of the Virginia plan, the chief speakers were, mainly in the affirmative: James Wilson [Pa.], James Madison [Va.], Charles Pinckney [S. C.], Alexander Hamilton [N. Y.], Hugh Williamson [N. C.], Elbridge Gerry [Mass.], Rufus King [Mass.], and Gov. Edmund Randolph [Va.]; mainly in the negative: John Lansing, Jr. [N. Y.], George Mason [Va.], Dr. William Samuel Johnson [Ct.], Judge Oliver Ellsworth [Ct.], Luther Martin [Md.], Gov. Benjamin Franklin [Pa.], George Read [Del.], Abraham Baldwin [Ga.], Gunning S. Bedford, Jr. [Del.], and Gouverneur Morris [Pa.].

STRONG OR WEAK GOVERNMENT?

CONSTITUTIONAL CONVENTION, JUNE 19-JULY 5, 1787

MR. LANSING.—I am clearly of opinion that I am not authorized to accede to a system which will annihilate the State governments, and the Virginia plan is declarative of such extinction.

317

It has been asserted that the public mind is not known. To some points it may be true; but we may collect from the fate of the requisition of the impost what it may be on the principles of a national government. When many of the States were so tenacious of their rights on this point, can we expect that thirteen States will surrender their governments up to a national plan? Rhode Island pointedly refused granting it. Certainly she had a federal right to do so; and I hold it as an undoubted truth, as long as State distinctions remain, let the national government be modified as you please, both branches of your legislature will be impressed with local and State attachments. The Virginia plan proposes a negative on the State laws where, in the opinion of the national legislature, they contravene the national government; and no laws can pass unless approved by them. They will have more than a law in a day to revise; and are they competent to judge of the wants and necessities of remote States?

This national government will, from their power, have great influence in the State governments; and the existence of the latter is only saved in appearance. And has it not been asserted that they expect their extinction? If this be the object, let us say so, and extinguish them at once. But remember, if we devise a system of government which will not meet the approbation of our constituents, we are dissolving the Union; but, if we act within the limits of our power, it will be approved of; and should it, upon experiment, prove defective, the people will intrust a future convention again to amend it. Fond as many are of a general government, do any of you believe that it can pervade the whole continent so effectually as to secure the peace, harmony, and happiness of the whole? The excellence of the British model of government has been much insisted on; but we are endeavoring to complicate it with State governments, on principles which will gradually destroy the one or the other. You are sowing the seeds of rivalship, which must at last end in ruin.

Mr. Mason.—The material difference between the two plans has already been clearly pointed out. The objection to that of Virginia arises from the want of power to institute it, and the want of practicability to carry it into effect. Will the first objection apply to a power merely recommendatory? In certain seasons of public danger it is commendable to exceed power. The treaty of peace, under which we now enjoy the blessings of freedom, was made by persons who exceeded their powers. It met the approbation of the public and thus deserved the praises of those who sent them. The impracticability of the plan is still more groundless. These measures are supported by one who, at his time of life, has little to hope or expect from any government. Let me ask: Will the people intrust their dearest rights and liberties to the determination of one body of men, and those not chosen by them, and who are invested both with the *sword* and *purse?* They never will—they never can—to a conclave, transacting their business secret from the eye of the public. Do we not discover by their public journals of the years 1778-9 and 1780 that factions and party spirit had guided many of their acts? The people of America, like all other people, are unsettled in their minds, and their principles fixed to no object, except that a republican government is the best and that the legislature ought to consist of two branches. The constitutions of the respective States, made and approved of by them, evince this principle. Congress, however, from other causes, received a different organization. What! would you use military force to compel the observance of a social compact? It is destructive to the rights of the people. Do you expect the militia will do it? or do you mean a standing army? The first will never, on such an occasion, exert any power; and the latter may turn its arms against the government which employs them. I never will consent to destroy State governments, and will ever be as careful to preserve the one as the other. If we should, in the formation of the latter, have omitted some necessary regulation, I will trust my posterity to amend it. That the one government will be productive of disputes and jealousies against the other, I believe; but it will produce mutual safety. I shall close with observing that, though some have expressed much warmth on this and former occasions, I can excuse it as the result of sudden passion; and hope that, although we may differ in some particular points, if we mean the good of the whole, that our good sense, upon reflection, will prevent us from spreading our discontent farther.

Mr. Wilson.—The question before us may admit of the three following considerations:

1. Whether the legislature shall consist of one or two branches.

2. Whether they are to be elected by the State governments or by the people.

3. Whether in proportion to State importance, or States individually.

Confederations are usually of a short date. The Amphictyonic council was instituted in the infancy of the Grecian re-

publics. As those grew in strength the council lost its weight
and power. The Achæan league met the same fate. Switzerland
and Holland are supported in their confederation, not by its intrinsic merit, but the incumbent pressure of surrounding bodies.
Germany is kept together by the house of Austria. True, Congress carried us through the war even against its own weakness.
That powers were wanting, you, Mr. President, must have felt.
To other causes, not to Congress, must the success be ascribed.
That the great States acceded to the Confederation, and that
they, in the hour of danger, made a sacrifice of their interest
to the lesser states, is true. Like the wisdom of Solomon, in
adjudging the child to its true mother, from tenderness to it, the
greater states well knew that the loss of a limb was fatal to the
Confederation: they, too, through tenderness, sacrificed their
dearest rights to preserve the whole. But the time is come when
justice will be done to their claims. Situations are altered.

Congress have frequently made their appeal to the people. I
wish they had always done it: the national government would
sooner have been extricated.

DR. JOHNSON.—It appears to me that the Jersey plan has for
its principal object the preservation of the State governments.
So far it is a departure from the plan of Virginia, which, although it concentrates in a distinct national government, is not
totally independent of that of the States. A gentleman from New
York, with boldness and decision, proposed a system totally different from both; and, though he has been praised by everybody,
he has been supported by none. How can the State governments
be secured on the Virginia plan? I could have wished that the
supporters of the Jersey system could have satisfied themselves
with the principles of the Virginia plan, and that the individuality of the States could be supported. It is agreed, on all hands,
that a portion of government is to be left to the States. How
can this be done? It can be done by joining the States, in their
legislative capacity, with the right of appointing the second
branch of the national legislature, to represent the States individually.

MR. WILSON.—If security is necessary to preserve the one it is
equally so to preserve the other. How can the national government be secured against the States? Some regulation is necessary. Suppose the national government had a competent number in the State legislature. But where the one government
clashed with the other the State government ought to yield, as
the preservation of the general interest must be preferred to
a particular. But let us try to designate the powers of each,

and then no danger can be apprehended, nor can the general government be possessed of any ambitious views to encroach on the State rights.

MR. MADISON.—I could have wished that the gentleman from Connecticut had more accurately marked his objections to the Virginia plan. I apprehend the greatest danger is from the encroachment of the States on the national government. This apprehension is justly founded on the experience of ancient confederacies, and our own is a proof of it.

The right of negativing, in certain instances, the State laws affords one security to the national government. But is the danger well founded? Have any State governments ever encroached on the corporate rights of cities? And if it was the case that the national government usurped the State government, if such usurpation was for the good of the whole, no mischief could arise. To draw the line between the two is a difficult task. I believe it cannot be done, and therefore I am inclined for a general government.

If we cannot form a general government, and the States become totally independent of each other, it would afford a melancholy prospect.

The second resolve was then put and carried—seven States for, three against, one divided.

The third resolve was then taken into consideration by the Convention.

After debate it was carried: 8 ayes, 2 noes, 1 State divided. The fourth resolution of the committee was now taken up.

MR. C. PINCKNEY.—There is more equality of rank and fortune in America than in any other country under the sun; and this is likely to continue as long as the unappropriated western lands remain unsettled. They are equal in rights, nor is extreme of poverty to be seen in any part of the Union. If we are thus singularly situated, both as to fortune and rights, it evidently follows that we cannot draw any useful lessons from the examples of any of the European states or kingdoms; much less can Great Britain afford us any striking institution, which can be adapted to our own situation—unless we indeed intend to establish an hereditary executive, or one for life. Great Britain drew its first rude institutions from the forests of Germany, and with them that of its nobility. These having originally in their hands the property of the state, the crown of Great Britain was obliged to yield to the claims of power which those large possessions enabled them to assert. The Commons were then too contemptible to form part of the national councils. Many parliaments were held without their being represented; until, in process of time, under the protection of the Crown, and forming distinct communities, they obtained some weight in the British government. From such discordant materials, brought casually together, those admirable checks and balances, now so much the boast of the British constitution, took their rise. But will we be able to copy from this original? Do not suppose that in the Confederation there are one hundred gentlemen of sufficient fortunes to establish a nobility; and the equality of others as to rank would never admit of the distinctions of nobility. I lay it therefore down as a settled principle that equality of condition is a leading axiom in our government. It may be said we must necessarily establish checks, lest one rank of people usurp the rights of another. Commerce can neither interfere with the government nor give a complexion to its councils. Can we copy from Greece or Rome? Have we their nobles or patricians? With them offices were open to few. The different ranks in the community formed opposite interests, and produced unceasing struggles and disputes. Can this apply to the free yeomanry of America? We surely differ from the whole. Our situation is unexampled; and it is in our power, on different grounds, to secure civil and religious liberty; and when we secure these we secure everything that is necessary to establish happiness. We cannot pretend to rival the European nations in their grandeur or power; nor is the situation of any two nations so exactly alike as that the one can adopt the regulations or government of the other. If we have any distinctions they may be divided into three classes:

1. Professional men.   2. Commercial men.   3. The landed interest.

The latter is the governing power of America, and the other two must ever be dependent on them. Will a national government suit them? No. The three orders have necessarily a mixed interest; and in that view—I repeat it again—the United States of America compose, in fact, but one order. The clergy and nobility of Great Britain can never be adopted by us. Our government must be made suitable to the people; and we are, perhaps, the only people in the world who ever had sense enough to appoint delegates to establish a general government. I believe that the propositions from Virginia, with some amendments, will satisfy the people. But a general government must not be dependent on the State governments.

The United States include a territory of about fifteen hundred miles in length, and in breadth about four hundred, the whole of which is divided into States and districts. While we were dependent on the Crown of Great Britain, it was in contemplation to form the whole into one; but it was found impracticable. No legislature could make good laws for the whole, nor can it now be done. It would necessarily place the power in the hands of the few nearest the seat of government. State governments must therefore remain, if you mean to prevent confusion. The general negative powers will support the general government. Upon these considerations I am led to form the second branch differently from the report. Their powers are important, and the number not too large, upon the principle of proportion. I have considered the subject with great attention; and I propose this plan [1] [*reads it*]; and if no better plan is proposed I will then move its adoption.

MR. WILSON.—The question now before us is whether the second branch of the general legislature shall, or shall not, be appointed by the State legislatures. In every point of view it is an important question. The magnitude of the objects is indeed embarrassing. The great system of Henry IV of France, aided by the greatest statesmen, is small when compared to the fabric we are now about to erect. In laying the stone amiss we may injure the superstructure; and what will be the consequence if the corner-stone should be loosely placed? It is improper that the State legislatures should have the power contemplated to be given them. A citizen of America may be considered in two points of view—as a citizen of the general government, and as a citizen of the particular State in which he may reside. We ought to consider in what character he acts in forming a general government. I am both a citizen of Pennsylvania and of the United States. I must therefore lay aside my State connections and act for the general good of the whole. We must forget our local habits and attachments. The general government should not depend on the State governments. This ought to be a leading distinction between the one and the other; nor ought the general government to be composed of an assemblage of different State governments. We have unanimously agreed to establish a general government—that the powers of peace, war, treaties, coinage, and regulation of commerce ought to reside in that government. And if we reason in this manner we shall soon see the

[1] See page 290.

impropriety of interference of State governments with the general government. Equality of representation cannot be established if the second branch is elected by the State legislatures. When we are laying the foundation of a building which is to last for ages, and in which millions are interested, it ought to be well laid. If the national government does not act upon State prejudices State distinctions will be lost. I therefore move that the second branch of the legislature of the national government be elected by electors chosen by the people of the United States.

JUDGE ELLSWORTH.—I think the second branch of the general legislature ought to be elected agreeably to the report. The other way, it is said, will be more the choice of the people. The one mode is as much so as the other. No doubt every citizen of every State is interested in the State governments; and elect him in whatever manner you please, whenever he takes a seat in the general government, it will prevail in some shape or other. The State legislatures are more competent to make a judicious choice than the people at large. Instability pervades their choice. In the second branch of the general government we want wisdom and firmness. As to balances, where nothing can be balanced it is a perfect Utopian scheme. But still great advantages will result in having a second branch endowed with the qualifications I have mentioned. Their weight and wisdom may check the inconsiderate and hasty proceedings of the first branch.

I cannot see the force of the reasoning in attempting to detach the State governments from the general government. In that case, without a standing army, you cannot support the general government but on the pillars of the State governments. Are the larger States more energetic than the smaller? Massachusetts cannot support a government at the distance of one hundred miles from her capital without an army; and how long Virginia and Pennsylvania will support their governments it is difficult to say. Shall we proceed like unskilful workmen, and make use of timber which is too weak to build a first-rate ship? We know that the people of the States are strongly attached to their own constitutions. If you hold up a system of general government, destructive of their constitutional rights, they will oppose it. Some are of opinion that, if we cannot form a general government so as to destroy State governments, we ought at least to balance the one against the other. On the contrary, the only chance we have to support a general government is to draft it on the State governments. I want to proceed on this ground, as the safest, and I believe no other plan is practicable. In this way, and in this way only, can we rely on the confidence and support of the people.

MR. MASON.—All agree that a more efficient government is necessary. It is equally necessary to preserve the State governments, as they ought to have the means of self-defence. On the motion of Mr. Wilson, the only means they ought to have would be destroyed.

The question was put for postponing, in order to take into consideration the 8th resolve, and lost—7 noes, 4 ayes.

Question on the 1st clause in the 4th resolve—9 States for, 2 against it.

The question of the constitution of the Senate now came before the convention.

MR. READ moved that the term of "nine years" be inserted, in triennial rotation.

MR. MADISON.—We are now to determine whether the republican form shall be the basis of our government. I admit there is weight in the objection of the gentleman from South Carolina; but no plan can steer clear of objections. That great powers are to be given there is no doubt; and that those powers may be abused is equally true. It is also probable that members may lose their attachments to the States which sent them; yet the first branch will control them in many of their abuses. But we are now forming a body on whose wisdom we mean to rely, and their permanency in office secures a proper field in which they may exert their firmness and knowledge. Democratic communities may be unsteady, and be led to action by the impulse of the moment. Like individuals they may be sensible of their own weakness, and may desire the counsels and checks of friends, to guard them against the turbulency and weakness of unruly passions. Such are the various pursuits of this life that, in all civilized countries, the interest of a community will be divided. There will be debtors and creditors, and an unequal possession of property; and hence arise different views and different objects in government. This, indeed, is the groundwork of aristocracy, and we find it blended in every government, both ancient and modern. Even where titles have survived property we discover the noble beggar haughty and assuming.

The man who is possessed of wealth, who lolls on his sofa or rolls in his carriage, cannot judge of the wants or feelings of

the day-laborer. The government we mean to erect is intended
to last for ages. The landed interest, at present, is prevalent;
but in process of time, when we approximate to the states and
kingdoms of Europe—when the number of landholders shall be
comparatively small, through the various means of trade and
manufactures—will not the landed interest be overbalanced in
future elections? and, unless wisely provided against, what will
become of your government? In England, at this day, if elections were open to all classes of people, the property of landed
proprietors would be insecure. An agrarian law would soon
take place. If these observations be just our government ought
to secure the permanent interests of the country against innovation. Landholders ought to have a share in the government,
to support these invaluable interests, and to balance and check
the other. They ought to be so constituted as to protect the
minority of the opulent against the majority. The Senate, therefore, ought to be this body; and, to answer these purposes, they
ought to have permanency and stability. Various have been the
propositions; but my opinion is, the longer they continue in
office, the better will these views be answered.

MR. HAMILTON.—This question has already been considered
in several points of view. We are now forming a republican government. Real liberty is neither found in despotism nor the extremes of democracy, but in moderate governments.

Those who mean to form a solid republican government ought
to proceed to the confines of another government. As long as
offices are open to all men, and no constitutional rank is established, it is pure republicanism. But if we incline too much to
democracy we shall soon shoot into a monarchy. The difference
of property is already great among us. Commerce and industry will still increase the disparity. Your government must
meet this state of things, or combinations will, in process of time,
undermine your system. What was the tribunitial power of
Rome? It was instituted by the plebeians, as a guard against
the patricians. But was this a sufficient check? No. The only
distinction which remained at Rome was, at last, between the
rich and poor. The gentleman from Connecticut forgets that
the democratic body is already secure in a representation. As
to Connecticut, what were the little objects of their government
before the revolution? Colonial concerns merely. They ought
now to act on a more extended scale: and dare they do this?
Dare they collect the taxes and requisitions of Congress? Such
a government may do well if they do not tax; and this is precisely their situation.

MR. GERRY.—It appears to me that the American people have the greatest aversion to monarchy; and the nearer our government approaches to it the less chance have we for their approbation. Can gentlemen suppose that the reported system can be approved of by them? Demagogues are the great pests of our government, and have occasioned most of our distresses. If four years are insufficient, a future convention may lengthen the time.

MR. WILSON.—The motion is now for nine years, and a triennial rotation. Every nation attends to its foreign intercourse; to support its commerce; to prevent foreign contempt; and to make war and peace. Our Senate will be possessed of these powers, and therefore ought to be dignified and permanent. What is the reason that Great Britain does not enter into a commercial treaty with us? Because Congress has not the power to enforce its observance. But give them those powers, and give them the stability proposed by the motion, and they will have more permanency than a monarchical government. The great objection of many is that this duration would give birth to views inconsistent with the interests of the Union. This can have no weight if the triennial rotation is adopted; and this plan may possibly tend to conciliate the minds of the members of the convention on this subject, which have varied more than on any other question.

The question was then put on Mr. Read's motion, and lost—8 noes, 3 ayes.

The question on five years and a biennial rotation was carried—7 ayes, 4 noes.

The 5th resolve, that each house have the right of originating bills, was taken into consideration, and agreed to.

The 6th resolve was postponed, in order to take into consideration the 7th and 8th resolves. The 1st clause of the 7th, which respected the suffrage of each State in the first branch of the legislature, was proposed for consideration. Says Judge Yates:

Mr. Martin, the attorney-general from Maryland, spoke on this subject upward of three hours. As his arguments were too diffuse, and in many instances desultory, it was not possible to trace him through the whole, or to methodize his ideas into a systematic or argumentative arrangement. I shall therefore note only such points as I conceive merit most particular notice.

The question is important (said Mr. Martin), and I have already expressed my sentiments on the subject. My opinion is that the general government ought to protect and secure the State governments. Others, however, are of a different sentiment, and reverse the principle.

The present reported system is a perfect medley of confederated and national government, without example and without precedent. Many, who wish the general government to protect the State governments, are anxious to have the line of jurisdiction well drawn and defined, so that they may not clash. This suggests the necessity of having this line well detailed: possibly this may be done. If we do this the people will be convinced that we meant well to the State governments; and should there be any defects they will trust a future convention with the power of making further amendments.

A general government may operate on individuals in cases of general concern, and still be federal. This distinction is with the States, as States, represented by the people of those States. States will take care of their internal police and local concerns. The general government has no interest but the protection of the whole. Every other movement must fail. We are proceeding, in forming this government, as if there were no State governments at all. The States must approve, or you will have none at all. I have never heard of a confederacy having two legislative branches. Even the celebrated Mr. Adams, who talks so much of checks and balances, does not suppose it necessary in a confederacy. Public and domestic debts are our great distress. The treaty between Virginia and Maryland, about the navigation of the Chesapeake and Potomac, is no infraction of the Confederacy. The corner-stone of a federal government is equality of votes. States may surrender this right; but if they do their liberties are lost. If I err on this point it is the error of the head, not of the heart.

The first principle of government is founded on the natural rights of individuals, and in perfect equality. Locke, Vattel, Lord Somers, and Dr. Priestley all confirm this principle. This principle of equality, when applied to an individual, is lost, in some degree, when he becomes a member of a society, to which it is transferred; and this society, by the name of *state* or *kingdom*, is, with respect to others, again on a perfect footing of equality

—a right to govern themselves as they please. Nor can any other state, of right, deprive them of this equality. If such a state confederates it is intended for the good of the whole; and if it again confederates those rights must be well guarded. Nor can any state demand a surrender of any of those rights; if it can, equality is already destroyed. We must treat, as free states, with each other, upon the same terms of equality that men originally formed themselves into societies. Vattel, Rutherford, and Locke are united in support of the position, that states, as to each other, are in a state of nature.

Thus, says Mr. Martin, have I traveled with the most respectable authorities in support of principles all tending to prove the equality of independent states. This is equally applicable to the smallest as well as the largest states, on the true principles of reciprocity and political freedom.

Unequal confederacies can never produce good effects. Apply this to the Virginia plan. Out of the number 90 Virginia has 16 votes, Massachusetts 14, Pennsylvania 12; in all 42. Add to this a State having four votes, and it gives a majority in the general legislature. Consequently, a combination of these States will govern the remaining nine or ten States. Where are the safety and independency of those States? Pursue this subject farther. The executive is to be appointed by the legislature, and becomes the executive in consequence of this undue influence; and hence flows the appointment of all your officers, civil, military, and judicial. The executive is also to have a negative on all laws. Suppose the possibility of a combination of ten States: he negatives a law; it is totally lost, because those States cannot form two-thirds of the legislatures. I am willing to give up private interest to the public good; but I must be satisfied first that it is the public interest; and who can decide this point? A majority, only, of the Union.

The Lacedemonians insisted, in the Amphictyonic council, to exclude some of the smaller states from a right to vote, in order that they might tyrannize over them. If the plan now on the table be adopted three States in the Union have the control, and they may make use of their power when they please.

If there exist no separate interests there is no danger in an equality of votes; and if there be danger the smaller States cannot yield. If the foundation of the existing Confederation is well laid powers may be added. You may safely add a third story to a house where the foundation is good. Read, then, the votes and proceedings of Congress on forming the Confederation. Virginia only was opposed to the principles of equality.

The smaller States yielded rights, not the large States. They gave up their claim to the unappropriated lands with the tenderness of the mother recorded by Solomon. They sacrificed affection to the preservation of others. New Jersey and Maryland rendered more essential services during the war than many of the larger States. The partial representation in Congress is not the cause of its weakness, but the want of power. I would not trust a government, organized upon the reported plan, for all the slaves of Carolina, or the horses and oxen of Massachusetts. Price says that laws made by one man, or a set of men, and not by common consent, is slavery. And it is so when applied to States, if you give them an unequal representation. What are called human feelings, in this instance, are only the feelings of ambition and the lust of power.

On federal grounds it is said that a minority will govern a majority; but on the Virginia plan a minority would tax a majority. In a federal government a majority of States must and ought to tax. In local government of States counties may be unequal: still numbers, not property, govern. What is the government now forming—over States or persons? As to the latter, their rights cannot be the object of a general government. These are already secured by their guardians, the State governments. The general government is, therefore, intended only to protect and guard the rights of the States as states.

This general government, I believe, is the first upon earth which gives checks against democracies or aristocracies. The only necessary check, in a general government, ought to be a restraint to prevent its absorbing the powers of the State governments. Representation, on federal principles, can only flow from State societies. Representation and taxation are ever inseparable—not according to the quantum of property, but the quantum of freedom.

Will the representatives of a State forget State interests? The mode of election cannot change it. These prejudices cannot be eradicated. Your general government cannot be just or equal, upon the Virginia plan, unless you abolish State interests. If this cannot be done, you must go back to principles purely federal.

On this latter ground the State legislatures and their constituents will have no interests to pursue different from the general government, and both will be interested to support each other.

Under these ideas, can it be expected that the people can approve the Virginia plan? But it is said the people, not the State legislatures, will be called upon for approbation—with an evident design to separate the interest of the governors from the governed. What must be the consequence? Anarchy and confusion. We lose the idea of the powers with which we are intrusted. The legislatures must approve.

By them it must, on your own plan, be laid before the people. How will such a government, over so many great States, operate? Wherever new settlements have been formed in large States they immediately want to shake off their dependency. Why? Because the government is too remote for their good. The people want it nearer home.

The basis of all ancient and modern confederacies is the freedom and the independency of the states composing it. The states forming the Amphictyonic council were equal, though Lacedemon, one of the greatest states, attempted the exclusion of three of the lesser states from this right. The plan reported, it is true, only intends to diminish those rights, not to annihilate them. It was the ambition and power of the great Grecian states which at last ruined their respectable council. The states, as societies, are ever respectable. Has Holland or Switzerland ever complained of the equality of the states which compose their respective confederacies? Berne and Zurich are larger than the remaining eleven cantons. So of many of the states of Germany; and yet their governments are not complained of. Berne alone might usurp the whole power of the Helvetic confederacy, but she is contented still with being equal.

The admission of the larger States into the Confederation, on the principles of equality, is dangerous. But on the Virginia system it is ruinous and destructive. Still it is the true interest of all the States to confederate. It is their joint efforts which must protect and secure us from foreign danger, and give us peace and harmony at home.

Here Mr. Martin entered into a detail of the comparative powers of each State, and stated their probable weakness and strength.

At the beginning of our troubles with Great Britain the smaller States were attempted to be cajoled to submit to the views of that nation, lest the larger States should usurp their rights. We then answered them, Your present plan is slavery, which, on the remote prospect of a distant evil, we will not submit to.

I would rather confederate with any single State than submit to the Virginia plan. But we are already confederated, and no power on earth can dissolve it but by the consent of *all* the contracting powers; and four States, on this floor, have already declared their opposition to annihilate it. Is the old Confederation dissolved, because some of the States wish a new Confederation?

MR. LANSING.—I move that the word "not" be struck out of the resolve, and then the question will stand on its proper ground; and the resolution will read thus: that the representation of the first branch be according to the Articles of the Confederation; and the sense of the convention on this point will determine the question of a federal or national government.

MR. MADISON.—I am against the motion. I confess the necessity of harmonizing; and if it could be shown that the system is unjust or unsafe, I would be against it. There has been much fallacy in the argument advanced by the gentleman from Maryland. He has, without adverting to many manifest distinctions, considered confederacies and treaties as standing on the same basis. In the one the powers act collectively, in the other individually. Suppose, for example, that France, Spain, and some of the smaller states in Europe should treat on war or peace, or on any other general concern; it would be done on principles of equality. But if they were to form a plan of general government, would they give, or are the greater states obliged to give to the lesser, the same and equal legislative powers? Surely not. They might differ on this point, but no one can say that the large states were wrong in refusing this concession. Nor can the gentleman's reasoning apply to the present powers of Congress; for they may, and do, in some cases, affect property—and in case of war the lives of the citizens. Can any of the lesser States be endangered by an adequate representation? Where is the probability of a combination? What the inducements? Where is the similarity of customs, manners, or religion? If there possibly can be a diversity of interest it is the case of the three large States. Their situation is remote, their trade different. The staple of Massachusetts is fish, and the carrying trade; of Pennsylvania, wheat and flour; of Virginia, tobacco. Can States thus situated in trade ever form such a combination? Do we find those combinations in the larger counties in the different State governments to produce rivalships? Does not the history of the nations of the earth verify it? Rome rivaled Carthage, and could not be satisfied before she was destroyed. The houses of Austria and Bourbon acted on the same view; and the wars of France and England have been waged through rivalship; and let me add that we, in a great measure, owe our independency to

those national contending passions. France, through this motive, joined us. She might, perhaps, with less expense, have induced England to divide America between them. In Greece the contention was ever between the larger states. Sparta against Athens—and these again, occasionally, against Thebes—were ready to devour each other. Germany presents the same prospects—Prussia against Austria. Do the greater provinces in Holland endanger the liberties of the lesser? And let me remark that the weaker you make your confederation, the greater the danger to the lesser States. They can only be protected by a strong federal government. Those gentlemen who oppose the Virginia plan do not sufficiently analyze the subject. Their remarks, in general, are vague and inconclusive.

Mr. WILLIAMSON.—If any argument will admit of demonstration, it is that which declares that all men have an equal right in society. Against this position, I have heard, as yet, no argument; and I could wish to hear what could be said against it. What is tyranny? Representatives of representatives, if you give them the power of taxation. From equals take equals, and the remainder is equal. What process is to annihilate smaller States I know not. But I know it must be tyranny, if the smaller States can tax the greater, in order to ease themselves. A general government cannot exercise direct taxation. Money must be raised by duties and imposts, etc., and this will operate equally. It is impossible to tax according to numbers. Can a man over the mountains, where produce is a drug, pay equal with one near the shore?

Mr. WILSON.—I should be glad to hear the gentleman from Maryland [Mr. Martin] explain himself upon the remark on Old Sarum, when compared with the city of London. He has allowed this to be an unjust proportion; as in the one place one man sends two members, and in the other one million are represented by four members. I would be glad to hear how he applies this to the larger and smaller States in America; and whether the borough, as a borough, is represented, or the people of the borough.

Mr. MARTIN rose to explain. Individuals, as composing a part of the whole of one consolidated government, are there represented.

Gov. FRANKLIN read some remarks acknowledging the difficulties of the present subject. Neither ancient nor modern history (said Gov. Franklin) can give us light. As a sparrow does not fall without divine permission, can we suppose that governments can be erected without his will? We shall, I am afraid, be disgraced, through little party views. I move *that we have prayers every morning.*

DR. JOHNSON.—States are political societies. For whom are we to form a government? for the people of America, or for those societies? Undoubtedly for the latter. They must, therefore, have a voice in the second branch of the general government if you mean to preserve their existence. The people already compose the first branch. This mixture is proper and necessary; for we cannot form a general government on any other ground.

JUDGE READ.—I would have no objection, if the government was more national; but the proposed plan is so great a mixture of both that it is best to drop it altogether. A State government is incompatible with a general government. If it was more national I would be for a representation proportionate to population.

MR. WILSON.—Some gentlemen are afraid that the plan is not sufficiently national, while others, that it is too much so. If this point of representation was once well fixed we would come nearer to one another in sentiment. The necessity would then be discovered of circumscribing more effectually the State governments, and enlarging the bounds of the general government. Some contend that States are sovereign, when in fact they are only political societies. There is a gradation of power in all societies, from the lowest corporation to the highest sovereign. The States never possessed the essential rights of sovereignty. These were always vested in Congress. Their voting, as States, in Congress, is no evidence of sovereignty. The State of Maryland voted by counties. Did this make the counties sovereign? The States, at present, are only great corporations, having the power of making by-laws, and these are effectual only if they are not contradictory to the general Confederation. The States ought to be placed under control of the general government— at least as much so as they formerly were under the King and British Parliament. The arguments, I observe, have taken a different turn, and I hope may tend to convince all of the necessity of a strong energetic government, which would equally tend to give energy to and protect the State governments. What was the origin of the military establishment of Europe? It was the jealousy which one state or kingdom entertained of another. This jealousy was productive of evil. In Rome the patricians were often obliged to excite a foreign war to divert the attention of the plebeians from encroaching on the senatorial rights. In England and France perhaps this jealousy may give energy to their governments, and contribute to their existence. But a state of danger is like a state of war, and it unites the various parts of the government to exertion. May not our distractions, however, invite danger from abroad? If the power is not immediately derived from the people, in proportion to their numbers, we may make a paper confederacy, but that will be all. We know the effects of the old Confederation, and without a general government this will be like the former.

MR. HAMILTON.—The course of my experience in human affairs might perhaps restrain me from saying much on this subject. I shall, however, give birth to some of the observations I have made during the course of this debate. The gentleman from Maryland has been at great pains to establish positions which are not denied. Many of them, as drawn from the best writers on government, are become almost self-evident principles. But I doubt the propriety of his application of those principles in the present discussion. He deduces from them the necessity that states entering into a confederacy must retain the equality of votes. This position cannot be correct. Facts plainly contradict it. The Parliament of Great Britain asserted a supremacy over the whole empire; and the celebrated Judge Blackstone labors for the legality of it, although many parts were not represented. This parliamentary power we opposed as contrary to our colonial rights. With that exception, throughout that whole empire, it is submitted to. May not the smaller and greater States so modify their respective rights as to establish the general interest of the whole, without adhering to the right of equality? Strict representation is not observed in any of the State governments. The Senate of New York are chosen by persons of certain qualifications, to the exclusion of others. The question, after all is, Is it our interest, in modifying this general government, to sacrifice individual rights to the preservation of the rights of an artificial being, called *states?* There can be no truer principle than this— that every individual of the community at large has an equal right to the protection of government. If, therefore, three States contain a majority of the inhabitants of America, ought they to be governed by a minority? Would the inhabitants of the great States ever submit to this? If the smaller States maintain this principle, through a love of power, will not the larger, from the same motive, be equally tenacious to preserve their power? They are to surrender their rights: for what?—for the preservation of an artificial being. We propose a free government. Can it be so if partial distinctions are maintained? I agree with the gentleman from Delaware that, if the State governments are to act in the general government, it affords the strongest reason for exclusion. In the State of New York five counties form a majority of representatives, and yet the government is in no danger, because the laws have a general operation. The small States exaggerate their danger, and on this ground contend for an unproportion of power. But their danger is increased if the larger States will not submit to it. Where will they form new alliances for their support? Will they do this with foreign powers? Foreigners are jealous of our increasing greatness, and would rejoice in our distractions. Those who have had opportunities of conversing with foreigners respecting sovereigns in Europe have discovered in them an anxiety for the preservation of our democratic governments, probably for no other reason but to keep us weak. Unless your government is respectable foreigners will invade your rights; and to maintain tranquillity you must be respectable; even to observe neutrality you must have a strong government. I confess our present situation is critical. We have just finished a war which has established our independence, and loaded us with a heavy debt. We have still every motive to unite for our common defence. Our people are disposed to have a good government; but this disposition may not always prevail. It is difficult to amend confederations. It has been attempted in vain, and it is perhaps a miracle that we are now met. We must therefore improve the opportunity, and render the present system as perfect as possible. Their good sense, and, above all, the necessity of their affairs, will induce the people to adopt it.

MR. GERRY.—It appears to me that the States never were independent; they had only corporate rights. Confederations are a mongrel kind of government, and the world does not afford a precedent to go by. Aristocracy is the worst kind of government, and I would sooner submit to a monarchy. We must have a system that will execute itself.

The question was then put on Mr. Lansing's motion, and lost—4 ayes, 6 noes, 1 State divided.

Question on the clause—6 ayes, 4 noes, and 1 State divided.

JUDGE ELLSWORTH.—I move that the consideration of the 8th resolve be postponed. Carried—9 ayes, 2 noes.

I now move the following amendment to the resolve—that, in the second branch, each State have an equal vote. I confess that the effect of this motion is to make the general government partly federal and partly national. This will secure tranquillity, and still make it efficient; and it will meet the objections of the larger States. In taxes they will have a proportional weight in the first branch of the general legislature. If the great States refuse this plan we will be forever separated. Even in the executive the larger States have ever had influence. The province of Holland ever had it. If all the states are to exist they must necessarily have an equal vote in the general government. Small communities, when associating with greater, can only be supported by an equality of votes. I have always found, in my reading and experience, that in all societies the governors are ever gradually rising into power.

The large States, although they may not have a common interest for combination, yet they may be partially attached to each other for mutual support and advancement. This can be more easily effected than the union of the remaining small States to check it; and ought we not to regard antecedent plighted faith to the Confederation already entered into, and by the terms of it declared to be perpetual? And it is not yet obvious to me that the States will depart from this ground. When in the hour of common danger we united as equals, shall it now be urged by some that we must depart from this principle when the danger is over? Will the world say that this is just? We then associated as free and independent States, and were well satisfied. To perpetuate that independence I wish to establish a national legislature, executive and judiciary; for under these we shall, I doubt not, preserve peace and harmony. Nor would I be surprised (although we made the general government the most perfect, in our opinion) that it should hereafter require amendment. But at present this is as far as I possibly can go. If this convention only chalk out lines of good government we shall do well.

Mr. BALDWIN.—It appears to be agreed that the government we should adopt ought to be energetic and formidable, yet I would guard against the danger of being too formidable. The second branch ought not to be elected as the first. Suppose we take the example of the Constitution of Massachusetts, as it is commended for its goodness. There the first branch represents the people, and the second its property.

Mr. MADISON.—I would always exclude inconsistent principles in framing a system of government. The difficulty of getting its defects amended are great, and sometimes insurmountable. The Virginia State government was the first which was made; and, though its defects are evident to every person, we cannot get it amended. The Dutch have made four several attempts to amend their system, without success. The few alterations made in it were by tumult and faction, and for the worse. If there was real danger I would give the smaller States the defensive weapons. But there is none from that quarter. The great danger to our general government is the great southern and northern interests of the continent being opposed to each other. Look to the votes in Congress, and most of them stand divided by the geography of the country, not according to the size of the States.

Suppose the first branch granted money; may not the second branch, from State views, counteract the first? In Congress the single State of Delaware prevented an embargo, at the time that all the other States thought it absolutely necessary for the support of the army. Other powers, and those very essential, besides the legislative, will be given to the second branch—such as the negativing all State laws. I would compromise on this question, if I could do it on correct principles, but otherwise not. If the old fabric of the Confederation must be the groundwork of the new we must fail.

Mr. WILSON.—The question now before us is of so much consequence that I cannot give it a silent vote. Gentlemen have said that, if this amendment is not agreed to, a separation to the north of Pennsylvania may be the consequence. This staggers me neither in my sentiments nor my duty. If a minority should refuse their assent to the new plan of a general government, and if they will have their own will, and without it separate the Union, let it be done; but we shall stand supported by stronger and better principles. The opposition to this plan is as 22 to 90, in the general scale—not quite a fourth part of the Union. Shall three-fourths of the Union surrender their rights for the support of that artificial being called *State interest?* If we must join issue, I am willing. I cannot consent that one-fourth shall control the power of three-fourths.

If the motion is adopted seven States will control the whole, and the lesser seven compose 24 out of 90. One-third must control two-thirds—24 overrule 66. For whom do we form a Constitution? For men, or for imaginary beings called States—a mere metaphysical distinction? Will a regard to State rights justify the sacrifice of the rights of men? If we proceed on any other foundation than the last our building will neither be solid nor lasting. Weight and numbers is the only true principle: every other is local, confined, or imaginary. Much has been said of the danger of the three larger States combining together to give rise to monarchy or an aristocracy. Let the probability of this combination be explained, and it will be found that a rivalship, rather than a confederacy, will exist among them. Is there a single point in which this interest coincides? Supposing that the executive should be selected from one of the larger States; can the other two be gratified? Will not this be a source of jealousy among them; and will they not separately court the interest of the smaller States, to counteract the views of a favorite rival? How can aristocracy arise from this combination, more than among the smaller States? On the contrary, the present claims of the smaller States lead directly to the establishment of an aristocracy, which is the government of the few over the many; and the Connecticut proposal removes only a small part of the objection. There are only two kinds of bad government —the one, which does *too much*, and therefore oppressive, and the other, which does *too little*, and therefore weak. Congress partakes of the latter, and the motion will leave us in the same situation, and as much fettered as ever we were. The people see its weakness, and would be mortified in seeing our inability to correct it.

The gentleman from Georgia [Mr. Baldwin] has doubts how to vote on this question, and wishes some qualification made. I admit there ought to be some difference as to the numbers in the second branch; and perhaps there are other distinctions which could, with propriety, be introduced; such, for example, as the qualifications of the elected, etc. However, if there are leading principles in the system which we adopt, much may be done in the detail. We all aim at giving the general Government more energy. The State governments are necessary and valuable. No liberty can be obtained without them. On this question depend the essential rights of the general Government and of the people.

JUDGE ELLSWORTH.—I have the greatest respect for the gentleman who spoke last. I respect his abilities, although I differ from him on many points. He asserts that the general government must depend on the equal suffrage of the people. But will this not put it in the power of the few States to control the rest? It is a novel thing in politics that the few control the many. In the British government the few, as a guard, have an equal share in the government. The House of Lords, although few in number, and sitting in their own right, have an equal share in the legislature. They cannot give away the property of the community, but they can prevent the Commons from being too lavish in their gifts. Where is, or was, a confederation ever formed, where equality of voices was not a fundamental principle? Mankind are apt to go from one extreme to another; and, because we have found defects in the Confederation, must we therefore pull down the whole fabric, foundation and all, in order to erect a new building, totally different from it, without retaining any of its materials? What are its defects? It is said equality of votes has embarrassed us. But how? Would the real evils of our situation have been cured had this not been the case? Would the proposed amendment on the Virginia plan, as to representation, have relieved us? I fancy not. Rhode Island has been often quoted as a small State, and by its refusal once defeated the grant of the impost. Whether she was right in doing so is not the question; but was it a federal requisition? And if it was not, she did not, in this instance, defeat a federal measure.

If the larger States seek security, they have it fully in the first branch of the general government. But can we turn the tables, and say that the lesser States are equally secure? In *commercial regulations* they will unite. If policy should require free ports they would be found at Boston, Philadelphia, and Alexandria. In the disposition of lucrative offices they would unite. But I ask no surrender of any of the rights of the great States; nor do I plead *duress* in the makers of the old Confederation, nor suppose they soothed the danger, in order to resume their rights when the danger was over. No; small States must possess the power of self-defence, or be ruined. Will any one say there is no diversity of interests in the States? And, if there is, should not those interests be guarded and secured? But if there is none, then the large States have nothing to apprehend from an equality of rights. And let it be remembered that these remarks are not the result of partial or local views. The State I represent is respectable, and in importance holds a middle rank.

MR. MADISON.—Notwithstanding the admirable and close reasoning of the gentleman who spoke last, I am not yet convinced that my former remarks are not well founded. I apprehend that he is mistaken as to the fact on which he builds one of his arguments. He supposes that equality of votes is the principle on which all confederacies are formed. That of Lycia, so justly applauded by the celebrated Montesquieu, was different. He also appeals to our good faith for the observance of the confederacy. We know we have found one inadequate to the purposes for which it was made. Why then adhere to a system which is proved to be so remarkably defective? I have impeached a number of States for the infraction of the Confederation; and I have not even spared my own State, nor can I justly spare his. Did not Connecticut refuse her compliance to the federal requisition? Has she paid, for the two last years, any money into the Continental treasury? And does this look like government, or the observance of a solemn compact? Experience shows that the Confederation is radically defective; and we must, in a new national government, guard against those defects. Although the large States in the first branch have weight proportionate to their population, yet, as the smaller States have an equal vote in the second branch, they will be able to control and leave the larger without any essential benefit. As peculiar powers are intended to be granted to the second branch, such as the negativing State laws, etc., unless the larger States have a proportionate weight in the representation they cannot be more secure.

Mr. WILSON.—I think the second branch ought not to be numerous. I will propose an expedient: Let there be one member for every 100,000 souls, and the smallest States not less than one member each. This would give about twenty-six members. I make this proposal, not because I belong to a large State, but in order to pull down a rotten house, and lay a foundation for a new building. To give additional weight to an old building is to hasten its ruin.

Gov. FRANKLIN.—The smaller States, by this motion, would have the power of giving away the money of the greater States. There ought to be some difference between the first and second branches. Many expedients have been proposed, and, I am sorry to remark, without effect. A joiner, when he wants to fit two boards, takes off with his plane the uneven parts from each side, and thus they fit. Let us do the same. We are all met to do something.

I shall propose an expedient: Let the Senate be elected by the States equally; in all acts of sovereignty and authority let the votes be equally taken—the same in the appointment of all officers, and salaries; but in passing of laws each State shall have a right of suffrage in proportion to the sums they respectively contribute. Among merchants, where a ship has many owners, her destination is determined in that proportion. I have been one of the ministers to France from this country during the war, and we should have been very glad if they would have permitted us a vote in the distribution of the money to carry on the war.

Mr. BEDFORD.—That all the States at present are equally sovereign and independent has been asserted from every quarter of this house. Our deliberations here are a confirmation of the position; and I may add to it that each of them acts from interested, and many from ambitious, motives. Look at the votes which have been given on the floor of this house, and it will be found that their numbers, wealth, and local views have actuated their determinations; and that the larger States proceed as if our eyes were already perfectly blinded. Impartiality, with them, is already out of the question; the reported plan is their political creed, and they support it, right or wrong. Even the diminutive State of Georgia has an eye to her future wealth and greatness. South Carolina, puffed up with the possession of her wealth and negroes, and North Carolina, are all, from different views, united with the great States. And these latter, although it is said they can never, from interested views, form a coalition, we find closely united in one scheme of interest and ambition (notwithstanding they endeavor to amuse us with the purity of their principle and the rectitude of their intentions) in asserting that the general government must be drawn from an equal representation of the people. Pretences to support ambition are never wanting. Their cry is, Where is the danger? and they insist that although the powers of the general government will be increased, yet it will be for the good of the whole; and, although the three great States form nearly a majority of the people of America, they never will hurt or injure the lesser States. *I do not, gentlemen, trust you.* If you possess the power, the abuse of it could not be checked; and what, then, would prevent you from exercising it to our destruction? You gravely allege that there is no danger of combination, and triumphantly ask, "How could combinations be effected? The large States," you say, "all differ in productions and commerce; and experience shows that, instead of combinations, they would be rivals, and counteract the views of one another." This, I repeat, is language calculated only to amuse us. Yes, sir, the larger States will be rivals, but not against each other—they will be rivals against the *rest of the States*. But it is urged that such a government would suit the people, and that its principles are equitable and just. How often has this argument been refuted, when applied to a *federal* government! The small States never can agree to the Virginia plan; and why, then, is it still urged? But it is said that it is not expected that the State governments will approve the proposed system, and that this House must directly carry it to the people for their approbation! Is it come to this, then, that *the sword* must decide this controversy, and that the horrors of war must be added to the rest of our misfortunes? But what have the people already said? "We find the Confederation defective. Go, and give additional powers to the Confederation—give to it the imposts, regulation of trade, power to collect the taxes, and the means to discharge our foreign and domestic debts."

Can we not, then, as their delegates, agree upon these points? As their ambassadors, can we not clearly grant those powers? Why, then, when we are met, must entire distinct and new grounds be taken, and a government of which the people had no idea be instituted? And are we to be told, if we won't agree to it, it is the last moment of our deliberations? I say, it is indeed the last moment, if we do not agree to this assumption of power. The States will never again be entrapped into a measure like this. The people will say, The *small* States would confederate, and grant further powers to Congress; but you, the *large* States, would not. Then the fault would be yours, and all the nations of the earth will justify us. But what is to become of our public debts, if we dissolve the Union? Where is your plighted faith? Will you crush the smaller States, or must they be left unmolested? Sooner than be ruined, there are *foreign powers who will take us by the hand.*

I say not this to threaten or intimidate, but that we should reflect seriously before we act. If we once leave this floor, and solemnly renounce your new project, what will be the consequence? You will annihilate your federal government, and ruin must stare you in the face. Let us, then, do what is in our power—*amend and enlarge the Confederation, but not alter the federal system.* The people expect this, and no more. We all agree in the necessity of a more efficient government—and cannot this be done? Although my State is small, I know and respect its rights, as much, at least, as those who have the honor to represent any of the larger States.

MR. KING.—I am in sentiment with those who wish the preservation of State governments; but the general Government may be so constituted as to effect it. Let the Constitution we are about forming be considered as a *commission* under which the general government shall act, and as such it will be the guardian of the State rights. The rights of Scotland are secure from all danger and encroachments, although in the Parliament she has a small representation. May not this be done in our general Government? Since I am up, I am concerned for what fell from the gentleman from Delaware [Mr. Bedford]—*"Take a foreign power by the hand!"* I am sorry he mentioned it, and I hope he is able to excuse it to himself on the score of passion. Whatever may be my distress, I never will court a foreign power to assist in relieving myself from it.

The question was put on Ellsworth's motion—5 ayes, 5 noes, 1 State divided. So the amendment was lost.

Mr. C. Pinckney.—As a professional man, I might say that there is no weight in the argument adduced in favor of the motion on which we are divided; but candor obliges me to own that equality of suffrage in the States is wrong. Prejudices will prevail, and they have an equal weight in the larger as in the smaller States. There is a solid distinction, as to interest, between the Southern and Northern States. To destroy the ill effects thereof, I renew the motion which I made in the early stage of this business. (See page 323.)

Gen. C. C. Pinckney moved for a select committee to take into consideration both branches of the legislature.

Mr. Martin.—It is again attempted to compromise. You must give each State an equal suffrage, or our business is at an end.

Mr. Sherman.—It seems we have got to a point that we cannot move one way or the other. Such a committee is necessary to set us right.

Mr. G. Morris.—The two branches, so equally poised, cannot have their due weight. It is confessed, on all hands, that the second branch ought to be a check on the first; for without its having this effect it is perfectly useless. The first branch, originating from the people, will ever be subject to *precipitancy, changeability,* and *excess.* Experience evinces the truth of this remark, without having recourse to reading. This can only be checked by *ability* and *virtue* in the second branch. On your present system, can you suppose that one branch will possess it more than the other? The second branch ought to be composed of men of great and established property—*aristocracy;* men who, from pride, will support consistency and permanency; and to make them completely independent they must be chosen *for life,* or they will be a useless body. Such an aristocratic body will keep down the turbulency of democracy. But if you elect them for a shorter period they will be only a name, and we had better be without them. Thus constituted, I hope they will show us the weight of aristocracy.

History proves, I admit, that the men of large property will uniformly endeavor to establish tyranny. How, then, shall we ward off this evil? Give them the second branch and you secure their weight for the public good. They become responsible for their conduct, and this lust of power will ever be checked by the democratic branch, and thus form a stability in your government. But if we continue changing our measures by the breadth of democracy, who will confide in our engagements? Who will trust us? Ask any person whether he reposes any confidence in the government of Congress, or that of the State of Pennsylvania, he will readily answer you, No. Ask him the reason, and he will tell you it is because he has no confidence in their stability.

You intend also that the second branch shall be incapable of holding any office in the general government. It is a dangerous expedient. They ought to have every inducement to be interested in your government. Deprive them of this right, and they will become inattentive to your welfare. The wealthy will ever exist; and you never can be safe unless you gratify them, as a body, in the pursuit of honor and profit. Prevent them by positive institutions, and they will proceed in some left-handed way. A son may want a place—you mean to prevent him from promotion. They are not to be paid for their services; they will in some way pay themselves; nor is it in your power to prevent it. It is good policy that men of property be collected in one body, to give them one common influence in your government. Let vacancies be filled up, as they happen, by the executive. Besides, it is of little consequence, on this plan, whether the States are equally represented or not. If the State governments have the division of many of the loaves and fishes, and the general government few, it cannot exist. This Senate would be one of the *baubles* of the general government. If you choose them for *seven* years, whether chosen by the people or the States, whether by equal suffrage or in any other proportion, how will they be a check? They will still have local and State prejudices. A government by compact is no government at all. You may as well go back to your congressional federal government, where, in the character of ambassadors, they may form treaties for each State.

I avow myself the advocate of a strong government; still I admit that the influence of the rich must be guarded; and a pure democracy is equally oppressive to the lower order of the community. This remark is founded on the experience of history. We are a commercial people, and as such will be obliged to engage in European politics. Local government cannot apply to the general government. These latter remarks I throw out only for the consideration of the committee who are to be appointed.

Gov. RANDOLPH.—I am in favor of appointing a committee; but, considering the warmth exhibited in debate, I have, I confess, no great hopes that any good will arise from it. Cannot a remedy be devised? If there is danger to the lesser States, from an unequal representation in the second branch, may not a check be found in the appointment of one executive, by electing him by an equality of State votes? He must have the right of interposing between the two branches, and this might give a reasonable security to the smaller States. Not one of the lesser States can exist by itself; and a dissolution of the Confederation, I confess, would produce contentions as well in the larger as in the smaller States. The principle of self-preservation induces me to seek for a government that will be stable and secure.

The motion was then put to appoint a committee to report upon the 8th resolve, and so much of the 7th as had not been agreed to. The motion was carried—9 States against 2.

The *grand committee* met on July 3. Mr. Gerry was chosen chairman. Says Judge Yates:

The committee proceeded to consider in what manner they should discharge the business with which they were intrusted. By the proceedings in the convention they were so equally divided on the important question of *representation in the two branches,* that the idea of a conciliatory adjustment must have been in contemplation of the house in the appointment of this committee. But still, how to effect this salutary purpose was the question. Many of the members, impressed with the utility of a general government, connected with it the indispensable necessity of a representation from the States *according to their numbers and wealth;* while others, equally tenacious of the rights of the States, would admit of no other representation but such as *was strictly federal,* or, in other words, *equality of suffrage.* This brought on a discussion of the principles on which the house had divided, and a lengthy recapitulation of the arguments advanced in the house in support of these opposite propositions. As I had not openly explained my sentiments on any former occasion on this question, but constantly, in giving my vote, *showed by attachment to the national government on federal principles, I took this occasion to explain my motives.*

These remarks gave rise to a motion of Dr. Franklin, which after some modification, was agreed to, and made the basis of the following report of the committee:

The committee to whom was referred the 8th resolution reported from the committee of the whole house, and so much of the 7th as had not been decided on, submit the following report:

"That the subsequent propositions be recommended to the convention, on condition that both shall be generally adopted.

"That, in the first branch of the legislature, each of the States now in the Union be allowed one member for every 40,000 inhabitants of the description reported in the 7th resolution of the committee of the whole house. That each State, not containing that number, shall be allowed one member.

"That bills for raising or apportioning money, and for fixing salaries of the officers of government of the United States, shall originate in the first branch of the legislature, and shall not be altered or amended by the second branch; and that no money shall be drawn from the public treasury but in pursuance of appropriations to be originated in the first branch.

"That, in the second branch of the legislature, *each State shall have an equal vote.*"

On July 5 the report of the committee was read to the convention. The astute manager of the "large States'" interests expressed either real or assumed displeasure with it.

Mr. MADISON.—I restrain myself from animadverting on the report, from the respect I bear to the members of the committee. I must confess I see nothing of concession in it.

The originating money bills is no concession on the part of the smaller States; for, if seven States in the second branch should want such a bill, their interest in the first branch will prevail to bring it forward. It is nothing more than a nominal privilege.

The second branch, small in number, and well connected, will ever prevail. The power of regulating trade, imposts, treaties, etc., is more essential to the community than raising money, and no provision is made for those in the report. We are driven to an unhappy dilemma. Two-thirds of the inhabitants of the Union are to please the remaining one-third by sacrificing their essential rights.

When we satisfy the majority of the people in securing their rights, we have *nothing* to fear; in any other way, *everything*. The smaller States, I hope, will at last see their true and real interest; and I hope that the warmth of the gentleman from Delaware [Mr. Bedford] will never induce him to yield to his own suggestion of seeking for foreign aid.

At this period (July 5, 1787) Messrs. Yates and Lansing left the convention, and the remainder of the session was employed to complete the Constitution, on the principles already adopted.

LETTER OF YATES AND LANSING TO GOV. CLINTON

After the Constitution was adopted Messrs. Yates and Lansing wrote a letter to Gov. George Clinton of New York justifying their course in leaving the convention. In it they state:

We have been reduced to the disagreeable alternative of either exceeding the powers delegated to us, and giving assent to measures which we conceive destructive to the political happiness of the citizens of the United States, or opposing our opinions to that of a body of respectable men, to whom those citizens had given the most unequivocal proofs of confidence. Thus circumstanced, under these impressions, to have hesitated would have been to be culpable. We therefore gave the principles of the Constitution, which has received the sanction of a majority of the convention, our decided and unreserved dissent; but we must candidly confess that we should have been equally opposed to any system, however modified, which had in object the consolidation of the United States into one government.

We beg leave, briefly, to state some cogent reasons, which, among others, influenced us to decide against a consolidation of the States. These are reducible into two heads:

1st. The limited and well-defined powers under which we acted, and which could not, on any possible construction, embrace an idea of such magnitude as to assent to a general Constitution, in subversion of that of the State.

2d. A conviction of the impracticability of establishing a general government, pervading every part of the United States, and extending essential benefits to all.

Our powers were explicit, and confined to the sole and express purpose of revising the Articles of Confederation, and reporting such alterations and provisions therein as should render the Federal Constitution adequate to the exigencies of government and the preservation of the Union. . . .

Exclusive of our objections originating from the want of power, we entertained an opinion that a general government, however guarded by declarations of rights, or cautionary provisions, must unavoidably, in a short time, be productive of the destruction of the civil liberty of such citizens as could be effectually coerced by it, by reason of the extensive territory of the United States, the dispersed situation of its inhabitants, and the insuperable difficulty of controlling or counteracting the views of a set of men (however unconstitutional and oppressive their acts might be) possessed of all the powers of government, and who, from their remoteness from their constituents, and necessary permanency of office, could not be supposed to be uniformly actuated by an attention to their welfare and happiness; that, however wise and energetic the principles of the general government might be, the extremities of the United States could not be kept in due submission and obedience to its laws, at the distance of many hundred miles from the seat of government; that, if the general legislature was composed of so numerous a body of men as to represent the interests of all the inhabitants of the United States, in the usual and true ideas of representation, the expense of supporting it would become intolerably burdensome; and that, if a few only were vested with a power of legislation, the interests of a great majority of the inhabitants of the United States must necessarily be unknown; or, if known, even in the first stage of the operations of the new government, unattended to.

These reasons were, in our opinion, conclusive against any system of consolidated government; to that recommended by the convention we suppose most of them very forcibly apply. . . .

We were not present at the completion of the new Constitution; but before we left the convention its principles were so well established as to convince us that no alteration was to be expected to conform it to our ideas of expediency and safety. A persuasion that our further attendance would be fruitless and unavailing rendered us less solicitous to return.

The retirement of Yates and Lansing as a protest against a strong government had a very depressing effect upon Washington. On July 10 he wrote as follows to Hamilton, who was in New York opposing the influence in that State of the two dissidents:

I *almost* despair of seeing a favorable issue to the proceedings of the convention, and do therefore repent having had any agency in the business.

The men who oppose a strong and energetic government are, in my opinion, narrow minded politicians, or are under the influence of local views.—The apprehension expressed by them that the people will not accede to the form proposed is the ostensible, not the real, cause of the opposition—but admitting that the present sentiment is as they prognosticate, the question ought nevertheless to be, is it, or is it not, the best form?—If the former, recommend it, and it will assuredly obtain mauger opposition.

I am sorry you went away. I wish you were back. The crisis is equally important and alarming, and no opposition under such circumstances should discourage exertions till the signature is fixed.

CHAPTER XIII

ON THE POWERS OF THE PRESIDENT, NATIONAL CONTROL OF COMMERCE, AND SLAVERY

[MINOR DEBATES IN THE CONSTITUTIONAL CONVENTION]

Debate on the Powers of the President—Debate on Congress's Power over Commerce, including Abolition of Slave Trade—Debate on Counting Slaves in Apportioning Representatives in Congress: in favor, Roger Sherman [Ct.], Oliver Ellsworth [Ct.], Gen. Charles Cotesworth Pinckney [S. C.], John Rutledge, Sr. [S. C.], Pierce Butler [S. C.]; opposed, Rufus King [Mass.], Gouverneur Morris [Pa.], James Wilson [Pa.], John Dickinson [Pa.], Jonathan Dayton [N. J.], George Mason [Va.]—Resolutions Adopted Are Referred to "Committee of Detail" to Draft Constitution—This Committee's Draft Referred to "Committee on Revision"—Finished Draft Signed and Sent to Congress—Letter to Congress—Dissolution of the Convention.

THE chief subjects of discussion after the settlement of the great question of the representation of the States in Congress were the nature and powers of the executive and the regulation by Congress of navigation, including the slave trade.

POWERS OF THE PRESIDENT

The organization of a supreme executive presented many difficulties, arising not merely from the nature of the subject, but from the complicated system of the government. The mode of choice, and whether to consist of one or more persons, the time for which the executive should be chosen, whether reëligible, and the powers to be granted to the person or persons who should administer the government were questions of new impression, and which the members of the convention found it extremely difficult to settle in a manner satisfactory even to themselves. After much deliberation,

351

on the 26th of July, a majority of the States, being six against three and one divided,[1] agreed to the following plan:

That a national executive be instituted—
To consist of a single person;
To be chosen by the national legislature;
For the term of seven years;
To be ineligible a second time;
With power to carry into execution the national laws;
To appoint to offices in cases not otherwise provided for;
To be removeable on impeachment and conviction of malpractice or neglect of duty;
To receive a fixed compensation for the devotion of his time to public service;
To be paid out of the public treasury.

This plan was referred to the committee appointed to prepare the Constitution, and was incorporated in the first draft reported by them.

This important subject remained undecided until the 31st of August, when it was referred to a committee of one from each State; and on the 4th of September the committee reported an entirely new plan, which, after some amendments, was adopted.

NATIONAL CONTROL OF COMMERCE

As the national legislature was invested with the exclusive power of regulating commerce with foreign nations, and of course could pass *navigation acts,* a difference arose between the navigating and non-navigating States respecting the exercise of this power. The latter were jealous that the former might be disposed to secure to themselves improper advantages in the carrying trade. In the first draft of the Constitution, therefore, the power of Congress was limited in this respect by a special provision, that *"no navigation acts should be passed, without the assent of two-thirds of the members present in each house."*

[1] New Hampshire, Connecticut, New Jersey, North Carolina, South Carolina, and Georgia were in the affirmative—Pennsylvania, Delaware, and Maryland, in the negative—and Virginia was divided. See also Hamilton's letter to Pickering on page 313.

Some of the slave-holding States also wished to secure to themselves the right of importing slaves, free from any tax or duty. A clause was therefore at first inserted, declaring that Congress should not prohibit the importation of such persons as the States might think proper to admit, nor lay any tax on the persons so imported.

The question was at last referred to a committee of one from each State. This committee, by way of compromise, reported that "the migration or importation of such persons as the several States *now existing* shall think proper to admit shall not be prohibited by the legislature prior to the year 1800; but a tax may be imposed on such migration or importation at a rate not exceeding the average of the duties laid on imports."

The same committee also reported against the provision requiring the assent of *two-thirds* of the members of each house to pass *navigation acts*. This report, after an amendment, extending the time of allowing such importation to 1808, and limiting the tax on each person to ten dollars, was adopted by a majority of the States, those in favor of allowing the importation of slaves until 1808 being New Hampshire, Massachusetts, Connecticut, Maryland, North Carolina, South Carolina, and Georgia—those against it being New Jersey, Pennsylvania, Delaware, and Virginia.

The adoption of this provision brought up the question of the counting of slaves when Representatives were to be assigned to the States in ratio of population. The following report of the discussion that ensued is taken from the "Madison Papers."

The chief speakers in favor of slave representation were: Roger Sherman and Oliver Ellsworth of Connecticut, Gen. Charles Cotesworth Pinckney, John Rutledge, Sr., and Pierce Butler of South Carolina, and Abraham Baldwin of Georgia; those opposed were: Rufus King of Massachusetts, Gouverneur Morris, James Wilson, and John Dickinson of Pennsylvania, Jonathan Dayton of New Jersey, and George Mason of Virginia.

DEBATE ON SLAVE REPRESENTATION

CONSTITUTIONAL CONVENTION, AUGUST 8-29, 1787

In the debate of August 8 on the adoption of the report of the committee.

MR. RUFUS KING (then of Massachusetts, afterward an eminent Senator from New York) wished to know what influence the vote just passed was meant to have on the succeeding part of the report concerning the admission of slaves into the rule of representation. He could not reconcile his mind to the article, if it was to prevent objections to the latter part. The admission of slaves was a most grating circumstance to his mind, because he had hoped that this concession would have produced a readiness which had not been manifested to strengthen the general government and to make a full confidence in it. The report under consideration had, by the tenor of it, put an end to all his hopes. In two great points the hands of the legislature were absolutely tied. The importation of slaves could not be prohibited. Exports could not be taxed. Is this reasonable? What are the great objects of the general system? First, defence against foreign invasion; second, against internal sedition. Shall all the States then be bound to defend each, and shall each be at liberty to introduce a weakness which will render defence more difficult? Shall one part of the United States be bound to defend another part, and that other part be at liberty, not only to increase its own danger, but to withhold a compensation for the burden? If slaves are to be imported, shall not the exports produced by their labor supply a revenue, the better to enable the general government to defend their masters? . . . He never could agree to let them be imported without limitation, and then be represented in the national legislature. Indeed, he could so little persuade himself of the rectitude of such a practice that he was not sure that he could assent to it under any circumstances.

MR. ROGER SHERMAN (of Connecticut) regarded the slave trade as iniquitous, but the point of representation having been settled after much difficulty and deliberation he did not think himself bound to make opposition, especially as the present article, as amended, did not preclude any arrangement whatever on that point in another place reported.

MR. GOUVERNEUR MORRIS moved to insert "free" before the word "inhabitants." Much, he said, would depend on this point. He never could concur in upholding domestic slavery. It was a nefarious institution. It was the curse of heaven on the States where it prevailed. Compare the free regions of the Middle States, where a rich and noble cultivation marks the prosperity and happiness of the people, with the misery and poverty which overspread the barren wastes of Virginia, Maryland, and the other States having slaves. Travel through the whole continent and you behold the prospect continually varying with the appearance and disappearance of slavery. . . . Upon what principle is it that the slaves shall be computed in the representation? Are they men? Then make them citizens and let them vote. Are they property? Why then is no other property included? The houses in this city (Philadelphia) are worth more than all the wretched slaves that cover the rice swamps of South Carolina. The admission of slaves into the representation, when fairly explained, comes to this: that the inhabitant of Georgia or South Carolina, who goes to the coast of Africa, and, in defiance of the most sacred laws of humanity, tears away his fellow-creatures from their dearest connections and dooms them to the most cruel bondage shall have more votes in a government instituted for the protection of the rights of mankind than the citizen of Pennsylvania or New Jersey, who views with a laudable horror so nefarious a practice. He would add that domestic slavery is the most prominent feature in the aristocratic countenance of the proposed Constitution. . . . Let it not be said that direct taxation is to be proportioned to representation. It is idle to suppose that the general government can stretch its hand directly into the pockets of the people scattered over so vast a country. They can only do it through the medium of exports, imports, and excises. For what then are all the sacrifices to be made? He would sooner submit himself to a tax, paying for all the negroes in the United States, than *saddle posterity with such a Constitution.*

MR. DAYTON (of New Jersey) seconded the motion. He did it, he said, that his sentiments on the subject might appear, whatever might be the fate of the amendment.

MR. SHERMAN did not regard the admission of negroes into the ratio of representation as liable to such insuperable objections, etc., etc.

GEN. C. C. PINCKNEY (of South Carolina) considered the fisheries and the western frontier as more burdensome to the United States than the slaves. He thought this could be demonstrated if the occasion were a proper one.

On the question on the motion to insert "free" before "inhabitants" it was disagreed to, New Jersey alone voting in the affirmative.

On Tuesday, August 21:

MR. LUTHER MARTIN (of Maryland) proposed to vary Article VII, Section 4, so as to allow a prohibition or tax on the importation of slaves. In the first place, as five slaves are to be counted as three freemen in the apportionment of representatives, such a clause would leave an encouragement to this traffic. In the second place, slaves weakened one part of the Union, which the other parts were bound to protect. The privilege of importing was therefore unreasonable. And, in the third place, *it was inconsistent with the principles of the Revolution, and dishonorable to the American character, to have such a feature in the Constitution.*

MR. RUTLEDGE (of South Carolina) did not see how the importation of slaves could be encouraged by this section. He was not apprehensive of insurrections and would readily exempt the other States from the obligation to protect the Southern against them. *Religion and humanity had nothing to do with this question. Interest* alone is the governing principle with nations, etc.

MR. ELLSWORTH (of Connecticut) was for leaving the clause as it stands, etc.

MR. PINCKNEY.—South Carolinia *can never receive the plan if it prohibits the Slave-Trade.* In every proposed extension of the powers of Congress that State expressly and watchfully excepted that of meddling with the importation of negroes. If the States should be all left at liberty on this subject, South Carolina may, perhaps by degrees, do of herself what is wished, as Virginia and Maryland have already done.

In the debate of the following day—the consideration of Article VII, Section 4, being resumed—Colonel George Mason gave utterance to the following sentiments:

This *infernal traffic* originated in the avarice of British merchants. The British Government has constantly checked the attempts of Virginia to put a stop to it. The present question concerned not the importing of slaves alone, but the whole Union. *The evil of having slaves was experienced during the late war. Had slaves been treated as they might have been by the enemy, they would have proved dangerous instruments in their hands.* But their folly dealt by the slaves as it did by the Tories. . . . Maryland and Virginia, he said, had already prohibited the importation of slaves. North Carolina had done the same in substance. All this would be vain if South Carolina and Georgia be at liberty to import. The Western people are already calling for slaves for their new lands, and will fill that country with slaves if they can be got through South Carolina and Georgia. Slavery discourages the arts and manufactures. The poor despise labor when performed by slaves. They prevent the emigration of whites who really enrich and strengthen a country. They produce the most pernicious effect on manners. Every master of slaves is born a petty tyrant. They bring the judgment of heaven on a country. *As nations can not be punished in the next world, they must be in this. By an inevitable chain of causes and effects Providence punishes national sins by national calamities.* . . . He held it essential in every point of view that the general government should have power to prevent the increase of slavery.

GENERAL PINCKNEY declared it to be his firm conviction that if himself and all his colleagues were to sign the Constitution and use their personal influence it would be of no avail toward obtaining the consent of their constituents. South Carolina and Georgia can not do without slaves. . . . He contended that the importation of slaves would be for the interest of the whole Union. The more slaves, the more products to employ the carrying trade; the more consumption also, and the more of this, the more revenue for the common treasury. He admitted it to be reasonable that slaves should be dutied like other imports, *but should consider a rejection of the clause as an exclusion of South Carolina from the Union.*

MR. BALDWIN has similar conceptions in the case of Georgia.

MR. WILSON (of Pennsylvania) observed that if South Carolina and Georgia were thus disposed to get rid of the importation of slaves in a short time, as had been suggested, they would never refuse to unite because the importation might be prohibited. As the section now stands, all articles imported are to be taxed. Slaves alone are exempt. This is, in fact, a *bounty* on that article.

MR. DICKINSON (of Delaware) expressed his sentiments as of a similar character. And MESSRS. KING and LANGDON (of New Hampshire) were also in favor of giving the power to the general government.

GENERAL PINCKNEY thought himself bound to declare candidly *that he did not think South Carolina would stop her importations of slaves in any short time,* but only stop them occasionally as she now does. He moved to commit the clause that slaves might be made liable to an equal tax with other imports which he thought right and which would remove one difficulty that had been started.

MR. RUTLEDGE seconded the motion of General Pinckney.

MR. GOUVERNEUR MORRIS wished the whole subject to be committed, including the clause relating to taxes on exports and the navigation act. These things may form a *bargain* among the Northern and Southern States.

MR. BUTLER (of South Carolina) declared that he would never agree to the power of taxing exports.

MR. SHERMAN said it was better to let the Southern States import slaves than to part with them if they made that a *sine quâ non.*

On the question for committing the remaining part of Sections 4 and 5, of Article VII, the vote was 7 in the affirmative; 3 in the negative; Massachusetts absent.

Upon slave representation James Madison had this to say in "The Federalist."

It were doubtless to be wished that the power of prohibiting the importation of slaves had not been postponed until the year 1808, or rather, that it had been suffered to have immediate operation. But it is not difficult to account either for this restriction on the general government or for the manner in which the whole clause is expressed. It ought to be considered as a great point gained in favor of humanity that a period of twenty years may terminate forever within these States a traffic which has so long and so loudly upbraided the barbarism of modern policy; that within that period it will receive a considerable discouragement from the Federal Government and may be totally abolished by the concurrence of the few States which continue the unnatural traffic in the prohibitory example which is given by so *large a majority of the Union.* Happy would it be for the unfortunate Africans if an equal prospect lay before them of being redeemed from the oppression of their European brethren. . . .

We subscribe to the doctrine, *might one of our Southern brethren observe,* that representation relates more immediately to persons, and taxation more immediately to property; and we join in the application of this distinction to the case of our slaves. But we deny the fact that slaves are considered *merely* as property, and in no respect whatever as persons. The true state of the case is that they partake of both these qualities, being considered by our laws in some respects as persons, and in other respects as property. In being compelled to labor, not merely for himself, but for a master—in being vendible by one master to another master, and being subject, at all times, to being restrained in his liberty and chastised in his body by the capricious will of his owner, the slave may appear to be degraded from the human rank and classed with that of the irrational animals which fall under the legal denomination of property. In being protected, on the other hand, in his life and in his limbs against the violence of all others, even the master of his labor and his liberty, and in being punished himself for all violence committed against others, the slave is no less regarded by the law as a member of society, not as a part of the irrational creation—as a moral person, not a mere object of property. The Federal Constitution, therefore, decides *with great propriety* on the case of our slaves when it views them in the mixed character of persons and property. This is, in fact, their true character. It is the character bestowed on them by the laws under which they live, and it will not be disputed that these are the proper criterion, because it is only under the pretext that the laws have transformed negroes into subjects of property that a place is denied to them in the computation of numbers, *and it is admitted that if the laws were to restore the rights which have been taken away the negroes would no longer be refused an equal share of representation with the other inhabitants.*

On August 29 Mr. Butler of South Carolina moved to insert after Article XV:

"If any person bound to service or labor in any of the United States shall escape into another State, he or she shall not be discharged from such service or labor in consequence of any regulations existing in the State to which they escape, but shall be delivered up to the person justly claiming their service or labor."

This, says Madison in his "Papers," was after some verbal modification agreed to, no one opposing.

In the debate in the North Carolina ratification convention in 1788:

MR. IREDELL begged leave to explain the reason of this clause (last clause, Section 2, Article IV). In some of the Northern States they have emancipated all their *slaves*. If any of our *slaves*, said he, go there and remain there a certain time, they would, by the present laws, be entitled to their freedom so that their masters could not get them again. This would be extremely prejudicial to the inhabitants of the Southern States, and to prevent it this clause is inserted in the Constitution. Though the word *slave* is not mentioned, this is the meaning of it. The Northern delegates, owing to their peculiar scruples on the subject of Slavery, did not choose the word *slave* to be mentioned.

General Chas. C. Pinckney said in the South Carolina ratification convention in 1788:

"I am of the same opinion now as I was two years ago that while there remained one acre of swamp land uncleared in South Carolina I would raise my voice against restricting the importation of negroes. . . . The Middle States and Virginia were for an immediate and total prohibition. We endeavored to obviate the objections which were urged in the best manner we could, and assigned reasons for our insisting on the importation, which there is no occasion to repeat, as they must occur to every gentleman in the House. A committee of the States was appointed in order to accommodate this matter and after a great deal of difficulty it was settled on the footing of the Constitution. By this settlement we have secured an unlimited importation of negroes for twenty years. Nor is it declared when that importation shall be stopped; it may be continued. We have a right to recover our slaves in whatever part of America they may take refuge. In short, considering all circumstances, we have made the best terms for the security of this species of property it was in our power to make. *We would have made better if we could, but on the whole, I do not think them bad.*"

We should here observe that amendments were proposed and even adopted until the day when the Constitution was signed. It will be remembered that in the arrangement with respect to the ratio of representation in the House there was to be one representative for every forty thousand inhabitants. This remained so until the last day of the session, when General Washington rose and said, in effect, that, "though he was sensible of the impropriety of the chairman's intermingling in the debates, yet he could not help observing that the small number which constituted the representative body appeared to him a defect in the plan—that it would better suit his ideas, and he believed it would be more agreeable to the people, if the number should be increased, and that the ratio should be one for every *thirty thousand*." The motion for reducing the ratio to this number was immediately put and almost unanimously carried. This is one instance of the influence of that great man in this assembly; and there can be no doubt his influence was also felt in other instances, though perhaps not in so direct a manner during the long deliberations of that body.

On July 23 the nineteen resolutions of the Virginia plan, with the amendments, were referred to a "committee of detail" to draft a Constitution in accordance with them. The plans of Pinckney and Paterson were also referred to the committee. The members composing the committees were elected by ballot: Rutledge, Randolph, Gorham, Ellsworth, and Wilson.

On the 6th of August the committee reported the draft it had agreed upon. (For the text of this, see Elliott's "Debates on the Federal Constitution," Vol. I, page 224.) This was debated upon until September 8, when a committee of five was chosen by ballot "to revise the style of and arrange the articles agreed to by the House." The members chosen were Johnson, Hamilton, Gouverneur Morris, Madison, and King.

On the 12th of September the committee submitted its draft, together with the draft of a letter to Congress. Both were approved, and the Constitution was ordered to be printed and copies furnished the members. This was done on the following day.

On September 17 the convention formally agreed to the Constitution, all the States voting "Ay," and ordered it to be transmitted to Congress to be laid before State conventions elected for the purpose of considering the ratification of the instrument, and that so soon as it was ratified by a constitutional majority Congress should take measures for the election of a President, and fix the time for beginning proceedings under it. The Journal of the Convention and other papers were deposited with its president (Washington) to be retained by him subject to the order of Congress if this body should be formed under the Constitution.

The members proceeded to sign the Constitution, and the convention then dissolved itself by an adjournment *sine die*.

The following is the text of the letter to Congress accompanying the Constitution:

THE LETTER TO CONGRESS

We have now the honor to submit to the consideration of the United States in Congress assembled that Constitution which has appeared to us the most advisable.

The friends of our country have long seen and desired that the power of making war, peace, and treaties; that of levying money and regulating commerce; and the correspondent executive and judicial authorities shall be fully and effectually vested in the general government of the Union. But the impropriety of delegating such extensive trust to one body of men is evident. Thence results the necessity of a different organization. It is obviously impracticable in the Federal Government of these States to secure all rights of independent sovereignty to each and yet provide for the interest and safety of all. Individuals entering into society must give up a share of liberty to preserve the rest. The magnitude of the sacrifice must depend as well on situation and circumstances as on the object to be obtained. It is at all times difficult to draw with precision the line between those rights which must be surrendered and those which may be reserved. And on the present occasion this difficulty was increased by a difference among the several States as to their situation, extent, habits and particular interests.

In all our deliberations on this subject we kept steadily in our view that which appeared to us the greatest interest of every true American—the consolidation of the Union—in which are involved our prosperity, felicity, safety, perhaps our national existence. This important consideration, seriously and deeply impressed on our minds, led each State in the convention to be less rigid in points of inferior magnitude than might have been otherwise expected. And thus the Constitution which we now present is the result of a spirit of amity and of that mutual deference and concession which the peculiarity of our political situation rendered indispensable.

That it will meet the full and entire approbation of every State is not perhaps to be expected. But each will doubtless consider that, had her interest alone been consulted, the consequences might have been particularly disagreeable and injurious to others. That it is liable to as few exceptions as could reasonably have been expected we hope and believe; that it may promote the lasting welfare of that country so dear to us all, and secure her freedom and happiness, is our most ardent wish.

CHAPTER XIV

Nation or Confederation?

[DEBATES IN STATE LEGISLATURES ON RATIFICATION OF THE CONSTITUTION]

Congress Submits the Constitution to the States for Ratification—Debate in the Massachusetts Convention: Speech of Fisher Ames: "Union, the Dyke of the Nation"—The Virginia Convention: Great Debate on "Consolidation or Confederation?" between Edmund Pendleton, Edmund Randolph, James Madison, George Wythe, John Marshall, *et al.*, Advocating Ratification, and Patrick Henry, George Mason, William Grayson, *et al.*, Opposing It—Debates in the New York Convention.

ON September 20, 1787, the Constitution was taken up by Congress, then sitting in City Hall, New York, and debated for eight days. The chief opposition to the Constitution was that it consolidated too much power in the general Government, thus endangering the independence of the States. Congress finally ordered, on September 28, that the "report (*i. e.,* the Constitution) of the convention lately assembled in Philadelphia" be "transmitted to the several legislatures in order to be submitted to a convention of delegates chosen in each State by the people thereof." In pursuance of this act the State legislatures called such conventions, which met in the course of the next three years.

Ratification was adopted unanimously by Georgia, New Jersey, and Delaware, and by large majorities in Pennsylvania, Connecticut, Maryland, and South Carolina. The State of Rhode Island for some time declined calling a convention, and it was for a while doubtful whether the other States would assent to it without previous amendments. Such, however, was the situation of the United States, without government, without funds, burdened with debt, and without the power or means of discharging it, despised abroad, and threatened with anarchy at home, that small majorities were at last induced to yield their assent, trusting to future amendments.

THE MASSACHUSETTS CONVENTION

In the convention of Massachusetts, which met in January, 1788, were men of the first talents who exerted their utmost energies in favor of the adoption of the Constitution. They encountered strong opposition from a class who had small personal interests at stake, and among these persons were eighteen or twenty who had actually been in Shay's army.

Fisher Ames delivered the most powerful of the speeches in favor of ratification. In the conclusion he said:

UNION, THE DYKE OF THE NATION

FISHER AMES

Shall we put every thing to hazard by rejecting this Constitution? Who is there that really loves liberty that will not tremble for its safety if the Federal Government should be dissolved? Can liberty be safe without government?

The Union is essential to our being as a nation. The pillars that prop it are crumbling to powder. The Union is the vital sap that nourishes the tree. If we reject the Constitution, to use the language of the country, we girdle the tree, its leaves will wither, its branches drop off, and the moldering trunk will be torn down by the tempest. What security has this single State against foreign enemies? Could we defend the mast country which the British so much desire? Can we protect our fisheries or secure by treaties a sale for the produce of our lands in foreign markets? Is there no loss, no danger, by delay? In spite of our negligence and perverseness, are we to enjoy *at all times* the privilege of forming a Constitution which no other nation has enjoyed at all? We approve our own form of government, and seem to think ourselves in safety under its protection. We talk as if there was no danger of deciding wrong. But when the inundation comes, shall we stand on dry land? The State government is a beautiful structure. It is situated, however, on the naked beach. The Union is the dyke to fence out the flood. That dyke is broken and decayed, and if we do not repair it when the next spring tide comes we shall be buried in one common destruction.

The question was taken on the adoption of the Constitution on February 6, 1788, and carried by a small majority.

The Virginia Convention

The convention of Virginia met on the 2nd of June, and the talented men of that large State were arranged on opposite sides. Patrick Henry, George Mason, William Grayson, James Monroe, and others were in the ranks of opposition, and they were met by Edmund Pendleton, Edmund Randolph, James Madison, John Marshall, Chancellor Wythe, and others. The debates as given to the public, though no doubt imperfect, exhibit a display of eloquence and talents, certainly at that time unequaled in this country.

The debates, though generally courteous, were often animated, sometimes violent.

The radical difference between the parties in Virginia and in other States respecting the new system was that it departed from the principles of a confederacy and constituted a consolidated national government vested with extensive powers operating, not upon the States, but upon individuals, and that the people themselves, on whom it was to operate, were not secured against the improper exercise of those powers by a bill of rights. The loss of sovereignty and of influence was felt by the large States, and led them to a more particular examination of the various powers transferred to the different departments of the new Government.

Consolidation or Confederation?

DEBATE IN THE VIRGINIA CONVENTION

All the talents and eloquence of Patrick Henry were exerted against a system which he deprecated. He commenced by inquiring why the Confederation had been

abandoned, and what authority the general convention
had to make a consolidated government:

I would make this inquiry of those worthy characters who
composed a part of the late federal convention. I am sure
they were fully impressed with the necessity of forming a
great consolidated government instead of a confederation.
That this is a consolidated government is demonstrably clear,
and the danger of such a government is to my mind very
striking. I have the highest veneration for those gentlemen,
but, sir, give me leave to demand what right had they to say
we, the people? My political curiosity, exclusive of my anxious
solicitude for the public welfare, leads me to ask who authorized
them to speak the language of *we, the people,* instead of *we,*
the States? States are the characteristics and the soul of a
confederation. If the States be not the agents of this compact, it must be one great consolidated government of the
people of all the States. I have the highest respect for those
gentlemen who formed the convention, and, were not some of
them here, I would express some testimonial of esteem for
them. America had, on a former occasion, put the utmost
confidence in them—a confidence which was well placed, and
I am sure, sir, I could give up any thing to them; I would
cheerfully confide in them as my representatives. But, sir!
on this great occasion I would demand the cause of their
conduct. Even from that illustrious man who saved us by his
valor I would have a reason for his conduct—that liberty which
he has given us by his valor tells me to ask this reason—
and sure I am, were he here, he would give us the information.
The people gave them no power to use their name. That they
exceeded their power is perfectly clear. It is not mere curiosity
that actuates me—I wish to hear the real actual existing danger
which should lead us to take these steps so dangerous in my
conception. Disorders have arisen in other parts of America,
but here, sir, no dangers, no insurrection or tumult has happened—everything has been calm and tranquil. But, notwithstanding this, we are wandering on the great ocean of human
affairs. I see no landmark to guide us. We are running we
know not whither. Difference of opinion has gone to a degree
of inflammatory resentment in some parts of the country which
has been occasioned by this perilous innovation. The federal
convention ought to have amended the old system—for this
purpose they were solely delegated; the object of their mission
extended to no other consideration.

To this direct inquiry Governor Randolph replied by saying:

The members of the general convention were particularly deputed to ameliorate the Confederation. On a thorough contemplation of the subject they found it impossible to amend that system; what was to be done? The dangers of America, which will be shown at another time by particular enumeration, suggested the expedient of forming a *new plan;* the Confederation has done a great deal for us, we will allow, but it was the danger of a powerful enemy, and the spirit of America, sir, and not the energy of that system, that carried us through that perilous war. For what were its best arms? The greatest exertions were made when the danger was most imminent. This system was not signed till March, 1781, Maryland having not acceded to it before, yet the military achievements and other exertions of America previous to that period were as brilliant, as effectual and successful as they could have been under the most energetic government. This clearly shows that our perilous situation was the cement of our Union.

How different the scene when this peril vanished and peace was restored! The demands of Congress were treated with neglect. One State complained that another had not paid its quota as well as itself. Public credit gone! For I believe, were it not for the private credit of individuals, we should have been ruined long before that time. Commerce languishing, produce falling in value, and justice trampled under foot. We became contemptible in the eyes of all foreign nations; they discarded us as little wanton boys who had played for liberty, but who had not sufficient solidity or wisdom to secure it on a permanent basis, and were therefore unworthy of their regard. It was found that Congress could not even enforce the observance of their own treaties. That treaty under which we enjoy our present tranquillity was disregarded. Making no difference between the justice of paying debts due to people here, and that of paying those due to people on the other side of the Atlantic, I wished to see the treaty complied with by the payment of the British debts, but have not been able to know why it has been neglected. What was the reply to the demands and requisitions of Congress? You are too contemptible; we will despise and disregard you. After meeting in convention the deputies from the States communicated their information to one another. On a review of our critical situation, and of the impossibility of introducing any degree of improvement into the old system, what ought they to have done?

Would it not have been treason to return without proposing some scheme to relieve their distressed country?

Mr. Henry, in renewing the discussion, declared the new system produced "a revolution as radical as that which separated us from Great Britain."

It is fully as radical if in this transition our rights and privileges are endangered and the sovereignty of the States be relinquished; and cannot we plainly see that this is actually the case? The rights of conscience, trial by jury, liberty of the press, all your immunities and franchises, all pretensions to human rights and privileges, so loudly talked of by some and inconsiderately by others, are rendered insecure, if not lost, by this change. Is this tame relinquishment of rights worthy of freemen? Is it worthy of that manly fortitude that ought to characterize republicans? It is said that eight States have adopted this plan. I declare that if twelve States and a half had adopted it, I would with manly firmness and in spite of an erring world reject it.

Should the system go into operation, Mr. Henry asked, "what will the States have to do? Take care of the *poor,* repair and make *highways,* erect *bridges,* and so on and so on. Abolish the State legislatures at once. For what purposes should they be returned?"

Mr. Henry in particular objected to the jurisdiction of the Supreme Court in controversies between a State and a foreign government. Would the foreign government in such a case, he asked, be bound by the decision? And would not the American State be barred from its claim if the federal judiciary thought it unjust? The exclusion of trial by jury in such cases would be destructive of the rights of the people of the State affected. And, if there is not to be this exclusion, would not juries empaneled in the proposed federal district, a territory only ten miles square, be mere tools of parties, especially since the right of challenging such juries is not secured in the Constitution. For his part, said Mr. Henry, sooner than trust his person or property to the mercy of such creatures, he would rather leave it to the court, unjust to his rights as a citizen of Virginia as this would be.

To these arguments John Marshall, afterwards to be the Chief-Justice for many years of the Supreme Court, replied, saying that, as the previous consent of both parties was necessary in bringing the case before the court, each would be bound in honor as well as in law to accept the decision of the tribunal. Accordingly the court would be a means of preventing disputes, instead of aggravating them, between the States and foreign nations. He continued:

The exclusion of trial by jury in such a case, says the honorable gentleman (Henry), would prostrate our rights. Does the word court mean only the judges? Does not the determination of a jury necessarily lead to the judgment of the court? Is there anything here which gives the judges exclusive jurisdiction of matters of fact? What is the object of a jury trial? To inform the court of the facts. When a court has cognizance of facts, does it not follow that they can make inquiry by a jury? It is impossible to be otherwise. I hope that in this country, where impartiality is so much admired, the laws will direct facts to be ascertained by a jury. But, says the honorable gentleman, the juries in the ten miles square will be mere tools of parties, with which he would not trust his person or property, which, he says, he would rather leave to the court. Because the Government may have a district ten miles square, will no man stay there but the tools and officers of the Government? Will nobody else be found there? Is it so in any other part of the world where a government has legislative power? Are there none but officers and tools of the government of Virginia in Richmond? Will there not be independent merchants and respectable gentlemen of fortune within the ten miles square? Will there not be worthy farmers and mechanics? Will not a good jury be found there as well as anywhere else? Will the officers of the Government become improper to be on a jury? What is it to the Government, whether this man or that man succeeds? It is all one thing. Does the Constitution say that juries shall consist of officers, or that the Supreme Court shall be held in the ten miles square? It was acknowledged by the honorable member that it was secure in England. What makes it secure there? Is it their constitution? What part of their constitution is there that the Parliament cannot change? As the preservation of this right is in the hands of Parliament, and it has ever been held sacred by them, will the Government of America be less honest than that of Great Britain? Here a restriction is to be found. The jury is not to be brought out of the State. There is no such restriction in that government, for the laws of Parliament decide everything respecting it. Yet gentlemen tell us that there is safety there, and nothing here but danger. It seems to me that the laws of the United States will generally secure trials by a jury of the vicinage, or in such manner as will be most safe and convenient for the people.

But it seems that the right of challenging the jurors is not secured in this Constitution. Is this done by our own Constitution, or by any provision of the English Government? Is it done by their Magna Charta or Bill of Rights? This privilege is founded on their laws. If so, why should it be objected to the American Constitution that it is not inserted in it? If we are secure in Virginia without mentioning it in our Constitution, why should not this security be found in the federal court?

A majority of the Virginia convention were in favor of very material amendments of the nature of a "Bill of Rights," and the question finally was whether the Constitution should be adopted previously or subsequently to such amendments.

After a debate of about twenty days, Mr. Wythe moved that the Constitution be ratified, with a preamble declaring that the powers granted by it were the gift of the people, and that every power not granted remained with them—that no right, therefore, of any denomination could be canceled, abridged, restrained, or modified by Congress, or any officer of the United States, except in those instances in which power was given by the Constitution for those purposes. Among other essential rights, liberty of conscience and of the press were mentioned, and it was declared that any imperfections which might exist in the Constitution ought rather to be examined in the mode therein prescribed for obtaining amendments than to bring the union in danger by a delay, with a hope of obtaining previous amendments.

On this motion the debate was renewed with increased zeal and animation. Mr. Henry, in opposition to it, observed:

With respect to subsequent amendments proposed by the worthy member, I am distressed when I hear the expression. It is a new one altogether, and such as stands against every idea of fortitude and manliness in the States or any one else. Evils admitted in order to be removed *subsequently,* and tyranny submitted to in order to be excluded by a *subsequent* alteration, are things totally new to me. But I am sure he meant nothing but to amuse the committee. I know his candor. His proposal is an idea dreadful to me. I ask: does experience warrant such a thing from the beginning of the world to this day? Do you enter into a compact of government first and afterwards settle the terms of the government? It is admitted by every one that this is a compact. Although the Confederation be lost, it is a compact, constitution, or something of that nature. I confess I never heard of such an idea before. It is most abhorrent to my mind. You endanger the tranquillity of your country, you stab its repose if you accept this government unaltered. . . .

I cannot conclude without saying that I shall have nothing to do with it if subsequent amendments be determined on. Oppressions will be carried on as radically by the majority when adjustments and accommodations will be held up. I say I conceive it my duty, if this government is adopted before it is amended, to go home. I shall act as I think my duty requires. Every other gentleman will do the same. Previous amendments, in my opinion, are necessary to procure peace and tranquillity. I fear, if they be not agreed to, every movement and operation of government will cease, and how long that baneful thing, civil discord, will stay from this country God only knows.

The language of Mr. Henry at the close of this debate and just before the final question was taken was dispassionate and patriotic.

If I shall be in the minority I shall have those painful sensations which arise from a conviction of being overpowered in a good cause. Yet I will be a peaceful citizen! My head, my hand, and my heart shall be at liberty to retrieve the loss of liberty and remove the defects of that system in a constitutional way. I wish not to go to violence, but will wait with hopes that the spirit which predominated in the Revolution is not yet gone, nor the cause of those who are attached to the Revolution lost. I shall therefore patiently wait in expectation of seeing that Government changed so as to be compatible with the safety, liberty, and happiness of the people.

The object of some opponents was that the States of Virginia, North Carolina, and New York should reject the system until their amendments were agreed to by the other States. This it was supposed would secure the adoption of such amendments as they required. This, on the other hand, was deemed too hazardous an experiment, and it was urged that it would place the Union itself in the greatest danger. To remarks of this kind Mr. Grayson replied:

The dangers of disunion are painted in strong colors. How is the fact? It is this: that if Virginia thinks proper to insist on previous amendments, joined by New York and North Carolina, she can procure what amendments she pleases. What is the geographical position of those States? New York commands the ocean. Virginia and North Carolina join the Spanish dominions. What would be the situation then of the other States? They would be topographically separated, though politically united with one another. There would be no communication between the center and the component parts. While these States were thus separated, of what advantage would commercial regulations be to them? Yet will gentlemen pretend to say that we must adopt first and then beg amendments? I see no reason in it. We undervalue our own importance. Consider the vast consequence of Virginia and North Carolina. What kind of connection would the rest of the States form? They would be carrying States without anything to carry. They would have no communication with the other Southern States. I therefore insist that if you are not satisfied with the paper as it stands it is as clear to me as that the sun shines that, by joining those two States, you may command such amendments as you think necessary for the happiness of the people. The late convention were not empowered totally to alter the present Confederation. The idea was to amend. If they have laid before us a thing quite different, we are not bound to accept it. There is nothing dictatorial in refusing it. We wish to remove the spirit of party. In all parts of the world there is a reciprocity in contracts and compacts. If one make a proposition to another, is he bound to receive it?

Six or seven States have agreed to it. As it is not their interest to stand by themselves, will they not with open arms receive us? Tobacco will always make our peace with them. I hope then that the gentleman will find on reconsideration that we are not at all in that dangerous situation he represented.

In my opinion the idea of subsequent amendments is preposterous—they are words without meaning. The little States will
not agree to an alteration. When they find themselves on an
equal footing with the other States in the Senate, and all power
vested in them, the executive mixed with the legislative, they
will never assent. Why are such extensive powers given to
the Senate? Because the little States gained their point. In
every light I consider subsequent amendments as unwise and
impolitic.

Speaking of the advantages Virginia was to derive
from the new system, Mr. Grayson asked:

Has Virginia any gain from her riches and commerce?
What does she get in return? I can see what she gives up,
which is immense. The little States gain in proportion as
we lose. Every disproportion is against us. If the effects of
such a contrariety of interests be happy, it must be extraordinary and wonderful. From the very nature of the paper,
one part whose interest is different from the other is to govern
it. What will be our situation? The Northern States are
carrying States. We are considered as productive States.
They will constantly carry for us. Are manufacturers favorable
to us? If they reciprocate the act of Charles II and say that
no produce of America shall be carried in any foreign bottom,
what will be the consequence? This—that all the produce of
the Southern States will be carried by the Northern States on
their own terms, which must be very high.

The reply of Mr. Madison to the first part of this
speech produced a powerful effect in favor of Mr.
Wythe's motion. He saw that the fate of the system
he had been so instrumental in forming depended on
the question then to be decided. He was too well acquainted with the difficulties in the general convention
to believe that the States could ever unite in the various
amendments which would be proposed. He said:

Nothing has excited more admiration in the world than the
manner in which free governments have been established in
America. For it was the first instance, from the creation of
the world to the American Revolution, that free inhabitants
have been seen deliberating on a form of government and
selecting such of their citizens as possessed their confidence
to determine upon and give effect to it. But why has this

excited so much wonder and applause? Because it is of so much magnitude, and because it is liable to be frustrated by so many accidents. If it has excited so much wonder that the United States have, in the middle of war and confusion, formed free systems of government, how much more astonishment and admiration will be excited should they be able peaceably, freely, and satisfactorily to establish one general government when there is such a diversity of opinions and interests, when not cemented or stimulated by any common danger? How vast must be the difficulty of concentrating in one government the interests, and conciliating the opinions of so many different heterogeneous bodies?

How have the confederacies of ancient and modern times been formed? As far as ancient history describes the former to us, they were brought about by the wisdom of some eminent sage. How was the imperfect union of the Swiss Cantons formed? By danger. How was the confederacy of the United Netherlands formed? By the same. They were surrounded by dangers. By these and one influential character, they were stimulated to unite. How was the Germanic system formed? By danger in some degree, but principally by the overruling influence of individuals. When we consider this Government, we ought to make great allowances. We must calculate the impossibility that every State should be gratified in its wishes, and much less that every individual should receive this gratification. It has never been denied by the friends of the paper on the table that it has its defects. But they do not think that it contains any real danger. They conceive that they will in all probability be removed when experience will show it to be necessary. I beg that gentlemen deliberating on this subject consider the alternative. Either nine States will ratify it or they will not. If nine States adopt it, can it be reasonably presumed or required that nine States, having freely and fully considered the subject and come to an affirmative decision, will, upon the demand of a single State, agree that they acted wrong and could not see its defects—tread back the steps which they have taken and come forward and reduce it to uncertainty whether a general system shall be adopted or not? Virginia has always heretofore spoken the language of respect to the other States, and she has always been attended to. Will it be that language to call on a majority of the States to acknowledge that they have done wrong? Is it the language of confidence to say that we do not believe that amendments for the preservation of the common liberty and general interest of the States will be consented to by them? This is neither the language of confidence nor respect. Virginia, when she speaks respectfully, will be as much attended to as she has hitherto been when speaking this language. It is a most awful thing that depends on our decision—no less than whether the thirteen States shall unite freely, peaceably, and unanimously for the security of their common happiness and liberty, or whether everything is to be put in confusion and disorder? Are we to embark in this dangerous enterprise, uniting various opinions to contrary interests, with the vain hopes of coming to an amicable concurrence?

It is worthy of our consideration that those who prepared the paper on the table found difficulties not to be described in its formation—mutual deference and concession were absolutely necessary. Had they been inflexibly tenacious of their individual opinions they would never have concurred. Under what circumstances was it formed? When no party was formed, or particular proposition made, and men's minds were calm and dispassionate. Yet under these circumstances it was difficult, extremely difficult, to agree to any general system.

Suppose eight States only ratify it, and Virginia proposes certain alterations as the previous condition of her accession. If they should be disposed to accede to her proposition, which is the most favorable conclusion, the difficulty attending it would be immense. Every State which has decided it must take up the subject again. They must not only have the mortification of acknowledging that they have done wrong, but the difficulty of having a reconsideration of it among the people, and appointing new conventions to deliberate upon it. They must attend to all the amendments, which may be dictated by as great a diversity of political opinions as there are local attachments. When brought together in one assembly they must go through and accede to every one of the amendments. The gentlemen who within this House have thought proper to propose previous amendments have brought no less than forty amendments—a bill of rights which contains twenty amendments and twenty other alterations, some of which are improper and inadmissible. Will not every State think herself equally entitled to propose as many amendments? And suppose them to be contradictory. I leave it to this convention, whether it be probable that they can agree to anything but the plan on the table, or whether greater difficulties will not be encountered than were experienced in the progress of the formation of this Constitution.

The motion of Mr. Wythe prevailed by a majority of ten, 89 to 79. In the form of ratification, after stating that every power not granted remained with the people, the convention added:

With these impressions, with a solemn appeal to the searcher of hearts for the purity of our intentions, and under the conviction that whatsoever imperfections may exist in the Constitution ought rather to be examined in the mode prescribed therein than to bring the Union into danger by a delay with a hope of obtaining amendments previous to the ratification.

The convention at the same time agreed upon a bill of rights, consisting of twenty articles, and the same number of amendments to the body of the Constitution. The most important of the latter were: that Congress should not lay direct taxes until the States had refused them; that members of the Senate and House should be incapable of holding any civil office under the authority of the United States; that no commercial treaty should be ratified without the concurrence of two-thirds of the whole number of the members of the Senate, and that no treaty ceding or suspending the territorial rights or claims of the United States, or any of them, or their rights to fishing in the American seas, or navigating the American rivers, should be but in cases of the most extreme necessity, nor should any such treaty be ratified without the concurrence of three-fourths of the whole number of the members of both Houses; that no navigation law or law regulating commerce should be passed without the consent of two-thirds of the members present in both Houses; that no person be capable of being President of the United States for more than eight years in any term of sixteen years; that the judicial power of the United States should extend to no case where the cause of action originated before the ratification of the Constitution except in disputes between persons claiming lands under grants of different States and suits for debts due to the United States; that Congress should not alter, modify, or interfere in the times, places, or manner of holding elections for Senators or Representatives, or either of them, except when the legislature of any State should neglect, refuse or be disabled by invasion or rebellion to prescribe the same; that the clauses which declare that Congress should not exercise certain powers be not interpreted to extend their powers, but be construed as making exceptions to the specified powers, or inserted merely for greater caution; that the laws ascertaining the compensations of the members be postponed in their operation until after the election of Representatives immediately succeeding the passage of the same; that some tribunal other than the Senate be provided to try impeachment of Senators.

NEW YORK CONVENTION

A majority of the convention of New York, which met on June 19, were strongly opposed to the new system of government. The most important point discussed was the proportion of representation fixed by the Constitution for the popular House. This divided the convention into the two camps of those inclined toward a strong government, and those who feared the centralization of power in the hands of a comparatively few men of ability and political prestige.

As ten States had ratified the Constitution, and it must necessarily go into operation, no alternative was left New York but to unite or secede. By a small majority the system was adopted and amendments recommended. These amendments were more numerous as well as more radical than those of any other State.

CHAPTER XV

DEFENCE OF THE CONSTITUTION

[LETTERS IN THE PRESS]

Letters of "Fabius" (John Dickinson of Pennsylvania)—"The Federalist" Papers, by Alexander Hamilton [N. Y.], James Madison [Va.], and John Jay [N. Y.]: Introduction by Hamilton; Digest of the Arguments; Conclusion, by Hamilton—Adoption of the Constitution.

MANY attacks on the proposed Constitution were made in the newspapers. To these John Dickinson replied in his "Letters of Fabius," and Alexander Hamilton, James Madison, and John Jay in articles over the common signature of Publius, which were collected and published under the title of "The Federalist." Dickinson wrote for the common people, and Hamilton, Madison, and Jay for persons of superior education.

The letters of "Fabius" were published early in 1788, while ratification of the Constitution was in doubt, in order to "simplify the subject so as to facilitate inquiries" regarding it and remove current objections to it. The substance of the papers is here presented in dialogue form, the language of the original being preserved so far as practicable.

THE LETTERS OF FABIUS

JOHN DICKINSON

Objection. The proposed system has such inherent vices as must necessarily produce a bad administration, and at length the oppression of a monarchy and aristocracy in the federal offices.

Reply. *The power of the people*, pervading the proposed system by frequent elections, together with the *strong con-*

379

federation of the States, forms an adequate security against *every* danger that has been apprehended.

The proof of the salutary, purifying, and preserving qualities of this popular rule removes all the particular objections to the Constitution as menacing liberty by unnecessary taxation, standing armies, the abolishment of trial by jury in federal judicial procedure, and limitations of freedom of the press and freedom of commerce, etc. The question then is: not what may be done, when the Government shall be turned into a tyranny, but *how* the Government can be so turned.

Objection. The number of federal officers is *too small.*

Reply. If this is a fault it will be remedied in the natural course of the country's development by the unavoidable multiplication of offices. The Senate continues the present representation of the sovereignties of the States, and through State jealousy it will never renounce its powers, including representation. The House of Representatives will grow only with the country's growth and corresponding legislative needs.

Objection. The federal officers hold their offices too long.

Reply. This cannot hold against the Representatives who are elected every two years. The Senators, from their smaller numbers, should serve a longer term, to balance, by their greater *experience* in legislation, the greater *power* of the Representatives (that of the purse).

Objection. The President will not be independent.

Reply. He is not chosen by the people, who have not the necessary information before them of the qualifications of men proposed for the office, nor by Congress, lest it should disturb the national councils, nor by *any standing body whatever,* for fear of undue influence, but by a specially appointed body of private citizens whose qualifications for such service are known by the people and who are uninfluenced by any other consideration than the worth of the men considered for the Presidency and Vice-Presidency.

Objection. The President may become a dictator.

Reply. Two-thirds of Congress may pass any law over his veto.

Objection. The Senate may become a dictator.

Reply. The terms of office of the Senators expire at different times, and the political complexion of the State legislatures which elect them will be constantly changing. Machiavel and Cæsar Borgia together could not form a conspiracy in such a Senate destructive to any but themselves and their accomplices.

Objection. The Constitution is not broad enough.

Reply. The people of the United States are *trebly* repre-sented in it. The *whole* Government is interested in the safety of every *part*.

Objection. But the sovereign will of the Government must of consequence destroy the subordinate sovereignties of the several States.

Reply. If so, we must abandon the *principle of all society* for the subordinate sovereignties, or, in other words, the *un-delegated rights* of the several States in a confederation stand upon the very same foundation with the undelegated rights of *individuals* in a society, the federated sovereign will being com-posed of the subordinated sovereign wills of the several con-federated States.

Why should we be alarmed when we know that the rights to be delegated by the several States to the Confederation are simple, defined, and so limited to particular objects that they cannot possibly be applied by any construction to other objects without such a distortion of interpretation, and such a viola-tion of propriety, as must offend every sound head and honest heart?

As some persons seem to think *a bill of rights* is *the best security* of rights, the *sovereignties* of the several States have *this* best security by the proposed Constitution, and *more than this* best security, for *they* are not barely *declared* to be rights, but are taken into it as *component parts* for *their* perpetual preservation—by *themselves*. In short, the government of each State is, and is to be, *sovereign* and *supreme* in *all* matters that *relate* to each state *only*. It is to be *subordinate* barely in *those* matters that relate to *the whole;* and it will be their own faults if the several States suffer the *federal sovereignty* to interfere in things of their respective jurisdictions. An instance of such interference with regard to *any single State* will be a dangerous *precedent as to all,* and therefore will be guarded against *by all,* as the trustees or servants of the several States will not dare, if they retain their senses, so to violate the *independent sovereignty* of their respective States, that justly darling object of *American* affections, to which they are responsible, besides being engaged by all the charities of life.

Trial by jury, and the dependence of taxation upon rep-resentation, those cornerstones of liberty, were not obtained by *a bill of rights* or any other records, and have not been and cannot be preserved by them. They and all other rights must be preserved, by *soundness of sense* and *honesty of heart*. Compared with *these,* what are a bill of rights or any characters drawn upon paper or parchment, those frail remembrances? Do we want to be reminded that the sun enlightens, warms, invigorates, and cheers? or how horrid it would be to have his rays intercepted by our being thrust for life into mines or dungeons? Liberty is the sun of society. Rights are the rays.

Objection. A very extensive territory cannot be ruled by a government of republican form.

Reply. It is true that extensive territory has in general been arbitrarily governed; and it is as true that a number of republics in such territory, *loosely connected,* must inevitably rot into despotism. But the proposed Constitution presents a government without a precedent, and therefore the historical argument does not apply to it. Where was there ever a confederacy which obliged by its direct authority every *individual* to contribute, when the public good necessarily required it, a just proportion of aid to the support of the commonwealth protecting him—*without disturbing him in the discharge of the duties owing by him to the State of which he is an inhabitant,* and at the same time was so amply, so anxiously provided for bringing the interests, and even the wishes of *every sovereignty* and of *every person* of the Union under all their various modifications and impressions into their full operation and efficacy in the national councils? The instance never existed. The conclusion ought not to be made.

The assertion has probably been suggested by reflections on the democracies of antiquity without making a proper distinction between them and the democracy of *the United States.*

In the democracies of antiquity the people assembled together and governed *personally.* This mode was incompatible with greatness of number and dispersion of habitation.

In the democracy of *the United States* the people act by their *representatives.* This improvement collects the will of millions upon points concerning their welfare with more advantage than the will of hundreds could be collected under the ancient form.

Representation which implies purity of election is a gentle remedy for every evil. It is at once a preservative against discontent and rashness on the part of the people and against negligence and usurpation on the part of their magistrates. All the curious contrivances and artful balances devised in ancient or modern times to supply its place have proved deficient. To mention no more, *Athens* and *Rome* perished for want of a representative government.

There is another improvement equally deserving regard, and that is the *varied representation* of sovereignties *and* people in the Constitution now proposed.

It has been said that this representation was a mere compromise.

It was not a mere compromise. *The equal representation of each State* with equal suffrage *in one branch of the legislature* was an original substantive proposition made in the convention at Philadelphia in 1787, very soon after the draft offered by *Virginia,* to which last mentioned State *United America* is much indebted not only in other respects, but for her merit in the origination and prosecution of this momentous business.

The proposition was *expressly* made by the delegate who brought it forward upon *this principle* that a territory of such extent as that of *United America* could not *be safely and advantageously governed,* but by a *combination* of republics, each *retaining* all the rights of supreme sovereignty, *excepting* such as ought to be contributed to the Union; that for the securer *preservation* of these sovereignties they ought to be represented in a body *by themselves* and with *equal suffrage,* and that they would be annihilated if both branches of the legislature were to be formed of representatives of the people in proportion to the number of inhabitants in each State.[1]

The principle lately mentioned appears to be well founded in reason. Why cannot a very extensive territory be ruled by a government of republican form? It is answered because its power must languish through distance of parts. Granted if it be not a "body by joints and bands having nourishment ministered and knit together." If it be such a body, the objection is removed. Instead of *such a perfect body* framed upon *the principle that commands men to associate and societies to confederate; that which by communicating and extending happiness corresponds with the gracious intentions of our Maker towards us his creatures;* what is proposed? *Truly, that the natural legs and arms of this body should be cut off because they are too weak and their places supplied by stronger limbs of wood and metal.*

America is, and will be, divided into several sovereign States, each possessing every power proper for governing *within its own limits for its own purposes* and also for acting *as a member of the Union.*

They will be *civil* and *military* stations *conveniently planted* throughout the empire with lively and regular com-

[1] See the plan of Charles Pinckney on page 290.

munications. A stroke, a touch upon any part, will be immediately felt by the whole. *Rome,* famed for imperial arts, had a glimpse of *this great truth,* and endeavored, as well as her hard-hearted policy would permit, to realize it in her colonies. They were miniatures of the capital, but wanted the *vital principle of sovereignty,* and were too small. They were melted down into or overwhelmed by the nations around them. Were they now existing, they might be called curious automatons—something like to our *living* originals. *These* will bear a remarkable resemblance to the mild features of *patriarchal* government, in which each son ruled *his own household,* and in *other matters* the whole family was directed by the common ancestor.

Can any government be devised that will be more suited to citizens who wish for *equal freedom* and *common prosperity,* better calculated for preventing corruption of manners,[1] for advancing the improvements that endear or adorn life, or that can be more conformed to the *understanding,* to the *best affections,* to the very *nature* of man? *What harvests of happiness may grow from the seeds of liberty that are now sowing?* The cultivation will indeed demand continual attention, unceasing diligence, and frequent conflict with difficulties, but to object against the benefits offered to us by our Creator, by excepting to the terms annexed, is a crime to be equaled only by its folly.

Objection. The Constitution is admittedly not perfect. Before it is adopted it should be thoroughly discussed that proper alterations may be made.

Reply. As to alterations a little experience will cast more light upon the subject than a multitude of debates. Whatever qualities are possessed by those who object, they will have the candor to confess that they will be encountered by opponents, not in any respect inferior, and yet differing from them in judgment upon every point they have mentioned.

Such untired industry to serve their country did the delegates to the federal convention exert that they not only labored to form the best plan they could, but *provided for making at any time amendments on the authority of the people* without shaking the stability of the Government.

Thus by a gradual progress we may from time to time *introduce every improvement in our Constitution* that shall be found suitable to our situation.

[1] Education is the best institution for preventing corruption of manners; and progress of knowledge the most successful foe to religious and civic despotism. By wise legislators, instruction will be relied on vastly more than punishments. Of these the most effectual regulation will be their certainty, not severity.—J. D.

The Federalist Papers

From October 27, 1787, to April 2, 1788, there appeared in *The Independent Journal* and other newspapers of New York a series of seventy-seven papers signed "Publius," explaining and justifying the Constitution. They created a great interest throughout the country, and were shortly afterwards collected and published in book form under title of "The Federalist," eight essays being added, making a total of eighty-five. They were written by Alexander Hamilton, James Madison and John Jay, to whose authorship have been assigned by the historians, respectively, 51, 29, and 5 of the essays. Hamilton discussed all phases of the subject, especially finance; Madison treated particularly of the relation between Federal and State powers; Jay dealt almost exclusively with foreign relations. Hamilton is credited with being the originator of the series, it being his intention to convert the State of New York, which was strongly inclined to reject the Constitution, to its adoption. Not only was this accomplished, but the papers had a profound influence in other States as well. In completeness of exposition, force of argument, and in literary style they far surpassed all other publications upon the subject, and remain to-day the most authoritative commentary on the Constitution, being recognized as such by the courts. Many editions of the work have been published, the most fully edited and indexed being that by Paul Leicester Ford (1898). A number of editions have been prepared as text-books on the Constitution, the handiest of these being by Henry Cabot Lodge (1888), the present Senator from Massachusetts. To these editions the reader of GREAT DEBATES who desires to pursue further the study of the Constitution is referred. Space is available here for only the introduction and conclusion by Hamilton, and a digest of the intervening argument.

In the "Introduction" Hamilton lays down the general principles upon which discussion should be conducted, and it therefore should be carefully perused by every one desiring to fit himself for public speaking.

INTRODUCTION TO THE FEDERALIST

ALEXANDER HAMILTON

After full experience of the insufficiency of the existing Federal Government you are invited to deliberate upon a new Constitution for the United States of America. The subject speaks its own importance, comprehending in its consequences nothing less than the existence of the Union, the safety and welfare of the parts of which it is composed, the fate of an empire, in many respects the most interesting in the world. It has been frequently remarked that it seems to have been reserved to the people of this country to decide by their conduct and example the important question whether societies of men are really capable or not of establishing good government from reflection and choice, or whether they are forever destined to depend for their political constitutions on accident and force. If there be any truth in the remark, the crisis at which we are arrived may, with propriety, be regarded as the period when that decision is to be made, and a wrong election of the part we shall act may, in this view, deserve to be considered as the general misfortune of mankind.

This idea, by adding the inducements of philanthropy to those of patriotism, will heighten the solicitude which all considerate and good men must feel for the event. Happy will it be if our choice should be directed by a judicious estimate of our true interests, uninfluenced by considerations foreign to the public good. But this is more ardently to be wished for than seriously to be expected. The plan offered to our deliberations affects too many particular interests, innovates upon too many local institutions, not to involve in its discussion a variety of objects extraneous to its merits and of views, passions, and prejudices little favorable to the discovery of truth.

Among the most formidable of the obstacles which the new Constitution will have to encounter may readily be distinguished the obvious interest of a certain class of men in every State to resist all changes which may hazard a diminution of the power, emolument, and consequence of the offices they hold under the State establishments . . . and the perverted ambition of another class of men who will either hope to aggrandize themselves by the confusions of their country or will flatter themselves with fairer prospects of elevation from the subdivision of the empire into several partial confederacies than from its union under one government.

It is not, however, my design to dwell upon observations

of this nature. I am aware it would be desingenuous to resolve indiscriminately the oppression of any set of men into interested or ambitious views merely because their situations might subject them to suspicion. Candor will oblige us to admit that even such men may be actuated by upright intentions, and it cannot be doubted that much of the opposition which has already shown itself or that may hereafter make its appearance will spring from sources blameless at least, if not respectable . . . the honest errors of minds led astray by preconceived jealousies and fears. So numerous indeed and so powerful are the causes which serve to give a false bias to the judgment that we, upon many occasions, see wise and good men on the wrong as well as on the right side of questions of the first magnitude to society. This circumstance, if duly attended to, would always furnish a lesson of moderation to those who are engaged in any controversy, however well persuaded of being in the right. And a further reason for caution in this respect might be drawn from the reflection that we are not always sure that those who advocate the truth are actuated by purer principles than their antagonists. Ambition, avarice, personal animosity, party opposition, and many other motives not more laudable than these are apt to operate as well upon those who support as upon those who oppose the right side of a question. Were there not even these inducements to moderation, nothing could be more ill-judged than that intolerant spirit which has at all times characterized political parties. For in politics as in religion it is equally absurd to aim at making proselytes by fire and sword. Heresies in either can rarely be cured by persecution.

And yet, just as these sentiments must appear to candid men, we have already sufficient indications that it will happen in this, as in all former cases of great national discussion. A torrent of angry and malignant passions will be let loose. To judge from the conduct of the opposite parties we shall be led to conclude that they will mutually hope to evince the justness of their opinions and to increase the number of their converts by the loudness of their declamations and by the bitterness of their invectives. An enlightened zeal for the energy and efficiency of government will be stigmatized as the offspring of a temper fond of power and hostile to the principles of liberty. An over-scrupulous jealousy of danger to the rights of the people which is more commonly the fault of the head than of the heart will be represented as mere pretence and artifice . . . the stale bait for popularity at

the expense of public good. It will be forgotten on the one
hand that jealousy is the usual concomitant of violent love
and that the noble enthusiasm of liberty is too apt to be infected with a spirit of narrow and illiberal distrust. On the
other hand it will be equally forgotten that the vigor of government is essential to the security of liberty; that in the contemplation of a sound and well-informed judgment their interests can never be separated, and that a dangerous ambition
more often lurks behind the specious mask of zeal for the
rights of the people than under the forbidding appearance
of zeal for the firmness and efficiency of government. History
will teach us that the former has been found a much more
certain road to the introduction of despotism than the latter,
and that of those men who have overturned the liberties of
republics the greatest number have begun their career by paying
an obsequious court to the people, commencing demagogues and
ending tyrants.

In the course of the preceding observations it has been
my aim, fellow-citizens, to put you upon your guard against
all attempts, from whatever quarter, to influence your decision
in a matter of the utmost moment to your welfare by any impressions other than those which may result from the evidence
of truth. You will no doubt at the same time have collected
from the general scope of them that they proceed from a source
not unfriendly to the new Constitution. Yes, my countrymen,
I own to you that after having given it an attentive consideration I am clearly of opinion it is your interest to adopt it.
I am convinced that this is the safest course for your liberty,
your dignity, and your happiness. I affect not reserves which
I do not feel. I will not amuse you with an appearance of
deliberation when I have decided. I frankly acknowledge to
you my convictions and I will freely lay before you the reasons
on which they are founded. The consciousness of good intentions disdains ambiguity. I shall not however multiply professions on this head. My motives must remain in the depository of my own breast; my arguments will be open to all and
may be judged of by all. They shall at least be offered in a
spirit which will not disgrace the cause of truth.

I propose in a series of papers to discuss the following interesting particulars: *The utility of the Union to your political
prosperity. The insufficiency of the present Confederation to
preserve that Union. The necessity of a government at least
equally energetic with the one proposed to the attainment of
this object. The conformity of the proposed Constitution to*

the true principles of republican government. Its analogy to your own State constitution, and, lastly, The additional security which its adoption will afford to the preservation of that species of government to liberty and to property.

In the progress of this discussion I shall endeavor to give a satisfactory answer to all the objections which shall have made their appearance that may seem to have any claim to attention.

It may perhaps be thought superfluous to offer arguments to prove the utility of the Union, a point, no doubt, deeply engraved on the hearts of the great body of the people in every State, and one which, it may be imagined, has no adversaries. But the fact is that we already hear it whispered in the private circles of those who oppose the new Constitution that the thirteen States are of too great extent for any general system, and that we must of necessity resort to separate confederacies of distinct portions of the whole. This doctrine will, in all probability, be gradually propagated till it has votaries enough to countenance its open avowal. For nothing can be more evident to those who are able to take an enlarged view of the subject than the alternative of an adoption of the Constitution or a dismemberment of the Union. It may, therefore, be essential to examine particularly the advantages of that Union, the certain evils and the probable dangers to which every State will be exposed from its dissolution. This shall accordingly be done.

DIGEST OF THE ARGUMENTS OF THE FEDERALIST

HAMILTON, MADISON, AND JAY

I. *The Utility of the Union to the Political Prosperity of the People.*

The Union will promote prosperity in political relations with *foreign nations* by removing the usual *just* causes of war (which are violations of compacts through trade), and by improving the administration of government through the employment of better men than those employed in State governments, through uniform interpretation of the compacts and treaties, and by avoidance of local temptation to bad faith to which a single State may yield, and the local prejudices to which it may be subject. *Nos. 1-5, J.*[1]

[1] This and the following similar annotations refer to the numbers of the papers and the authors; H = Hamilton, M = Madison, and J = Jay, as the papers are assigned in Jefferson's MS. notes.

Peace will be secured through the Union's greater ability to settle amicably a war (if it should arise) by reason of absence of local pride and prejudices, the greater strength of the States when united, the Union's removal beyond the influences of *unjust* causes (such as superior power of neighboring nations and jealousy of foreign powers from successful trade) and by preventing European alliances with our rival nations.

Prosperity will also be promoted by the Union's abolition of *interstate hostilities* arising from the jealousy and power of commercial competition and individual passions and influences.

Nos. 6-9, H.

These States, if disunited, would be tempted to war by *internal disputes* (such as those of the Western lands, New Hampshire grants, etc.), by *commercial rivalry* (such as jealousy against New York and New Jersey), by *apportionment of the federal debt* among the States, by *local laws* violating private contracts between citizens of different States, and by *alliances between individual States and foreign powers* incompatible with the interests of other States.

These interstate hostilities will lead primarily to great destruction of life and property, and ultimately to the establishment of standing armies, extension of the power of the executive, and elevation of the military over the civil power.

The Union will afford a barrier to *domestic faction and insurrection* (to which republics are liable and upon which the advocates of despotism rely for argument), by causing every citizen to possess the same opinions, passions, and interests.

When the faction is a *minority*, both a Union and a confederacy can control it by a regular vote, but when it is a *majority,* only the Union can do so, because of its distinguishing ability to *divide* the prevailing influences and prevent their *concentration.* This ability is *increased* in ratio of *territorial extension.*   *No. 10, M.*

The Union will increase *commerce* with *foreign nations* by securing *uniformity of trade relations,* by establishing a *federal navy* to enforce respect of commercial rights, such as in the *fisheries,* and the navigation of *Western lakes* and the *Mississippi River,* and by the development of a *merchant marine.*

Nos. 11-13, H.

The Union will afford a better system of national revenue by substituting *indirect taxation* for direct taxation, to which the "genius of the people" is opposed.

The Union will increase national revenue by preventing

illicit trade, and interstate rivalry to secure trade by *reduction of customs duties,* and so will obviate the necessity of *real estate taxation,* which is oppressive, of *excise duties,* which are small in the agricultural States and hard to collect, and of *personal property,* which is difficult to trace.

The Union will also increase national revenue by greater *economy* in administration: there will be but one *civil* and one *military* list in place of several which would result from a number of confederacies.

The Constitution supplies an ideal form of government of *extensive territory* and *additions* thereto in its limitation of federal jurisdiction to objects of *general* interest and its provisions for organizing *new States.*   *No.* 14, *M.*

The Union will facilitate *interstate transportation.*

Since all the States are on the frontier, the Union will equally provide for *defence against foreign aggression.*

II.   *The Insufficiency of the Confederation.*

The general admission of this, even by the opponents of the Constitution, proves their inconsistency.   *Nos.* 15-16, *H.*

The legislation of the Confederacy is defective in *raising men and money.*

The Confederacy lacks that authority over the *persons of the citizens* which is the essential foundation of a government. It cannot inflict *penalties* on offenders against federal laws, such as magistrates.

The Confederacy cannot coerce by arms *States* offending against federal laws. Breaches of these laws are certain to arise by reason of the passions and interests of *individual members* of the States who are in power, and by the impatience of control which arises from the *sovereign power* of the States. Such offences have already occurred. If coercion is attempted by the Confederation, it would be productive of constant *wars* through counter-alliance, either of the offending States or of an offending State or States with a foreign nation or nations, and these wars would ultimately lead to a *military despotism* and the death of liberty.

The Union being established on the responsibility of in-dividual citizens who elect the national representatives, thus placing them in national matters above individuals in power in the State governments, would be enabled to *coerce* by arms offenders against national laws, the State governments being powerless to interfere by reason of *public opinion* against such interference.

The Federal Government under the Constitution would not

invade the reserved rights of the States, first, because of lack of inducement, and, secondly, because the federal representatives of the States could frustrate such invasion if it were attempted.

Nos. 17-19, M.

There is greater danger that the delegated rights of the Federal Government will be invaded by the State governments because of their more immediate influence over the people of the diffusive construction of the Federal Government, and of the superior intensity of popular interest in local over national interests.

The Confederacy is defective because of the total want of a *sanction* to its laws, having no power to exact obedience or punish disobedience, since it has received no express delegation of authority to use force against the States.   *No. 21, M.*

The Confederacy is defective because there is no *mutual guaranty* of the States to obey its federal laws, nor has it authority to assist a State in enforcing the State's own laws as in the case of Shay's Rebellion.

The Confederacy is defective because the State *contributions* to the common treasury are by *quotas*. This rule is based on a false presumption that there is a common measure of national wealth, and it is therefore inequitable. The national government should raise its revenues by duties on consumption which will be equitably raised from individuals throughout the entire Union, provided that the dutiable articles will be so selected that each citizen can regulate his consumption of them according to his resources. The rates of the duties will not become oppressive, since if they are either too high or too low the total revenue therefrom will be diminished. Indirect taxation of this sort is preferable to direct taxation proportioned either on the value of land or population, because it is an "Herculean task" to obtain a valuation of land, especially in an unsettled and rapidly improving country such as the United States, and because population, while a better and more convenient standard, is still not a true measure of wealth.

The Confederacy is defective because of the want of a power to regulate commerce by the formation of *commercial treaties*.

Nos. 22-35, H.

The Confederacy is defective because of its raising *troops* by *quotas*, which is very *expensive, inadequate* for defence, and *unequal* in the burden it imposes on the various States.

Representation in the Confederacy is unjust to the more populous States. A majority of the small States contains a minority of the population of all, and the large States would in time rebel against their domination.

The Confederacy is defective because of want of a *judiciary* power, to expound and define the true meaning and operation of the laws, to construe foreign treaties, and to secure uniformity in legal decisions.

The Confederacy is defective in that it has never been *ratified* by the people.

III. *The Necessity of a Constitution at Least Equally Energetic to the One Proposed to Preserve the Union.*

Such a Constitution must provide for the *common defence.* The power to do so should be *without limitation,* because of *unforeseen exigencies* which may arise.

There is no adequate provision for the common defence in the Confederation, hence its failure.

A *standing army* is no menace, since it will be controlled by the legislative department elected by the people. The power of Congress to provide for the common defence is expressly *limited* by the Constitution. The constant danger of the United States from *foreign and Indian hostilities* and the demand of our growing *commerce* for protection are justifications of this power.

It would be an inversion of the primary principle of our association to place the common defence in the care of the individual States, since this would be oppressive to some of the States, and *dangerous* to all, and create *jealousies* between them. Besides, it would afford a temptation to the States to *invade the constitutional authority* of the Union.

The militia of the States is inadequate for the common defence, lacking vigor and stability, and being uneconomical.

A standing army in times of external peace is sometimes necessary—witness present disorders in Pennsylvania, and recent ones in Massachusetts. It will not threaten the liberties of the people, since Congress has authority in the matter, and the subject must be reconsidered every two years, thus preventing *conspiracy,* which requires time to be matured.

The standing army will not as a rule be required to enforce the laws of the Union, since the *people* will obey the Federal Government voluntarily—more willingly perhaps than the State governments, since the former will be the better administered. This superior administration will arise from the greater *latitude* in the choice of federal officers, causing the *most intelligent* men to be sent to the House and Senate, as well as the *most patriotic,* and therefore the least inclined to faction. The

Federal Government having public opinion behind it will be able to suppress sedition in the States without force, employing the ordinary magistracy of each State in the execution of its laws. The mere knowledge that the Federal Government can, if it will, use a force sufficient to execute its laws will prevent the occasion for employing this force.

In any form of federal government force would have to be employed at times. The present form, where this force is controlled by the people through Congress, is the best for the purpose. If Congress betrays the people, there is left the same recourse to self-defence as when a State legislature betrays the people, and, in addition, the assistance of the State against the federal usurpation.

A *general power of taxation* is necessary in every constitution to obviate official plunder and general atrophy of the government. The want of it in the Confederation has produced disaster. This power should extend to *internal taxation,* or the national revenues will be insufficient, causing recourse to the vicious system of *requisitions* upon the States. This system is vicious because (1) it cannot be depended on, (2) it diverts to Federal uses funds that would otherwise be used for needed State purposes, (3) it destroys public credit, (4) it renders loans difficult to be procured, and (5) it tends toward general disaster. On the contrary, internal taxation will (1) develop the resources of the country, (2) and render loans to supply deficiencies easy to procure, because of the increase of national credit by the new power delegated to the national Government.

The power of internal taxation delegated to a Federal Government *will not interfere with State levies of money,* since the good sense of the people, expressed through their representatives in Congress, will be a barrier to the oppressive use of this power; the hazard of provoking State resentment will be a second barrier, and the recognition by Congress that the Union is founded on the prosperity of its parts a third. Besides, the States would still retain an *independent and uncontrollable* authority to raise their own revenues. The sovereignty of the Federal Government is limited to grants made in *express terms* in the Constitution, (1) similar to, but not conflicting with those in the States, (2) expressly prohibitory of like authority in the States, and (3) implicitly contradictory and repugnant to similar authority in the States. The only *exclusive* power of taxation delegated to the Federal Government is that of imposing taxes on imports, and therefore the States may freely impose all other taxes. This concurrent authority is a necessary result of the division of the sovereign power made by the Constitution.

The *incidental* powers in connection with taxation possessed by Congress under the Constitution are necessary to any form of national government. Power to *levy taxes* carries with it the authority to *enforce* the power. This executive power is expressed in the Constitution, not because it was necessary, but by way of caution. The exercise of the taxing power is in the *discretion* of Congress, whose constituents are the ultimate judges of it. The constitutionality of any measure, such as of taxation, would be determined by the nature of the power on which it was founded. Thus, if Congress, on the pretence of an interference with national revenues, should undertake to abrogate a land tax imposed by a State, it would be evident that this was an invasion of concurrent jurisdiction of Union and State. Acts of Congress *not pursuant* to the Constitution are usurpations, and should and would be resisted.

The taxing power of the Union must be *supreme* to be operative, since all laws must be supreme to those to whom they apply; therefore, concurrent authority concerning all taxation save customs duties was the only device which would be adopted to make the Union effective and at the same time prevent the entire subordination of the States.

This coördinate sovereignty is entirely practicable, as proved by its successful operation in the Roman empire, where the difficulties interfering with its execution were greater than in the United States.

Greater power in raising revenue is needed by the Federal Government than by the States, since it must provide for various purposes and future contingencies such as the *public defence* and payment of *national debts,* with which the State governments are not concerned.

The jurisdiction of the national Government in revenue matters should not be restricted to particular objects, since this would oppress particular branches of industry and distribute the burden of taxation unequally. If the jurisdiction is limited to a tariff, duties might be raised too high in the false hope that this would produce greater revenue, thus really decreasing revenue, as well as fostering monopolies in manufacture, diverting industry from its natural channels, and oppressing the merchant by impairing his capital through his inability to shift the tax upon consumers, and so operating against the citizens of importing States and in favor of those of non-importing and manufacturing States.

Representation in the House of Representatives is sufficiently large to represent adequately all classes in the country. Merchants, because of their better education, are the national representatives of the mechanic and manufacturing classes, whose interests are at one with their own. Members of the learned professions have no distinct interests in society, and will be indiscriminately the choice of community, according to their talents. The large landholder and the middling farmer are affected in the same manner by legislation, and, judging by the choice of State legislators, the latter is more apt to be sent to Congress than the former. The merchants and the landholders will represent broadly the industrial and agricultural interests of the country, with the professional men as arbiters between them. The best representative is he who, whatever his profession, has the most extensive information, especially in matters pertaining to political economy, and who has a sympathetic knowledge of the interests and feelings of the people.

It is not necessary that every *locality* be represented in Congress. Members from each State can obtain the necessary information about its interests and desires.

The Constitution empowers Congress to levy a *direct tax* upon each State in proportion to its population. This power need not be exercised, and, if it proves inconvenient, the old system of requisitions may be resorted to.

While it is true that the Federal Government may *duplicate taxes* imposed by the State government, and so increase expense of collection, and excite the indignation of the people, these very results are likely to prevent Congress from attempting anything of the kind, and to cause it to rely for revenue upon its exclusive power to levy customs duties.

A proper Federal Government requires the power of regulating the *militia* and of commanding its services in times of insurrection and invasion, since uniformity in organization and discipline can be obtained only in this manner. The authority retained by the States to appoint the officers of the militia is a sufficient safeguard against the wrongful employment of the militia against a State.

IV. *The Conformity of the Proposed Constitution to the True Principles of Republican Government.*

Allowances should be made for the *inherent difficulties* in framing the Constitution: such as the difficulty of combining the requisite stability and energy in government with a due regard to liberty and the republican form; the difficulty of marking the proper line of partition between the authority of the general Government and that of the State governments; the difficulty arising from the interfering pretensions of the larger and the smaller States; and the difficulty arising from other combinations of the States resulting from a difference of local position and policy. *No. 36, H.*

On the other hand, the convention was free from party animosities, and all the demands of the various deputations were finally satisfied.

All former national constitutions have been framed by a *single individual,* to which fact were due their defects, which therefore may be presumed to be absent in the workings of this Constitution.

The errors of the present Constitution will arise because of *lack of experience* in the innovations introduced in it, rather than because of *want of thought* in preparing them.

Nos. 37-58, M.

The Constitution is certainly an improvement on the Articles of Confederation; if it is not, let the objectors to it improve on it. Their objections certainly apply with more point against the old Articles than against the Constitution.

The proposed Constitution conforms to the *standard of republican government* as fixed by the governments of Holland, England, etc., in (1) the tenure of its offices, and (2) its prohibition of titles of nobility.

It will be founded on the *ratification* by the several States.

The sources of power of the proposed government are: (1) the people of America, as represented in the House of Representatives; (2) the States, as represented in the Senate; and (3) people and States, as represented in the Executive. These are also the sources of authority for the amendments to the Constitution.

The convention acted in framing the Constitution *within its authority,* which was "to establish in these States a firm national government, adequate to the exigencies of government and the preservation of the Union," "by making alterations and provisions in the articles of confederation," the same to be submitted to Congress and the States for ratification. The proposed system is therefore harmless until so ratified and, even if the convention exceeded its powers, this defect will be cured by such ratification.

The *aggregate* of the power given by the Constitution to the Federal Government is no less than it should be.

A Federal Government ought to have discretionary powers, in peace as well as in war, to provide against foreign danger, as well as the power of levying and borrowing money. Such powers are given in the Constitution. They are, indeed, copied from the old system, differing only therefrom in being made effective, though with all proper *restrictions* cast about them.

So, too, such a government should have power to send and receive ambassadors and consuls and to make treaties; to punish piracies and felonies on the high seas, and offences against the law of nations; and to regulate foreign commerce. These powers are given in the Constitution. Owing to objections of certain States, the regulation of the slave trade was deferred until after a not distant year [1808], and before this time it may be regulated, or even abolished, with the concurrence of the objecting States.

Such a government should have power to maintain harmony and proper *intercourse between the States*. To this end the Constitution regulates trade with the Indians, coins money, and punishes counterfeiters, fixes the standard weights and measures, establishes a uniform rule of naturalization and a uniform law of bankruptcy, establishes a rule for proving the acts of the several States and determining their effect in other States, and establishes post-offices and post-roads.

Such a government should have power to pass *patent and copyright* laws, to legislate over the federal district, to punish *treason,* to *admit new States,* to govern the territories and other public property, to guarantee every State a republican form of government, to protect the States against invasion and domestic violence, to assume and control the payment of the *public debt,* and to provide for *amendments* to the Constitution, all of which powers are provided in the Constitution.

The provision that the Constitution shall be adopted upon the ratification of nine States is as just as it is necessary, since the dissenting States are left voluntarily in their present position save that the former contract of the confederation has already been legally dissolved, and may rightly be declared to have been dissolved because of its many infractions by the very dissenting States. The Constitution is silent on what relations shall exist between the Union and the dissenting States. This is for Congress and the dissenting States to decide, and it will undoubtedly, in view of common interest, be arranged with moderation on one side and prudence on the other.

The Constitution, in further enforcement of its sovereign powers, *restricts the authority* of the several States as to treaty-making, war-making, coinage and currency, the passage of bills of attainder, etc., as well as to the passage of such acts injurious to popular democratic rights as *ex post facto* laws, laws impairing contracts, and establishment of titles of nobility, and it denies them the power delegated exclusively to Congress of levying customs duties.

A Federal Government should have the authority to make all laws necessary to execute its rightful powers. This the Constitution gives. The people, by their power over their Representatives in Congress, will prevent all usurpation which might result from such authority.

The Constitution rightly requires, in self-defence, that the various officers of the State governments, no less than of the Federal Government, be bound by oath to support it.

The Constitution will not prove fatal to the State governments, because of the tendency in all confederacies to diminish rather than increase the federal powers. Since the State governments possess more influence among the people, the State employees are more numerous than the national, and the State powers are greater than the national.

The proposed changes consist less in the addition of new powers to the Union than in the invigoration of its *old* ones. The State and the Federal Governments are only different agents for the people, with different powers and for different purposes. If popular favor should rest on the Federal Government, it would be only because it was better *administered*. There would be no danger of the Federal Government coercing the people, because of the high impossibility of collecting a force for such a purpose, and, if it should be collected, because of the superior power of the militia to overcome it.

In such a government the three parts, the legislative, executive, and judicial, should be separate and distinct, and yet, at the same time, be so far connected and blended as to give to each a constitutional control over the others, without any one possessing the supremacy. Mr. Jefferson proposed to counteract the tendency of the legislature to gain dominance by an appeal to the people, by two-thirds of the members of the other departments. This would be ineffective in opposing a combination of two branches of the Government for control, and unwise in that frequent appeals would impair the confidence of the people in the Government and disturb the public peace, while the legislature, which, as the people's representatives, would have to put their will into effect, would still control the decision. The best way in which to prevent the dominance of one branch over the others is *constitutional*. Thus the members of each branch should have little to do in the appointment of members of the others or with their emoluments, and the executive, in particular, should have a *veto* over legislation. This is the plan of the present Constitution.

The House of Representatives is made by the Constitution the popular branch of Congress. In order not to interfere with the suffrage systems of the States, the Constitution fixed the qualifications of electors of Representatives in each State as those of the electors of the most numerous branch of the legislature of that State. Elections to the House were made biennial, *frequent elections* being considered a necessity for the proper voicing of the will of the people, yet *annual elections*, being thought too frequent for a body of legislators in whom experience in national legislation is a desirable qualification.

The apportionment of Representatives among the States was made on *population* in order that it be truly popular.

In this apportionment *three-fifths* of the *slaves* were reckoned, slaves partaking partly of the nature of persons and partly of the nature of property, even in the laws of the slave-holding States. Now it is right that *property* as well as *persons* should be represented in Congress. There will be no inducement for falsifying the census in the matter of slave population, as the measure for representation is also the measure of taxation.[1]

The *number* of Representatives is not too small for thorough discussion and freedom from combination for improper purposes, nor too large for well-considered and temperate debate. As the country grows the representation will keep pace with its needs.

Since the members of the House will be elected *by* all classes and conditions of citizens, they will naturally be selected *from* all classes and conditions, and the desire for reëlection will cause them to legislate *for* all classes and conditions, the more, too, because their *private interests* will be affected by the legislation in the same manner as the private interests of their constituents.

A bare majority of Representatives properly forms a quorum, and a bare majority of the quorum properly passes measures, since, if a two-thirds majority were required, the principle of democracy might be violated by an obstructing minority.

Power is given Congress to regulate its elections, because of the primary right of *self-preservation.* Otherwise the existence of the Union would be entirely at the mercy of the State governments. If Congress should attempt to promote the election of some favorite class of men, this design would be frustrated by an immediate revolt of the people, led by their State governments, as well as the Senate. *Nos. 59-61, H.*

The Senate is made by the Constitution the peculiar repre-

[1] See this argument in full on page 358.

sentation of the States in the national legislature, the mixed
character of the Federal Government requiring a mixed representation. The recognition of State sovereignty in the Senate
furnishes a security against legislation destructive of the equal
rights of the States. The Senate is also a check against all hasty
and ill-considered legislation. Its membership does not change
so often as that in the House of Representatives, thus giving the
element of stability in our laws which is demanded, especially
by the business interests.

The Senate will add a conservative force in our national
councils which will attract the respect of foreign nations and
enable us to form advantageous political and commercial relations with them.

The Senate will also defend the people against their own
temporary errors and delusions.   *Nos. 62, 63, M.*

History informs us of no long-lived republic which had not
a senate. It also proves the objection groundless that the Senate
will gradually acquire a dangerous preëminence in the Government and finally transform it into a tyrannical aristocracy. Besides, the House of Representatives will be a sufficient check
against such an usurpation.

The important treaty-making power has been given the Senate rather than the House of Representatives from the more intimate acquaintance by the Senate with public affairs, and its
farther removal from the influence of the temporary passions
of the people. Its proceedings will undoubtedly be secret, and
secrecy and despatch are often required in foreign relations.

Treaties are international bargains and are, therefore, made
supreme laws, above mere legislative acts, in order not to be
subject to repeal at the passing whim of the people. Since all
the States are equally represented in the Senate, there is no
fear, in treaties or other acts in which it has a deciding vote,
that the interests of one State will be unfairly dealt with.

The Senate, rather than the Supreme Court, has been made
the court of impeachment. The Supreme Court, with its limited
membership, might not possess the fortitude or credit with the
people requisite to execute the duties of the trust, and, as impeachment will not end the proceedings, it would be improper
to bring the offender twice before the same court. *No. 64, J.*

The remaining numbers, 65 to 85, are by Hamilton.

The objection that legislative and judicial authority should
not be united in the same body is ill-founded—witness the suc-

cessful working of this union in the constitution of New York State.

In appointments the Senate does not *choose*, but merely *ratifies*, and so there is no fear that it will be too lenient a judge of officers.

Because of its *joint-agency* with the President in treaty-making, in which two-thirds of the Senate must concur, there is little danger of corrupt or perfidous action and of the consequent result that Senators may be called on to impeach themselves for such action. Indeed, there would be no need of impeachment, since they already would be disgraced.

The President is designed by the Constitution to possess the dignity and power due to the head of the nation, without the prerogatives of a monarch. It was desirable that the sense of the people should operate in choosing him; and yet that the choice be made by competent persons, guarded from all chance of cabal, intrigue, and corruption. This was arranged for, both in his case, and that of the Vice-President.

The President is elected for four years and is reëligible as often as the people shall think him worthy of their confidence. Such reëlection of the chief magistrate is common in State governments, where a dangerous influence is far more likely to be formed than in the nation, and it has not been found an evil practice.

As a check upon executive tyranny the President is made liable to impeachment, trial, removal from office, and subsequent imprisonment, unlike the Governors of Maryland and Delaware.

The President has the power to veto an act of Congress, which, nevertheless, Congress may pass over his veto by a two-thirds majority. This is the case with the Governor of Massachusetts in respect to the legislature.

The President is Commander-in-Chief of the army and navy, just as the Governor of New York is of the State militia.

He has power to pardon offenders against the law, *except in cases of impeachment*. The Governor of New York may pardon in these excepted cases, when they are not treason and murder.

The President may adjourn Congress only in case of disagreement about the time of adjournment. The Governor of New York may prorogue the legislature in any case for a limited time.

The President, as the recognized head of the nation, has the power of making treaties and appointing ministers, but only with the concurrence of the Senate. In this his authority differs in nature from that of a State executive, and necessarily so because of the Union's exclusive sovereignty on the point.

For convenience the President is authorized to receive foreign ministers, Congress not always being in session.

No defender, therefore, of the State constitutions can rightly object to the powers of the national executive.

The Constitution wisely has placed the executive power in the hands of *one* man, thus concentrating energy of action and responsibility for conduct, as well as reducing expense.

The Constitution has wisely rendered the President independent in his actions, by his reasonably long term of office, and by his coördinate powers with the other two branches of government.

The heads of the various executive departments, being deputies of the President, are rightly appointed by him and responsible to him. When the person of the executive changes, these will probably change. Therefore stability in government will be promoted by continuance of the same man in the office of President.

Eligibility to reëlection is also a good feature in that it affords inducements to good behavior.

The emolument of the President is fixed by Congress, thus making him independent of Congress, whose tool he might be if they determined his compensation.

A veto power is given him in order to defend himself from legislative aggressions, and the people from improper legislation, and yet this veto is *limited* to prevent executive usurpation. The Governor of Massachusetts has a similar power.

The President is assisted by a cabinet composed of heads of the executive departments, from whom he may require opinions.

He has the power of *pardoning offenders* against the laws of the Union. The criminal code of every country partakes so much of necessary severity that, without an easy access to exceptions in favor of unfortunate guilt, justice would wear a countenance too sanguinary and cruel. Concurrence of the legislature in cases of *treason* is not required, since a well-timed offer of pardon to insurgents may quell a rebellion, which would have made too much headway before the legislature could be convened.

Since treaty-making is both an *executive* and *legislative* function, it is committed to the President and the Senate in combination.

The appointment of certain officers is given to the President in connection with the Senate because it would be impracticable to leave it to the people. The delegation of this to *one man* will beget a livelier sense of duty and greater regard to reputation on the part of the officers. The necessary concurrence by the Senate will afford a check on the favoritism of the executive, and the prohibition of a Senator to hold office will prevent an improper use of this check. To add to the concurrence of the House of Representatives in appointments would occasion infinite delays and embarrassments.

The President has the necessary executive powers of communicating to Congress information (which he receives through the departments) of the state of the Union, recommending measures which he deems expedient, convening one or both branches of Congress on extraordinary occasions, adjourning Congress in case of a disagreement concerning time of adjournment, receiving ambassadors and other public ministers, executing the laws of the Union, and commissioning all the officers of the United States.

The tenure by which the Federal judges hold their offices is unobjectionable because similar to that of the judiciary in several States. Being the weakest of the three departments of government, the executive holding the sword, and the legislative the purse, it is made completely *independent* of the other two, both in powers and emolument. Its authority to pronounce legislative acts void because contrary to the Constitution does not indicate superiority to the legislature except in cases where the legislature is violating the will of the people as previously determined upon. The Constitution ought to be preferred to the statute; the intention of the people to the intention of their agents.

The Federal judiciary is designed to be an intermediate body between the people and the legislature, to keep the latter within its assigned limits and protect the rights of individuals from laws.

The court is designed also to intervene, in times of popular passion, between the Constitution and both legislature and people, in order to prevent changes in the fundamental law of the land except by the process laid down in the Constitution, and to protect the rights of individuals guaranteed in it.

In order to prevent corruption among these judges they may be impeached for malconduct by the House of Representatives and tried by the Senate. To impeach them for *inability*, except in the case of insanity, gives an opportunity for abuse of legislative power and, hence, this was not permitted.

The powers of the judiciary necessarily extend to all cases: (1) which concern the execution of the provisions in the Constitution; (2) in which the United States are a party; (3) which involve the peace of the Union (foreign and interstate relations) ; (4) which are of maritime jurisdiction; and (5) wherein State tribunals cannot be supposed to be impartial and unbiased (territorial disputes).

The Constitution provides for "one court of supreme and final jurisdiction," and inferior courts, thus securing adjudication of important cases by the *greater legal ability.*

Congress cannot rectify the effect of these adjudications except in the future, when it can do so by the passage of *new laws.*

Original jurisdiction in the supreme court is only in diplomatic affairs, and in cases in which a State is a party.

It is inherent in the nature of a sovereignty not to be amenable to the suit of an *individual* without the sovereign's consent. Hence an assignment of the public securities of one State to the citizens of another would not enable these citizens to sue that State in the Federal courts.

The supreme court has "appellate jurisdiction, both as to law and fact." This does not necessarily imply a reëxamination in *common law* cases of facts decided by juries in the inferior courts, for such is not the legal custom; in *civil law* cases, however, reëxamination of facts is agreeable to usage. Congress certainly has power to prohibit reëxamination of facts in the former cases.

The State courts will *retain* the jurisdiction they now have, except where it has been expressly delegated to the Federal courts. There is thus *concurrent* State and Federal jurisdiction as well as legislation.

Congress may commit certain legislation to the jurisdiction of the Federal courts without divesting the State courts of their primitive jurisdiction further than may relate to an appeal, nor of the right to take cognizance of causes which may arise out of such legislation.

An appeal will lie from the State courts to the supreme court of the United States.

The Constitution does not provide for trial by jury in civil cases, because, while trial by jury is essential in criminal cases, it is of relative unimportance in civil cases, as is indicated by the varying usage among the States.

The Constitution could not with probity adopt the system of one State, and therefore left the question in abeyance, to be settled by Congress.

The Constitution contains no special *Bill of Rights,* since this is unnecessary, these rights being both expressly and implicitly contained in the body of the instrument, which itself is a bill of rights.   Besides, the people will surrender none of these rights in adopting the Constitution, and their future interest in them will be protected by their Representatives in Congress.   Indeed, the statement of a bill of rights would be dangerous as implying the grant to the Federal Government of all powers not expressly withheld therefrom.

The Constitution does not provide for debts due to the United States.   This is unnecessary, as it is an established rule of national law that "States neither lose any of their rights, nor are discharged from any of their obligations, by a change in the form of their civil government."

The proposed government is *economical*, the number of State officers being diminished to the extent of the addition of Federal, and the sessions of State legislatures being diminished in number and shortened in duration by the sessions of Congress.

V.   Additional Securities to Republican Government

The additional securities to republican government, to liberty, and to property, to be derived from the adoption of the plan under consideration, consist chiefly in the restraints which the preservation of the Union will impose on local factions and insurrections, and on the ambition of powerful individuals in single States, who might acquire credit and influence enough, from leaders and favorites, to become the despots of the people; in the diminution of the opportunities to foreign intrigue, which the dissolution of the Confederacy would invite and facilitate; in the prevention of extensive military establishments, which could not fail to grow out of wars between the States in a disunited situation; in the express guaranty of a republican form of government to each; in the absolute and universal exclusion of titles of nobility; and in the precautions against the repetition of those practices on the part of the State governments which have undermined the foundations of property and credit, have planted mutual distrust in the breasts of all classes of citizens, and have occasioned an almost universal prostration of morals.

VI.   Adopt the Constitution and Amend It Afterward.

It is susceptible of absolute demonstration that it will be far more easy to obtain subsequent than previous amendments to the Constitution.   The moment an alteration is made in the present plan it becomes, to the purpose of adoption, a new one, and must undergo a new decision of each State.   To its complete establishment throughout the Union it will therefore require the concurrence of thirteen States.   If, on the contrary, the Constitution proposed should once be ratified by all the States as it stands, alterations in it may at any time be effected by nine States. Here, then, the chances are as thirteen to nine [1] in favor of subsequent amendments, rather than of the original adoption of an entire system.

This is not all. Every Constitution for the United States must inevitably consist of a great variety of particulars, in which thirteen independent States are to be accommodated in their interests or opinions of interest. We may of course expect to see, in any body of men charged with its original formation, very different combinations of the parts upon different points. Many of those who form a majority on one question may become the minority on a second, and an association dissimilar to either may constitute the majority on a third. Hence the necessity of moulding and arranging all the particulars which are to compose the whole, in such a manner as to satisfy all the parties to the compact; and hence, also, an immense multiplication of difficulties and casualties in obtaining the collective assent to a final Act. The degree of that multiplication must evidently be in a ratio to the number of particulars and the number of parties.

But every amendment to the Constitution, if once established, would be a single proposition, and might be brought forward singly. There would then be no necessity for management or compromise, in relation to any other point; no giving, nor taking. The will of the requisite number would at once bring the matter to a decisive issue. And, consequently, whenever nine, or rather ten, States were united in the desire of a particular amendment, that amendment must infallibly take place. There can, therefore, be no comparison between the facility of effecting an amendment and that of establishing in the first instance a complete Constitution.

In opposition to the probability of subsequent amendments, it has been urged that the persons delegated to the administration of the national Government will always be disinclined to yield up any portion of the authority of which they were once possessed. [But] any amendments which may, upon mature consideration, be thought useful will be applicable to the organization of the Government, not to the mass of its powers; and the intrinsic difficulty of governing thirteen States at any rate, independent of calculations upon an ordinary degree of public spirit and integrity, will constantly *impose* on the national rulers the *necessity* of a spirit of accommodation to the reasonable ex-

---

[1] It may rather be said *ten*, for, though two-thirds may set on foot the measure, three-fourths must ratify.

pectations of their constituents. But there is yet a further consideration, which proves beyond the possibility of doubt that the observation is futile. It is this, that the national rulers, whenever nine States concur, will have no option upon the subject. By the fifth article of the plan, the Congress will be *obliged*, "on the application of the legislatures of two-thirds of the States" (which at present amount to nine) "to call a convention for proposing amendments, which *shall be valid* to all intents and purposes, as part of the Constitution, when ratified by the legislatures of three-fourths of the States, or by conventions in three-fourth thereof." The words of this article are peremptory. The Congress "*shall* call a convention." Nothing in this particular is left to the discretion of that body. And, of consequence, all the declamation about the disinclination to a change vanishes in air. Now, however difficult it may be supposed to unite two-thirds, or three-fourths, of the State legislatures in amendments which may affect local interests, can there be any room to apprehend any such difficulty in a union on points which are merely relative to the general liberty or security of the people? We may safely rely on the disposition of the State legislatures to erect barriers against the encroachments of the national authority.

VII. *Appeal to the People.*

It may be in me a defect of political fortitude, but I acknowledge that I cannot entertain an equal tranquillity with those who affect to treat the dangers of a longer continuance in our present situation as imaginary. A nation without a national government is, in my view, an awful spectacle. The establishment of a Constitution, in time of profound peace, by the voluntary consent of a whole people, is a prodigy, to the completion of which I look forward with trembling anxiety. I can reconcile it to no rules of prudence to let go the hold we now have, in so arduous an enterprise, upon seven out of the thirteen States;[1] and after having passed over so considerable a part of the ground to recommence the course. I dread the more the consequences of new attempts, because I know that powerful individuals, in this and in other States, are enemies to a general national government in every possible shape.

ADOPTION OF THE CONSTITUTION

The ratification of the Constitution by the State of New Hampshire, being the ninth in order, was laid be-

[1] When this letter was written seven States had ratified the Constitution.

fore Congress on the 2d of July, 1788, and, with the ratifications of the other States, referred to a committee to report an act for carrying the new system into operation. An act for this purpose was reported on the 14th of the same month, but, in consequence of a division as to the place where the first Congress should meet, did not pass until the 13th of September following. By this act the electors of the President were to be appointed on the first Wednesday of January, 1789, and to give in their votes on the first Wednesday of the succeeding February; the first Wednesday of March, being the 4th day of that month, was fixed as the *time*, and the city of New York as the *place,* for beginning proceedings under the new Constitution.

CHAPTER XVI

THE CONSTITUTION AND ITS AMENDMENTS

Text of the Constitution—History of the Amendments to the Constitution—
Text of Amendments.

THE CONSTITUTION OF THE UNITED STATES
OF AMERICA

*W*E *the people of the United States in order to form
a more perfect union, establish justice, ensure domestic tranquillity, provide for the common defence, promote the general welfare, and secure the blessings of
liberty to ourselves and our posterity, do ordain and establish
this Constitution for the United States of America.*

ARTICLE I

SECTION I

All legislative powers herein granted shall be vested in a
Congress of the United States, which shall consist of a Senate
and House of Representatives.

SECTION II

The House of Representatives shall be composed of members
chosen every second year by the people of the several States, and
the electors in each State shall have the qualifications requisite
for electors of the most numerous branch of the State legislature.

No person shall be a Representative who shall not have attained to the age of twenty-five years, and been seven years a
citizen of the United States, and who shall not, when elected, be
an inhabitant of that State in which he shall be chosen.

Representatives and direct taxes shall be apportioned among
the several States which may be included within this Union, according to their respective numbers, which shall be determined

by adding to the whole number of free persons, including those bound to service for a term of years, and excluding Indians not taxed, three-fifths of all other persons. The actual enumeration shall be made within three years after the first meeting of the Congress of the United States, and within every subsequent term of ten years, in such manner as they shall by law direct. The number of Representatives shall not exceed one for every thirty thousand, but each State shall have at least one Representative; and until such enumeration shall be made the State of *New Hampshire* shall be entitled to choose three, *Massachusetts* eight, *Rhode Island* and *Providence Plantations* one, *Connecticut* five, *New York* six, *New Jersey* four, *Pennsylvania* eight, *Delaware* one, *Maryland* six, *Virginia* ten, *North Carolina* five, *South Carolina* five, and *Georgia* three.

When vacancies happen in the representation from any State, the Executive authority thereof shall issue writs of election to fill such vacancies.

The House of Representatives shall choose their speaker and other officers; and shall have the sole power of impeachment.

SECTION III

[The Senate of the United States shall be composed of two Senators from each State, chosen by the legislature thereof, for six years; and each Senator shall have one vote.[1]]

Immediately after they shall be assembled in consequence of the first election, they shall be divided, as equally as may be, into three classes. The seats of the Senators of the first class shall be vacated at the expiration of the second year, of the second class at the expiration of the fourth year, and of the third class at the expiration of the sixth year, so that one-third may be chosen every second year; [and if vacancies happen by resignation or otherwise, during the recess of the legislature of any State, the executive thereof may make temporary appointments, until the next meeting of the legislature, which shall then fill such vacancies.[1]]

No person shall be a Senator who shall not have attained to the age of thirty years, and been nine years a citizen of the United States, and who shall not, when elected, be an inhabitant of that State for which he shall be chosen.

The Vice-President of the United States shall be President of the Senate, but shall have no vote unless they be equally divided.

The Senate shall choose their other officers, and also a Presi-

[1] Text within brackets has been supplanted by XVIIth Amendment.

dent pro tempore, in the absence of the Vice-President or when he shall exercise the office of President of the United States.

The Senate shall have the sole power to try all impeachments: when sitting for that purpose, they shall be on oath or affirmation. When the President of the United States is tried the Chief Justice shall preside: and no person shall be convicted without the concurrence of two-thirds of the members present.

Judgment in cases of impeachment shall not extend farther than to removal from office and disqualification to hold and enjoy any office of honor, trust, or profit under the United States: but the party convicted shall nevertheless be liable and subject to indictment, trial, judgment, and punishment, according to law.

SECTION IV

The times, places, and manner of holding elections for Senators and Representatives shall be prescribed in each State by the legislature thereof; but the Congress may at any time by law make or alter such regulations, except as to the places of choosing Senators.

The Congress shall assemble at least once in every year and such meeting shall be on the first Monday in December unless they shall by law appoint a different day.

SECTION V

Each House shall be the judge of the elections, returns, and qualifications of its own members, and a majority of each shall constitute a quorum to do business; but a smaller number may adjourn from day to day, and may be authorized to compel the attendance of absent members, in such manner and under such penalties as each House may provide.

Each House may determine the rules of its proceedings, punish its members for disorderly behavior, and, with the concurrence of two-thirds, expel a member.

Each House shall keep a journal of its proceedings, and from time to time publish the same, excepting such parts as may in their judgment require secrecy; and the yeas and nays of the members of either House on any question shall, at the desire of one-fifth of those present, be entered on the journal.

Neither House, during the session of Congress, shall, without the consent of the other, adjourn for more than three days, nor to any other place than that in which the two Houses shall be sitting.

SECTION VI

The Senators and Representatives shall receive a compensation for their services, to be ascertained by law, and paid out of the treasury of the United States. They shall in all cases, except treason, felony, and breach of the peace, be privileged from arrest during their attendance at the session of their respective Houses, and in going to and returning from the same; and for any speech or debate in either House they shall not be questioned in any other place.

No Senator or Representative shall, during the time for which he was elected, be appointed to any civil office under the authority of the United States, which shall have been created, or the emoluments whereof shall have been increased during such time: and no person holding any office under the United States shall be a member of either House during his continuance in office.

SECTION VII

All bills for raising revenue shall originate in the House of Representatives; but the Senate may propose, or concur with, amendments, as on other bills.

Every bill which shall have passed the House of Representatives and the Senate shall, before it become a law, be presented to the President of the United States; if he approve he shall sign it, but if not he shall return it, with his objections, to that House in which it shall have originated, who shall enter the objections at large on their journal, and proceed to reconsider it. If after such reconsideration two-thirds of that House shall agree to pass the bill, it shall be sent, together with the objections, to the other House, by which it shall likewise be reconsidered, and, if approved by two-thirds of that House, it shall become a law. But in all such cases the votes of both Houses shall be determined by yeas and nays, and the names of the persons voting for and against the bill shall be entered on the journal of each House respectively. If any bill shall not be returned by the President within ten days (Sundays excepted), after it shall have been presented to him, the same shall be a law, in like manner as if he had signed it, unless the Congress by their adjournment prevent its return, in which case it shall not be a law.

Every order, resolution, or vote to which the concurrence of the Senate and House of Representatives may be necessary (except on a question of adjournment) shall be presented to the President of the United States; and, before the same shall take effect, shall be approved by him, or, being disapproved by him, shall be repassed by two-thirds of the Senate and House of Representatives, according to the rules and limitations prescribed in the case of a bill.

SECTION VIII

The Congress shall have power to lay and collect taxes, duties, imposts, and excises, to pay the debts and provide for the common defence and general welfare of the United States; but all duties, imposts, and excises shall be uniform throughout the United States;

To borrow money on the credit of the United States;

To regulate commerce with foreign nations, and among the several States, and with the Indian tribes;

To establish an uniform rule of naturalization, and uniform laws on the subject of bankruptcies throughout the United States;

To coin money, regulate the value thereof, and of foreign coin, and fix the standard of weights and measures;

To provide for the punishment of counterfeiting the securities and current coin of the United States;

To establish post-offices and post roads;

To promote the progress of science and useful arts by securing for limited times to author. and inventors the exclusive right to their respective writings and discoveries;

To constitute tribunals inferior to the supreme court;

To define and punish piracies and felonies committed on the high seas and offences against the law of nations;

To declare war, grant letters of marque and reprisal, and make rules concerning captures on land and water;

To raise and support armies, but no appropriation of money to that use shall be for a longer term than two years;

To provide and maintain a navy;

To make rules for the government and regulation of the land and naval forces;

To provide for calling forth the militia to execute the laws of the Union, suppress insurrections, and repel invasions;

To provide for organizing, arming, and disciplining the militia, and for governing such part of them as may be employed in the service of the United States, reserving to the States respectively the appointment of the officers and the authority of training the militia according to the discipline prescribed by Congress;

To exercise exclusive legislation in all cases whatsoever over such district (not exceeding ten miles square) as may, by cession of particular States, and the acceptance of Congress, become the seat of the government of the United States, and to exercise like authority over all places purchased by the consent of the legislature of the State in which the same shall be for the erection of forts, magazines, arsenals, dock-yards, and other needful buildings;—And

To make all laws which shall be necessary and proper for carrying into execution the foregoing powers, and all other powers vested by this constitution in the government of the United States, or in any department or officer thereof.

SECTION IX

The migration or importation of such persons as any of the States now existing shall think proper to admit shall not be prohibited by the Congress prior to the year eighteen hundred and eight, but a tax or duty may be imposed on such importation not exceeding ten dollars for each person.

The privilege of the writ of *Habeas Corpus* shall not be suspended, unless when, in cases of rebellion or invasion, the public safety may require it.

No bill of attainder or ex post facto law shall be passed.

No capitation, or other direct tax shall be laid, unless in proportion to the census or enumeration hereinbefore directed to be taken.

No tax or duty shall be laid on articles exported from any State.

No preference shall be given by any regulation of commerce or revenue to the ports of one State over those of another: nor shall vessels bound to, or from, one State be obliged to enter, clear, or pay duties in another.

No money shall be drawn from the treasury, but in consequence of appropriations made by law; and a regular statement and account of the receipts and expenditures of all public money shall be published from time to time.

No title of nobility shall be granted by the United States; and no person holding any office of profit or trust under them shall, without the consent of the Congress, accept of any present, emolument, office, or title, of any kind whatever, from any King, prince, or foreign state.

SECTION X

No State shall enter into any treaty, alliance, or confederation; grant letters of marque and reprisal; coin money, emit bills of credit; make anything but gold and silver coin a tender in payment of debts; pass any bill of attainder, ex post facto law; or law impairing the obligation of contracts; or grant any title of nobility.

No State shall, without the consent of the Congress, lay any imposts or duties on imports or exports, except what may be absolutely necessary for executing its inspection laws: and the net produce of all duties and imposts, laid by any State on imports or exports, shall be for the use of the Treasury of the United States; and all such laws shall be subject to the revision and control of the Congress.

No State shall, without the consent of Congress, lay any duty of tonnage, keep troops or ships of war in time of peace, enter into any agreement or compact with another State, or with a foreign power, or engage in war, unless actually invaded, or in such imminent danger as will not admit of delay.

ARTICLE II

SECTION I

The executive power shall be vested in a President of the United States of America. He shall hold his office during the term of four years, and, together with the Vice-President, chosen for the same term, be elected as follows:

Each State shall appoint, in such manner as the legislature thereof may direct, a number of electors equal to the whole number of Senators and Representatives to which the State may be entitled in the Congress; but no Senator or Representative, or person holding an office of trust or profit under the United States shall be appointed an elector.

The electors shall meet in their respective States and vote by ballot for two persons, of whom one at least shall not be an inhabitant of the same State with themselves. And they shall make a list of all the persons voted for, and of the number of votes for each; which list they shall sign and certify and transmit sealed to the seat of the Government of the United States, directed to the president of the Senate. The president of the Senate shall, in the presence of the Senate and House of Representatives, open all the certificates, and the votes shall then be counted. The person having the greatest number of votes shall be the President, if such number be a majority of the whole number of electors appointed; and if there be more than one who have such majority, and have an equal number of votes, then the

House of Representatives shall immediately choose, by ballot, one of them for President; and if no person have a majority, then from the five highest on the list the said House shall, in like manner, choose the President. But in choosing the President the votes shall be taken by States, the representation from each State having one vote; a quorum for this purpose shall consist of a member or members from two-thirds of the States, and a majority of all the States shall be necessary to a choice. In every case, after the choice of the President, the person having the greatest number of votes of the electors shall be the Vice-President. But if there should remain two or more who have equal votes the Senate shall choose from them by ballot the Vice-President.

The Congress may determine the time of choosing the electors, and the day on which they shall give their votes; which day shall be the same throughout the United States.

No person except a natural born citizen, or a citizen of the United States at the time of the adoption of this Constitution, shall be eligible to the office of President; neither shall any person be eligible to that office who shall not have attained to the age of thirty-five years, and been fourteen years a resident within the United States.

In case of the removal of the President from office, or of his death, resignation, or inability to discharge the powers and duties of the said office, the same shall devolve on the Vice-President, and the Congress may, by law, provide for the case of removal, death, resignation, or inability, both of the President and Vice-President, declaring what officer shall then act as President, and such officer shall act accordingly, until the disability be removed or a President shall be elected.

The President shall, at stated times, receive for his services a compensation, which shall neither be increased or diminished during the period for which he shall have been elected, and he shall not receive within that period any other emolument from the United States, or any of them.

Before he enter on the execution of his office he shall take the following oath or affirmation: *"I do solemnly swear (or affirm) that I will faithfully execute the office of President of the United States, and will, to the best of my ability, preserve, protect, and defend the Constitution of the United States."*

SECTION II

The President shall be commander-in-chief of the army and navy of the United States, and of the militia of the several

States, when called into the actual service of the United States; he may require the opinion, in writing, of the principal officer in each of the executive departments upon any subject relating to the duties of their respective offices; and he shall have power to grant reprieves and pardons for offences against the United States, except in cases of impeachment.

He shall have power, by and with the advice and consent of the Senate, to make treaties, provided two-thirds of the Senators present concur; and he shall nominate, and by and with the advice and consent of the Senate, shall appoint ambassadors, other public ministers and consuls, judges of the supreme court, and all other officers of the United States, whose appointments are not herein otherwise provided for, and which shall be established by law: But the Congress may, by law, vest the appointment of such inferior officers as they think proper in the President alone, in the courts of law, or in the heads of departments.

The President shall have power to fill up all vacancies that may happen during the recess of the Senate, by granting commissions which shall expire at the end of their next session.

SECTION III

He shall, from time to time, give to the Congress information of the state of the Union, and recommend to their consideration such measures as he shall judge necessary and expedient; he may, on extraordinary occasions, convene both Houses, or either of them, and, in case of disagreement between them, with respect to the time of adjournment, he may adjourn them to such time as he shall think proper; he shall receive ambassadors and other public ministers; he shall take care that the laws be faithfully executed, and shall commission all the officers of the United States.

SECTION IV

The President, Vice-President, and all civil officers of the United States shall be removed from office on impeachment for, and conviction of, treason, bribery, or other high crimes and misdemeanors.

ARTICLE III

SECTION I

The judicial power of the United States shall be vested in one Supreme Court, and in such inferior courts as the Congress may from time to time ordain and establish. The judges, both of the supreme and inferior courts, shall hold their offices during good behavior, and shall, at stated times, receive for their services a compensation, which shall not be diminished during their continuance in office.

SECTION II

The judicial power shall extend to all cases in law and equity, arising under this Constitution, the laws of the United States, and the treaties made, or which shall be made, under their authority; to all cases affecting ambassadors, other public ministers, and consuls; to all cases of admiralty and maritime jurisdiction; to controversies to which the United States shall be a party; to controversies between two or more States—between a State and citizens of another State—between citizens of different States—between citizens of the same State, claiming lands under grants of different States—and between a State or the citizens thereof and foreign states, citizens, or subjects.

In all cases affecting ambassadors, other public ministers, and consuls, and those in which a State shall be a party, the supreme court shall have original jurisdiction. In all the other cases before mentioned the supreme court shall have appellate jurisdiction, both as to law and fact, with such exceptions and under such regulations as the Congress shall make.

The trial of all crimes, except in cases of impeachment, shall be by jury; and such trial shall be held in the State where the said crimes shall have been committed; but, when not committed within any State, the trial shall be at such place or places as the Congress may by law have directed.

SECTION III

Treason against the United States shall consist only in levying war against them, or in adhering to their enemies. giving them aid and comfort. No person shall be convicted of treason unless on the testimony of two witnesses to the same overt act, or on confession in open court.

The Congress shall have power to declare the punishment of treason, but no attainder of treason shall work corruption of blood, or forfeiture, except during the life of the person attained.

ARTICLE IV

SECTION I

Full faith and credit shall be given in each State to the public acts, records, and judicial proceedings of every other State. And the Congress may, by general laws, prescribe the manner in which such acts, records, and proceedings shall be proved, and the effect thereof.

SECTION II

The citizens of each State shall be entitled to all the privileges and immunities of citizens in the several States.

A person charged in any State with treason, felony, or other crime, who shall flee from justice and be found in another State, shall, on demand of the executive authority of the State from which he fled, be delivered up, to be removed to the State having jurisdiction of the crime.

No person held to service or labor in one State under the laws thereof, escaping into another, shall, in consequence of any law or regulation therein, be discharged from such service or labor, but shall be delivered up on claim of the party to whom such service or labor may be due.

SECTION III

New States may be admitted by the Congress into this Union; but no new State shall be formed or erected within the jurisdiction of any other State; nor any State be formed by the junction of two or more States, or parts of States, without the consent of the legislatures of the States concerned as well as of the Congress.

The Congress shall have power to dispose of and make all needful rules and regulations respecting the territory or other property belonging to the United States; and nothing in this Constitution shall be so construed as to prejudice any claims of the United States, or of any particular State.

SECTION IV

The United States shall guaranty to every State in this Union a republican form of government, and shall protect each of them against invasion; and, on application of the legislature, or of the executive (when the legislature cannot be convened), against domestic violence.

ARTICLE V

The Congress, whenever two-thirds of both Houses shall deem it necessary, shall propose amendments to this Constitution, or, on the application of the legislatures of two-thirds of the several States, shall call a convention for proposing amendments, which, in either case, shall be valid to all intents and purposes as part of this Constitution when ratified by the legislatures of three-fourths of the several States, or by conventions in three-fourths thereof, as the one or the other mode of ratification may be proposed by the Congress; provided that no amendment which may be made prior to the year one thousand eight hundred and eight shall, in any manner, affect the first and fourth clauses in the ninth section of the first article; and that no State, without its consent, shall be deprived of its equal suffrage in the Senate.

ARTICLE VI

All debts contracted and engagements entered into before the adoption of this Constitution shall be as valid against the United States under this Constitution as under the Confederation.

This Constitution, and the laws of the United States which shall be made in pursuance thereof; and all treaties made, or which shall be made, under the authority of the United States, shall be the supreme law of the land; and the judges in every State shall be bound thereby, anything in the Constitution or laws of any State to the contrary notwithstanding.

The Senators and Representatives before mentioned, and the members of the several State legislatures, and all executive and judicial officers, both of the United States and of the several States, shall be bound, by oath or affirmation, to support this Constitution: but no religious test shall ever be required as a qualification to any office or public trust under the United States.

ARTICLE VII

The ratification of the conventions of nine States shall be sufficient for the establishment of this Constitution between the States so ratifying the same.

AMENDMENTS TO THE CONSTITUTION

The subject of amending the Constitution was brought before Congress during its first session by petitions from the States of Virginia and New York, requesting that another convention might be called to take into consideration and report such amendments as they might think proper and best calculated "to promote our common interests, and to secure to ourselves and our latest posterity the great and unalienable rights of mankind." The States of Virginia and New York were both opposed to the Constitution without the amendments proposed in their respective conventions. This opposition was strongly manifested in the legislature of Virginia in the first choice of Senators. Mr. Madison, who had been so instrumental, not only in forming the new system, but in procuring its ratification, though a candidate, lost his election. His opponents, Richard Henry Lee and William Grayson, were chosen. Madison, however, was elected to the House of Representatives. The same legislature requested another general convention.

Congress, however, had no authority to call a convention. Mr. Madison submitted to the House several amendments which, together with those presented by the several States, were referred to a committee consisting of one member from a State with general instructions. Amendments were reported by this committee, and after long debates and various alterations twelve articles were agreed to by both Houses to be submitted to the States, and were so submitted on September 25, 1789.

In the course of the next three years ten of these amendments were ratified by the constitutional majority of the States, an article proposing a *fixed* ascending scale of Representatives according to population, and an article prohibiting changes in compensation for members of Congress until after an election had intervened, being rejected.

In the course of the discussion in Congress a debate occurred as to whether the amendments should be interwoven into the Constitution or added as a supplement (see "Annals of Congress," August 13, 1789). The supplementary form was decided upon chiefly out of reverence for the Constitution which had already come to be regarded as an "Ark of the Covenant," not to be touched even to steady it.

Article XI, in reference to the judicial power, was passed by Congress in 1794, and declared ratified by three-fourths of the States in 1798.

This amendment arose out of a decision made by the Supreme Court in February 1793. Four of the five judges decided that a State was liable to a suit in favor of an individual. This important and interesting question came before the court in a suit instituted by a citizen of South Carolina (Mr. Chisholm) against the State of Georgia. The State of Georgia did not appear, and the question was argued solely by the Attorney-General of the United States (Edmund Randolph) in favor of the plaintiff.

The decision was grounded on that part of the Constitution establishing the Federal judiciary, which reclares that the judicial power should extend among other cases "to controversies between a State and citizens of another State." The court were of opinion that this was not limited to controversies where the State was plaintiff.

In consequence of this decision, in the summer of 1793, a suit was also commenced by an individual against the State of Massachusetts, and suits against other States were no doubt in contemplation. Therefore Congress at the following session passed the Eleventh Amendment.

Article XII, in reference to Presidential and Vice-Presidential elections, was passed by Congress in 1803, and declared ratified in 1804.

Article XIII, in reference to slavery, was passed by Congress and submitted to the States February 1, 1865, and declared ratified on December 18 of that year. For the debate on this amendment see Volume VI, chapter XIV.

Article XIV, in reference to rights of citizenship, was

passed by Congress June 16, 1866, and declared ratified on July 28, 1868. For the debate on this amendment, see Volume VII, chapter XII.

Article XV, in reference to equal manhood suffrage, was passed by Congress on February 27, 1869, and declared ratified on March 30, 1870. For the debate on this amendment, see Volume VIII, chapter III.

Article XVI, in reference to the income tax, was passed by Congress on July 12, 1909, and declared ratified on February 25, 1913. For the debate on this amendment, see Volume XII, chapter XVII.

Article XVII, in reference to the popular election of Senators, was passed by Congress on May 15, 1912, and was declared ratified on May 31, 1913. For the debate on this amendment, see Volume IX, chapter XII.

ARTICLE I

Congress shall make no law respecting an establishment of religion, or prohibiting the free exercise thereof; or abridging the freedom of speech, or of the press; or the right of the people peaceably to assemble, and to petition the Government for a redress of grievances.

ARTICLE II

A well-regulated militia being necessary to the security of a free State, the right of the people to keep and bear arms shall not be infringed.

ARTICLE III

No soldier shall, in time of peace, be quartered in any house without the consent of the owner, nor in time of war but in a manner to be prescribed by law.

ARTICLE IV

The right of the people to be secure in their persons, houses, papers, and effects against unreasonable searches and seizures shall not be violated; and no warrants shall issue but upon probable cause, supported by oath or affirmation, and particularly describing the place to be searched and the persons or things to be seized.

ARTICLE V

No person shall be held to answer for a capital or otherwise infamous crime, unless on a presentment or indictment of a grand jury, except in cases arising in the land or naval forces, or in the militia when in actual service, in time of war or public danger; nor shall any person be subject, for the same offence, to be twice put in jeopardy of life or limb, nor shall be compelled in any criminal case to be a witness against himself; nor be deprived of life, liberty, or property, without due process of law; nor shall private property be taken for public use without just compensation.

ARTICLE VI

In all criminal prosecutions the accused shall enjoy the right to a speedy and public trial, by an impartial jury of the State and district wherein the crime shall have been committed, which district shall have been previously ascertained by law; and to be informed of the nature and cause of the accusation; to be confronted with the witnesses against him; to have compulsory process for obtaining witnesses in his favor; and to have the assistance of counsel for his defence.

ARTICLE VII

In suits at common law, where the value in controversy shall exceed twenty dollars, the right of trial by jury shall be preserved; and no fact tried by a jury shall be otherwise reëxamined in any court of the United States than according to the rules of the common law.

ARTICLE VIII

Excessive bail shall not be required, nor excessive fines imposed, nor cruel and unusual punishments inflicted.

ARTICLE IX

The enumeration in the Constitution of certain rights shall not be construed to deny or disparage others retained by the people.

ARTICLE X

The powers not delegated to the United States by the Constitution, nor prohibited by it to the States, are reserved to the States respectively, or to the people.

ARTICLE XI

The judicial power of the United States shall not be construed to extend to any suit in law or equity commenced or prosecuted against one of the United States by citizens of another State, or by citizens or subjects of any foreign state.

ARTICLE XII

The electors shall meet in their respective States and vote by ballot for President and Vice-President, one of whom, at least, shall not be an inhabitant of the same State with themselves; they shall name in their ballots the person voted for as President, and in distinct ballots the person voted for as Vice-President, and they shall make distinct lists of all persons voted for as President, and of all persons voted for as Vice-President, and of the number of votes for each, which lists they shall sign and certify, and transmit sealed to the seat of the government of the United States, directed to the president of the Senate. The president of the Senate shall, in presence of the Senate and House of Representatives, open all the certificates and the votes shall then be counted. The person having the greatest number of votes for President shall be the President, if such number be a majority of the whole number of Electors appointed; and, if no person have such majority, then, from the persons having the highest numbers not exceeding three on the list of those voted for as President, the House of Representatives shall choose immediately, by ballot, the President. But, in choosing the President, the votes shall be taken by States, the representation from each State having one vote; a quorum for this purpose shall consist of a member or members from two-thirds of the States, and a majority of all the States shall be necessary to a choice. And if the House of Representatives shall not choose a President whenever the right of choice shall devolve upon them, before the fourth day of March next following, then the Vice-President shall act as President, as in the case of the death or other constitutional disability of the President. The person having the greatest number of votes as Vice-President shall be the Vice-

President, if such number be a majority of the whole number of Electors appointed, and, if no person have a majority, then from the two highest numbers on the list the Senate shall choose the Vice-President; a quorum for the purpose shall consist of two-thirds of the whole number of Senators, and a majority of the whole number shall be necessary to a choice. But no person constitutionally ineligible to the office of President shall be eligible to that of Vice-President of the United States.

ARTICLE XIII

Section 1. Neither slavery nor involuntary servitude, except as a punishment for crime whereof the party shall have been duly convicted, shall exist within the United States, or any place subject to their jurisdiction.

Section 2. Congress shall have power to enforce this article by appropriate legislation.

ARTICLE XIV

Section 1. All persons born or naturalized in the United States and subject to the jurisdiction thereof are citizens of the United States and of the State wherein they reside. No State shall make or enforce any law which shall abridge the privileges or immunities of citizens of the United States; nor shall any State deprive any person of life, liberty, or property, without due process of law; nor deny to any person within its jurisdiction the equal protection of the laws.

ARTICLE XV

Section 1. The right of citizens of the United States to vote shall not be denied or abridged by the United States or by any State on account of race, color, or previous condition of servitude.

Section 2. The Congress shall have power to enforce this article by appropriate legislation.

ARTICLE XVI

The Congress shall have power to lay and collect taxes on incomes, from whatever source derived, without apportionment among the several States, and without regard to any census or enumeration.

ARTICLE XVII

The Senate of the United States shall be composed of two Senators from each State, elected by the people thereof, for six years; and each Senator shall have one vote. The electors in each State shall have the qualifications requisite for electors of the most numerous branch of the State legislatures.

When vacancies happen in the representation of any State in the Senate, the executive authority of such State shall issue writs of election to fill such vacancies: *Provided*, That the legislature of any State may empower the executive thereof to make temporary appointments until the people fill the vacancies by election as the legislature may direct.

This amendment shall not be so construed as to affect the election or term of any Senator chosen before it becomes valid as a part of the Constitution.

I've always loved you, he had said to her that day, the day they had learned that Matthew was still alive. *Always*, he had repeated as they had danced together, one last dance. *Always and for ever*.

Houses crumbled, but love lasted. Love threaded them together, her and her family. From her vantage point on the grassy slope, Esme watched the dancers: Coral and Stephen, Zoe and Ben, Matthew and Susan. Her sprawling, complicated, disputatious family; their love for each other now extended halfway round the world, as strong as the ivy that clung to the walls of Rosindell. Her love for Devlin and Devlin's love for her would stay with her until the day she died.

In the end, what remained was love. Esme walked down the lawn, back to her family.

The wind ripples through the grass and murmurs over the overgrown ruins of loggia and terrace, where decades ago other lovers once danced. It rustles a heap of dead leaves, making them skirl and scatter, and it reveals a glint of gold – a bracelet or an earring perhaps, lost by someone long ago.

The breeze finds its way into the house and a window rattles. There is an echo of laughter, though no one is there. A door opens and closes, and then the house becomes quiet again.